Debates in Continental Philosophy

John D. Caputo, *series editor*

PERSPECTIVES IN
CONTINENTAL
PHILOSOPHY

RICHARD KEARNEY

Debates in Continental Philosophy
Conversations with
Contemporary Thinkers

FORDHAM UNIVERSITY PRESS
New York ■ 2004

Perspectives in Continental Philosophy Series, No. 37
ISSN 1089-3938

Library of Congress Cataloging-in-Publication Data

Kearney, Richard.
  Debates in continental philosophy : conversations with contemporary thinkers / Richard Kearney.—1st ed.
     p. cm.—(Perspectives in continental philosophy, ISSN 1089-3938 ; no. 37)
  Includes bibliographical references and index.
  ISBN 0-8232-2317-5 (hard)—ISBN 0-8232-2318-3 (pbk.)
  1. Philosophy, Modern—20th century. 2. Philosophy, European—20th century.
3. Philosophers—Europe—20th century—Interviews. I.
Title. II. Series.
B804.K43 2004
190.'9'04—dc22

                                                                                2003023772

Printed in the United States of America
08 07 06 05 04   5 4 3 2 1
First edition

Contents

Preface

The present volume brings together twenty-one dialogues which I conducted over recent years in the area of Continental thought.

Part 1 features previously unpublished exchanges, ranging from the conversation with Georges Dumézil, one of the founding fathers of structural anthropology, to more recent debates with Jacques Derrida, Paul Ricœur, and Jean-Luc Marion. Part 2 contains interviews held with Continental thinkers originally published in 1984 by Manchester University Press under the title *Dialogues with Contemporary Continental Thinkers: The Phenomenological Heritage.* While some of these have since been anthologized, the original volume has been out of print since the early 1990s. The third part of the book features a selection of interviews from two of my later volumes, *Visions of Europe: Conversations on the Legacy and Future of Europe* (1992) and *States of Mind* (1995). This section includes conversations with Julia Kristeva, Umberto Eco, George Steiner, and Paul Ricœur, recorded between 1991 and 1993 as part of a series for Irish Public Television (RTE). It also contains two subsequent exchanges with Jean-François Lyotard and Hans-Georg Gadamer conducted between 1994 and 1995. The fourth and final part of the book adds six new colloquies on my own work, which took place at a number of recent international symposia.

I am very grateful to all those who participated in the organizing and editing of these dialogues—John Manoussakis, Todd Sadowski,

Brian Gregor, John Cleary, Stephen Costello, Mark Manolopoulos, Sean Connolly, Fabrizio Turoldo, Eoin Cassidy, and Ian Leask. Sadly, five of my original interlocutors have passed away since we recorded our dialogues—Marcuse, Levinas, Gadamer, Dumézil, and Lyotard. Their intellectual generosity is something I will always cherish, and I would like to dedicate this volume to their memory.

Richard Kearney
Boston College
October 2003

PART I

Recent Debates

Jacques Derrida
Terror, Religion, and the New Politics

RK: In the interview with Dominique Janicaud (*Heidegger en France* [Heidegger in France]), you talk about deconstruction as being a preference for discontinuity over continuity, for *différance* over reconciliation, and so on. These two traits are always at work in your thought. I was wondering, at the practical level, what this preference might mean in the current political situation. In the wake of September 11, there is much talk of the West versus Islam. In Northern Ireland, there was much negotiation over decommissioning of arms. And there are all these tensions between Pakistan and India and, of course, between Palestine and Israel. My instinct here is to ask: Don't we need reconciliation in these areas of the world? It is perhaps a naïve question but also a pragmatic one. What I am really saying is: Where could the hermeneutics of reconciliation meet the deconstruction of difference on these issues—the issues of agreement, consensus, and reconciliation between enemies?

JD: It is a very good question. First the quick answer. Of course, politically and socially speaking, I have nothing against reconciliation, and I think we should do whatever we can to reach a reconciliation worthy of that name, be it the end of war, the end of violence, and so on. And I think, since you gave us these examples of what is going on today in the world—with a war which is not a war in the classical sense, a terrorism which is not terrorism in the classical sense, all these forms of new violence which challenge the old concepts of war, terrorism, and even nation-state—given, then, the fact that you referred to these examples, of course my political choice will be toward reconciliation. But a reconciliation which would not be simply a compromise in which the other (as it is always the case) in this or that way loses his or her singularity, identity, desire, and so on; a reconciliation also that will not be simply a sort of "deal" in order to take advantage of the other. So, if there were a reconciliation that could be just, then of course I would be interested in reconciliation. Each time my choice will be on the side of life and not of death. Now, if we try to do justice to both sides of all the examples you cite, I suppose we would have to acknowledge that many think that they act for a just cause. Those who hijacked the airplanes on September 11 or those who spread the anthrax think probably that their actions were provoked by an act of terrorism from the opposite side, an act of state terrorism on the part of the United States. So if there were a kind of reconciliation that would signal a stop which could bring violence to a halt and reach an agreement or a common conviction, then why not? But if reconciliation is just a pretext for a cease-fire so that tomorrow violence can start again, the violence of the one trying to prove that it is stronger than the other, then I would be very reluctant. Since we cannot avoid the reference to September 11 and since I cannot start any public speech or discussion without reference to these unspeakable events that have been named after that date, I think that today the type of violence is such that there will be no reconciliation before violence stops.

RK: Is that a precondition?

JD: Let me say that I do not find the United States innocent, but, given what is going on, whatever the purpose might be, we cannot reach a reconciliation before this type of violence (either through military or the police agents) stops. But the terrain has changed. Assuming that we manage to identify the criminals behind these attacks— let's say, bin Laden or some of his followers—and capture them or kill them, this would not change the situation. The terrain of reconciliation requires a radical change in the world; I would say a revolution of some sort. Any reconciliation worthy of that name requires not only that someone stops the violence through military or police force, or, as they call them, the peacekeeping forces. It requires more—a political change in the minds of the strongest.

RK: But who is the strongest?

JD: In the present situation the strongest becomes the weakest, and the weakest the strongest. Take, for example, the case of biological war, which, by the way, as we all know, was initially provided by the United States. If you only read, among other sources, [Noam] Chomsky's book on the rogue states, you will see that the United States provided Saddam Hussein with the skills as well as the substance. That's why some people are so nervous about Iraq, because they know that Saddam has the substance and the ability to create it. That's why I said that no one is innocent in this affair. Nevertheless, being myself on the side of democracy, democracy to come, I wish only one thing: that the process of radical reconciliation—implying a total transformation of the political situation—would start with a major cessation of all violence. Although I remain suspicious of American policies, I think today they cannot do anything else but protect themselves and try to destroy the source of this terrorism, a terrible but unavoidable thing. Now, about reconciliation itself. For everything said so far was at the level of the current political situation. Now, on a more radical kind of reconciliation, beyond the political—the political is just a layer—I would not suspend every relation with the other for the sake of hope, salvation, or resurrection (I have been reading your admirable book these days on this subject). This is perhaps a difference between us: this indeterminacy of the messianic leaves you unsatisfied. To speak roughly, you, Richard, would not give up the hope of redemption, resurrection, and so forth; and I would not either. But I would argue that when one is not ready to suspend the determination of hope, then our relation with the other becomes again economical. . . .

RK: . . . Because hope interprets this relation in terms of horizons of expectation, interpretation?

JD: My feeling is, and this is not political—when I am political, juridical, and perhaps ethical, I am with you—that when I try to think the most rigorous relation with the other I must be ready to give up the hope for a return to salvation, the hope for resurrection, or even reconciliation. In the pure act of giving and forgiving we should be free from any hope of reconciliation. I must forgive, if one forgives . . .

RK: Unconditionally.

JD: . . . unconditionally, without the hope of reconstituting a healthy and peaceful community. That's where reconciliation is for me problematic. When I am for any kind of negotiating between these unconditional and absolute thoughts and the conditional, then I become juridical and political—then I am of course with the side of the best possible reconciliation—which is, nevertheless, always very difficult. Reconciliation is difficult. It has to be negotiated through transactions, analyses of contexts and times: unpredictability of all kinds. But at least we have the feeling of a possible compromise. That is what is happening in life.

RK: To come back to the conclusion you drew earlier and play devil's advocate. When you say we cannot have a genuine, radical reconciliation worthy of its name until we cease violence, this seems disturbingly reminiscent of certain phrases made, for example, by [Ariel] Sharon of Israel, refusing to speak with the Palestinians until we have peace; or the Unionists in Northern Ireland saying, "We cannot talk to Sinn Fein until they put away their guns." I can understand, of course, the logic behind that, but it seems like asking for the impossible *too soon*, and not accepting the muddiness and murkiness of political situations. The Palestinians are slow to abandon the gusher of arms unconditionally until they see what is going to happen, etc. Deconstruction's position is, as I understand it, that *nothing* is pure; everything is contaminated, mixed, ambiguous. And so we will never reach a point of pure nonviolence where we can have reconciliation. Unless we compromise. Unless we accept some kind of negotiated settlement *before* we reach perfect peace and nonviolence.

JD: I totally agree with you. Perhaps what I said was oversimplified. That's why reconciliation in the political sense always occurs during some lasting violence. Now when I mention the fact that the Americans have to respond to the events of September 11, I did not exclude that they have already transformed the situation. On the one hand, they said that they were ready to help poor Afghans by dropping food and providing similar kinds of humanitarian aid, and on the other hand, they are already discussing the prospect of a Palestinian state. You remember, perhaps, Sharon saying, "We do not want to become the 'Czechoslovakia' of today." Before World War II, peace was made with Hitler at the expense of Czechoslovakia, and Sharon is afraid that if the Western coalition needs to expand to include more Arab states, this could happen at the expense of Israel. I do not judge anyone now. Perhaps the United States is making a terrible mistake in what they are doing. I cannot judge. Since television is under censorship, we cannot really know. In fact, what I say is simply that the United States could not remain immobile. They couldn't say, "Let's wait and see." They had to do something, whether we call it "retaliation" or just an attempt to stop the terror. At the same time, without waiting for the total destruction of the violent side, they have already, at least, promised that they would change their policy. I think they are trying to change, however indirectly, but their premises are very complicated. They ask: "Why do they hate us?" They will have to try to understand these feelings of hatred and try to change them. I hope that the Europeans—because we will have to come back to Europe on this issue—that the European allies should exercise a pressure on the United States, that not only the States but the whole Western world should change its policy toward the Arabs, if only in order to demonstrate that they are right when they say that bin Laden does not represent Islam or the Palestinians. If they want this to be true, they have to take a number of steps. And I don't mean that they will necessarily have to stop the violence, but even before that, and at the same time with that, they will have to start changing their policy.

RK: Pursuing this question of *the other* and the European as sort of a middleman, between the so-called Middle East and America, I take it you are suggesting that because Europe has a much closer relationship with the Mediterranean world and Arab culture generally, it is more aware of all the different variations of Islam, and that Europe has, therefore, an obligation to try to communicate this understanding to America and to mediate between East and West, as it were. Since US citizens are asking, "Why do they hate us," they are asking for an answer. So we in Europe might be able to help "translate" between the two. I have been working on similar issues in my book *On Stories*, where there is a section on the construction of national narratives. I try to explore how Rome was founded on the exclusion of the Etruscans; how the British and the Irish constituted themselves within a dialectic of otherness with each other; and then how America founded its new world identity on the basis of its particular *other*—starting with the native Indians, then going onto the slaves, emigrants, and finally aliens as the other (there is an obsession with aliens from outer space). After September 11, there was a front-page headline in *Newsweek*, "A Nation Indivisible." The other had struck. It seems to me that there was an immediate need to put a face on it, to situate it geographically, to identify enemies out there, because to have enemies *within* was so disturbing. Perhaps that is why the scare about anthrax was so disturbing. Once the other is also located *within* the nation, it is harder to project the other back "out there." How do you see this dialectic playing out?

JD: There are at least two or three questions in what you have said. First, a vast problem, let's call it "translation." Can Europe help in translating? I think there are two ways to look into things, to estimate what is going on here. First, there is the short one: to understand the premises of the Cold War. We are still paying the price of the Cold War, because it is precisely for that reason—the reason of having an enemy—that the United States had to surround themselves with so many nondemocratic countries (as allies). At the same time there was this polarity, and by means of this polarity the United States had made a number of terrible mistakes in strategy that boomeranged. So now we face these consequences of the Cold War. We shouldn't forget that bin Laden was trained according to American models.

The longest way will be the study of the history and embodiment of Islam. How can we explain that this religion—one that is now in terms of demography the most powerful—and those nations which embody its beliefs, have missed something in history, something that it is not shared with Europe—namely, Enlightenment, science, economy, development? They are poor countries. Even if some Arabs are extremely rich by virtue of the oil industry, they still have not the necessary infrastructure. What is, then, that which places them economically on the wrong side? Is it the religion? Now, of course, I am oversimplifying. But it took some centuries, during which Christianity and Judaism succeeded in associating with the techno-scientific-capitalistic development while the Arabic-Islamic world did not. They remained poor, attached to old models, repressive, even more phallocentric than the Europeans (which is already something). So without an understanding of history, without a new kind of historical investigation about what happened with Islam during the last five centuries, we will not be able to understand what is going on today.

RK: You have several references in your work to monotheism as Judeo-Christian-Islamic. You always reintroduce this hyphen that many of us forget, and that complicates the scenario in a very refreshing way. You remind people that Islam shares a common monotheistic heritage in religion and philosophy (see for example the case of Avicena). At its inception, Islam does not look so alien from ourselves . . .

JD: In my short essay "Faith and Knowledge" I ask the question of Islam in relation to the other religions. We have the Judeo-Christian couple as opposed to Islam, but, on the other hand, we have the Judeo-Islamic couple as opposed to Christianity. The death of God is Christian; neither Jew nor Muslim would ever say that God is dead.

There is, then, this confrontation between the three Abrahamic traditions. If we want seriously to understand what is happening today, we have to go back to the origins and ask what has happened since the Middle Ages. Why—in spite of the fact that the Arabic world has incorporated Western scholarship, science, and culture—has it not developed socially, historically, as Europe has? I do not have an answer to that. But if we do not go back to this period, to this question, we cannot make sense of today's situation.

RK: Does that statement include Buddhism, Hinduism? These religions did not seem to have such a problem.

JD: No. I'm not sure that we could call them, strictly speaking, "religion." This is a point that I make in "Faith and Knowledge" about the *mondialatinisation*[1] of *religion*.

RK: Maybe it is because Islam in its origins is somehow more connected with us here in Europe. The departure from us (the West and Europe) came at a later point. The battle of Vienna, when the Islamic forces were defeated by the Germans and the Poles, was in 1682. It is not long since Islam was in the heart of Europe. The Balkans, Spain, Greece. Islam was a part of us, and we were a part of it.

JD: It is without doubt a great civilization, a great culture. Nevertheless, they did not articulate the possibility of what we define as power, as technoscience, capitalism.

RK: How do we raise this question of Islam while avoiding [Samuel] Huntington's binary thesis of the good Western Empire against the evil Islamic Empire?

JD: I think there is the expressed wish in Islam and among Muslims, among theologians, to dissociate Islam from a more violent form. I know that there is this desire to come back to an Islam that would be totally devoid of violence. These differences, however, within Islam, cannot be developed efficiently without a development of the institution of the political, of the transformation of the *structures* of the society. Of course, we will always find an interesting Muslim scholar or theologian who will say, "Islam is not bin Laden." But these people remain powerless because what has power is precisely *this* nondemocratic, violent regime. It is a strange situation today. Well, I think Europe—not the old question of Europe, the spirit of Europe, Husserl's Europe, Heidegger's Europe, not even the European Community or the Europe of Tony Blair—but perhaps there is something in Europe today, a possibility of taking a certain distance from both sides (the United States and Islam); even if there is an alliance in NATO [North Atlantic Treaty Organization], there is something in Europe which could or should avoid these theocratic struggles, the theocratic duel. In order to give some image of this schema, I would return to the question of the death penalty, which, as you know, obsesses me. Imagine that they capture bin Laden; they may treat him, if he is captured by the United States . . . they may capture him as a foreign soldier or enemy. They could judge him, then, according to their own laws of justice and probably sentence him to death. Or would he be transferred to an International Penal Court according to the new law of the United Nations? In that case, he couldn't be sentenced to death, because the New International Penal Court has of course judged crimes against humanity, crimes of war, but it cannot enforce death or pass the death sentence. This case locates the difference between, let's say, the spirit of Europe and the United States. The fact that the European Community has abolished the death penalty makes a difference. A real difference and a difference in principle.

RK: If, say, British forces took bin Laden, they couldn't extradite him to the United States.

JD: No, they couldn't and they shouldn't. Nor the French—they will never extradite someone to a country where the death penalty is accepted. Whether bin Laden would be killed as a "soldier," as an "enemy," or would be judged as a "terrorist." All these concepts are now shaken. To come back to the last part of your question about the refoundation of a sovereign, single nation, I am struck by the new reunification of this country. Speaking of assimilation, the African Americans of this country are now fully Americans, at least for the moment. As long as they are against bin Laden. Perhaps one day people will consider September 11 as the refoundation of the United States, because, precisely, the United States was struck by an unidentified enemy, not a state, not an individual (it is not bin Laden himself, alone). This attack has become the center for a new foundation of the nation. This aggression has rebuilt the nation; this terrible scar has provoked such a self-defense that it serves almost as a reconstitution, an economy, a sort of therapy, and so on. Americans are becoming reconciled with themselves. There is reconciliation with immigrants and other underprivileged groups of society. You have probably seen a TV advertisement where a number of people of various backgrounds and nationalities announce to the camera, "I am an American." It is amazing and it is true. You cannot but admire this wonderful thing going on: despite all the tragedy and all the hypocrisy, there is still an idea of democracy. No doubt. I remember when I was here in 1971, in Baltimore; the "war with blacks" was terrible. There were rebellions in prisons, terrible violence. I thought that there would be a real revolution. And they succeeded through violence, because a number of black militants, leaders of the black community, were killed. The despair was terrible. But after the depression they started with the act of integration, with the struggle for civil rights. There was progress. It is always not enough, of course. There is always a lot of hypocrisy: racism, for example, still exists. And yet the idea of this progress cannot be denied.

RK: This polarization works. Much of the Islamic world seems to have forgotten, on a popular level, a sort of a fraternity with the West. On the other hand, the Americans are certainly a reconciled, rejuvenated nation once again. In terms of these polar extremes — complementary enemies playing off against each other, both calling each other the "Evil Empire" — I would call the European position a middle one, a hermeneutics of mediation. But I suspect that you would be slow to use either of these terms: *hermeneutics* and *mediation.* That is what I would endorse. But your tendency is to focus more on the gaps and holes. This is an absolutely indispensable move, but not the whole story. I suppose, if there is a difference between us — I mention this in the fourth chapter of *The God Who May Be* — it is a difference of emphasis rather than of kind. Maybe it is because of the experience of Northern Ireland.

JD: We will need lots of time to make these traits more specific. I think that there is already an act of mediation in Europe. Although Europe is predominantly Christian, Europe as community is less theocratic than the United States. Europe is more secular, and by being the ally of the States and being more attentive and respectful to difference than the States, it could, and I hope that it will, play a role of mediation. It should exercise some pressure on the United States. I agree with you on this level. Europe is not this factual, Christian Europe simply led by Christianity — this is something that needs to be reelaborated. And here we come to the difference between you and me. It is easier to think of what I put under the word *khōra* in Europe than in any other place in the world. Now, it may also happen in some parts of the United States, but this will be the dimension of "Europe" in the States. Something may happen in the United States thanks to some American thinkers. But it would have to do with a way of freeing yourselves not from "a God who may be" but rather from a God that is, in the direction of what I call *khōra*. When I say *khōra*, I am not excluding anything, but I am referring also to the politics of *khōra*, the absolute indeterminacy, which is the only possible groundless ground for a universal—if not for reconciliation—at least for a universal politics beyond cosmopolitanism.

RK: I suppose I could see the "God who may be" emerging from *khōra*, from that space. If I had to try to locate it, this God, I would place it somewhere between the God of messianism and Being on the one hand, and *khōra*, on the other. The "God who may be" hovers and suffers between these two. It is not identical with *khōra*. This is the sort of dialogue I develop throughout the book with you and Jack Caputo. I am aware of our differences on the issue of how does one speak about God. For me it is a hermeneutic problem: How do you speak and name and identify a god without falling back to metaphysics and ontotheology, and yet without saying "God is *khōra*"?

JD: I never said that.

RK: I know you never said that, but you see the problematic . . .

JD: I try to address these various issues by reading your book. The differences between us are so thin that we cannot in a short discussion do justice to them. These thin and sometimes imperceptible differences or nuances could be translated into politics. But we cannot reduce them to that. I felt very close to everything you said in this book—up to a certain moment where you yourself rigorously define the thinnest difference, that is, on resurrection. I am not against resurrection. I would share your hope for resurrection, reconciliation, and redemption. But I . . . I think I have a responsibility as someone who thinks deconstructively, even if I dream of redemption . . . I have the responsibility to acknowledge, to obey the necessity of the possibility that there is *khōra*, rather than a relationship with the anthropotheologic God of revelation. At some point, you, Richard, translate your faith into something determinable, and then you have to keep the "name" of the resurrection. My own understanding of faith is that there is faith whenever one gives up not only any certainty but also any determined hope. If one says that resurrection is the horizon of one's hope, then one knows what one names when one says "resurrection"—faith is not pure faith. It is already knowledge. That's why sometimes you call me an atheist . . .

RK: Someone who rightly passes for an atheist.

JD: Sometimes I would argue that you have to be an atheist of this sort in order to be true to faith, to pure faith. So it is a very complicated logic.

RK: In *The God Who May Be,* I say that "where the religious so offends, I would call myself a seeker of love and justice *tout court.*"[2]

JD: Me too. A seeker of love and justice. It is not that I am happy with this. It is a suffering.

RK: For me, this is the crux of the dialogue between hermeneutics and deconstruction. My diacritical hermeneutics are different from Gadamer's and Heidegger's and even Ricœur's in certain respects. But what I have tried to explore and develop in *The God Who May Be* and *Strangers, Gods and Monsters* is the hermeneutic-deconstructive interface. One thing that I would like to mention here on the question of God is something you said in Villanova that I very much identified with. During the roundtable discussion, you said that "if I am interested in God, it would be the God who is powerless. . . ."

JD: Absolutely. First of all, I would like to tell you that I found your book powerful; it is powerful in its powerlessness. I was impressed and grateful to see what is happening with the history that we share, and we share twenty years now. Your book formalizes questions in a way that is absolutely wonderful. I read your book in agreement all the time with this tiny difference on the question of the power. The "may-be." There are two ways to understand the "may." "I may" is the "perhaps"; it is also the "I am able to" or "I might." The "perhaps" *(peut-être)* refers to the unconditional beyond sovereignty. It is an unconditional which is the desire of powerlessness rather than power. I think you are right to attempt to name God not as sovereign, as almighty, but as precisely the most powerless. Justice and love are precisely oriented to this powerlessness. But *khōra* is powerless too. Not powerlessness in the sense of poor or vulnerable. Powerlessness as simply no-power. No power at all.

RK: Can we, then, kneel and pray before *khōra?*

JD: No. No. This is precisely the difference. But I would immediately add that if we are to pray, if I pray, I have at least to take into account that *khōra enables* me to pray. That spacing, the fact that there is this spacing—a neutral, indifferent, impassible spacing—that enables me to pray. Without *khōra* there would be no prayer. We should think that without *khōra* there would be no God, no *other,* no spacing. But you can address a prayer only to some*thing* or some*one,* not to *khōra.* To come back to your question, I have nothing against all these things: reconciliation, prayer, redemption, and so on. But I think that these things would not be possible without this indifferent, impassible, neuter, interval spacing of *khōra:* the "there is" beyond being.

RK: Which is prior to all differences and yet makes difference possible . . .

JD: Yes.

RK: And this can lead to a new politics, another kind of cosmopolitanism.

JD: *Beyond* cosmopolitanism, since cosmopolitanism implies a state, a citizen, the cosmos. *Khōra* opens up a universality beyond cosmopolitanism. That's where at some point I am planning to examine the political consequences of the thought of *khōra,* which I think are urgent today. And if one day there will be a reconciliation between the terrible enemies, it would be because of some space, of some *khōra,* an empty, mutual space that is not the cosmos, not the created world, not the nation, state, global dimension, but just that: *khōra.*

New York City,
October 16, 2001

Jean-Luc Marion
The Hermeneutics of Revelation

I. Boston College, October 2, 2001

RK: They are many similarities between your work, Jean-Luc, and mine: Both of us owe a great deal of our philosophical formation to the phenomenologies of Husserl and Heidegger; we have both engaged ourselves in close dialogue with Levinas, Ricœur, and Derrida. Given these evident similarities, it would be more fruitful and interesting, it seems to me, if we take a look here into some of the *differences* in our respective positions in regards to the phenomenology of God. One question that I would like to put to you, Jean-Luc, and which, in fact, I have put in a more elaborate form on p. 33 of *The God Who May Be,* is the question of the hermeneutical status of the saturated phenomenon. It seems to me that if there is a difference between us, given all our common readings and assumptions, it is this: I would pass from phenomenology to hermeneutics more rapidly than you would. It strikes me that your approach is more strictly phenomenological, since for you the saturated phenomenon is fundamentally *irrégardable,* a pure event without horizon or context, without "I" or agent. As such it appears to *defy* interpretation. You do of course make some concessions to hermeneutics, as when you say—on the very last page of your essay "The Saturated Phenomenon"—that this phenomenon is communal and communicable and historic. Here you do seem to acknowledge the possibility of a hermeneutic response, but my suspicion, and please correct me if I'm mistaken, is that the example you privilege—revelation—requires a *pure phenomenology of the pure event*, whereas I would argue that there is no pure phenomenon as such, that appearing—no matter how iconic or saturated it may be—always already involves an interpretation of some kind. Phenomenological description and intuition, in my account, always imply some degree of hermeneutic reading, albeit that of a prereflective, preunderstanding, or preconscious affection for the most part. My question, then, would be: How do we interpret—and by extension, how do we judge—the saturated phenomenon without betraying it?

M: This is an old question. The first version of "The Saturated Phenomenon" was written as a paper just after *Reduction and Givenness;* then a more elaborate version followed, as it is now found in *Étant Donné [Being Given].* The first to raise this question was Jean Grondin, a specialist on Gadamer at the University of Montreal; after him Jean Greisch asked me the same question, and although I am stubborn and narrow-minded, I am not completely closed to critical remarks! Let us put aside for a moment the question of Christian revelation, which is not directly related to the saturated phenomenon. The saturated phenomenon is a kind of phenomenon that is characterized by a deficit in *concept* vis-à-vis *intuition:* such phenomena include *the event, the idol, the flesh,* and *the other.* In all these cases, there is a surplus of intuition over intention. It is precisely because of this surplus of intuition, I have argued, that we need hermeneutics. Why? Because hermeneutics is always an inquiry for further concepts: hermeneutics is generated when we witness an excess of information rather than its lack. In *Étant Donné,* where I discuss the four types of saturated phenomena, I say that the icon is "the icon of endless hermeneutics." Why an endless hermeneutics? Precisely because there is here a conceptual deficit. I have learned my hermeneutics with Ricœur, and Ricœur is very clear on this: if we are to have hermeneutics, it has to be an endless hermeneutics. There where the need of hermeneutics arises, it is completely impossible to imagine that we may get at any moment an adequate, final concept. Subjectivity, history, and the question of God—the question of history is very important for our discussion here, for the historical event is the most simple kind of saturated phenomenon—in all these cases, the question of hermeneutics is totally unavoidable. Hermeneutical investigation never completes its mission. It is never finished and should never be finished, and that is why there cannot be a hermeneutics of what I call the *common range* phenomenon. It is why, for example, the history of mathematics is not a part of mathematics, why the history of science in general is not *science*. Because, in the case of pure mathematics or pure science, there is no deficit of phenomenality, there is no saturated phenomenon, and thus no need of hermeneutics.

RK: In two of your texts, *De surcroît [In Excess: Studies of Saturated Phenomena]* and *Étant Donné,* you delineated the four types of saturated phenomena, all of them characterized by a superabundance of intuition over intention. As you say, they do not necessarily point towards a theological turn—actually, they could be quite atheological—but you have also written of the saturated phenomenon as a theological event. Since we are focusing our discussion here on the phenomenology and hermeneutics of God, let me come back to this theme and ask: Can we have a hermeneutics of God qua saturated phenomenon? For example, in some texts you speak of the saturated phenomenon in terms of a superabundance that surpasses all narration and predication and fills us with a certain stupor and terror whose very "incomprehensibility imposes on us." Regarding this notion of incomprehensibility, you would seem to suggest an *absence of hermeneutics* and point to a theology of absence where the role of narratives and images and even of conceptual interpretations appears to be a betrayal, in some sense, of the very unconditional absoluteness of the religious event. In *God Without Being,* you actually speak of a "eucharistic hermeneutics"; but here again we are faced with what you call the "unspeakable word," which seems to mean that we find the Word already given, gained, and available. In addition to that, there is the question of the theologian who, by definition, ultimately has the *last word* of interpretation. Such a view seems to me to delimit the notion of an endless hermeneutics. Moreover, those who do not participate in the praxis of the Eucharistic phenomenon seem to be excluded not only from its experience but also from its interpretation.

M: Let us go back, then, to the theological character of the saturated phenomenon. My final position on that is that the four types of saturated phenomena mentioned above could all be recapitulated in the field of a phenomenology of revelation. Nevertheless, if we are allowed to take revelation—a theological concept—as a phenomenological question, then, I think, it should be done to the degree that revelation can be described as the combination of the four types of saturated phenomena. I refer here to the Judeo-Christian revelation; to describe it you, I would need to employ (1) *event*—since it always occurs as an event; (2) the *idol*—since it bedazzles us with its appearance when it appears; (3) the *flesh*—since it is always an appearance that has to appeal to our senses; and finally, (4) the *other*, that is, the otherness of the other. Revelation combines and recapitulates in itself all of the four types; it is, we might say, a phenomenon saturated to the square. The kind of hermeneutics that we would need to employ vis-à-vis revelation is already at work on each of these kinds of saturated phenomena. I would say that revelation is a rather good paradigmatic case of what I call the saturated phenomenon. What is given in revelation is precisely what surpasses any expectation. The fact that we face something beyond any expectation and any final conception solicits an endless hermeneutics. That is why the field of hermeneutics is absolutely and widely open to any possible direction and to any level of interpretation. Take, for example, the Creed, the Apostolic *credo*. Strictly speaking it is a document that reveals a set of doctrines shared in common by all the churches and all the theologians; on the other hand, however, it is open to different interpretations which are not always consistent with each other, even within the same church or the same tradition. I see these differences of interpretation as many different hermeneutic possibilities. I would also say that the Jesuit spirituality is another example of a possible interpretation, of another type of hermeneutics within the tradition of Catholic spirituality.

RK: Would you, then, admit to a comparative phenomenology of the religious, along the lines of someone like Mircea Eliade? Do you think that the phenomenon of God can be experienced outside a specifically monotheistic context? Is there something in the notion of revelation as an absolute saturated phenomenon that requires a Judeo-Christian theology? It is not just *any* God that appears in revelation, is it? And how can we tell the difference?

M: I think that the "game," so to speak, is completely open to anyone who has to do what he can do and as much as his abilities allow. What happens at the moment of the revelation is like a tremendous explosion: it affects everyone, from those at the ground zero to those at the remotest periphery. But no matter where we stand, or how much or how little of intuition we receive, each one of us has to take that much and make out if it whatever we can. And this is an ongoing process; it is a story that never reaches its end.

RK: So one could have a Buddhist or Hindu hermeneutics of the phenomenon of God?

M: I do think that the question of God is so great that, to some extent, we have to admit that all the different traditions, including those that are apparently foreign to the biblical heritage, are needed in order to say something about God. Buddhism is a way of living the experience of the infinite prior to or beside the phenomenon of revelation; Buddhism concerns itself with what we would call "natural revelation." And this too is needed. It is like putting the question of revelation in a different way: What would have happened if no revelation had happened?

RK: You say "different" as negative to positive or as different to same?

M: It cannot be completely different because what is at stake here, that is, the human being, is the same, in the sense that it is *us* who raise the question of revelation. It can be raised differently, but it is always raised within the common structures of human experience. The experience of the infinite, with or without revelation, does not compel us to choose this or that tradition.

RK: Why do you say "without revelation"? Are there not kinds of revelations and epiphanies—as well as all kinds of saturated phenomena—that do *not* presuppose any theological or monotheistic given . . .

M: Yes.

RK: . . . and which are surely available to non-monotheistic traditions . . .

M: There could be.

RK: . . . whether it is a work of art or an icon or a sacred moment in some Eastern religion or simply an act of love or justice, giving a cup of cold water to a thirsty person?

M: Yes. I have no authority to decide whether the Buddhist, for example, would or should use this or that interpretation of his experience of the infinite. My point regarding the relation of the saturated phenomenon to revelation is an old issue between theology and metaphysics.

RK: To clarify, when you say "revelation," do you mean "Revelation"—with a capital "R"—that is, a monotheistic Revelation, or you mean "revelation" in the phenomenological sense, which is obviously more inclusive?

M: My answer will have to be a long one. An old question that concerned me for some time was why metaphysics since the sixteenth century became so interested in explaining the very notion of natural revelation—not a terribly consistent concept anyway. When in modern times philosophy was understood as the doctrine of the a priori, it became immediately apparent that if there are a priori, then any possible experience must be limited and admitted by them. Within this context, very roughly sketched here, the question of revelation needed to be addressed, because in the mode of revelation the limitations of our experience are supposed to be given by revelation itself, or by the One revealed through revelation, and not controlled by the modalities of the transcendental apparatuses. The conflict between these two horizons was an unavoidable one, and the final conclusion reached, in different ways by both [Johann Gottlieb] Fichte and Kant, was the limitation of religion "within the limits of reason alone." Let us recall here Fichte's criticism of any possible concept of revelation, Christian or non-Christian alike, and the answer that Hegel gave, where the Concept allows revelation to happen, but at the end it is the Concept itself that *is* the truth of revelation. The moral of this story was that philosophy *alone* is responsible for deciding what is acceptable as "revelation" and what is not. With the advent of the crisis in metaphysics, however, what we know today as "the end of metaphysics," the picture changes. The question that led metaphysics into crisis was precisely the one that questioned the role of metaphysics as the ultimate authority that decides which kind of phenomena are admissible to philosophical discourse and which are not, which questions the legitimacy of metaphysics and, along with all this, the question of the possibility of revelation. Together with the crisis in metaphysics, or as a consequence of this very crisis, the question of revelation per se was reopened. Under this light, the experience of a Buddhist, for example, faces the same problem and the same critique as the question of experience of the (Judeo-Christian) revelation. Neither can be taken as "rational" by the standards of philosophical and scientific rationality. On the other hand, Buddhists as well as Christians think that they have the right to be taken as reasonable and capable of performing sound reasoning and philosophical questioning, regardless of their faith. Obviously, a broader and less rigid concept of rationality is in order here. If you want to focus on the interreligious discourse (understood not in the sense of ecumenism, but as the question of what constitutes, or not, revelation), such a matter can only be addressed when you assume that revelation nullifies any natural experience. But to assume that you must already know what revelation is or does is the same as saying that the hermeneutics of revelation is now over, that revelation has nothing to reveal any more, and thus, by definition, that there is no revelation. If we speak of revelation, then, we have to accept that hermeneutics is still going on, that revelation is open, as history is still in the making. There is no contradiction in saying that everything was fully revealed and achieved but that, even today, we don't know, we can't know, how far it reaches.

RK: Would you, at this point in your work, revise your position in *God Without Being* regarding the hermeneutics of the text as being conditioned by the community itself? How do you feel now, for example, about this passage that you wrote? "Hermeneutic of the text by the community . . . thanks to the service of the theologian, but on the condition that the community itself be interpreted by the Word and assimilated to the place where theological interpretation can be exercised, thanks to the liturgical service of the theologian par excellence, the bishop," for it is "only the bishop that merits in its full sense the title of theologian" (152–53). The God without Being is undoubtedly inscribed within a monotheistic tradition. Is this theological position one which you would still defend? Or do you think that the brackets have to be opened again to an "interfaith" phenomenon of revelation?

M: I would like to say this. When I said that "only the bishop merits the title of the theologian," I was not, of course, taking sides in the present-day differences between, say, bishops and theologians; I was referring back to the tradition where most of our great theologians were, at the same time, bishops in their communities. I am thinking here of examples such as the two Gregorys, Basil the Great, or John the Chrysostom. For a long time in the common tradition of the church, the *place* to teach theology was the pulpit from which the bishop, during the liturgy, had to explain the Gospel. All of our great patristic books were in fact connected to these homiletic practices.

RK: But some of these books were burned by the bishops. Meister Eckhart was on the Index, as was John Scotus Eruigena. Even Aquinas at one point! These were great teachers and hermeneuts. But none of them were bishops!

M: But this very situation was the symptom of a corruption of what I am trying to explain here. It is difficult for us to think today about how theology was originally not supposed to be the outcome of intellectual curiosity, logical dexterity, or academic career. Theology grew out of the task of commenting on the scriptures, not because you chose to be a professional exegete of the scriptures, but because that was an essential part of the liturgy, of the Eucharistic gathering of the faithful. In this sense, theology was a communal event. It was the theology of a community and not the solitary research task of a theologian. The great theologians of the tradition were not writing books because they wished to get published but because they needed to address specific questions that were of importance in their communities. Their theology was built in direct relation to their pastoral service. With the advent of the universities, we are in a new, terrible situation where you have, on the one side the bishop who has administrative power (and often a rather low level of scholarship), and on the other side, the university professor who has a high level of scholarship but who is removed from the believing community and its act of celebration. The result is that each one uses his old weapons to get rid of the other in the struggle over the monopoly of truth. The academic claims that the bishop is deeply involved in politics and thus unable to do serious theology, while the bishop says that we should not take seriously all these uncommitted professors and researchers. Things have radically changed.

II. Dublin, January 11, 2003

M: I take the opportunity of this seminar to answer a comment made by Richard Kearney, which is very fruitful, and which is a very good example of how far the concept of the saturated phenomenon can be applied.

If we consider, as Kearney does in his hermeneutic reading of Exodus 3:14 in chapter 2 of *The God Who May Be*, it is very fascinating, because there are three possible interpretations. The first interpretation is the *kataphatic:* we take "I am who I am" as "I am an *ousia*," and, more than that, "I am Being itself," and so on. Then you have the negative or *apophatic* interpretation: "I am who I am, and you will never know who I am," which is a very old and traditional interpretation too. And there is a third one, which is beyond both affirmation and negation, namely, the hyperbolical one, where the two previous readings are both surpassed and assumed—"I am the One who shall be. Forever." Shall be what? He who can say, "Here I am," because "Here I am" is the name under which the encounter between God and man is made, throughout all revelation. So, "I will be the One always able to answer or to call." And so, with the same words of Exodus 3:14, the same intuition, to some extent, we have three possible significations, and we need at least those three. This is mystical theology. It is also a saturated phenomenon. And it is, finally, also the possibility of an endless hermeneutic. The Exodic revelation may be repeated for other *logia*. I think we, Richard and I, agree on this issue.

RK: Yes, we are in agreement here. But I would like to expand a little further. In *The God Who May Be*, I tried to explore how Meister Eckhart revisits certain metaphysical terms —*sum, ego, qui est,* etc.— and reinterprets them in a way that opens them up to a postmetaphysical, eschatological interpretation. And I think we could apply this move more generally to a variety of postmetaphysical movements in contemporary philosophy and theology. Maybe this is a slight difference of emphasis I have with Jean-Luc Marion, Heidegger, and Derrida. Rather than affirming the metaphysics of presence, or ontotheology, which from Aristotle to Husserl is caught up in a metaphysics of "conceptual idolatry," what I try to advance with my notion of "diacritical hermeneutics" is the suggestion that, in spite of the language of cause, substance, ground, *essentia, esse,* which easily lends itself to conceptual idolatry, there is also within metaphysics a metaphysical desire to understand, to conceptualize, to reason with, to reckon with, to make sense of, to debate with, questions of the ultimate. That metaphysical desire, it seems to me, is utterly respectable, and it can be recognized in most of the great metaphysicians. There are two ways of approaching Plato, for example. On the one hand, there is Plato as ontotheology and the metaphysics of presence. But on the other hand, there is Plato as Levinas revisits him, as the exponent of a metaphysics of eros, of desire. In that sense, when Levinas speaks of metaphysical desire in *Totality and Infinity,* he is not saying we should return to Aristotelian or Scholastic metaphysics qua speculative system. He's saying that there is some drive within all metaphysical attempts to name the unnameable, which is retrievable and which can be reread eschatologially. That's not just true of Plato; it's true of Augustine, where there is this restless desire for God; and it is true of Descartes too. As Levinas and Jean-Luc Marion have both pointed out, Descartes's "idea of the Infinite" is something that comes through metaphysics, but it can't be contained *within metaphysics.*

So, I would make that differentiation. Does this bring us close to something like process theology? As a metaphysical desire for God, yes. But not as a need to form a system, with grounds and causes and reasons and concepts that tend towards a pantheism, where there's a beginning, middle, and end, and a master narrative which reduces

God to an immanent, historical process. I don't have any quarrel with the description of God as an immanent, historical process up to a point, but I think it is only half of the story. It's the story of us responding to the call of God and trying to work towards the kingdom. But there's another side to the story, which I don't really see recognized in [Charles] Hartshorne or [Alfred North] Whitehead, and that relates how historical becoming is a *response* to a call that comes from *beyond* history. So the question is: Is there a notion in process theology of God as radical transcendence, ulteriority, exteriority, alterity? Does process theology sufficiently acknowledge the *difference* between immanence and transcendence?

M: There is no contradiction between Eckhart saying *Gott wirt und Gott entwirt* and the saturated phenomenon. The very experience of the *excess* of intuition over signification makes clear that the excess may be felt and expressed as a disappointment. The experience of disappointment means that I make an experience which I cannot understand, because I have no concept for it. So the excess and the disappointment can come together. The saturated phenomenon doesn't mean that we never have the experience of being in the desert. The reverse is the case: the desertification is an excess, in some way. The experience of something that is unconditional is, for me, something occasioned by the fact that I am disappointed, that I am in the situation of encountering something without having the possibility to understand it. This is not nothing. This is a very important figure of phenomenality.

And so back to desire now. I would not be so optimistic about desire as some are. Indeed, in philosophy from the beginning, there is something that is not purely conceptual, working "behind," being the secret energy of the system, the desire of knowing things. Desire of knowing. There are two possibilities opened up here: first, desire is quite different from knowledge itself—"All men desire to know," as Aristotle says. Second, desire is finally incorporated into the knowledge itself. To some extent, this is done with Hegel, where knowledge— rooted in the dialectic—includes in itself the desire to know. And so at that moment, desire is recalled and recollected, confirmed within metaphysics. Or you may argue—and I think it was part of Levinas's argument about Plato—that the desire is prior to the philosophical intention to know and is to be taken seriously as such. So you may try to focus your attention on desire "as such." This can explain an aspect of neo-Platonism, for instance, regarding desire "as such." But the question is whether desire does not claim far more than mere philosophy understood as a theory of knowledge. Perhaps the question of desire is too serious to be explained within the same horizons as the question of knowledge. Perhaps the question of desire can not only not be answered, but not even be asked in the horizon of Being. So this is a reason why I think desire is the "backstage" of metaphysics, something never enlightened by metaphysics (which is unable to do so). And so we have now, perhaps, to open a new horizon where the question of desire may be taken seriously. And it is not taken seriously, for instance, in psychoanalysis—because psychoanalysis can consider and describe desire—but it takes desire as simply a drive, an unconscious drive; it is nothing more than a drive, largely and maybe forever. But there is perhaps a deep rationality and consciousness of desire which is other than, and goes far beyond, mere unconsciousness. To open this new horizon, we have to get rid of the horizon of Being, which is, at the end of metaphysics, quite unable, because not broad enough, to do justice to desire.

RK: Perhaps we could link the notions of "desert" and "desire." Take Eckhart's notion of *Abgescheidenheit* as the abandonment of desire, the experience of releasement and dispossession. This is not incompatible with the experience of the saturated phenomenon but may actually be concomitant with it. I think there are two ways of approaching the divine, saturated phenomenon. One is ecstasy—the traditional beatific vision of the fusion with the God; mystical *jouissance*. But there is also *Abgescheidenheit*, the sense of being disinherited, disinvested—John of the Cross's dark night of the soul. Sometimes the saturated phenomenon seems closer to Augustine's or Dante's beatific vision; sometimes it approximates more to the experience of the desert, devastation, the void. Other times again, it can be both together.

In the transfiguration of Christ, for example, if we can take that as a divine saturated phenomenon, we witness an extraordinary fascination with the *whiteness* of the event, but also an experience of fear, such that the voice from the clouds has to say, "Do not be afraid." There is fascination but also recoil. Jesus cautions his disciples to keep a distance from the event, not to say anything to anyone about it, not to construct a monument or memorial. All these are ways, it seems to me, of acknowledging the importance of *Abgescheidenheit*. One is very close to something that could burn us up. We need a distance, and to be faithful to it we need to be cautious, discreet, and diffident. So I think it's a complex double move of ecstasy and *Abegescheidenheit*, of attraction and disappropriation.

Relating this back to desire, I think it's important to distinguish between two different kinds — ontological and eschatological. Ontological desire comes from lack, which is, I think, the Hegelian and Lacanian definition of desire, but it also goes back, in fact, to Plato. One interpretation of Plato in *The Symposium* is that *eros* is the offspring of Poros and Penia, of fullness and lack, and therefore is a lack striving to be fulfilled. This *ontological* notion of desire strives for possession, fusion, atonement, and appropriation. I would oppose this to *eschatological* desire, which doesn't issue from lack, but from superabundance, excess, and surplus. This latter is also operative in Plato. But it's most emphatically evident, I think, in a biblical text like the *Song of Songs*, where there's a sort of theo-erotic drama between the divine and the human.

M: If I may comment about that. You know the formulation in the commentary on the *Song of Songs* by Gregory of Nyssa? What is eternity in paradise? It is the fulfillment of pleasure, where each fulfillment is a new *archē*, without end. That is exactly the reverse of our experience of biological desire, which cannot survive its fulfillment. And in that nonbiological, nonontical desire, which is not based on lack, the reverse is true: the more it is fulfilled, the more there is a rebirth of desire, without end. This kind of desire — which is nourished by excess, not destroyed by it — is quite different. When we feel that kind of desire, it's very clear that the original Platonic model, which is, I think, ruling all of metaphysics up to Lacan, is quite insufficient and cannot match the requirement of what is beyond even the way of knowledge. This is true for the question of will also. Because will, according to metaphysics — as will of will, will for knowledge, will to power — is quite different from the will involved in the question of meeting the other person, the question of love. So there is a real equivocity about concepts like will, desire, and so on. And that equivocity is further evidence that there is really some limitation to metaphysics.

RK: Taking up Gregory of Nyssa's point, we might mention his notion of *perichōresis* to describe the love between the three persons of the Trinity. This is a telling analogy, because what you've got here in the Three Persons is a love, a desire, a loving desire, that cedes the place *(cedere)*, that gives room. But it is also a movement of attraction *towards* the other *(sedere)*, a movement of immanence. Father to Son, Son to Spirit, and so on, in an endless circle. Hence the ambivalence of the double Latin translation as both *circum-in-Cessio* and *circum-in-Sessio*. But what is this movement that both yields and attracts? What does the *peri* or *circum* refer to? Around what? *Khōra*, an empty space, a space of detachment and distance and disappropriation. The immanent movement in the free play of each person towards the other is accompanied by a movement of desire which is also a granting or ceding of a place to the other. And it's that double move of ecstasy—*Abgescheidenheit*—that you find within the very play of divine desire, which then translates into human-divine desire.

Just a comment on Hegel. Where I would have a difference with Hegel is on the question of the "Ruse of Reason." Whether Hegel's desire is an ontological drive or an eschatological one is open to interpretation. But certainly in the *Phenomenology* it seems to me that it's still caught in a kind of metaphysical totality. The movement is there, and the energy and dynamism is there, within the dialectic. But in the final analysis, there's a *cunning of reason* that has rigged the game. All the stakes are already set. Where I have a big problem with Hegel is not just with the definition of God as absolute consciousness—a God who has really decided everything before the play has even begun—but also with his notion of evil. It's the question of theodicy, where everything is ultimately justified within the system. In contrast to Hegel, I propose a diacritical hermeneutics which approaches the problem of evil in a less extreme, more tolerant way, a way that allows for greater understanding. This is a very undogmatic claim, a hypothesis, a wager. It is a suggestion that this is a better way of doing things, as a description and as an interpretation. But the only way it can be shown to be better (or worse)—because I'm just part of a dialogue that others have begun long before me and will continue long after me—is through the intersubjective community of dialogue. In other words, it works if people are persuaded by this as an accurate description. As Merleau-Ponty says about the evidence of phenomenology, you read Husserl, you read Heidegger, and either you're persuaded by their descriptions or you're not. There are no extraphenomenological or extrahermeneutical criteria that you can appeal to as a metaphysical foundation or ground or cause that proves you right and the others wrong. So in that sense it is always tentative. Indeed, it seems to me that the virtue of philosophy is this tentativeness—which doesn't mean being relativist or uncommitted. We all operate from beliefs, faiths, and commitments; all our philosophizing is preceded and followed by conviction. Before we enter the realm of philosophy, we are already hermeneutically engaged. We come out the other end—no one being able to live by philosophy alone; we recommit to our convictions, our beliefs, and so on. But the important point is that one acknowledges when one goes into the philosophical debate that these are one's hermeneutical presuppositions, prejudices, and prejudgments—temporally and methodologically suspended for the sake of the conversation. Maybe when you come back to your commitments again, you do so with a greater sensitivity to a plurality of interpretations. This is not relativism; it is a democracy of thought.

M: Yes, may I repeat that point in another way. There is no other argument to choose between different interpretations of the same data than the power of one interpretation in front of the other. This is a very fair battle, where the winner, posited at the end, is the one able to produce more rationality than the other, and you are convinced simply by the *idea vera index sui et fallacia*. The hypothesis that produces more rationality than the other is the winner. And it is why it is a weakness in philosophy always to stick to a narrow interpretation of a situation, which is unable to make sense out of large parts of experience and to say, "well, you have no right to go beyond that limit." For me, it is the defeat of reason, of philosophy, when a philosopher says, "you have no right to make sense of that part of experience; this is meaningless, and should remain meaningless." It is an improvement in philosophy when a new field, which was taken to be meaningless, suddenly makes sense. For instance, you begin with a situation where everyone has an even chance. Everyone can say, "This sunset is a question of biology" or of aesthetics or of religion. Everyone has his possible interpretation, his constitution of the phenomenon. And everyone tries to go as far as they can. The result and the conviction which is gained, or not, is the result only of the power of that interpretation. Let us take the example of Levinas. The question of the *other* remained a puzzling issue until the move made by Levinas, considering that in the case of the phenomenon of the other, we cannot understand it unless we *reverse the intention*. In that case, we no longer have an intention coming from me to the other as the objective, the object, but there is a reverse intentionality, and we have to reconstruct all of the phenomenon that way. By saying that, suddenly a large range of phenomena were available — I would say — for the first time in the history of philosophy. There is no other demonstration than the simple visibility of the phenomenon of the *other*.

RK: I agree. I don't think that the different hermeneutics have to be seen as conflicting or competitive or incompatible. If that were the case, then you'd have to say, "My hermeneutic is right, the saturated phenomenon is God, and Heideggereans are wrong to call it *Ereignis*, and deconstructionists are wrong to call it *khōra*." That's not what it's about. I would rather use the term *equi-primordial* here. For example, say you are depressed. You go to a Heideggerian philosopher, and s/he will tell you this is *angst;* it's an existential experience of your being-towards-death. You go to a psycho-pharmaceutical therapist, and s/he will give you Prozac. The thing is, it's not a question of saying one is right and one is wrong. Here, I think, Julia Kristeva is quite right. If you're to be more fully responsive to the pain of the sufferer, it is not a debate as to whether this is a biochemical crisis or an existential one. It can be both. And you can be helped at both levels. But it is not a matter of saying they're the same thing. They're operating at different levels. I think that's *important* to recognize the different claims, interests, and levels of interpretation.

M: The question of love is also very crucial. For instance, to fall in love implies a very special type of reduction, a self-reduction, but at the level of an erotic reduction, and it is very true that the experience of the other in love is the experience of the saturated phenomenon *par excellence.* It's absolutely clear that you will "see" the other before knowing him or her. On the other hand, "blessed are those who believe without seeing." What does that mean exactly? It may be, to some extent, the distinction between philosophy and theology, simply that. Because in philosophy we have to "see" to believe. What does that mean, to believe? For us, because we start from a philosophical point of view, we spontaneously think that to believe is to take for true, to assume something as if it were true, without any proof. This is our interpretation of belief. In that case, it is either belief or seeing. But is this the real meaning of belief? In fact, belief is also to commit yourself, and in that case it is also, perhaps, a theoretical attitude. Because by committing yourself to somebody else, you open a field of experience. And so it's not only a substitute for not knowing; it is an act which makes a new kind of experience possible. It is because I believe that I will see, and not as a compensation. It's the very fact that you believe which makes you see new things, which would not be seen if you did not believe. It's the *credo ut intelligam.* So all this makes clear that what is at stake with the end of metaphysics, and with phenomenology, is that the distinction between the theoretical attitude and the practical attitude should be questioned. At the end of metaphysics, both theory and practical situations are quite different. But I think there are practical or ethical requirements even in a theoretical point of view. There is no pure theoretical point of view. You assume a complete attitude towards the world. And this has to be questioned. It is why questions about what is given, and what you believe, of love, are perhaps the unavoidable issues now.

RK: On this question of seeing, I think it's important to recognize hermeneutically that there is a plurality of seeing. We can see in different ways. The empiricist sees the burning bush as a fact. John Locke would probably describe it in terms of impressions, and John Searle would probably start cooking sausages. That is a certain approach: a positivist, materialist, pragmatist approach. By contrast, Husserl or Heidegger, for example, might see it as a manifestation, a *Lichtung*, or disclosure of Being. For Husserl, it would be a kind of categorial seeing: we're not just looking at the fire as it burns us, as it lights up; we're also looking at the *being* of the fire. Heidegger would deepen this ontological seeing. But then we could add a third mode of seeing, with a third reduction, which would be an eschatological seeing, where you hear the voice and you see the fire as a manifestation of the divine. Either you see it or you don't. And it doesn't mean, philosophically, that one is right and one is wrong. John Locke and the empiricists would come to Mount Horeb to describe the impression of a fire, unlike Moses, who came with a burning question: How do I liberate my people from bondage in Egypt? Moses is lost; he is disoriented; his people are enslaved; he's looking for liberty, for hope. He comes with the desire for a promise, the desire for revelation. And so Moses sees something that the empiricist is not going to see. There are different modes of seeing. They're not incompatible. Maybe Moses initially saw the fire empirically (you have to, to even approach it), but then he hears the voice. And that hearing and seeing *otherwise* is what trips the hermeneutic switch. Belief and desire are indispensable to interpretation.

As you know yourselves, when you're talking to someone about a difficult concept—love, beauty, the sublime, Being, God—you tend, even colloquially, to say, "Do you see what I mean?" Now, it's that "seeing-as," that "Do you see it *as* I see it?" that signals a different mode of seeing. In all modes of seeing, there is a "seeing-as," and therefore a belief, a presupposition, a reading (no matter how spontaneous or prereflective). In the case of Moses, there is what we might call a theological-eschatological "seeing-as": he sees the burning bush *as* a manifestation of God. For Moses and for subsequent believers, that is what it is; that is how it strikes them. But for someone who doesn't come with that faith, they're not going to see it that way.

M: Is that "seeing-as" simply the application of the same phenomenological "as-structure" in Heidegger, in *Sein und Zeit [Being and Time]*?

RK: Yes, although not at exactly the same level. It would be confessional rather than purely existential.

M: You suggest that the case of seeing-as according to faith is a variation of *die Als-Struktur?*

RK: Yes, but you will interpret the seeing eschatalogically, as a seeing of something that precedes you and overwhelms you and exceeds you.

M: What is very important to make clear against [Karl] Barth's or [Rudolf] Bultmann's way of thinking is that there is some continuity between the general structure of hermeneutics and the case of faith, which is not irrational. This is my point. There is a deep rationality in the operations of faith, understanding, and interpretation, which cannot be reduced to the usual rules of hermeneutics and phenomenology. But there is a connection. I think we are no longer in a situation where you have "reason or faith." Reason is a construct. It is not optional; it is done. I would say that the difficulty for Christian theology now is perhaps that Christian theology assumes too much of the former figure of metaphysics and philosophy, which is already deconstructed. And this opens, I think, new fields for creative theology. But many theologians, if I may say so, have not taken quite seriously deconstruction and the end of metaphysics, and so they miss open opportunities. It is perhaps surprising that philosophers are maybe more aware of new possibilities open to theology than theologians (or at least some them).

RK: An afterthought on the question of the hermeneutic "as." I would say the everyday way of seeing the world is always inscribed by an "as." We see everything "as." Wittgenstein, of course, makes the same point. Seeing is always seeing as. But when we go to practice philosophical hermeneutics, we bring the everyday "as" of prereflective lived experience (what Heidegger calls our preunderstanding/*Vor-verständnis*) to a level of conscious clarification and critical reflection. I think we then switch the hermeneutic "as" into an "as if." There we enter into a position where we pretend we don't have our belief structures; we act "as if" we were free of convictions or presuppositions. It is a version of methodological bracketing or suspension. We put our everyday lived beliefs into parenthesis—not to renounce them, not to disown them, but to see them all the better. We go into a methodological laboratory of possibilities where our faith commitments and convictions—and it doesn't have to be religious faith; it can be political or cultural faith, etc.—become certain ones amongst others. The so-called neutrality of philosophical hermeneutics is therefore strategic, artificial, contrived—but very helpful as a pull toward common understanding or consensus. I acknowledge the "seeing as" of my everyday preunderstanding; I put that on the table, and then I act *as if* I'm now open to empathizing with and listening to, with an open mind, these other perspectives. Then finally, of course, one returns after the thought experiment of the hermeneutic "as if" to the former convictions of one's lived world. After the detour of methodological suspension, one returns to one's primordial "seeing as"—but hopefully with a more enlarged, amplified, and attentive attitude. An attitude more sensitive and open to other points of view.

M: We should emphasize, before concluding, that there is also a *temporality* in the experience of the saturated phenomenon. We may be in quite different situations in front of the saturated phenomenon. Some saturated phenomena will, after a certain time, perhaps be reduced to average objects. Perhaps after more information, other concepts, we shall be able to constitute them as objects. So there are some states—like admiration, according to Descartes—which change. Some admiration should disappear after time: when there is no surprise any more, complete understanding, no admiration left. We have that possibility. But there is the other possibility with saturated phenomena that the more we understand them, the more they keep appearing *as* saturated phenomena. For example, the saturated phenomena of the *ur*-impression of time: it is always renewed. Or the experience of living and knowing the other, when it is successful: the more you know the other, the more it remains a saturated phenomenon. And you may perhaps assume the same about the historical event: the more you study the historical event, the more it appears again and again as a nonobjective phenomenon, a saturated phenomenon. So I think there are a lot of different epistemological situations. The saturated phenomenon does not stop epistemological enquiry; it makes it quite different.

Paul Ricœur
On Narrative Imagination

On Life Stories

RK: You have written much about the power of narrative to provide people with a sense of identity and cohesion. You have also written much about the fact that human existence is always in quest of narrative by way of providing us with a historical memory or future. Do you believe that narrative has a positive therapeutic potential?

PR: Well, Hannah Arendt claims that "all sorrows may be borne if you may put them into a story or tell a story about them." She uses Isak Dinesen's beautiful proverb as the epigraph to her great chapter "Action" in *The Human Condition*. Now this chapter is based on the remarkable theme of the "disclosure of the agent in speech and action" (section 24), followed by its corollary that it is in narrative that the disclosure of the "who" is fulfilled, thanks to its weaving of the web of relationships between agents and the circumstances of action. What is lost, at least for a moment (it is explored a little later in "The Frailty of Human Affairs," section 26), is the burden of these "sorrows" in the epigraph. Whence my question: What resources does the "story" have to make sorrows *bearable?*

It is in examining this question that I would like to enrich and reinforce the conclusions of your *On Stories.* I will do this by adding to the adjective *acting* that of *suffering,* referring to the acting and suffering person. This topic is not absent in *On Stories.* Its three "case histories" —

33

Joyce's Daedalus, Freud's Dora, and [Steven] Spielberg's representation of Schindler compared with [Claude] Lanzmann's *Shoah*—are
about sorrows, whether they be the torments of hysteria or of the
unspeakable horror of the death camps. In this way sorrow is in each
case the answer to the question which opens your book: "Where Do
Stories Come From?" However, in none of these cases does the "story"
make sorrow bearable: Molly's final soliloquy in *Ulysses* does not achieve
this effect; similarly, Dora is not cured (perhaps because her case was
used to verify a theory which would take shape more so in Freud's
biography), and the sufferings of extermination exceed the resources
of narrative—cinematic as much as literary. If sorrow is neither absent
nor resolved in your journey through personal narratives, it goes no
differently in the national narratives, those founding Roman myths,
those humiliating representations of the Irish by the British until recently,
those relating to the distorted relationships of the Americans with their
others, the border crossings that prove to be the source of an alienation
that makes neighbors into strangers.

What then can I add to this ensemble of stories generated in some
way or other by the innumerable figures of sorrow? I propose a reflection on the capacity "to bear"—to *endure*—that is generated by narrative. A void indeed remains to be filled in the vigorous concluding chapter of *On Stories*, entitled "Narrative Matters." This chapter remains
centered, like Arendt's chapter "Action," on the relationship between
the narrative and the acting person. You show yourself to be concerned
by the postmodern criticism of traditional narratives, be they fiction
or history (coinciding paradoxically, though for opposite reasons, with
the negationist criticism of the *Shoah*). At stake in the quarrel is the
persistence of the very capacity to *narrate* in a time of fragmentation
and the dispersion of human experience in its totality. In this response,
you find support from that which seems to validate the persistence of
the capacity to narrate, exemplified in the perennial nature of the categories of narrative theory drawn from Aristotle's *Poetics;* it is the
link between narrative and action that is at the center of the theory,
which is a matter of *mythos, mimesis,* or *catharsis.* The basic argument
is that life itself is in search of narrative "because it strives to discover a pattern to cope with the experience of chaos and confusion."
Cast in these terms, the argument leaves me enough leeway to join suffering to action. However, following Aristotle, what is said of life is
recentered on action in order to introduce the topic of mimesis, which
is the mimesis of action, by virtue of the thesis taken from the anthropological part of the *Nicomachean Ethics,* according to which action "is

always conducted in view of some end." It is thus permitted to affirm that "each human life is always already an implicit story."

But does not sorrow come to cast its shadow on the finalist version of human action that secures the primacy of action in the theory of narrative? Does it not place in doubt the assertion according to which it would be the life of each person that would "always already" be an implicit story? My suggestion here is that the arguments that follow the definition of narrative as "mimesis of action" or "acting persons" would emerge reinforced by the addition of suffering to action, whether it be a matter of redefining *mimesis* as "re-creation," *catharsis* as "release," *phronesis* as "wisdom," and finally *ethos* as an "ethics" concerned with a persisting "self-identity," which perdures through a life of our memories, projects, and presence in the world.

How would this widening of the referential base of narrative be carried out? It would need, I suggest, to recapture the theme of mourning by revealing its narrative component.

To this end, I will rely on the rapprochement, suggested in *La mémoire, l'histoire, l'oubli* [Memory, History, the Lapse of Memory], between *(a)* what Freud says in "Mourning and Melancholia" about the distinctive features of mourning compared to melancholia, and *(b)* his comments in "Recollection, Repetition, and Working Through" on the distinctive features of recollection when "working through" frees it from repetition. But as you have done in *On Stories*, I will not make psychoanalysis the only resource for a reflection on the narrative component of mourning. Psychoanalysis operates under the restrictive conditions that comprise the rule of "telling all," the abandon of free association, the role of transference and countertransference. I want to hold up the experience of analysis as a model and guide concerning the ways of facing tragedy and sorrow in the normal circumstances of life, let us say, those of ordinary neurosis. It was these circumstances of tragedy which I took as my reference point in my essay "Evil, a Challenge to Philosophy and Theology" (1986), included in *Lectures 3* (and in *Figuring the Sacred*).

I return to my attempt to learn a lesson from the rapprochement between "Mourning and Melancholia" and "Recollection, Repetition, and Working Through." The title of the first essay does not evoke narrative at all, but introduces the idea of the "work of mourning," onto which I will graft my theme of the work of narrative as applied to sorrow. The situations to which mourning reacts are indeed situations of sorrow: the loss of a loved one or of an abstraction set up in place of this person. As for the work of mourning it consists of this: "the test of reality showed that the loved object ceased existing and the entire *libido* is commanded to give up the bond which attached it to this object. It is against this that there is an understandable revolt." There follows Freud's description of the "large cost of time and cathectic energy" that this obedience of the libido to the orders of reality requires, in spite of the continued existence of the lost object in psychic intimacy. "The detailed realization of each order laid down by reality is the work of mourning." Is it not to a work of memory that the work of mourning can in its turn cathect? Is the feeling of mourning not based on complaints that melancholy has transformed into accusations *(Ihre Klagen sind Anklagen)*? Is it not these complaints and accusations that narrative struggles to *tell differently?*

This suggestion finds support precisely in Freud's second essay. Here it is the tendency to act out *(passer à l'act)*, which Freud sees as a "substitute for memory," that occasions a transition towards narrative; the patient, says Freud, "does not reproduce the forgotten fact in the form of remembering but in the form of action; he *repeats* it, obviously without knowing that he repeats it." Freud explains the phenomenon in terms of the link between the compulsion to repeat and resistances. This is where the obstacle to remembering resides. It is then the "translaboration" or "working out" which makes recollection a work, the work of memory. Is this not, once again, a contact point for a narrative that should be called a labor of narrative? Does this work of narrative not lie in the transition between what I call in *Time and Narrative* the "configuration" constitutive of emplotment and the "refiguration" of life by the practice of narrative? The work of narrative would thus be the narrative form of "working through."

It is in widening this breach in the direction of the work of mourning with which all acting and suffering beings are someday or other confronted that I return to your closing statement in *On Stories* in order to amplify it and reinforce it. Yes, "all sorrows can be borne if you put them into a story or tell a story about them." But these narratives that are able to make sorrows *bearable* and to make us able to endure them constitute but one element of the work of mourning. Peter Homans, in *The Ability to Mourn,* shows that this work, which all of psychoanalysis seeks to explore, extends to the whole of our archaic and infantile beliefs, to our disappointments and disillusions, and in general to everything in our existence that bears the mark of *loss.* Loss is the overarching pattern into which sorrow fits. It is this that was implied in my 1986 essay on evil. It spoke initially about mourning, to address speculative explanations in the form of theodicy, and evoked a *broken dialectic* perhaps close to what you are developing elsewhere with your "God who may be." The essay continued by referring to work carried out in the field of action (evil is that which *must* be fought) and completed in the transformation of *feeling:* at this point I evoked the work of mourning put at the service of appeasing the complaint.

It is here that the work of narrative constitutes an essential element of the work of mourning, understood as the acceptance of the irreparable.

My conviction is that the final chapter of *On Stories*, "Narrative Matters," emerges reinforced by the addition of suffering to acting, of sorrow to praxis. It works better than ever, thanks to this expanding of the ways "of *making* our lives into life-stories."

Paris, May 2003
Trans. Boyd Blundell

On the Crisis of Authority

RK: One of my main arguments in both *On Stories* and *Strangers, Gods and Monsters* was that we live in a time of crisis—crisis of identity, crisis of legitimation, crisis of authority. In recent years in American and Western society, we have witnessed the collapse of a number of major national and international institutions—from the Catholic Church (due to abuse scandals) and corporate capitalism (Enron and Wall Street post-September 11) to the basic practice of the United Nations around the Iraq debacle. How do you think philosophy might best respond to this climate of crisis?

PR: A key problem today is authority. Authority is disappearing from our world. When Hannah Arendt asks, "What *is* authority?" she immediately adds, "What *was* authority?" But what has vanished? I would say it is the right to be ordered or obeyed without having to be legitimated, because the great problem of authority is legitimation. Especially after the 1970s, there was suspicion of anyone having authority. This crisis laid bare the very structure of authority, which is the role of hierarchical relationship amongst equalitarian relations—or, to put it in a spatial metaphor, a vertical relationship crossing a horizontal one. Living together as equals on the one hand and obeying orders on the other. Authority has to be legitimated. It is the capacity to give reasons in a situation which is now in crisis. Before, too, of course, one had to give reasons, but, in a sense, authority worked by a kind of social inertia because it was learned. The antiquity of authority was considered enough because it had a long past in itself. Authority relied on memory.

Nowadays people need explanations for authority. In his book *On Justification,* the French sociologist Luc Boltanski argues that today everyone must be able to justify what she or he does and that this necessity to be justified in each situation is new. In the past, the very fact that there was "authorized" authority meant that "it was so." But today authority is always in question. As we say in French, *"Qui t'a fait roi?"* We always look for another authority behind authority. So it is regressive. We ask where is the end point? Is there something indefinite in authority, or a kind of ultimate point where something will be authorized by itself? It is the lack of this ultimate point of reference that defines our modern situation. To go beyond these generalities, I should distinguish between some typical situations, because authority does not work the same way according to different circles of allegiance. Following Luc Boltanski, we may distinguish between five or six different "worlds" or "cities." Concerning the grammar of *grandeur,* we could say that in a traditional society the model would be the king. But in a modern democratic society, what is the paradigm of *grandeur?* We are not "great" in every respect. We are great according to certain rules of estimation. In a city of creativity or inspiration, for example, amongst artists and writers, the paradigm of greatness is the recognition of creativity, and we have many criteria for this. It must be something which has to do with the capacity to produce something new. But if you speak of the city of fame, if you speak of sports—a great cyclist, for example—you are great according to quite different rules—for example, recognized performance, because fame here is to be recognized in the opinion of others. You are not necessarily great in domestic relationships, because fame is something larger than the family. Still now, in our modern society, the model of the couple involves what the Greeks would have called the *oikos* (the home). The relationship between father, mother, and child is one part of it, the relationship between the sexes another part. In medieval society, for the traditional aristocracy for example, we could say that the model of the home was prevalent. The French or British court was both a *house* and the central *power.* The model of the home absorbed the political relationship. Then in the merchant bourgeois relationship, the capacity to exchange and to invent new modes of exchange, became the prevalent model of the city. Today the Internet is the typical model of a world expansion of the relationship of merchants. Everything is merchandise.

* * *

So where does authority now reside? Today, political relationships are part of our system, but they are only partial relationships, in the sense that we are not always concerned with voting, giving our opinion in opinion poles, or taking part in political meetings. But we remain citizens; the authority of the state still obtains. It concerns only part of our activity, but at the same time it is the condition of all the other relationships of the modern nation-state—this is especially so in Europe. Here the problem of authority is brought to its extreme. Why? Because there is no end to the problem of legitimacy. What makes the authority of the governing power from Hobbes and Machiavelli to Hegel, for instance, is the recurring question: Who or what possesses the right to corrupt others? Because the problem of authority becomes that of *sovereignty,* what is so supreme that there is nothing higher? Then we come back to the core problem: What makes the legitimacy of hierarchical relationship in our democratic tradition of equality? This was the problem of [Alexis de] Tocqueville especially, in his famous book *Democracy in America,* because, coming from Europe where there was the presupposition of aristocratic superiority, he encountered a society in America where there was no theoretical supremacy, no superiority. Where, therefore, was the recognition of superiority to come from? That was Tocqueville's question. And then we have Rousseau, of course, speaking of the "labyrinth of politics."

Now today we have the additional question of international authority. We know how the nation-state works, but the state is afraid of political authority; it has limits of its own; its space is closed. There are two central features of the nation-state. On the one hand, we have the fact that the state has appropriated and absorbed the evils of revenge. As Hegel and Max Weber say, it has the monopoly of violence. But it has the power of implementing its decisions, whereas international society today doesn't have this power. It relies only on the good will, especially of the great powers. But there already we have a silent progression of the international lobby, particularly after the great criminal trials of the middle of the twentieth century—Nuremberg, Tokyo, Buenos Aires—where the tyrants were judged by the victors. The winners of the Great War were able to establish a tribunal which had a certain authority. I think this is a new phenomena. The idea that criminal law could cover the entire globe. As in the Pinochet case, we see how for the first time all the other states have a right to say something about what happens within the boundaries of the Chilean state. Why? Because we recognize that nation-state sovereignty is not absolute; it has rules of its own. The first rule of the sovereign state is to provide security for all its members. In tyrannies, the state has failed to provide this security, so, therefore, this failure gives a right to all the other states to intervene. You have now an international right of intervention in the affairs of particular nations. This involves a certain *external* limitation of sovereignty.

There was a time when, after a certain period, a crime was forgotten, but now, even decades later, you can be judged. This was only made possible after the victory of the democratic states over the Nazis, on the one hand, and the communist tyranny, on the other. This is new and positive. We can judge people who were guilty many years ago because there is a world public opinion.

So how is world opinion linked to the question of authority? How does it work? We could say that there is a trial going on at the level of authority beyond the tribunals. The sentences of tribunals have to be recognized by public opinion. And it is in this process of recognition that something new happens. Before, we did not have this global judgment, this support of international opinion. Maybe it existed within certain quarters in the eighteenth century, under the French intellectual domination of Europe — to a certain extent at the time of Enlightenment, for instance — but today we are witnessing a new world enlightenment.

If we turn, on the other hand, to the whole question of regionalism in the emerging federal project for a Europe of regions, we encounter the problem of the *internal* limitations of the nation-state. Here we witness the growth of intermediary powers at subnational levels, so we witness two systems of limitation: the international limitation of the absoluteness of sovereignty and the regional limits to state sovereignty from within. We now have a very complex system and many options, going from a real plurality of subsystems, as in federal states like Germany or the United States, to the very subtle conjunction between regional governments and national governments in a country like Spain, for example, between the Catalans and the Spanish state, or in Italy between several regional authorities. France is arguably the most resistant to this plurality of substates. Sorting out the various relations between international, national, and subnational power is a good example of practical wisdom in the political field.

Or take, finally, the quarrels between one province and another in Canada: this cannot be decided *from outside.* It is a negotiation between powers and the peoples concerned. The big problem is whether they are consulted in a free and fair way.

Authority involves the crucial question of *legislation* — and this arises at critical moments in the life of a state, usually after a civil war or constitutional crisis. In France, we had seven or eight procedures of amnesty — after the Commune in 1871, after the First World War, after the war of Algeria. Sometimes this can involve a big lie — "nothing happened." But it can also be a way of saying, "We are not in war," a way of preserving peace. I would say it is a matter of official forgetfulness, institutional forgetfulness, *"un oubli institutionnel."* The Americans use the word *pardon.* When Ford gave a pardon to Nixon, it is a remnant of a regal right, the right of grace, but in Europe it has disappeared. In France, only the President of the Republic is allowed to give such a "pardon"; we call it *"grâce."* It's a remnant of the right of the king. But it has already been criticized by Kant in his theory of rights, where he says that *"le droit de grace"* is a privilege of the king; if he uses it for the benefit of culprits, it would be a great injustice. Why? Because then victims would be deprived of the right to be recognized and the law would be despised.

A purely utilitarian practice of amnesty would be a way of saying that the war did not appear, that the war between citizens did not occur; it would be a way of effacing *"le tort,"* the harm done. Such amnesty would be a denial of harms. We are not allowed to speak about it. The first model of this is to be found in the Greek city in 403 B.C. There was a decree in Athens: You will not speak about the evils — *ta kaka.* There was an oath: "I shall not speak, notice, or even remember." It was a censorship of memory. It was a "big lie," because the harm done and the suffering was not recognized; there was an injustice, because there was a lack of recognition. It was a harm done to truth. It is interesting to see in a Greek tragedy how it is the poetry which preserves the memory of suffering. In all the great tragedies, we have the problem of the harm of the powerful and the memories of great families and so on. We could say that politics starts with the prose of peace pitted against the poetry of war. There is a kind of truthfulness in the preservation by poetry of the memory of harm and suffering, while in denial in the prose of political life.

At one level, then, this forgetfulness, this amnesty of crimes of the past, is not a good thing. It seems better to remember. There is the work of mourning. Amnesty and forgetfulness may prevent mourning. They can prevent a second suffering of harm done, but also the suffering of mourning, which is a working through, a creative process. I make an allusion here again to the important essay by Freud, "Mourning and Melancholia," where he speaks of the necessity of preserving mourning from being swallowed up by melancholia. When we prevent mourning, we succumb to melancholia. As we see in Europe after the French Revolution, there was a law of forgetfulness with the end of the Napoleonic wars, after which we had the spleen of the romantic generation.

So it is not harmless to implement amnesty. What I am saying is at the best *"un moindre mal,"* the lesser of two evils. Two great sufferings are prevented—hate and revenge—at the expense of the suffering of memory and the liberating power of this suffering. But we should not underestimate *mourning*. It is a way of giving people the right to start anew by remembering in such a way that we may overcome obsessive or compulsive repetition. It is a matter of the right balance between memory and forgetting.

Narrative has a crucial role here. I speak, especially now, of narrative at the public level, because collective memory and collective identity are based on stories concerning the founding events, and because founding events have civil dates whereby memory is both created and preserved by telling stories. As a result, history has the function of adjudicating commemorations in a kind of public ritual.

Does this found authority? All kinds of authority are ways of telling the story and repeating and therefore preserving what I call the social inertia of the past, by providing a kind of effectiveness of the past. In spite of all the changes in one's society, this is a matter of preserving the invisible roots of community by telling stories.

Paris, April 2001

The Power of the Possible

RK: A central theme explored in *The God Who May Be* is that of "possibility." While I was dealing there primarily with eschatological and ontological notions of the possible, ranging from Cusanus to Heidegger and Derrida, I am aware that you have dealt with this theme in a number of your writings and that you expressed to me recently the wish to write a last book—if you have the time and energy—entitled *L'homme capable*. What sorts of things would you likely explore in such a book?

PR: As I get older, I have been increasingly interested in exploring certain metaphysics of potency and act. In *Oneself as Another,* I broach this in my analysis of the *capacity* to speak, narrate, and act. This phenomenology of the "I can," in turn, brings me to Aristotle's attempt in the *Metaphysics* E 2 to outline metacategories of potentiality and actuality in line with his commitment to a plurality of meanings of *being.* So in this respect, I no longer subscribe to the typically antimetaphysical Protestant lineage of Karl Barth (though it is true that in early works like *The Symbolism of Evil,* I was still somewhat under this influence).

But if I am on the side of metaphysics here, it is, admittedly, in the somewhat minority camp of those who prefer the categories of possibility and actuality to that of "substance." If the mainstream and official tradition of Western metaphysics has been substantialist, this does not preclude other metaphysical paths, such as those leading from Aristotle's *dunamis* to Spinoza's *conatus* and [Friedrich] Schelling's and Leibniz's notions of potentiality *(puissance)*. Here we find a dynamic notion of being as potency and action (Spinoza reformulates substance as a *substantia actuosa*), which contrasts sharply with the old substantialist models of Scholasticism or the mechanistic models of Descartes. This is a matter of dynamism versus mechanism. The idea of a dynamic in being that grows towards consciousness, reflection, community. Here I think it is important to think ontology in close rapport with ethics. And that is why in *Thinking Biblically,* I endeavor to unravel some of the ontological and eschatological implications of the "I am who am" episode in Exodus 3:14. We encounter in this passage a notion of being which is alien to the Greek usage, and so its translation into Greek language and thought signals an alteration of the existing meaning of being to include new notions of being-with, being-faithful, being-in-accompaniment with one's community or people (which is precisely what Yahweh promises Moses when he says "I am he who will be with you"). Now Aristotle had never considered this signification of being when he wrote the *Metaphysics.* But that didn't and doesn't prevent the enlargement of Greek ontology to accommodate and respond to such "other" meanings: a better solution, it seems to me, than setting up an unbridgeable antagonism between Hellenic and Hebraic meanings of being and then having to choose one or the other. What I am exploring in *Thinking Biblically* is a sort of philosophical theology or theological philosophy—not an easy task in a contemporary intellectual culture which still wants people to say whether they are "philosophers" *or* "theologians" and is uncomfortable with overlaps. This recent return to religious thinking is intimately linked with my growing interest in the whole field of action and *praxis,* which increasingly drew me away from the abstract universalism of Kant towards a more Aristotelian ethics of the "good life" *(bien vivre).* And, of course, I would not deny for a moment here the important Heideggerian analysis of "care" and the whole post-Heideggerian retrieval of Greek thinking. Not that I have ever found my ontological feet in any final or absolute sense. It is no accident that the title of the last chapter of *Oneself as Another* is in the form of an interrogation rather than an assertion—"Towards Which Ontology?" Here I try to explore possibilities of an ethical ontology beyond the Heideggerian model of *ontology without ethics* and the Levinasian model of *ethics without ontology*. By trying to think ethics in terms of action *(praxis/pragma)* and action in terms of being as potency and act, I am seeking ways beyond the either/or of Heidegger/Levinas. The ultimate purpose of hermeneutic reflection and attestation, as I see it, is to try to retrace the line of intentional capacity and action behind mere objects (which we tend to focus on exclusively in our natural attitude) so that we may recover the hidden truth of our operative acts—of *being capable*, of being *un homme capable*. So if hermeneutics is right, in the wake of Kant and Gadamer, to stress the finitude and limits of consciousness, it is also wise to remind ourselves the tacit potencies and acts of our lived existence. My bottom line is a *phenomenology of being able*.

RK: It is remarkable that you should begin your philosophical career by reflecting on the nature of *l'homme faillible* (fallible man) and conclude by shifting the focus to *l'homme capable*. One might have expected it the other way around! But could you tease out a little more what you mean by this idea of a phenomenology of "I am able" *(une phénoménologie du je peux)*? As you know, in my own work on the possible, from *Poétique du Possible* (1984) to *The God Who May Be* (2001), I have been trying to develop a post-Heideggerean hermeneutics of possibility, inspired in part by Heidegger's reversal of the old metaphysical priority of act *(energeia)* over potency *(dunamis)*. I wonder if our respective paths are not converging more and more on this question.

PR: I believe that the ontology and analogy of action which I am trying to think through plays itself out on the basis of a differentiated phenomenology of "I can speak," "I can act," "I can narrate," and "I can designate myself as imputable"*(imputabilité)*. What all these instances of "I am able to . . ." articulate is the basic capacity of a human being to act and suffer. I am interested here in an anthropology of potency and impotency *(puissance et impuissance)*. And in one sense what I find intriguing about Spinoza's notion of *conatus* is that it refuses the alternative between act and potency, between *energeia* and *dunamis*. For Spinoza, each concrete thing or event is always a mélange of act and possibility. And I would be closer here to Spinoza or Heidegger than to Aristotle, for what is the meaning of an "architect in potency," to take Aristotle's example, if it is not already an architect who is thinking architecturally, making plans, preparing to realize a building project, and so on? I would hold to the idea of a profound continuity between *dunamis* and *energeia*, since *energeia* is the *ergon*, and this, as we know from the *Ethics*, can be translated as the *task*. Whether being an architect, doctor, musician, etc., is exercised or not, it remains an *ergon*. So that possibility as "capacity" to realize a task is by no means the same thing as possibility as an abstract or logical "virtuality." Think of the sprinter poised on the starting block. There are different modalities of the possible—the possible that is not yet possible, the possible that is on the way to being realized, the possible that is already a certitude, etc.

RK: Unlike Aristotle, then, who argues that we can only know possibility through actuality, you would say that "attestation" is already a way of knowing possibility *(puissance)*.

PR: Yes, I would say that, and I think this has important ethical consequences. I would insist, for example, that certain people who are deprived of their rights or means to exercise their capacities—for example, the imprisoned or the mentally ill—nonetheless are worthy of respect, because they still possess these capacities as possibilities. Likewise, if I say that I can speak a certain foreign language, I do not have to be actually speaking it to have this capacity or skill. Or, indeed, when it comes to language generally: it is true that I *can* speak and use all sorts of different words and constructions, even if I am not actually doing so and will arguably never be in a position to speak *all* of language. And here it might be useful to rethink the Aristotelian notion of *dunamis* and Spinoza's notion of *conatus* in rapport with Leibniz's notion of *appetites*—possibility as a dynamic tendency or inclination. These philosophers, and Heidegger and yourself, too, of course, offer great resources for a new thinking about the possible. But my own interest in these questions is ultimately inseparable from the *moral* question—How do we relate a phenomenology of "being able" to the ethical events of "imputability" and "attestation"? And I might even concede here a point made recently by my young colleagues Dominico Jervolino and Fabrizio Turoldo that my thought is not so removed from certain religious and biblical issues as my standard policy of "conceptual ascetism" might have been prepared to admit in the past. I am not sure about the absolute irreconcilability between the God of the Bible and the God of Being (understood with Jean Nabert as "primary affirmation" or with Spinoza as *"substantia actuosa"*). The tendency of modern French thought to eclipse the Middle Ages has prevented us from acknowledging certain very rich attempts to think God and being in terms of each other. I no longer consider such conceptual asceticism tenable.

RK: Would you say that there is difference between your early and late thinking?

PR: Is there a difference between the beginning and the end? It's true that I have changed in the last fifty years. I have read lots of new books, and the whole philosophical climate has altered in all kinds of important ways. I began in an era of existentialism, traversed structuralism, and now find myself before a "post-I-know-not-what," deconstruction, etc. A long life like mine has meant passing through a great variety of philosophical landscapes, and negotiating with my contemporaries—sometimes friends, sometime adversaries—is each time different according to the specific nature and singularity of the encounter. And yet perhaps history will link these different situations in some way?

Recorded by Fabrizio Turoldo and Richard Kearney, Paris 1995 and 2003

Imagination, Testimony, and Trust

Q: I am sure that Professor Ricœur realizes that in a country like Ireland, we have a particular interest in the idea of obsessive memorization and in repetition and ritual in political terms, so if we could retell stories—if we could recreate a narrative and liberate ourselves from this—we would be looking to a better future. But the problem of retelling the narrative is that it is told and retold so that you get not one agreed narrative but two narratives, and the competing narratives simply duplicate the conflicting ideologies from which they come. How, in this country, can you get a shared narrative about identity?

PR: This problem of a common narrative calls for an ethics of discussion. In so-called discourse ethics, developed by people like [Jürgen] Habermas and [Karl-Otto] Apel, we argue one against the other, but we understand the argument of the other without assuming it. This is what John Rawls calls "reasonable disagreements." I take the example of the relationship between Europe and the Islamic world, where we distinguish between those Islamic speakers with whom we can discuss and others with whom we cannot. We make the difference between reasonable disagreement and intractable disagreement. A common or identical history cannot be reached—and should not be attempted—because it is a part of life that there are conflicts. The challenge is to bring conflicts to the level of discourse and not let them degenerate into violence, to accept that they tell history in their own words as we tell our history in our own words and that these histories compete against each other in a kind of competition of discourse—what Karl Jaspers called a loving conflict. But sometimes consensus is a dangerous game, and if we miss consensus, we think that we have failed. To assume and live conflicts is a kind of practical wisdom.

Q: You speak, in relation to Freud, of repetition as an obstruction to memory. But might it not also be, in certain instances, a way of constructing a memory one could be comfortable with?

PR: This is why Freud speaks of patience. The work of memory is a slow transformation of compulsive repetition into a talking cure, a liberation from pathological obsession into words as free association. Freud provides some historical examples where repressed feelings and memories were allowed to be brought to the surface, and it is quite possible that the positive side of commemoration has, in a sense, to do with this "acting out," which is a form of substitution, allowing for healthy memory. This sort of patience is very important: to let time do its own work, which is not destruction but a diluting resistance.

Q: I'd like to raise the question of historical retrieval.

PR: Let me cite a situation where there are several different interpretations of the same past event. I take the case of the French Revolution, since, over nearly two centuries, it has been a bone of contention among French historians. We have many stories of the French Revolution, and it is the competition between these stories that makes for historical education. There are two extreme approaches. The first is that of claiming the event as the beginning of everything, a new creation of a new human being. Some of the revolutionary leaders even tried to invent a new calendar with a new way of dividing times and years and months and weeks (a week of ten days and so on). So it claimed to be the master of time and history. The opposite interpretation claims the French Revolution to have been only an acceleration of the centralizing trend of the monarchy, or a mere prefiguration of the Bolshevik Revolution. Here, the French Revolution is not seen as a unique event but a mere variation on a larger historical movement. By acknowledging that the history of an event involves a conflict of several interpretations and memories, we in turn open up the future. And this retrieval-projection of history has ethical and political implications. Different political projects concerning the future invariably presuppose different interpretations of the past. Utopian projects, for instance, are about unkept promises of the historical past being reprojected, reanimated in terms of a better future which might realize such lost opportunities or unfulfilled, betrayed, possibilities. So here we have to connect past and future in an exchange between memory and expectation. The German historian Reinhart Koselleck put this past-future relation well in saying that there is a permanent tension between what he calls the space of experience *(erfahrungsfeld)* and the horizon of expectation. This critical exchange between memory and expectation is, I believe, fundamental.

Q: You say utopias are places where we reactivate unkept promises of the past. Does that mean there are no new dreams to dream and that the future is just a recollection of past historical movements, fulfilled or unfulfilled?

PR: The epistemic status of utopia is very complex. I tried to explore this issue in my book *Lectures on Ideology and Utopia.* There I argued that ideology usually reasserts the historical field of past experience in a gesture of reassurance. Utopia, by contrast, attempts a kind of excursion out of time, a radical break into the future. There is a moment of madness in utopia which is irreducible to mere repetition. Utopia claims to be imagination of the new, of a pure beginning. But the opposition is not so simple. No historical period ever exhausted its own dreams. What happened in the past is only a partial realization of what had been projected. We may say this of the Greek city which failed and of the Roman Empire which was rescued by the Catholic Church as the Holy Roman Empire, before it collapsed again. The promise of an historical event is always more than what was actually realized. There is more in the past than what happened. And so we have to find the *future of the past,* the unfulfilled potential of the past. That is why Raymond Aron argues that one of the tasks of the historian is to return to the moment of time when the actors did not know what would happen later and therefore to assume the state of uncertainty in which these actors were positioned, exploring the multiplicity of their expectations, few of which were ever fulfilled. Even Habermas approaches the Enlightenment in this way, as a still unfulfilled project. There is something still unfulfilled in the Greek heritage, in the Christian heritage, in the Enlightenment heritage, in the romantic heritage. There is never pure rupture. There is always reactualization to some degree or another.

Q: In Ireland, we have a saying: If you want to know what happened, ask your father, and if you want to know what people say happened, ask your mother. There is this double attitude to the history of the past—what actually happened (history) and the way in which people interpreted what happened (story). Do we not always select and edit memories? Is it not true that to remember everything, as the Irish playwright Brian Friel says, is a form of madness?

Q: Following on from the previous question, if you allow many different interpretations of your own memory and of the memories of the nation, and if you claim that the healthy thing is a conflict of interpretations which disallows any final consensus—since there is no one who has the perspective from which to say what *really* happened—how can you talk of the *abuse* of memory, either on a personal level or on the level of the nation? If there are only competing interpretations, each with a claim on truth, how can we speak of truth or untruth in history? To speak of abuse assumes you have some perspective from which you can judge that someone is making a proper use of memory, and that someone is making an improper use of memory.

PR: In relation to both questions, allow me to refer to my essay "Memory and Forgetting," in which I spoke of the truth claim of memory. This should not be forgotten. There could be no *good* use of memory if there were no aspect of truth. So, in a sense, what "really happened" must keep concerning us. And here I am faithful to the German school of historians of the nineteenth century in saying that we have to tell things as they really happened *(wie es eigentlich gewesen)*. This is a very difficult problem, because we have two ways of speaking of the past. The past is something that is no longer there but which has been there, which once was there. So the grammar of the past is a twofold grammar. It is no longer, and yet it *has been*. In a sense we are summoned by what was, beyond the loss of what is, no longer to be faithful to what happened. Here we confront problems of historical representation and reference to the past, but we must never eliminate the truth claim of what has been. This is so for ethical as well as epistemological reasons.

Q: You are not saying that history is a matter of a pure relativism of interpretations, where anything goes?

PR: No. This crucial issue brings us to the borderline between imagination and memory. In his book on imagination, *The Psychology of Imagination*, [Jean-Paul] Sartre said that imagination is about the unreal, and memory is about the (past) real. So there is a positing act in memory, whereas there is an unrealizing of history in imagination. It is very difficult to maintain the distinction, but it must be kept, at least as a basic recognition of two opposite claims about the past, as *unreal* and *real*. In that sense, memory is on the side of perception, whereas imagination is on the side of fiction. But they often intersect. There are so-called revisionist historians, those who, like [Robert] Faurisson, deny the existence of extermination camps, ignore this problem of "factual" truth. This is why historical memory needs to be supplemented by documentary and archival evidence. The Popperian criterion of falsifiability must be observed. This is not to ignore the fact that sometimes fictions come closer to what really happened than do mere historical narratives, where fictions go directly to the *meaning* beyond or beneath the facts. It is puzzling. But, finally, we have to return to a body count. You have to accurately *count* the corpses in the death camps as well as offering vivid narrative *accounts* that people will remember.

Q: Is it possible to get a balance between the two approaches, between a narrative retelling (which evokes in us the feeling of the horror of what happened) and a critical, scientific, objective distance (which informs us of the "facts" of what happened). Is this not a paradox?

PR: I would say that the paradox is not on the side of memory but of imagination. This is the case because imagination has two functions. The first is to bring us outside of the real world—into unreal or possible worlds. But it has a second function, which is to put memories *before our eyes*. Bergson touches on this in the second chapter of *Matter and Memory*. He says that pure memory is virtual and has to be brought back into the field of consciousness *as* an image. This is why writing history as memory is so difficult. We are dealing with memory-images where imagination serves as a kind of *mise-en-scène* of the past. The reality of history is made "visible" again through images, and this makes memory a reproduction, a sort of second production. Yet at the same time, the difference *remains* between the unreal and the real. So the paradox of imagination-memory is very puzzling indeed. Many philosophers, such as Spinoza, have treated memory as a province of imagination. And we also have the view, expressed by [Blaise] Pascal and [Michel de] Montaigne, that memory is a form of imagination which is to be guarded against. This is why I stress so strongly the reality claims of memory to remain faithful to our *debt* to the past, to the pastness of the past. Which brings me finally to the indispensable issue of *testimony*. Testimony is the ultimate link *between* imagination and memory, because the witness says "I was part of the story. I was there." At the same time, the witness tells a story that is a living presentation, and therefore deploys the capacity of imagination to place the events before our eyes, as if we were there. Testimony would be a way of bringing memory and imagination together. It is very difficult, of course. I am struggling with this difficulty at present. Maybe it has to do with the two meanings of pastness—no longer there and still there, absent and present (or quasi-present). How do we make the past visible as if it were present, while acknowledging our debt to the past as it actually happened? That is my main ethical question of memory.

Q: Is it not the case that testimonies can be manipulated and distorted to serve certain interests? If so, what critical tools must we avail ourselves of to unmask such manipulation?

PR: In order to answer this, we must refer to the epistemological structure of historical knowledge. The fundamental objective of the *good* historian is to enlarge the sphere of archives; that is, the conscientious historian must open up the archive by retrieving traces which the dominant ideological forces attempted to suppress. In admitting what was originally excluded from the archive, the historian initiates a critique of power. He gives expression to the voices of those who have been abused, the victims of intentional exclusion. The historian opposes the manipulation of narratives by telling the story differently and by providing a space for the confrontation between opposing testimonies. We must remember, however, that the historian is also embedded in history: he belongs to his own field of research. The historian is an actor in the plot. Our condition dictates that we can never be in a state of pure indifference. The historian's testimony is therefore not completely neutral. It is a selective activity. It is, however, far less selective than the testimony of the dominant class. Here we should invoke what John Rawls calls "reflective equilibrium." He speaks of the need for reflective equilibrium between predominantly held beliefs and the findings of critical minds, represented by professional people such as historians. Such a mechanism helps us to distinguish good from bad history. In the final analysis, however, we must emphasize the role of trust. When I testify to something, I am asking the other to trust that what I am saying is true. To share a testimony is an exchange of trust. Beyond this we cannot go. Most institutions rely fundamentally on the trust they place in the word of the other.

Q: How do you reconcile the emphasis which you place on the role of trust with what you call "the hermeneutics of suspicion"?

PR: The hermeneutics of suspicion functions against systems of power which seek to prevent a confrontation between competing arguments at the level of genuine discourse. In such discourse, we bring together diverse and opposing *interests* with the hope that they will engage at the level of rigorous argumentation. Habermas sees in such a strategy an "ethics of discussion." Such an ethics of discourse obliges me to give my best argument to my enemy in the hope that he will in turn articulate his resentment and aggression in the form of an equally plausible argument. It is through discussion of this sort that suspicion between opposing interests gives way to trust and a certain level of consensus.

Q: How can an "ethics of discussion" help us to forgive and forget?

PR: It is always better to give expression to anger or hatred than to repress it. It is good that the wounds of history remain open to thought. There is indeed something healthy in the expression of anger. To repress grievances is certainly bad. Expression and discussion are ways of healing. Psychoanalysis relies precisely on this expressive function of language. To hear the anger of other people forces us to confront our wrongdoings, which is the first step towards forgiveness. We must have trust in language as a weapon against violence, indeed, the best weapon there is against violence.

Our thanks to the following for contributing to this dialogue, held at University College Dublin in April 1998 and first published in *Questioning Ethics*, ed. Richard Kearney and Mark Dooley (London and New York: Routledge, 1999): Brian Cosgrave, Gayle Freyne, David Scott, Imelda McCarthy, Redmond O'Hanlon, Brian Garvey, John Cleary, Margaret Kelleher, Dermot Moran, and Maeve Cooke, in addition to the two editors.

Georges Dumézil
Myth, Ideology, Sovereignty

RK: There is still some debate as to how exactly your work should be situated and classified. Is it primarily philosophical, sociological, anthropological, theological, or linguistic? After your early research, you begin to define your study of ancient myths and religions as "the comparative study of the Indo-European religions" or simply "Indo-European civilization," in contradistinction to the earlier title of "comparative mythology." How does this change in nomenclature describe your specific approach to myth and religion?

GD: My work is primarily linguistic, or, to be more precise, philological. That is, the classification and interpretation of ancient myths in terms of textual structures or types. My first concern was to discover what the earliest texts of the various Indo-European civilizations might have in common, what similarities of *function* might exist in different mythic or religious orders to suggest a shared source. Eventually, I discerned the "Ideology of the Three Functions"—Sovereignty, Force, and Fecundity—firstly in texts representative of diverse layers of Vedic, Germanic, and Roman civilization. And this led me to ascertain that there existed a specific conception of the three functions in all of the Indo-European cultures from India to Ireland. So my original philological preoccupation to better understand the texts of Indian and classical poets, for instance, developed into a passion to understand the unrevealed ways of thought of their common ancestors. In short, *philology* enabled me to posit the existence of an underlying Indo-European *ideology*.

This development meant of course that my work could no longer be accurately termed *comparative mythology*, since the ideology of the three functions proved to be one of the chief characteristics of Indo-European civilization as a whole; it is not, for example, present in any articulate way in African, American Indian, Chinese, or even biblical texts. And if they are present to a degree in the Aniki tradition of Polynesia, that probably results from very ancient and strong Indian components. Moreover, "mythology" itself became too limited a rubric, for the ideology of the three functions was also to be found in the religious, literary, philosophical, and even at times social, structures of Indo-European societies.

RK: How does this approach differ, for instance, from the "anthropological" method of Claude Lévi-Strauss or the "comparative phenomenological" method of Mircea Eliade?

GD: Both Eliade's and Lévi-Strauss's readings of the world of myth are very different from my own. Eliade's approach to myth strikes me as being primarily that of a man of letters. He interprets myth as a poet might, in terms of its inexhaustible mystery and sacredness. To see this, one only has to read his reflections on the myths of cyclical time and eternal return. But he differs of course from the ordinary poet in that he is a philosophising poet. He is concerned with the comparative study of the myths and rituals of different world civilizations in order to identify what he would see as the universal characteristics of man as a *homo religiosus*. Lévi-Strauss, on the contrary, is before all else a philosopher. His philosophy is essentially a *critical* philosophy, that is, a critical interrogation of the systems and structures which enable men to understand their world. Hence the term *structuralist*, which is applied to him.

RK: If you differ from Eliade and Lévi-Strauss in terms of *method*—philological rather than poetic or philosophical—is it not true that you also differ in respect of *subject matter*?

GD: Certainly. Eliade, though he began as a specialist of Eastern European culture (which he knew intimately as a Romanian) and Indian folklore (of which he also had firsthand acquaintance from his visits there in the 1930s), analyzes material from all or most of the world religions. He was also a talented philologist and linguist. But his overriding interest is a "comparative phenomenology," that is, a reflective description of the "essential meaning" of the totality of ancient myths, rituals, and symbols still available to modern research. Lévi-Strauss, for his part, specializes in the study of the religions of peoples *without writing*. This is what he calls "savage thought" *(la pensée sauvage)* with no derogatory intent, because it precedes and precludes historical transposition into a developing or evolving literature (what he calls "diachronic" culture). Lévi-Strauss's principal subject matter is, accordingly, the culture of the Latin-American Indian, where the symbolic and ritual structures have resisted time and change, remaining the same throughout the centuries ("synchronic"). To put it briefly, I differ from Eliade in that my research is confined to the ideological structures of Indo-European civilization and from Lévi-Strauss in that this Indo-European civilization is a historically developing and diachronic one—in direct contrast to the *"pensée sauvage"* of the American Indians. That said, I must point out that there is absolutely no conflict between our three approaches. They operate on three heterogeneous planes without collision. I have great respect for the work of both Eliade, with whom I have been associated, and of Lévi-Strauss, who so kindly received me at the Académie française and whose work I see as wholly compatible with my own, though some of his disciples have claimed otherwise.

RK: What would you consider to be the relationship between the ideology of the three functions and history? Would you consider yourself an historian?

GD: I like to think of myself as an historian of sorts, though many historians would object to this. The study of Indo-European ideology does not exclude the study of history. On the contrary, I believe that history as we know it is ultimately founded on an *ultrahistory*. This ultrahistory consists of an interpretation of the historical facts. To be more precise, it comprises the tripartite ideological functions which structure the historical facts available to us. For what is the Ideology of the Three Functions but the way in which the Indo-Europeans *explained* their world, giving the facts of existence an explicit meaning, order, or coherence. Thus historical facts, as rendered or recorded in Indo-European texts, are already conceptual interpretations of history. For example, in the last six songs of the *Aeneid*, the articulation of Aeneas, Tarchon, and Latinus is given coherence by being modelled on the tripartite structure of Romulus (the religious sovereignty of the proto-Romans), Lucumon (the warrior force of the Etruscans) and Tatius (the wealth and the gift of the Sabines), which had been itself produced as an expression of the tripartite scheme. But these ideological divisions exist not only in mythic and literary structures but also in the *ensemble* of religious, social, and philosophical structures of a society. They cut right through a culture and give it its specific sense of order. Thus when I speak of ideology, I do not mean it in the habitual sense of a "theory of illusions" opposed to the reality of history. I mean rather the comprehensive sense of a body of structural formations and functions to be found in a society's myths (mythology), deities (theology), ideals (philosophy), and even at times in the organization of its social history. In this respect, I would say that my homeland of research resides somewhere between the philologists and the historians, somewhere between the text and the historical facts that are being conceptualised or harmonized in the text — their ultrahistory.

RK: But how does this ultrahistorical ideology of a culture correspond to its empirical or sociological institutions? Lévi-Strauss's "social anthropology" indicates a direct connection between sociological and mythological structures. In your own work, what is the rapport, if any, between ideology and sociology?

GD: This is an extremely complex question. First, one must remember that every form of ideology — be it mythological, theological, or philosophical — is somehow a response to social reality. However, while in some Indo-European societies, for instance the Indian, one can detect a clear correlation between the tripartite ideology and the real tripartite division of that society into priests, warriors, and labourers, this is not always the case in other societies. Indeed, I would be tempted to say that where such a correspondence does exist, it is but one amongst other applications of the ideology. In other words, social organization conditions the ideology less than it is conditioned by it. I say this because I am struck by the fact that in many cultures the ideology of the three functions can survive at the level of religion or myth or literature without any corresponding social organization. This is true of the Scythians, the Ossetes, or the Celts. For example, the tripartite ideology is manifest in the old Welsh legend of the Mabinogi of Math (eleventh century), even though the tripartite division no longer operated in the social practices of the Welsh people. Similarly, as Jean-Pierre Vernant and others have demonstrated, the tripartite ideology perdured in Greece, even though its social instantiation had virtually disappeared. The same is true of Rome, where ideology represented by the three gods — Jupiter (the sacred), Mars (the military), and the more complex Quirinus (partially the productive) — bears no relation to the binary social division into Patricians and Plebians. One could argue, accordingly, that the tripartite ideology teaches us that there can be a realm of values and explanations beyond the purely economic order.

RK: So you would hold that the tripartite ideology can go beyond socio-economic facts and become autonomous?

GD: I believe that the ideology of functions can ultimately free itself from the social or economic determinations of a society. This does not mean that at one time the ideological and sociological structures were synonymous. Nor, on the other hand, does it mean that ideology ceases to function as a structural interpretation of man's biological, social, or existential needs. I am convinced that the tripartite ideology corresponds to three fundamental biological needs which every human group must satisfy in order to survive: every man has *a brain, hands,* and *a mouth,* which correspond to his natural needs for control (sovereignty), protection (force), and nourishment (fecundity and plenty). Even animals and insects must operate according to the three basic functions as soon as they begin to organize in groups. One can see this by examining a beehive or ant colony. So it is undeniable that the tripartite ideology has some basis or beginning in nature. The natural needs of nourishment, power, and survival are at the root of the ideology of the three functions and constitute its "primary matter." But there is a radical difference between the material needs of nature or human society, from which the three functions may originate, and the formulated ideology of these functions which can go beyond material needs and enjoy considerable autonomy. The three functions always operate as natural needs, but it is only in the old Indo-European cultures that they assume an *explicit conceptual form* by means of which a society can provide itself with an ideological raison d'être.

RK: But how would you account for this distinction between the three functions as biological needs and ideological forms? What enables the human spirit to make this leap from nature to culture, from the real to the ideal? I noted, for example, that in *Mythe et épopée* [Myth and Epic] you speak of myths as "dreams of mankind," as "creations that testify above all to the fertility of the human mind." You seem to suggest that the ideology of myth cannot be exhaustively explained in terms of its biological, socio-economic, or unconscious origins (what Paul Ricœur calls the "archaeological" or reductive hermeneutic). Do you believe, then, that ideology can be seen as a creative projection or invention whereby humans express their desire to transcend the given facts of existence towards a more coherent or perfect model of explanation which often has no place *(u-topos)* in the world of historical contingency? This latter interpretation is what Ricœur calls the "teleological" hermeneutic of hope—meaning that myths, dreams, or symbols can be read as signs of man's striving towards a future goal *(telos* or *eschaton)*, rather than as mere symptoms of a determining past or origin *(archē)*. In short, is myth the product of social and biological determination or of a creative and utopian imagination?

GD: These are really questions for the philosophers. It is true that in my youth I experienced the enthrallment and enthusiasm of philosophy, particularly the philosophy of Bergson. This early experience is one that I have attempted to both assimilate and suppress. And insofar as I have assimilated it, I would say that Bergson's notion of the *élan vital* always tempted me to suppose the existence of a teleological dimension, in addition to an archaeological one, in the creation of ideology. I think that both dimensions exist. But these are things which we can never scientifically prove or demonstrate. We can only "dream" about them.

RK: Your conviction that ideology can sometimes transcend the conditioning empirical facts of history and society would certainly seem to corroborate the teleological interpretation. But I would like to tackle the relationship between ideology and philosophy from another angle. In the preface to *Mythe et épopée,* you describe the ideology of the three functions as a "philosophy" and affirm that "these reflections of the old thinkers merit this name (philosophy) just as much as the speculations of the pre-Socratics." What do you mean exactly by such a comparison?

GD: I am taking philosophy here, in its largest and most generous sense, to mean the explanation of human experience in terms of conceptual structures. Therefore, just as the pre-Socratics explained their experience of nature and the cosmos in terms of the cycle of the four elements—air, fire, water, earth—or in terms of dialectical pairings such as love/hate or light/darkness, the ideology of the three functions proffers an equally coherent structuring of experience with its division into (1) *the sacred,* (2) *the martial,* and (3) *the productive.* Thus in Greek mythology we find an interpretation of the world quite as ordered and complex as the pre-Socratic explanation of things. In the description of the Judgment of Paris, to take just one example, we witness the ideology of the three functions represented by Hera (sovereignty),

Athena (victory), and Aphrodite (love). And this ideological division survives in Greece even though the tripartite social division into priests, warriors, and producers had disappeared. Even Plato, the speculative philosopher *par excellence,* drew on this ideology of the three functions in his ideal partition of society in *The Republic.* So the line separating "speculation" and "ideology" is not always a clear one.

RK: Did the Indo-European ideology disappear in France with the demise of the Gallo-Roman Empire?

GD: Probably. But there has been something like a reinsemination of the tripartite ideology in the ninth century in France when the three functions reappear in the Latin texts as *Oratores/Bellatores/Laboratores.* And later again, they appear in the three orders of the Middle Ages, namely, *Clergy, Nobility,* and the *Third Estate (Tiers Etat)* of productive labourers and peasants. Indeed, as Joël Grisward showed in a recent book, in the thirteenth century one finds that the legendary cycle of Emery of Narbonne presents the same form of tripartite structure as the Indian legend of Yayati and his sons. There are three possible ways in which the Indo-European ideology found its way back into France. First, it could have come through the Germanic, especially Visigoth, invasions; second, it could have come through the Anglo-Saxon channels of influence; or third, through Irish monasticism, which contributed much to the intellectual renaissance in Europe (for example, John Scotus Eriugena, who spearheaded the Palatine school at Laon in the ninth century). Early Christianity — as Proinsias McCana and others have remarked — tolerated and often preserved the Celtic ideology of the three functions by means of the creative coexistence of the pagan Druid and *File* with the Christian monk.

RK: How does the tripartite ideology as such relate to monotheism? Some critics have argued that it is the exclusive preserve of polytheistic paganism. Would you agree?

GD: It is unquestionable that the rise of Judeo-Christian monotheism in Europe did much to dispense with the Indo-European explanation of things. Naturally, monotheism insisted on the all-powerfulness of the One God, rather than apportioning the divine functions to different deities. In 1959, John Brough wrote a study entitled "The Tripartite Ideology of the Indo-Europeans and the Bible: An Experiment in Method," in which he tried to demonstrate that the tripartite ideology operated in the Bible also. The complete failure of his demonstration at every level (for example, the qualifications of the God of the Bible, of the twelve tribes of Israel, of Solomon, etc.) suggests that Judaic theology has no need to transpose the three natural necessities of sovereignty, force, and abundance into a corresponding tripartite ideological system. Yahweh is the one and only God. And such a monotheistic explanation of the world is hardly likely to accommodate a pluralistic ideology of functions. This also applies to Islamic and Christian monotheism. Attempts to read the Christian trinity in terms of the tripartite Indo-European ideology are meaningless. (It was once suggested to me that the Holy Spirit represented the third function of phallic fecundity!) However, the impossibility of reducing monotheistic theology to the Indo-European ideology does not mean that monotheistic and Indo-European elements cannot coexist within the same culture or society.

RK: We have already mentioned the compatibility of Celtic paganism and Christianity in ancient Ireland. Do you believe that the Indo-European ideology can have a positive significance for contemporary society?

GD: I think it can, so long as it remains at the philosophical or aesthetic level as part of our collective or communal memory, as the stuff of our dreams. However, it cannot and should not be inserted into contemporary politics because the modern organization of Western society is alien to a tripartite hierarchy of priests, warriors, and workers. The ideology of the three functions is something of the past. But precisely as such it has *descriptive*, not *normative*, value. To suggest that the ideology could be revived in order to serve as the blueprint for a new political order is most dangerous. We know what happened in Nazi Germany when the ideology of the warrior-hero was rehabilitated and deformed in order to mislead an entire people.

RK: So the Indo-European ideology is not some "privileged dream" which, as the New Right like to believe, might denote the superiority of one culture or people over another?

GD: Absolutely not. As I mentioned, the three natural necessities of human survival constitute the "primary matter" of all ideologies — be they theological, sociological, or mythological. Consequently, every culture or society — Indo-European or not — could *de jure* formulate an ideology of the three functions. So the ideological formulation of the three functions is potentially universal qua "primary matter." However, de facto it was only the Indo-European peoples who achieved such a formulation, who transposed the tripartite natural structure of human needs into a corresponding conceptual one. This formulation is only one of the many possible explanations of human existence; the Hebrew, the Chinese, the Babylonian, and the American Indian, to name but some, offered very different conceptual ideologies. Though all cultures share the same material and biological necessities, they "dream" differently. And no culture or civilization has the right to declare its dream a privileged one.

Paris, 1982

PART II

From *Dialogues:*
The Phenomenological Heritage, 1984

Emmanuel Levinas
Ethics of the Infinite

RK: Perhaps you could retrace your philosophical itinerary by identifying some of the major influences on your thought?

EL: Apart from the great masters of the history of philosophy—in particular Plato, Descartes, and Kant—the first contemporary influence on my own thinking was Bergson. In 1925, in Strasbourg University, Bergson was being hailed as France's leading thinker. For example, [Maurice] Blondel, one of his Strasbourg disciples, developed a specifically Bergsonian psychology quite hostile to Freud—a hostility which made a deep and lasting impression on me. Moreover, Bergson's theory of time as concrete duration *(la durée concrète)* is, I believe, one of the most significant, if largely ignored, contributions to contemporary philosophy. Indeed, it was this Bergsonian emphasis on temporality that prepared the soil for the subsequent implantation of Heideggerian phenomenology into France. It is all the more ironic, therefore, that in *Being and Time* Heidegger unjustly accuses Bergson of reducing time to space. What is more, in Bergson's *L'Évolution créatrice [Creative Evolution]*, one finds the whole notion of technology as the destiny of the Western philosophy of Reason. Bergson was the first to contrast technology, as a logical and necessary expression of scientific rationality, with an alternative form of human expression which he called creative intuition or impulse—the *élan vital*. All of Heidegger's celebrated analyses of our technological era as the logical culmination of Western metaphysics and its forgetfulness of Being came after Bergson's reflections on the subject. Bergson's importance to contemporary Continental thought has been somewhat obfuscated; he has been suspended in a sort of limbo; but I believe it is only a temporary suspension.

RK: Could you describe how, after Bergson, you came under the influence of the German phenomenologists Husserl and Heidegger?

EL: It was in 1927 that I first became interested in Husserl's phenomenology, which was still unknown in France at that time. I traveled to the University of Freiburg for two semesters in 1928–29 and studied phenomenology with Husserl and also, of course, with Heidegger, who was then the leading light in German philosophy, after the publication of *Sein und Zeit [Being and Time]* in 1927. Phenomenology represented the second, but undoubtedly most important, philosophical influence in my thinking. Indeed, from the point of view of philosophical method and discipline, I remain to this day a phenomenologist.

RK: How would you characterize the particular contribution of phenomenology to modern philosophy?

EL: The most fundamental contribution of Husserl's phenomenology is its methodical disclosure of how meaning comes to be, how it emerges in our consciousness of the world, or, more precisely, in our becoming conscious of our intentional rapport *(visée)* with the world. The phenomenological method enables us to discover meaning within our lived experience; it reveals consciousness to be an intentionality always in *contact* with objects outside of itself, other than itself. Human experience is not some self-transparent substance or pure *cogito*; it is always intending or tending towards something in the world which preoccupies it. The phenomenological method permits consciousness to understand its own preoccupations, to reflect upon itself and thus discover all the hidden or neglected horizons of its intentionality. In other words, by returning to the implicit horizons of consciousness, phenomenology enables us to explicate or unfold the full intentional meaning of an object, which would otherwise be presented as an abstract and isolated entity cut off from its intentional horizons. Phenomenology thus teaches us that consciousness is at once tied to the object of its experience and yet free to detach itself from this object in order to return upon itself, focusing on those *visées* of intentionality in which the object emerges as *meaningful*, as part of our lived experience. One might say that phenomenology is a way of becoming aware of where we are in the world, a *sich besinnen* which consists of a recovery of the origin of meaning in our life-world or *Lebenswelt*.

RK: Your second major work was entitled *En découvrant l'existence avec Husserl et Heidegger [Discovering Existence with Husserl and Heidegger]*. If Husserl introduced you to the phenomenological method, how would you assess your debt to Heidegger?

EL: Heidegger's philosophy was a shock for me, and for most of my contemporaries in the late twenties and thirties. It completely altered the course and character of European philosophy. I think that one cannot seriously philosophize today without traversing the Heideggerian path in some form or other. *Being and Time*, which is much more significant and profound than any of Heidegger's later works, represents the fruition and flowering of Husserlian phenomenology. The most far-reaching potentialities of the phenomenological method were exploited by Heidegger in this early work and particularly in his phenomenological analysis of anguish as the fundamental mood of our existence. Heidegger brilliantly described how this existential mood, or *Stimmung*, revealed the way in which we were attuned to Being. Human moods, such as guilt, fear, anxiety, joy, or dread are no longer considered as mere physiological sensations or psychological emotions, but are now recognized as the ontological ways in which we feel and find our being-in-the-world, our being-there as *Befindlichkeit*.

RK: This phenomenological analysis of our existential moods was, of course, something which you yourself used to original effect in your descriptions of such human dispositions as need, desire, effort, laziness, and insomnia in *Existence and Existents*. But to return to Husserl and Heidegger, how would you define the main difference of style in their employment of phenomenology?

EL: Husserl's approach was always more abstract and ponderous—one really had to have one's ears cocked if one wished to understand his lectures! Husserl was primarily concerned with establishing and perfecting phenomenology as a method, that is, as an epistemological method of describing how our logical concepts and categories emerge and assume an essential meaning. What is the relation between our logical judgments and our perceptual experience? This was Husserl's question—and phenomenology was his method of responding, by means of rigorous and exact descriptions of our intentional modes of consciousness. Phenomenology was thus a way of suspending our preconceptions and prejudices in order to disclose how essential truth and meaning are generated; it was a methodical return to the beginnings, to the origins of knowledge. On the other hand, Heidegger, the young disciple, brought the phenomenological method to life and gave it a contemporary style and relevance. Heidegger's existential analyses possessed a poetic quality and force which enchanted and astonished the mind, while preserving all the while the rigorous contours of the master's method. So that I would say, by way of summary, that if it was Husserl who opened up for me the radical possibilities of a phenomenological analysis of knowledge, it was Heidegger who first gave these possibilities a positive and concrete grounding in our everyday existence. Heidegger showed that the phenomenological search for eternal truths and essences ultimately originates in time, in our temporal and historical existence.

RK: Your first study of phenomenology, *The Theory of Intuition in Husserl's Phenomenology*, published in 1930, was the first complete work on Husserl in French. Your seminal study of Heidegger in *La Revue Philosophique* in 1931 was another milestone in contemporary French philosophy. Sartre and Merleau-Ponty were soon to follow suit, exploring further possibilities of the phenomenological method known today as French existentialism. As the discreet inaugurator of the French interest in phenomenology, what exactly was your relationship with Sartre and Merleau-Ponty?

EL: I have always admired the powerful originality of Merleau-Ponty's work, however different from my own in many respects, and had frequent contact with him at Jean Wahl's philosophical meetings in the Collège de Philosophie in the thirties and forties and also whenever I contributed to *Les Temps Modernes* while he was still co-editor with Sartre. But it was Sartre who guaranteed my place in eternity by stating in his famous obituary essay on Merleau-Ponty that he, Sartre, "was introduced to phenomenology by Levinas." Simone de Beauvoir tells how it happened in one of her autobiographical works. One day in the early thirties, Sartre chanced upon a copy of my book on Husserl in the Picard bookshop just opposite the Sorbonne. He picked it up, read it, and declared to Beauvoir, "This is the philosophy I wanted to write!" Afterwards, he reassured himself that my analysis was far too didactic and that he could do better himself! And so he applied himself to a sustained study of Husserl and Heidegger. The result was a host of enterprising phenomenological analyses ranging from *L'Imaginaire [Imagination]* (1940) to *Being and Nothingness* (1945). I was extremely interested in Sartre's phenomenological analysis of *the other,* though I always regretted that he interpreted it as a threat and a degradation, an interpretation which also found expression in his fear of the God question. In fact, Sartre's rejection of theism was so unequivocal that his final statements, in the *Nouvel Observateur* interviews just before his death, about the legitimacy of Jewish history as a belief in the existence of God seemed incredible to those who knew him or had studied him. In Sartre, the phenomenon of the other was still considered, as in all Western ontology, to be a modality of unity and fusion, that is, a reduction of the other to the categories of the same. This is described by Sartre as a teleological project to unite and totalize the for-itself and the in-itself, the self and the other-than-self. It is here that my fundamental philosophical disagreement with Sartre resides. At a personal level, I always liked Sartre. I first met him in Gabriel Marcel's house just before the war and had further dealings with him after the war on the controversial question of Israel's existence. Sartre had refused the Nobel Prize for Literature, and I felt that someone who had the courage to reject such a prize for ethical reasons had certainly conserved the right to intervene and to try to persuade Nasser, the Egyptian leader at the time, to forgo his threats to Israel and embark upon dialogue. What I also admired in Sartre was that his philosophy was not confined to purely conceptual issues but was open to the possibility of ethical and political commitment.

RK: What are the origins of the religious dimensions in your own thinking?

EL: I was born in Lithuania, a country where Jewish culture was intellectually prized and fostered and where the interpretation and exegesis of biblical texts was cultivated to a high degree. It was here that I first learned to read the Bible in Hebrew. It was at a much later date, however, that I became actively interested in Jewish thought. After the Second World War, I encountered a remarkable master of Talmudic interpretation here in Paris, a man of exceptional mental agility who taught me how to read the Rabbinic texts. He taught me for four years, from 1947 to 1951, and what I myself have written in my *Talmudic Lectures* has been written in the shadow of his shadow. It was this postwar encounter which reactivated my latent—I might even say dormant—interest in the Judaic tradition. But when I acknowledge this Judaic influence, I do not wish to talk in terms of belief or nonbelief. *Believe* is not a verb to be employed in the first person singular. Nobody can really say *I believe*—or *I do not believe*—or for that matter, that God exists. The existence of God is not a question of an individual soul uttering logical syllogisms. It cannot be proved. The existence of God, the *Sein Gottes,* is sacred history itself, the sacredness of man's relation to man, through which God may pass. God's existence is the story of his revelation in biblical history.

RK: How do you reconcile the phenomenological and religious dimensions of your thinking?

EL: I always make a clear distinction, in what I write, between philosophical and confessional texts. I do not deny that they may ultimately have a common source of inspiration. I simply state that it is necessary to draw a line of demarcation between them as distinct methods of exegesis, as separate languages. I would never, for example, introduce a Talmudic or biblical verse into one of my philosophical texts to try to prove or justify a phenomenological argument.

RK: Would you go so far as to endorse Heidegger's argument that genuine philosophical questioning requires one to suspend or bracket one's religious faith? I am thinking in particular of Heidegger's statement in his Introduction of Metaphysics that a religious thinker cannot ask the philosophical question, "Why is there something rather than nothing?" since he already possesses the answer: "Because God created the world." Hence Heidegger's conclusion that a religious (in the sense of Christian or Jewish) philosophy is a square circle, a contradiction in terms.

EL: For me, the essential characteristic of philosophy is a certain, specifically Greek, way of thinking and speaking. Philosophy is primarily a question of language, and it is by identifying the subtextual language of particular discourses that we can decide whether they are philosophical or not. Philosophy employs a series of terms and concepts—such as *morphē* (form), *ousia* (substance), *noos* (reason), *logos* (thought), or *telos* (goal), etc.—which constitute a specifically Greek lexicon of intelligibility. French and German, and indeed all of Western philosophy, is entirely shot through with this specific language; it is a token of the genius of Greece to have been able to thus deposit its language in the basket of Europe. But although philosophy is essentially Greek, it is not exclusively so. It also has sources and roots which are non-Greek. What we term the Judaeo-Christian tradition, for example, proposed an alternative approach to meaning and truth. The difficulty is, of course, to speak of this alternative tradition given the essentially Greek nature of philosophical language. And this difficulty is compounded by the fact that Judaeo-Christian culture has, historically, been incorporated into Greek philosophy. It is virtually impossible for philosophers today to have recourse to an unalloyed religious language. All one can say is that the Septennium is not yet complete, that the translation of biblical wisdom into the Greek language remains unfinished. The best one can do by way of identifying the fundamental difference between the Greek and biblical approaches to truth is to try to define the distinctive quality of Greek philosophy before the historical incursion of Jewish and Christian cultures. Perhaps the most essential distinguishing feature of the language of Greek philosophy was its equation of truth with an intelligibility of presence. By this I mean an intelligibility which considers truth to be that which is present or copresent, that which can be gathered or synchronized into a totality which we would call the world or cosmos. According to the Greek model, intelligibility is what can be rendered present, what can be represented in some eternal here-and-now, exposed and disclosed in pure light. To thus equate truth with presence is to presume that however different the two terms of a relation might appear (for example, the divine and the human) or however separated over time (for example, into past and future), they can ultimately be rendered commensurate and simultaneous, the same, englobed in a history which totalizes time into a beginning or an end, or both, which is presence. The Greek notion of Being is essentially this presence.

RK: Would you agree then with Heidegger's critique of Western metaphysics as a philosophy of presence?

EL: I don't think Heidegger is entirely consistent on this point. For me, Heidegger never really escaped from the Greek language of intelligibility and presence. Even though he spent much of his philosophical career struggling against certain metaphysical notions of presence — in particular the objectifying notion of presence as *Vorhandenheit,* which expresses itself in our scientific and technological categorization of the world — he ultimately seems to espouse another, more subtle and complex, notion of presence as *Anwesen,* that is, the coming-into-the-presence of Being. Thus, while Heidegger heralds the end of the metaphysics of presence, he continues to think of Being as a coming-into-presence; he seems unable to break away from the hegemony of presence which he denounces. This ambiguity also comes to the surface when Heidegger interprets our being-in-the-world as history. The ultimate and most authentic mission of existence or *Dasein* is to recollect *(wiederholen)* and totalize its temporal dispersal into past, present, and future. *Dasein* is its history to the extent that it can interpret and narrate its existence as a finite and contemporaneous story *(histoire)*, a totalizing copresence of past, present, and future.

RK: How does the ethical relation to the other, so central a theme in your philosophy, serve to subvert the ontology of presence in its Greek and Heideggerian forms?

EL: The interhuman relationship emerges with our history, without being-in-the-world as intelligibility and presence. The interhuman realm can thus be construed as a part of the disclosure of the world as presence. But it can also be considered from another perspective — the ethical or biblical perspective which transcends the Greek language of intelligibility — as a theme of justice and concern for the other as other, as a theme of love and desire which carries us beyond the finite Being of the world as presence. The interhuman is thus an interface: a double axis where what is "of the world" *qua phenomenological intelligibility* is juxtaposed with what is "not of the world" *qua ethical responsibility.* It is in this ethical perspective that God must be thought and not in the ontological perspective of our being-there or of some Supreme Being and Creator correlative to the world, as traditional metaphysics often held. God, as the God of alterity and transcendence, can only be understood in terms of that interhuman dimension which, to be sure, emerges in the phenomenological-ontological perspective of the intelligible world, but which cuts through and perforates the totality of presence and points towards the absolutely Other. In this sense one could say that biblical thought has, to some extent, influenced my ethical reading of the interhuman, whereas Greek thought has largely determined its philosophical expression in language. So I would maintain, against Heidegger, that philosophy can be ethical as well as ontological, can be at once Greek and non-Greek in its inspiration. These two sources of inspiration coexist as two different tendencies in modern philosophy, and it is my own personal task to try to identify this dual origin of meaning — *der Ursprung des Sinnhaften* — in the interhuman relationship.

RK: One of the most complex and indeed central themes in your philosophy is the rapport between the interhuman and time. Could you elucidate this rapport by situating it in terms of the ethics/ontology distinction?

EL: I am trying to show that man's ethical relation to the other is ultimately prior to his ontological relation to himself (egology) or to the totality of things which we call the world (cosmology). The relationship with the other is *time:* it is an untotalizable diachrony in which one moment pursues another without ever being able to retrieve it, to catch up with or coincide with it. The nonsimultaneous and nonpresent is my primary rapport with the other in time. Time means that the other is forever beyond me, irreducible to the synchrony of the same. The temporality of the interhuman opens up the meaning of otherness and the otherness of meaning. But because there are more than two people in the world, we invariably pass from the ethical perspective of alterity to the ontological perspective of totality. There are always at least three persons. This means that we are obliged to ask who is the other, to try to objectively define the undefinable, to compare the incomparable in an effort to juridically hold different positions together. So that the first type of simultaneity is the simultaneity of equality, the attempt to reconcile and balance the conflicting claims of each person. If there were only two people in the world, there would be no need for law courts, because I would always be responsible for, and before, the other. As soon as there are three, the ethical relationship with the other becomes political and enters into the totalizing discourse of ontology. We can never completely escape from the language of ontology and politics. Even when we deconstruct ontology, we are obliged to use its language. Derrida's work of deconstruction, for example, possesses the speculative and methodological rigor of the philosophy which he is seeking to deconstruct. It's like the argument of the skeptics: How can we know that we can't know anything? The greatest virtue of philosophy is that it can put itself in question, try to deconstruct what it has constructed, and unsay what it has said. Science, on the contrary, does not try to unsay itself, does not interrogate or challenge its own concepts, terms, or foundations; it forges ahead, progresses. In this respect, science attempts to ignore language by constructing its own abstract nonlanguage of calculable symbols and formulae. But science is merely a secondary bracketing of philosophical language, from which it is ultimately derived; it can never have the last word. Heidegger summed this up admirably when he declared that science *calculates* but does not *think*. Now, what I am interested in is precisely this ability of philosophy to think, to question itself, and ultimately to unsay itself. And I wonder if this capacity for interrogation and for unsaying *(dédire)* is not itself derived from the preontological interhuman relationship with the other. The fact that philosophy cannot fully totalize the alterity of meaning in some final presence or simultaneity is not for me a deficiency or fault. Or to put it in another way, the best thing about philosophy is that it fails. It is better that philosophy fail to totalize meaning—even though, as ontology, it has attempted just this—for it thereby remains open to the irreducible otherness of transcendence. Greek ontology, to be sure, expressed the strong sentiment that the last word is unity, the many becoming one, the truth as synthesis. Hence Plato defined love—*eros*—as only half-divine, insofar as it lacks the full coincidence or unification of differences which he defined as divinity. The whole romantic tradition in European poetry tends to conform to this Platonic ontology by inferring that love is perfect when two people become one. I am trying to work against this identification of the divine with unification or totality. Man's relationship with the other is *better* as difference than as unity: sociality is better than fusion. The very value of love is the impossibility of reducing the other to myself, of coinciding into sameness. From an ethical perspective, two have a better time than one *(on s'amuse mieux à deux)!*

RK: Is it possible to conceive of an eschatology of noncoincidence, wherein man and God could coexist eternally, without fusing into oneness?

EL: But why eschatology? Why should we wish to reduce time to eternity? Time is the most profound relationship that man can have with God, precisely as a going towards God. There is an excellence in time, which would be lost in eternity. To desire eternity is to desire to perpetuate oneself, to go on living as oneself, to *be* always. Can one conceive of an eternal life that would not suspend time or reduce it to a contemporaneous presence? To accept time is to accept death as the impossibility of presence. To be in eternity is to be *one*, to be *oneself* eternally. To be in time is to be for God *(être à Dieu)*, a perpetual leave-taking *(adieu)*.

RK: But how can one be for God or go towards God as the absolutely Other? Is it by going towards the human other?

EL: Yes, and it is essential to point out that the relation implied in the preposition *towards (à)* is ultimately a relation derived from time. Time fashions man's relation to the other, and to the absolutely Other or God, as a diachronic relation irreducible to correlation. "Going towards God" is not to be understood here in the classical ontological sense of a return to, or reunification with, God as the Beginning or End of temporal existence. "Going towards God" is meaningless unless seen in terms of my primary "going towards the other person." I can only go towards God by being ethically concerned by and for the other person—I am not saying that ethics presupposes belief. On the contrary, belief presupposes ethics as that disruption of our being-in-the-world which opens us to the other. The ethical exigency to be responsible for the other undermines the ontological primacy of the meaning of Being; it unsettles the natural and political positions we have taken up in the world and predisposes us to a meaning that is other than Being, that is otherwise than Being *(autrement qu' être)*.

RK: What role does your analysis of the "face" *(visage)* of the other play in this disruption of ontology?

EL: The approach to the face is the most basic mode of responsibility. As such, the fact of the other is verticality and uprightness; it spells a relation of rectitude. The face is not in front of me *(en face de moi)* but above me; it is the other before death, looking through and exposing death. Secondly, the face is the other who asks me not to let him die alone, as if to do so were to become an accomplice in his death. Thus the face says to me: You shall not kill. In the relation to the face, I am exposed as a usurper of the place of the other. The celebrated "right to existence," which Spinoza called the *conatus essendi* and defined as the basic principle of all intelligibility, is challenged by the relation to the face. Accordingly, my duty to respond to the other suspends my natural right to self-survival, *le droit vital.* My ethical relation of love for the other stems from the fact that the self cannot survive by itself alone, cannot find meaning within its own being-in-the-world, within the ontology of sameness. That is why I prefaced *Totality and Infinity* with Pascal's phrase, *"Ma place au soleil, le commencement de toute usurpation."* Pascal makes the same point when he declares that *"le moi est haïssable."* Pascal's ethical sentiments here go against the ontological privileging of "the right to exist." To expose myself to the vulnerability of the face is to put my ontological right to existence into question. In ethics, the other's right to exist has primacy over your own, a primacy epitomized in the ethical edict: you shall not kill; you shall not jeopardize the life of the other. The ethical rapport with the face is asymmetrical in that it subordinates my existence to the other. This principle recurs in Darwinian biology as the "survival of the fittest," and in psychoanalysis as the natural instinct of the "id" for gratification, possession, and power — the *libido dominandi.*

RK: So I owe more to the other than to myself . . .

EL: Absolutely, and this ethical exigency undermines the Hellenic endorsement, still prevalent today, of the *conatus essendi.* There is a Jewish proverb which says that "the other's material needs are my spiritual needs"; it is this disproportion or asymmetry which characterizes the ethical refusal of the first truth of ontology — the struggle to *be*. Ethics is, therefore, *against nature* because it forbids the murderousness of my natural will to put my own existence first.

RK: Does going towards God always require that we go against nature?

EL: God cannot appear as the cause or creator of nature. The word of God speaks through the glory of the face and calls for an ethical conversion or reversal of our nature. What we call "lay morality," that is, humanistic concern for our fellow human beings, already speaks the voice of God. But the moral priority of the other over myself could not come to be if it were not motivated by something beyond nature. The ethical situation is a human situation, beyond human nature, in which the idea of God comes to mind *(Gott fällt mir ein)*. In this respect, we could say that God is the other who turns our nature inside out, who calls our ontological will-to-be into question. This ethical call of conscience occurs, no doubt, in other religious systems besides the Judeo-Christian, but it remains an essentially religious vocation. God does indeed go against nature for He is not of this world. God is other than Being.

RK: How does one distill the ethico-religious meaning of existence from its natural or ontological sedimentation?

EL: But your question already assumes that ethics is derived from ontology. I believe, on the contrary, that the ethical relationship with the other is just as primary and original *(ursprünglich)* as ontology — if not more so. Ethics is not derived from an ontology of nature; it is its opposite, a meontology which affirms a meaning beyond Being, a primary mode of non-Being *(me-on)*.

RK: And yet you claim that the ethical and the ontological coexist as two inspirations in some way?

EL: Already in Greek philosophy one can discern traces of the ethical breaking through the ontological, for example, in Plato's idea of the "Good existing beyond Being" *(agathon epekeina tes ousias)*. (Heidegger, of course, contests this ethical reading of the Good in Plato, maintaining that it is merely one among other descriptions of Being itself.) One can also cite in this connection Descartes's discovery of the "Idea of the Infinite," which surpasses the finite limits of human nature and the human mind. And similarly supraontological notions are to be found in the pseudo-Dionysian doctrine of the *via eminentiae*, with its surplus of the divine over Being, or in the Augustinian distinction in the *Confessions* between the truth which challenges *(veritas redarguens)* and the onto-logical truth which shines *(veritas lucens)*, etc.

RK: Do you think that Husserl's theory of temporality points to an otherness beyond Being?

EL: However radically Husserl's theory of time may gesture in this direction, particularly in *The Phenomenology of Internal Time Con-sciousness*, it remains overall a *cosmological* notion of time; temporality continues to be thought of in terms of the present, in terms of an ontol-ogy of presence. The present *(Gegenwart)* remains for Husserl the cen-tralizing dimension of time, the past and the future being defined in terms of intentional re-presentations *(Vergegenwärtigen)*. To be more precise, the past, Husserl claims, is retained by the present, and the future is precontained in, or protended by, the present. Time past and time future are merely modifications of the present; and this double extension of the present into the past (retention) and the future (pro-tension) reinforces the ontology of presence as a seizure and appro-priation of what is other or transcendent. Heidegger, who actually edited Husserl's lectures on time, introduced an element of alterity into his own phenomenological description of time in *Being and Time,* when he analyzed time in terms of our anguish before death. Temporality is now disclosed as an ecstatic being-towards-death which releases us from the present into an ultimate horizon of possibles, rather than as a holding or seizing or retaining of the present.

RK: But is not Heidegger's analysis of temporality as a being-towards-death still a subtle form of extending what is mine, of reduc-ing the world to my ownmost *(eigenst)* authentic *(eigentlich)* existence? Death is for Heidegger always *my* death. *Dasein* is always the Being which is *mine.*

EL: This is the fundamental difference between my ethical analy-sis of death and Heidegger's ontological analysis. Whereas for Hei-degger, death is *my* death, for me it is the *other's* death. In *The Letter on Humanism,* Heidegger defines *Dasein* in almost Darwinian fashion as "a being which is concerned for its own being." In paragraph 9 of *Being and Time,* he defines the main characteristic of *Dasein* as that *of mineness (Jemeinigkeit),* the way in which Being becomes mine, imposes or imprints itself on *me. Jemeinigkeit* as the possession of my Being as *mine* precedes the articulation of the *I. Dasein* is only "I" *(Ich)* because it is already *Jemeinigkeit.* I become I only because I possess my own Being as primary. For ethical thought, on the contrary, *le moi,* as this primacy of what is mine, is *haïssable*. Ethics is not, for this reason, a depersonalizing exigency. I am defined as a subjectivity, as a singular person, as an "I," precisely because I am exposed to the other. It is my inescapable and incontrovertible answerability to the other that makes me an individual "I." So that I become a responsible or ethical "I" to the extent that I agree to depose or dethrone myself—to abdicate my position of centrality—in favor of the vulnerable other. As the Bible says, "He who loses his soul gains it." The ethical I is a being who asks if he has a right to be, who excuses himself to the other for his own existence.

RK: In the structuralist and poststructuralist debates which have tended to dominate Continental philosophy in recent years, there has been much talk of the disappearance or demise of the subject. Is your ethical thought an attempt to preserve subjectivity in some form?

EL: My thinking on this matter goes in the opposite direction to structuralism. It is not that I wish to preserve, over and against the structuralist critique, the idea of a subject who would be a substantial or mastering center of meaning, an idealist self-sufficient *cogito*. These traditional ontological versions of subjectivity have nothing to do with the entomological version of subjectivity that I put forward in *Autrement qu'être [Otherwise than Being]*. Ethical subjectivity dispenses with the idealizing subjectivity of ontology which reduces everything to itself. The ethical "I" is subjectivity precisely insofar as it kneels before the other, sacrificing its own liberty to the more primordial call of the other. For me, the freedom of the subject is not the highest or primary value. The heteronomy of our response to the human other, or to God as the absolutely Other, precedes the autonomy of our subjective freedom. As soon as I acknowledge that it is "I" who am responsible, I accept that my freedom is anteceded by an obligation to the other. Ethics redefines subjectivity as this heteronymous responsibility in contrast to autonomous freedom. Even if I deny my primordial responsibility to the other by affirming my own freedom as primary, I can never escape the fact that the other has demanded a response from me *before* I affirm my freedom not to respond to his demand. Ethical freedom is *une difficile liberté*, a heteronymous freedom obliged to the other. Consequently, the other is the richest and the poorest of beings: the richest, at an ethical level, in that it always comes before me, its right-to-be preceding mine; the poorest, at an ontological or political level, in that without me it can do nothing—it is utterly vulnerable and exposed. The other haunts our ontological existence and keeps the psyche awake, in a state of vigilant insomnia. Even though we are ontologically free to refuse the other, we remain forever accused, with a bad conscience.

RK: Is not the ethical obligation to the other a purely negative ideal, impossible to realize in our everyday being-in-the-world? After all, we live in a concrete historical world governed by ontological drives and practices, be they political and institutional totalities or technological systems of organization and control. Is ethics practicable in human society, as we know it? Or is it merely an invitation to apolitical acquiescence?

EL: This is a fundamental point. Of course we inhabit an ontological world of technological mastery and political self-preservation. Indeed, without these political and technological structures of organization, we would not be able to feed mankind. This is the great paradox of human existence: we must use the ontological *for the sake of the other;* to ensure the survival of the other, we must resort to the technico-political systems of means and ends. This same paradox is also present in our use of language, to return to an earlier point. We have no option but to employ the language and concepts of Greek philosophy, even in our attempts to go beyond them. We cannot obviate the language of metaphysics and yet we cannot, ethically speaking, be satisfied with it: it is necessary but not enough. I disagree, however, with Derrida's interpretation of this paradox. Whereas he tends to see the deconstruction of the Western metaphysics of presence as an irredeemable crisis, I see it as a golden opportunity for Western philosophy to open itself to the dimension of otherness and transcendence beyond Being.

RK: Is there any sense in which language can be ethical?

EL: In *Autrement qu'être,* I pose this question when I ask, "What is saying without a said?" Saying is ethical sincerity insofar as it is exposition. As such, this *saying* is irreducible to the ontological definability of the *said.* Saying is what makes the self-exposure of sincerity possible; it is a way of giving everything, of not keeping anything for oneself. Insofar as ontology equates truth with the intelligibility of total presence, it reduces the pure exposure of saying to the totalizing closure of the said. The child is a pure exposure of expression insofar as it is pure vulnerability; it has not yet learned to dissemble, to deceive, to be insincere. What distinguishes human language from animal or child expression, for example, is that the human speaker can remain silent, can refuse to be exposed in sincerity. The human being is characterized as human not only because he is a being who can speak but also because he is a being who can lie, who can live in the duplicity of language as the dual possibility of exposure and deception. The animal is incapable of this duplicity; the dog, for instance, cannot suppress its bark, the bird its song. But man can repress his saying, and this ability to keep silent, to withhold oneself, is the ability to be political. Man can give himself in saying to the point of poetry—or he can withdraw into the non-saying of lies. Language as *saying* is an ethical openness to the other; as that which is *said*—reduced to a fixed identity or synchronized presence—it is an ontological closure to the other.

RK: But is there not some sort of morality of the *said* which might reflect the ethics of saying in our everyday transactions in society? In other words, if politics cannot be ethical insofar as it is an expression of our ontological nature, can it at least be moral (in your sense of that term)?

EL: This distinction between the ethical and the moral is very important here. By morality I mean a series of rules relating to social behavior and civic duty. But while morality thus operates in the socio-political order of organizing and improving our human survival, it is ultimately founded on an ethical responsibility towards the other. As *prima philosophia,* ethics cannot itself legislate for society or produce rules of conduct whereby society might be revolutionized or transformed. It does not operate at the level of the manifesto or *rappel à l'ordre;* it is not *a savoir vivre.* When I talk of ethics as a disinterestedness *(dés-inter-essement),* I do not mean that it is indifference; I simply mean that it is a form of vigilant passivity to the call of the other which precedes our interest in Being, our *inter-esse* as a being-in-the-world, attached to property and appropriating what is other than itself to itself. Morality is what governs the world of political "interestedness," the social interchanges between citizens in a society. Ethics, as the extreme exposure and sensitivity of one subjectivity to another, becomes morality and hardens its skin as soon as we move into the political world of the impersonal "third"—the world of government, institutions, tribunals, prisons, schools, committees, etc. But the norm which must continue to inspire and direct the moral order is the ethical norm of the interhuman. If the moral-political order totally relinquishes its ethical foundation, it must accept all forms of society, including the fascist or totalitarian, for it can no longer evaluate or discriminate between them. The state is usually better than anarchy—but not always. In some instances—fascism or totalitarianism, for example—the political order of the state may have to be challenged in the name of our ethical responsibility to the other. This is why ethical philosophy must remain the first philosophy.

RK: Is not the ethical criterion of the interhuman employed by you as a sort of Messianic eschatology, wherein the ontological structures of possession and totality would be transcended towards a face-to-face relation of pure exposure to the absolutely Other?

EL: Here again I must express my reservations about the term *eschatology*. The term *eschaton* implies that there might exist a finality, an end *(fin)* to the historical relation of difference between man and the absolutely Other, a reduction of the gap which safeguards the alterity of the transcendent, to a totality of sameness. To realize the *eschaton* would therefore mean that we could seize or appropriate God as a *telos* and degrade the infinite relation with the other to a finite fusion. This is what Hegelian dialectics amounts to, a radical denial of the rupture between the ontological and the ethical. The danger of eschatology is the temptation to consider the man-God relation as a state, as a fixed and permanent state of affairs. I have described ethical responsibility as *insomnia* or *wakefulness* precisely because it is a perpetual duty of vigilance and effort which can never slumber. Ontology as a state of affairs can afford sleep. But love cannot sleep, can never be peaceful or permanent. Love is the incessant watching over of the other; it can never be satisfied or contented with the bourgeois ideal of love as domestic comfort or the mutual possession of two people living out an *égoïsme-à-deux*.

RK: If you reject the term *eschatology*, would you accept the term *Messianic* to describe this ethical relation with the other?

EL: Only if one understands Messianic here according to the Talmudic maxim that "the doctors of the law will never have peace, neither in this world nor in the next; they go from meeting to meeting discussing always—for there is always more to be discussed." I could not accept a form of Messianism which would terminate the need for discussion, which would end our watchfulness.

RK: But are we not ethically obliged to struggle for a perfect world of peace?

EL: Yes, but I seek this peace not for me but for the other. By contrast, if I say that "virtue is its own reward," I can only say so *for myself.* As soon as I make this a standard for the other, I exploit him, for what

I am then saying is: be virtuous towards me—work for me, love me, serve me, etc.—but don't expect anything from me in return. That would be rather like the story of the Czar's mother who goes to the hospital and says to the dying soldier: "You must be very happy to die for your country." I must always demand more of myself than of the other, and this is why I disagree with [Martin] Buber's description of the I-Thou ethical relation as a symmetrical copresence. As Alyosha Karamazov says in *The Brothers Karamazov* by [Fyodor] Dostoevsky, "We are all responsible for everyone else—but I am more responsible than all the others." And he does not mean that every "I" is more responsible than all the others, for that would be to generalize the law for everyone else—to demand as much from the other as I do from myself. This essential asymmetry is the very basis of ethics: not only am I more responsible than the other, but I am even responsible for everyone else's responsibility!

RK: How does the God of ethics differ from the "God of the philosophers," that is, the God of traditional ontology?

EL: For ethics, it is only in the infinite relation with the other that God passes *(se passe)*, that traces of God are to be found. God thus reveals himself as a trace, not as an ontological presence, which Aristotle defined as a Self-Thinking Thought and Scholastic metaphysics defined as an *Ipsum Esse Subsistens* or *Ens Causa Sui.* The God of the Bible cannot be defined or proved by means of logical predictions and attributions. Even the superlatives of wisdom, power, and causality advanced by medieval ontology are inadequate to the absolute otherness of God. It is not by superlatives that we can think of God, but by trying to identify the particular interhuman events which open towards transcendence and reveal the traces where God has passed. The God of ethical philosophy is not God the Almighty Being of Creation but the persecuted God of the prophets who is always in relation with man, and whose difference from man is never indifference. This is why I have tried to think of God in terms of desire, a desire that cannot be fulfilled or satisfied—in the etymological sense of *satis*, measure. I can never have enough in my relation to God for He always exceeds my measure, remains forever incommensurate with my desire. In this sense, our desire for God is without end or term: it is interminable and infinite because God reveals Himself as absence rather than presence. Love is the society of God and man, but man is happier for he has God as company, whereas God has man! Furthermore, when we say that God cannot satisfy our desire, we must add that the insatisfaction is itself sublime! What is a defect in the finite order becomes an excellence in the infinite order. In the infinite order, the absence of God is better than His presence; and the anguish of our concern and searching for God is better than consummation or comfort. As Kierkegaard put it, "The need for God is a sublime happiness."

RK: Your analysis of God as an impossibility of Being or being-present would seem to suggest that the ethical relation is entirely utopian and unrealistic.

EL: This is the great objection to my thought — "Where did you ever see the ethical relation practiced?" people say to me. I reply that its being utopian does not prevent it from investing our everyday actions of generosity or goodwill towards the other: even the smallest and most commonplace gestures, such as saying "after you" as we sit at the dinner table or walk through a door, bear witness to the ethical. This concern for the other remains utopian in the sense that it is always "out of place" (u-topos) in this world, always other than the "ways of the world," but there are many examples of it in the world. I remember meeting once with a group of Latin American students well versed in the terminology of Marxist liberation and terribly concerned by the suffering and unhappiness of their people in Argentina. They asked me rather impatiently if I had ever actually witnessed the utopian rapport with the other which my ethical philosophy speaks of. I replied, "Yes, indeed, here in this room."

RK: So you would maintain that Marxism bears witness to a utopian inspiration?

EL: When I spoke of the overcoming of Western ontology as an "ethical and prophetic cry" in "Dieu et la philosophie" ["God and Philosophers"] (De Dieu qui vient à l'idée [of God who comes to mind]), I was in fact thinking of Marx's critique of Western idealism as a project to understand the world rather than to transform it. In Marx's critique, we find an ethical conscience cutting through the ontological identification of truth with an ideal intelligibility and demanding that theory be converted into a concrete praxis of concern for the other. It is this revelatory and prophetic cry which explains the extraordinary attraction which the Marxist utopia exerted over numerous generations. Marxism was, of course, utterly compromised by Stalinism. The 1968 revolt in Paris was a revolt of sadness, because it came after the Khrushchev Report and the exposure of the corruption of the Communist Party. The year of 1968 epitomized the joy of despair, a last grasping at human justice, happiness, and perfection after the truth had dawned that the communist ideal had degenerated into totalitarian bureaucracy. By 1968 only dispersed groups and rebellious pockets of individuals remained to seek their surrealist forms of salvation, no longer confident in a collective movement of humanity, no longer assured that Marxism could survive the Stalinist catastrophe as the prophetic messenger of history.

RK: What role can philosophy serve today? Has it in fact reached that end which so many contemporary Continental philosophers have spoken of?

EL: It is true that philosophy, in its traditional forms of ontotheology and logocentrism—to use Heidegger's and Derrida's terms—has come to an end. But it is not true of philosophy in the other sense of critical speculation and interrogation. The speculative practice of philosophy is by no means near its end. Indeed the whole contemporary discourse of overcoming and deconstructing metaphysics is far more speculative in many respects than metaphysics itself. Reason is never so versatile as when it puts itself in question. In the contemporary end of philosophy, philosophy has found a new lease of life.

Paris, 1981

Herbert Marcuse
The Philosophy of Art and Politics

RK: As a Marxist thinker of international renown and inspira-
tional mentor of student revolutions in both the United States and
Europe in the sixties, you have puzzled many by the turn to primarily
aesthetic questions in your recent works. How would you explain or
justify this turn?

HM: It seems to have become quite evident that the advanced
industrial countries have long since reached the stage of wealth and
productivity which Marx projected for the construction of a socialist
society. Consequently, a quantitative increase in material productivity
is now seen to be insufficient in itself, and a qualitative change in society as a whole is seen to be necessary. Such a qualitative change presupposes, of course, new and unalienating conditions of labor, distribution and living, but that *alone* is not enough. The qualitative change
necessary to build a truly socialist society, something we haven't yet
seen, depends on other values — not so much economic (quantitative)
as aesthetic (qualitative) in character. This change in turn requires
more than just a gratification of needs; it requires, in addition, a change
in the nature of these needs themselves. This is why the Marxian
revolution in our age must look to art also, if it is to succeed.

RK: If art, then, is to play such a central role in the revolutionary
transition to a new society, why didn't Marx himself say that?

HM: Marx did not say that because Marx lived over a hundred years ago and so did not write in an age when, as I have just maintained, the problems of the material culture could in fact be resolved by the establishment of genuinely socialist institutions and relationships. Consequently, he did not fully realize that a purely economic resolution of the problem can never be enough, and so lacked the insight that a twentieth-century revolution would require a different type of human being and that such a revolution would have to aim at, and, if successful, implement, an entirely new set of personal and sexual relationships, a new morality, a new sensibility, and a total reconstruction of the environment. These are, to a great extent, aesthetic values (aesthetic to be understood in the larger sense of our sensory and imaginative culture which I outlined in *Eros and Civilization,* following Kant and [Friedrich] Schiller), and that is why I think that one viewing the possibility of struggle and change in our time recognizes the decisive role which art must play.

RK: You spoke there, rather dangerously it seems to me, about the possible necessity of "implementing" these new personal relationships, etc., which would characterize the qualitatively new society. How can art or culture be instrumental in this implementation without becoming the tool of some dictatorial elite (which would see it as its role to determine what should be "implemented") and without, consequently, degenerating into propaganda?

HM: Art can never and never should become *directly* and immediately a factor of political praxis. It can only have effect indirectly, by its impact on the consciousness and on the subconsciousness of human beings.

RK: You are saying therefore that art must always maintain a critical *and* negative detachment from the realm of everyday political practice?

HM: Yes, I would claim that all authentic art is negative, in the sense that it refuses to obey the established reality, its language, its order, its conventions, and its images. As such, it can be negative in two ways: either insofar as it serves to give asylum or refuge to defamed humanity and thus preserves in another form an alternative to the "affirmed" reality of the establishment *or* insofar as it serves to negate this "affirmed" reality by denouncing both it and the defamers of humanity who have affirmed it in the first place.

RK: Is it not true, however, that in many of your writings (I think particularly of *An Essay on Liberation* and *Eros and Civilization*) you suggest that art can play a more directly political and indeed positive role, by helping to point the way to a socialist utopia?

HM: Art can give you the "images" of a freer society and of more human relationships, but beyond that it cannot go. In this sense, the difference between aesthetic and political theory remains unbridgeable: art can say what it wants to *say* only in terms of the complete and formal fate of individuals in their struggle with their society in the medium of *sensibility;* its images are felt and imagined rather than intellectually formulated or propounded, whereas political theory is necessarily *conceptual.*

RK: How then would you view the role of reason in art—I refer not to *Verstand* (reason in the narrow Enlightenment sense of strictly logical, mathematical, and empirico-metric calculation) but to the Kantian and Hegelian concept of *Vernunft* (reason in the larger sense of a critical and regulative faculty), concerned primarily with those realms of human perception, intuition, evaluation, and ethical deliberation so central, it would seem, to the concerns of any cultural aesthetic?

HM: I believe that you cannot have the liberation of human sensitivity and sensibility without a corresponding liberation of our rational faculty *(Vernunft)*. Any liberation effected by art signifies, therefore, a liberation of both the senses and reason from their present servitude.

RK: Would you be opposed then to the emotionally euphoric and Dionysian character of much of contemporary popular culture—rock music, for example?

HM: I am wary of all exhibitions of freewheeling emotionalism, and as I explained in *Counter-revolution and Revolt,* I think that both the living-theater movement (the attempt to bring theater out into the street and make it immediate by "tuning in" to the language and sentiments of the working class) and the rock cult are prone to this error. The former, despite its noble struggle, is ultimately self-defeating. It tries to blend the theater and the revolution, but ends up blending a contrived immediacy with a clever brand of mystical humanism. The latter, the rock-group cult, seems open to the danger of a form of commercial totalitarianism which absorbs the individual into an uninhibited mass, where the power of a collective unconscious is mobilized but left without any radical or critical awareness. It could, at times, prove a dangerous outburst of irrationalism.

RK: Accepting the fact, then, that a revolutionary liberation of the senses requires also a liberation of reason, the question still remains as to who is to decide what is rational, what criteria, in turn, are to be deployed in such a decision and, also, who is consequently to endorse and implement this rational liberation? In other words, how do you obviate the unsavory prospect of a benevolent, "rational" dictator or elite imposing their criteria on the manipulated and "irrational" masses?

HM: The aesthetic liberation of the rational and sensible faculties (at present repressed) will have to begin with individuals and small groups, trying, as it were, such an experiment in unalienated living. How it then gradually becomes effective in terms of the society at large and makes for a different construction of social relationships in general, we cannot say. Such premature programming could only lead to yet another example of ideological tyranny.

RK: Would you then disagree with your former colleague, Walter Benjamin, when he urges that popular culture, and particularly the cinema (which he held enables the critical and receptive attitudes of the public to coincide), be used in a politically committed fashion to aid and abet the socialist revolution?

HM: Yes, I would have to disagree with Benjamin there. Any attempt to use art to effect a mass conversion of sensibility and consciousness is inevitably an abuse of its true functions.

RK: Its true functions being . . .

HM: Its true functions being (1) to negate our present society, (2) to anticipate the trends of future society, (3) to criticize destructive or alienating trends, and (4) to suggest images of creative and unalienating zones.

RK: And this fourfold function of *negation, anticipation, critique,* and *suggestion* would presumably be aimed at the individual or small group?

HM: Yes, that is correct.

RK: Would you wish to retract your allegiance to the Frankfurt school's Marxist aesthetic, as expressed in the following formulation? "We interpret art as a kind of a code language for processes taking place within society which must be deciphered by means of critical analysis."

HM: Yes, that seems to me to be too reductive. Art is more than a code or puzzle which would *reflect* the world in terms of a second-order aesthetic structure. Art is not just a mirror. It can never only imitate reality. Photography does that much better. Art has to transform reality so that it appears in the light (1) of what it does to human beings, and (2) of the possible images of freedom and happiness, which it might provide for these same human beings; and this is something photography cannot do. Art, therefore, does not just mirror the present; it leads beyond it. It preserves, and thus allows us to remember, values which are no longer to be found in our world; and it points to another possible society in which these values may be realized. Art is a code only to the extent that it acts as a mediated critique of society. But it cannot as such be a direct or immediate indictment of society—that is the work of theory and politics.

RK: Would you not say that the works of Orwell, Dickens, or the French surrealists, for example, were directly an indictment of their society?

HM: Well, the surrealists were never, it seems to me, *directly* political; Orwell was not a great writer; and Dickens, like all great writers, was far more than a political theorist—reading him gives us positive pleasure and thereby ensures that there is a reader for the book in the first place. This is one of the central dilemmas of art conceived as an agent of revolution. Even the most radical art cannot, in its denunciation of the evils of society, dispense with the element of entertainment. That is why Bertolt Brecht always maintained that even the work which most brutally depicts what is going on in the world must also please. And one additional point to be remembered here is that even when certain works of art *appear* directly social or political in *content*—for example, Orwell and Dickens, but also [Emile] Zola, [Henrik] Ibsen, [Georg] Büchner, [Eugène] Delacroix, [Pablo] Picasso—they are never so in *form*, for the work always remains committed to the structure of art, to the form of the novel, drama, poem, and painting, etc., and thereby testifies to a distance from reality.

RK: What is your opinion then of the notion of a "proletarian" art?

HM: I think it is false for several reasons. Its attempt to transcend the distancing forms of classical and romantic art and to unite art and reality by providing in their stead a "living art" or "anti-art" rooted in the actions, slang, and spontaneous sensations of the oppressed folk, seems to me to be doomed to failure, as I have argued in *Counter-revolution and Revolt.* Although in earlier works I stressed the political potential of the linguistic rebellion of the blacks, witnessed in their folk music, dance, and particularly language (whose very obscenity I interpreted as a legitimate protest against their misery and repressed cultural tradition), I now believe that such a potential is ultimately ineffective, for it has become standardized and can no longer be identified as the expression of frustrated radicals, but all too often as the futile gratification of aggressiveness which too easily turns against sexuality itself. (For instance, the obligatory verbalization of the genital sphere in "radical" speech has not been a political threat to the establishment so much as a debasement of sexuality, for example, if some radical exclaims, "Fuck Nixon," he is associating the term for the highest gratification with the highest member of the oppressive establishment!)

RK: What is your view of "living" or "natural" music which has always been associated with the oppressed masses in the West and particularly with the black culture?

HM: Well, it seems to me that here again one finds the same thing occurring. What originally started out as an authentic cry and song of the oppressed black community has since been transformed and commercialized into white rock, which, by means of contrived performances, serves as an orgiastic group-therapy, which removes all the frustrations and inhibitions of the audiences, but only *temporarily* and without any socio-political foundation.

RK: I take it then that you would not support the idea of an art of the masses, an art devoted to the working-class struggle?

HM: No, it seems to me that, rather than being a particular code of the struggle of the proletariat or working class, art can transcend any *particular* class interest without eliminating such an interest. It is always concerned with history but history is the history of *all* classes. And it is this generality which accounts for that universal validity and objectivity of art which Marx called the quality of "prehistory" and which Hegel called the "continuity of substance" from the beginning of art to the end—the truth which links the modern novel and the medieval epic, the facts and possibilities of human existence, conflict and reconciliation between man and man, man and nature. A work of art will obviously contain a class content (to the extent to which it reflects the values, situations, and sentiments of a feudal, bourgeois, or proletarian worldview), but it becomes transparent as the condition of the universal dreams of humanity. Authentic art never *merely* acts as a mirror of a class or as an automatic, spontaneous outburst of its frustrations and desires. The very sensuous immediacy which art expresses presupposes, however surreptitiously (and this is something which most of our popular culture has forgotten), a complex, disciplined, and formal synthesis of experience according to certain universal principles which alone can lend to the work more than a purely private significance. It is because of this universal dimension of art that some of the greatest political radicals have displayed the most apolitical stances and tastes in art (for example, the famous sympathizers of the Paris Commune of 1871, or even Marx himself). Many of the apparently *formless* works of modern art (those of [John] Cage, [Karlheinz] Stockhausen, [Samuel] Beckett, or [Allen] Ginsberg) are in fact highly intellectual, constructivist, and formal. And indeed this fact hints, I believe, at the passing of anti-art and the return to *form*. It is because of this universal significance of art as form that we may find the meaning of revolution better expressed in Bertolt Brecht's most perfect lyrics than in his explicitly political polemics, in Bob Dylan's most "soulful" and deeply personal songs rather than in his propagandist manifestos. Both Brecht and Dylan have one message: to make an end with things as they are. Even in the event of a total absence of political content, their works can invoke, for a vanishing moment, the image of a liberated world and the pain of an alienated one. Thus, the aesthetic dimension assumes a political and revolutionary value, but without becoming the mouthpiece of any particular class interest.

RK: A certain detachment from the political reality would seem then almost prerequisite for a genuinely revolutionary art, would it not?

HM: Yes, art must always remain alienated to some extent, and this precludes an identification of art with revolutionary praxis. As I argued in *Counter-revolution and Revolt*, art cannot represent the revolution; it can only invoke it in another medium, in an aesthetic structure in which the political content becomes metapolitical, governed by the formal necessity of art. And so the goal of all revolution—a world of tranquility and freedom—can appear in a totally unpolitical medium under the aesthetic laws of beauty and harmony.

RK: Would it be fair to conclude, therefore, that you reject the various attempts by Lenin, [Georg] Lukács, and other Marxist dialecticians to formulate the possibility of progressive art as a weapon of class war?

HM: The belief that only a proletarian literature can fulfill the progressive function of art and develop a revolutionary consciousness seems to me a mistaken one in our age. Today the working class shares the same worldview and values as those of a large part of other classes, especially the middle class. The conditions and goals of a revolution against global monopoly capitalism today cannot therefore be adequately articulated in terms of a proletarian revolution, and so if this revolution is to be present in some way as a goal in art, such art could not be typically proletarian. Indeed, it seems to me more than a matter of personal preference that both Lenin and Trotsky were critical of the notion of a "proletarian culture." But even if you could argue for a proletarian culture, you would still be left asking whether there is such a thing as a proletariat (as Marx described it) in our age. In the United States, for example, one finds that the working people are often apathetic, if not totally hostile, to socialism, while in Italy and France, strongholds of the Marxist tradition of labor, the workers seem to be ruled by a Communist Party and trade unionism manipulated very often by the USSR and committed to the minimum strategy of compromise or tolerance. In both situations, that is, in the United States and in Europe, it would seem that a large part of the working class has become a class of bourgeois society, and their proletarian socialism, if it exists at all, no longer appears as a definitive negation of capitalism. Consequently, the attempt to turn the emotions of the working class into a standard for authentic radical and socialist art is a regressive step and can only result in a superficial adjustment of the established order and a perpetuation of the prevailing atmosphere of oppression and alienation. For instance, authentic "black literature" is revolutionary, but it is not a "class" literature as such, and its *particular* content is at the same time a *universal* one. One finds here in the particular situation of an alienated radical minority the most universal of all needs: the need of the individual and his group to exist as human beings.

RK: We seem to have returned again to the notion of "aesthetic" revolution as something centered around individuals and small groups in its advocation of, and experimentation with, unalienated living. Are you in fact suggesting that it might be possible for certain individuals and small groups to live in a nonalienated manner in an alienated world? (I think here in particular of certain dissenting artists, intellectuals, ecologists, antinuclear pacifists, or the advocates of alternative modes of cooperative community existence.)

HM: No. One cannot actually live in a nonalienated manner in an alienated world. You can *experiment* with it; you can *remember* it; you can in your own little circle try your best to develop it, but beyond that you cannot go.

RK: Would you agree that it is by means of the aesthetic imagination that one can transcend one's alienated world, in order to experiment with and remember alternative forms of life as you suggest?

HM: Yes, that is *correct*, and imaginative remembrance is particularly important, for it is by remembering the values and desires which, unable over the ages to express themselves in a politically corrupt world, took refuge in art and thus preserved themselves that we shall be able to find hints of a direction out of our present alienation.

RK: This notion of art as hinting at a new direction would seem to me to be a positive one, but have you not already on many occasions, and even in this interview, confirmed the view, held by Brecht, Beckett, and Kafka, to name but a few, that art must be negative ("estranged") and alienating if it is to remain authentic?

HM: Yes, indeed, I did and still do support that view. Art must never lose its negative and alienating power, for it is there that its most radical potential lies. To lose this negating power is, in effect, to eliminate the tension between art and reality and so also the very real distinctions between subject and object, quantity and quality, freedom and servitude, beauty and ugliness, good and evil, future and present, justice and injustice. Such a claim to a final synthesis of these historical oppositions in the here and now would be the materialist version of absolute idealism. It would signal a state of perfect barbarism at the height of civilization. In other words, to do away with these distinctions between value and fact is to deny present reality and forestall our search for another more human one. Indeed, the common negative force of a piece of music by Verdi and Bob Dylan, a piece of writing by [Gustave] Flaubert and [James] Joyce, or a painting by [Jean Auguste Dominique] Ingres and Picasso is precisely that hint of beauty which acts as refusal of the commodity world and of the performances, attitudes, looks, and sounds required by it.

RK: So the artistic imagination, you would say, can in no way be revolutionary in a positive sense?

HM: Art, as we know it, cannot transform reality and cannot, therefore, submit to the actual requirements of the revolution without denying itself. It is only as a negative and alienating power that it can in fact negate, dialectically, the alienation of the political reality. And, as such, as the negation of the negation, to use Hegel's term, it is indeed revolutionary. That is why in *Counter-revolution and Revolt* and elsewhere, I described the relation between art and politics as a unity of opposites, an antagonistic unity which must always remain antagonistic.

RK: In *An Essay on Liberation*, you speak at one point about technology being used by the revolutionary in the same way as the painter uses his canvas and brush. Does not this analogy suggest a direct and positive relationship to the socio-political reality?

HM: In some limited sense I suppose it does. It is true, I believe, that technology should, ideally, be used creatively and imaginatively to reconstruct nature and the environment.

RK: But according to what criteria?

HM: According to the criterion of beauty.

RK: But who decides this criterion? Is it universal for all men and women? And if so, in what way does it, as aesthetic criterion, differ from a theological or ontological system of value?

HM: I think that the striving for beauty is simply an essential part of human sensibility.

RK: But surely, if our world is to undergo a revolutionary reconstruction in the name of and for the sake of beauty, one must be quite sure in advance what this "beauty" is—whether it is in fact the universal and absolute goal of all human striving, or merely the subjective and particular goal of one revolutionary leader/artist or an elite of revolutionary leaders/artists. If the latter, then how does one deny the charge of totalitarian imposition, manipulation, and tyranny?

HM: A revolution cannot be waged for the sake of beauty. Beauty is but one criterion which plays a leading role in one element of the revolution, that is, the restoration and reconstruction of the environment. It cannot be used to "reconstruct" men, without, as you correctly infer, running the risk of totalitarianism. It simply cannot presume to go that far.

RK: In *Eros and Civilization*, it certainly seems, however, as if you are suggesting that beauty is no less than the ultimate end, or *telos*, of all human struggle, and that this teleological struggle is itself synonymous with Freud's "metapsychological" interpretation of *eros* or Kant's view that "all aesthetic endeavor seeks beauty as its final purpose."

HM: No. Beauty is only one amongst other goals.

RK: You would not wish, then, in any sense, to ascribe an absolute character to beauty?

HM: No, beauty can never be absolute. Nevertheless, I think that certain evaluative criteria can be established in rotation to it.

RK: How then would you react to Martin Jay's assertion in his book on the Frankfurt school, *The Dialectical Imagination,* that your repeated attempts to describe human desire for an ideal utopia are rooted in the latent Judeo-Messianic optimism of the Frankfurt school, which, in fact, consisted almost exclusively of German Jewish intellectuals, for example, [Theodor W.] Adorno, [Erich] Fromm, [Max] Horkheimer, Benjamin, and, of course, yourself, who wished to synthesize the intuitions of two other Jews, Marx and Freud?

HM: I do not recall on any occasion having described or even attempted to describe such a thing as utopia. The relationships which I indicate as essential for qualitative change are certainly aesthetic, but they are not utopian.

RK: So you would deny any link between your political optimism about a new society and the Messianic optimism of Judaism?

HM: Absolutely.

RK: Another current interpretation of the striving for universal and objective value-criteria in your writings on the "aesthetic revolution" is that you are in fact returning, albeit surreptitiously, to the fundamental ontology of your original mentor, Martin Heidegger — seeking a new kind of "poetic dwelling on Earth." Do you see your later works as a return to your early attempts in the thirties to reconcile a Heideggerean phenomenology of subjective historicity with a Marxist dialectics of collective history?

HM: That Heidegger had a profound influence on me is without any doubt, and I have never denied it. He taught me a great deal about what real phenomenological "thinking" is, about how thinking is not just a logical function of "representing" what is, here and now in the present, but operates at deeper levels in its "recalling" of what has been forgotten and its *projecting* what might yet come to pass in the future.

That appreciation of the temporal and intentional nature of phenomena has been extremely important for me, but that is as far as it goes.

RK: Evidently art has, in your opinion, a radical role to play in detaching individuals from their mindless slavery to the present conditions of work, competition, performance, advertising, mass media, etc., and thereby educating them in their own reality. Indeed, you have spoken very often of late about art as education. Would you like to comment on this relationship?

HM: Such an education in the reality of one's repressed faculties — sensory, imaginative, and rational — and in our repressive environmental and working conditions would have to be based not on a mass education plan (that again would be to abuse art by turning it into propaganda) but in small communal projects of *auto-critique*. Such auto-critique would not, of course, replace a general education. It could not be a question of substituting one for the other, of abandoning the traditional tools of education altogether; not so much a question of *deschooling* as *reschooling*.

RK: Such an aesthetic reschooling, which as you say would not be alternative, but supplementary to a general basic education, would presumably be concerned with those ethical and existential areas of human relations which constitute the locus of a qualitative leap to another society, would it not?

HM: Yes it would.

RK: And presumably you would like to be able to base such an aesthetic education on certain universal principles whose objectivity would preclude the danger of an ideological indoctrination of the "ignorant" and "gullible" masses by some enlightened elite, an abuse of education which is directly conducive to totalitarianism and fascism.

HM: Yes, that is certainly a very real danger. And in order to be as objective as possible, one must try to determine objectively what are the seats of power today and how they influence what they have established as reality. This objectivity would then be based on what is the reality of our present society and not on ideological constructions.

RK: But I suspect that in your projection of the images of a new society, you tend to go behind an objectivity founded in what is, to an objectivity founded in what ought to be; and so we return to the old question: What is this "ought" which would govern the aesthetic transformation of human beings and their relations with one another?

HM: There is no such thing as an absolute prescriptive criterion for change. If a man is happy in the society in which he presently finds himself, then he has condemned himself. This problem has never bothered me. A human being who today still thinks that the world ought not to be changed is below the level of discussion. I have no problems about the "is" and the "ought"; it is a problem invented by philosophers.

RK: But if the question is so unproblematical, what is it that separates human desire for a freer and unalienated society from the animals? I mean, why doesn't an animal feel the imperative need to change its world into a qualitatively better one?

HM: It cannot, but it does at least have enough instinct to realize that when its environment is lacking in food, warmth, and a mate it must migrate to another.

RK: How then would you account for the difference between the human desire to change his world and the animal's?

HM: An animal has no reason, whereas a human being has and so can outline, indirectly by means of art and directly by means of political theory, *possible* directions for future improvement.

RK: Humans, therefore, would seem by virtue of their reason *(Vernunft)* to possess some universal orientation towards a future society — something which you frequently spoke of in your early writings — which the animal does not possess. But by viewing our rational imagination in this way, as a power capable of transcending the immediate continuum of history and of projecting alternative possibilities for a future society, you would seem once again, would you not, to have moved beyond the strictly empirical realm of the "is"? How would you account then for this exigency, so manifest in the passion of artists and intellectuals, to transcend the given mores and conventions of our present society in search of new and better ones?

HM: Everyone searches for something better. Everyone searches for a society in which there is no more alienated labor. There is no need for a guiding principle or goal; it is simply a matter of common sense.

RK: Would you wish to equate the striving for beauty and the ideal society with the abolition of alienated labor?

HM: Of course not. Once the problem of alienated labor is solved there will be many others which remain. The creative and imaginative faculties of man will never be redundant. If art is something which among other things can point to the images of a political utopia, it is inevitably something which can never cease to be. Art and politics will never finally coalesce because the ideal society which art strives for in its negation of all alienated societies presupposes an ideal reconciliation of opposites, which can never be achieved in any absolute or Hegelian sense. The relationship between art and political praxis is therefore dialectical. As soon as one problem is solved in a synthesis, new problems are born and so the process continues without end. The day when men try to identify opposites in an ultimate sense, thus ignoring the inevitable rupture between art and revolutionary praxis, will sound the death-knell for art. Man must never cease to be an artist, to criticize and negate his present self and society and to project by means of his creative imagination alternative images of existence. He can never cease to imagine for he can never cease to change.

San Diego, 1976

Paul Ricœur
The Poetics of Language and Myth

The Creativity of Language

RK: How do your later works on metaphor (*La Métaphore vive [The Rule of the Metaphor]*, 1975) and narrativity (*Temps et récit, vol. 1 [Time and Narrative]*, 1983) fit into your overall program of philosophical hermeneutics?

PR: In *La Métaphore vive*, I tried to show how language could extend itself to its very limits, forever discovering new resonances within itself. The term *vive* (living) in the title of this work is all-important, for it was my purpose to demonstrate that there is not just an epistemological and political imagination, but also, and perhaps more fundamentally, a *linguistic* imagination which generates and regenerates meaning through the living power of metaphoricity. *La Métaphore vive* investigated the resources of rhetoric to show how language undergoes creative mutations and transformations. My work on narrativity, *Temps et récit*, develops this inquiry into the inventive power of language. Here, the analysis of narrative operations in a literary text, for instance, can teach us how we formulate a new structure of "time" by creating new modes of plot and characterization. My chief concern in this analysis is to discover how the act of *raconter*, of telling a story, can transmute *natural* time into a specifically *human* time, irreducible to mathematical, chronological "clock time." How is narrativity, as the construction or deconstruction of paradigms of storytelling, a perpetual search for new ways of expressing human time, a production or creation of meaning? That is my question.

RK: How would you relate this hermeneutics of narrativity to your former phenomenology of existence?

PR: I would say, borrowing Wittgenstein's term, that the "language game" of narration ultimately reveals that the meaning of human existence is itself narrative. The implications of narration as a retelling of history are considerable, for history is not only the story *(histoire)* of triumphant kings and heroes, of the powerful; it is also the story of the powerless and dispossessed. The history of the vanquished dead crying out for justice demands to be told. As Hannah Arendt points out, the meaning of human existence is not just the power to change or master the world, but also the ability to be remembered and recollected in narrative discourse, to be *memorable.* These existential and historical implications of narrativity are very far-reaching, for they determine what is to be "preserved" and rendered "permanent" in a culture's sense of its past, of its own "identity."

RK: Could you outline some such implications for a political rereading of the past? How, for example, would it relate to a Marxist interpretation?

PR: Just as novelists choose a certain plot *(intrigue)* to order the material of their fiction into a narrative sequence, so too historians order the events of the past according to certain choices of narrative structure or plot. While history has traditionally concerned itself with the plot of kings, battles, treaties, and the rise and fall of empires, one finds alternative readings emerging from the nineteenth century onwards whose narrative selection focuses on the story of the victims—the plot of suffering rather than that of power and glory. [Jules] Michelet's romantic historiography of the "people" was a case in point. And a more obvious and influential example is the Marxist rereading of history according to the model of the class struggle, which champions the cause of the oppressed workers. In such ways, the normal narrative ordering of history is reversed and the hero is now the slave, rather than the master as before; a new set of events and facts are deemed to be relevant and claim our attention; the relations of labor and production take precedence over the relations between kings and queens. But here again one must remain critical lest the new heroes of history become abstractions in their turn, thus reducing an alternative liberating plot to another reified version of events, which might only deepen the illusion that history somehow unfolds of its own accord, independently of the creative powers of the laboring human subject. After such a manner, Marxism as an ideology of liberation, of the powerless, can easily become—as happened with the German Social Democrats or with Stalin—an ideology which imposes a new kind of oppressive power: the proletariat thus ceases to be a living human community of subjects and becomes instead an impersonal, abstracted concept in a new system of scientific determinism.

RK: Is narrative language primarily an intentionality of subjective consciousness, as phenomenology argued, or is it an objective and impersonal structure which predetermines the subjective operations of consciousness, as structuralism maintained?

PR: It is both at once. The invaluable contribution made by structuralism was to offer an exact scientific description of the codes and paradigms of language. But I do not believe that this excludes the creative expression of consciousness. The creation of meaning in language comes from the specifically *human* production of new ways of expressing the objective paradigms and codes made available by language. With the same grammar, for example, we can utter many novel and different sentences. Creativity is always governed by objective linguistic codes which it continually brings to their limit in order to invent something new. Whereas I drew from the objective codes of rhetoric in my analysis of the creative power of metaphor, in my study of narrativity I refer to the linguistic structures disclosed by the Russian Formalists, the Prague school, and more recently by the structuralism of Lévi-Strauss and [Gerard] Genette. My philosophical project is to show how human language is *inventive* despite the objective limits and codes which govern it, to reveal the diversity and potentiality of language which the erosion of the everyday, conditioned by technocratic and political interests, never ceases to obscure. To become aware of the metaphorical and narrative resources of language is to recognize that its flattened or diminished powers can always be rejuvenated for the benefit of all forms of language usage.

RK: Can your research on narrativity also be considered as a search for a shared meaning beyond the multiplicity of discourses? In other words, does the act of narrating history render it universal and common to all?

PR: This problem of unity and diversity is central to narrativity and can be summarized in terms of the two following, conflicting interpretations. In the *Confessions*, Augustine tells us that the "human body is undone," that human existence is in discord insofar as it is a temporal rupturing and exploding of the present in contrast to the eternal presence of God. To this Augustinian reading of human existence as *dispersion*, I would oppose Aristotle's theory of tragedy, in *The Poetics*, as a way of *unifying* existence by retelling it. Narrativity can be seen in terms of this opposition: the discordance of time *(temps)* and the concordance of the tale *(récit)*. This is a problem which faces all historians, for example. Is history a narrative tale which orders and constructs the fragmentary, empirical facts offered by sociology? Can history divorce itself from the narrative structure of the tale, in its *rapprochement* to sociology, without ceasing to be history? It is interesting that even Fernand Braudel, who champions the sociological approach to history in his preface to *The Mediterranean in the Time of Philippe II*, still retains the notion of history as temporal duration; he stops short of espousing atemporal paradigms, à la Lévi-Strauss, for that would spell the demise of history. Lévi-Strauss's social anthropology can afford to dispense with history since it is only concerned with "cold societies": societies without historical or diachronic development, whose customs and norms—the incest taboo, for example—are largely unaffected by temporal change. History begins and ends with the reciting of a tale *(récit)*, and its intelligibility and coherence rest upon this recital. My task is to show how the narrative structures of history and of the story (that is, of the novel or fiction) operate in a parallel fashion to create new forms of human time, and therefore new forms of human community, for creativity is also a social and cultural act; it is not confined to the individual.

RK: What exactly do you mean by "human" time?

PR: I mean the formulation of two opposing forms of time: public time and private time. Private time is mortal time, for, as Heidegger says, to exist is to be a being-towards-death *(Sein-zum-Tode)*, a being whose future is closed off by death. As soon as we understand our existence as this mortal time, we are already involved in a form of private narrativity or history; as soon as the individual comes up against the finite limits of its own existence, it is obliged to recollect itself and to make time its *own*. On the other hand, there exists public time. Now, I do not mean public in the sense of physical or natural time (clock time), but the time of language itself, which continues on after the individual's death. To live in human time is to live between the private time of our mortality and the public time of language. Even [Bruno]

Chénu, who tends towards a quantitative assessment of history, acknowledges that the kernel of history is demography, that is, the regeneration of generations, the story *(histoire)* of the living and the dead. Precisely as this recollection of the living and the dead, history—as public narrativity—produces human time. To summarize, I would say that my analysis of narrativity is concerned with three interrelated problems: (1) narration as history, (2) narration as fiction, and (3) narration as human time.

RK: What can this analysis contribute to your study of the biblical patterns of narration in *La Symbolique du mal [The Symbolism of Evil]*?

PR: The hermeneutics of narration is crucial to our understanding of the Bible. Why is it, for example, that Judeo-Christianity is founded on narrative episodes or stories? And how is it that these succeed in becoming *exemplary,* co-coordinated into laws, prophecies, and psalms, etc.? I think that the biblical coordination of narratives can perhaps best be understood in terms of Kristeva's notion of *intertextuality:* the idea that every text functions in terms of another. Biblical narratives operate in terms of other prescriptive texts. The kernel of biblical hermeneutics is this conjunction of narrativity and prescription.

RK: What is the rapport between your earlier analysis of the "creative imagination" as an "eschatological hope" for the "not yet" of history, and your more recent analysis of narrativity as the production of human time and history?

PR: Whereas the analysis of creative imagination dealt with creativity in its prospective or futural aspect, the analysis of narrativity deals with it in a retrospective fashion. Fiction has a strong relation to the past. Camus' *L'Etranger [The Stranger]*, like most other novels, is written in the past tense. The narrative voice of a novel generally retells something that has taken place in a fictional past. One could almost say that fictional narration tends to suspend the eschatological in order to inscribe us in a meaningful past. And I believe that we must have a sense of the meaningfulness of the past if our projections into the future are to be more than empty utopias. Heidegger argues in *Being and Time* that it is because we are turned towards the future that we can possess and repossess a past, both our personal past and our cultural heritage. The structure of narrativity demonstrates that it is by trying to put order on our past, by retelling and recounting what has been, that we acquire an identity. These two orientations—towards the future and towards the past—are not, however, incompatible. As Heidegger himself points out, the notion of "repeating" *(Wiederholung)* the past is inseparable from the existential projection of ourselves towards our possibilities. To "repeat" our story, to retell our history, is to re-collect our horizon of possibilities in a resolute and responsible manner. In this respect, one can see how the retrospective character of narration is closely linked to the prospective horizon of the future. To say that narration is a recital which orders the past is not to imply that it is a conservative closure to what is new. On the contrary, narration preserves the meaning that is behind us so that we can have meaning before us. There is always *more* order in what we narrate than in what we have actually already lived, and this narrative excess *(surcroît)* of order, coherence and unity, is a prime example of the creative power of narration.

RK: What about the modernist texts of Joyce and Beckett, etc., where the narrative seems to disperse and dislocate meaning?

PR: These texts break up the habitual paradigms of narrative in order to leave the ordering task of creation to the reader himself. And ultimately it is true that the reader composes the text. All narrative, however, even Joyce's, is a certain call to order. Joyce does not invite us to embrace chaos but an infinitely more complex order that he calls "chaosmos." Narrative carries us beyond the oppressive order of our existence to a more liberating and refined one. The question of narrativity, no matter how modernist or avant-garde, cannot be separated from the problem of order.

RK: What compelled you to abandon the Husserlian phenomenology of consciousness, with its claim to a direct and immediate apprehension of meaning, and to adopt a hermeneutic phenomenology where the meaning of existence is approached indirectly through myth, metaphor, or narrativity, that is, through the detour of mediation?

PR: I think that it is always through the mediation of structuring operations that one apprehends the fundamental meaning of existence, what Merleau-Ponty called *l'être sauvage.* Merleau-Ponty sought this *être sauvage* throughout his philosophical career and consistently criticized its deformation and obfuscation in science. I for my part have always attempted to identify those mediations of language which are not reducible to the dissimulations of scientific objectivity, but which continue to bear witness to creative linguistic potentialities. Language possesses deep resources which are not immediately reducible to knowledge (particularly the intellectualist and behaviorist forms of knowledge which Merleau-Ponty rejected). And my interest in hermeneutics, and its interpretation of language, which extends to the limits of logic and the mathematical sciences, has always been an attempt to detect and describe these resources. I am convinced that all figurative language is potentially conceptualizable and that the conceptual order can possess a form of creativity. This is why I insisted, at the end of *La Métaphore vive*, upon the essential connection or intersection between speculative and poetic discourse—evidenced, for example, in the whole question of analogy. It is simplistic to suggest that conceptualization is per se antagonistic to the meaning of life and experience; concepts can also be open, creative, and living, though they can never constitute a knowledge which would be immediately accessible to some self-transparent *cogito*. Conceptualization cannot reach meaning directly or create meaning out of itself *ex nihilo;* it cannot dispense with the detour of mediation through figurative structures. This detour is intrinsic to the very working of concepts.

RK: In study 8 of *La Métaphore vive*, you raised the complex philosophical problem of "reference" in language. How does narrativity relate to this problem of reference?

PR: This question brings us to the intersection between history, which claims to deal with what actually happens, and the novel, which is of the order of fiction. Reference entails a conjunction of history and fiction. And I reckon that my chances of demonstrating the validity of reference are better in an analysis of narrativity than in one of metaphoricity. Whereas it is always difficult to identify the referent of poetic or metaphorical discourse, the referent of narrative discourse is obvious—the order of human action. Now of course human action itself is charged with fictional entities such as stories, symbols, rites, etc. As Marx pointed out in *The German Ideology*, when men produce their existence in the form of *praxis*, they represent it to themselves in terms of fiction, even at the limit in terms of religion (which for Marx is the model of ideology). There can be no praxis which is not already symbolically structured in some way. Human action is always figured in signs, interpreted in terms of cultural traditions and norms. Our narrative fictions are then added to this primary interpretation or figuration of human action, so that narrative is a redefining of what is already defined, a reinterpretation of what is already interpreted. The referent of narration, namely human action, is never raw or immediate reality but an action which has been symbolized and resymbolized over and over again. Thus narration serves to displace anterior symbolizations onto a new plane, integrating or exploding them as the case may be. If this were not so, if literary narrative, for example, were closed off from the world of human action, it would be entirely harmless and inoffensive. But literature never ceases to challenge our way of reading human history and praxis. In this respect, literary narrative involves a creative use of language often ignored by science or by our everyday existence. Literary language has the capacity to put our quotidian existence into question; it is *dangerous* in the best sense of the word.

RK: But is not the hermeneutic search for mediated and symbolized meaning a way of escaping from the harsh, empirical reality of things? Is it not always working at one remove from life?

PR: [Marcel] Proust said that if play was cloistered off in books, it would cease to be formidable. Play is formidable precisely because it is loose in the world, planting its mediations everywhere, shattering the illusion of the immediacy of the real. The problem for a hermeneutics of language is not to rediscover some pristine immediacy but to mediate again and again in a new and more creative fashion. The mediating role of imagination is forever at work in lived reality *(le vécu)*. There is no lived reality, no human or social reality, which is not already *represented* in some sense. This imaginative and creative dimension of the social, this *imaginaire social,* has been brilliantly analyzed by [Cornelius] Castoriadis in his book, *L'Institution imaginaire de la société [The Imaginary Institution of Society]*. Literature supplements this primary representation of the social with its own narrative representation, a process of *iconographic augmentation.* But literature is not the only way in which fiction can iconographically mediate human reality. There is also the mediating role of models in science or of utopias in political ideologies. These three modes of fictional mediation—literary, scientific and political—effectuate a metaphorization of the real, a creation of new meaning.

RK: Which returns us to your original question: What is the meaning of creativity in language and how does it relate to the codes, structures, or laws imposed by language?

PR: Linguistic creativity constantly strains and stretches the laws and codes of language that regulate it. Roland Barthes described these regulating laws as "fascist" and urged the writer and critic to work at the limits of language, subverting its constraining laws, in order to make way for the free movement of *desire,* to make language festive. But if the narrative order of language is replete with codes, it is also capable of creatively violating them. Human creativity is always in some sense a response to a regulating order. The imagination is always working on the basis of already established laws, and it is its task to make them function creatively, either by applying them in an original way or by subverting them; or indeed both—what [André] Malraux calls "regulated deformation." There is no function of imagination, no *imaginaire*, that is not structuring or structured, that is not said or about-to-be-said in language. The task of hermeneutics is to charter the unexplored resources of the to-be-said on the basis of the already-said. Imagination never resides in the unsaid.

RK: How would you respond to Lévi-Strauss's conclusion, in *L'Homme nu [The Naked Man]*, that the structures and symbols of society originate in "nothing" *(rien)?*

PR: I am not very interested in Lévi-Strauss's metaphysics of nothingness. The great contribution made by Lévi-Strauss was to identify the existence of enduring symbolic structures in what he called "cold societies," that is, societies (mainly South-American Indian) resistant to historical change. The Greek and Hebraic societies which combined to make up our Western culture are, by contrast, "hot societies"; they are societies whose symbolic systems change and evolve over time, carrying within themselves different layers of interpretation and reinterpretation. In other words, in "hot" societies the work of interpretation is not—as in "cold" societies—something which is introduced from without, but an internal component of the symbolic system itself. It is precisely this diachronic process of reinterpretation that we call "tradition." In the Greek *Iliad*, for example, we discover a myth that is already reinterpreted, a piece of history that is already reworked into a narrative order. Neither Homer nor Aeschylus invented their stories; what they did invent were new narrative meanings, new forms of retelling the same story. The author of the *Iliad* has the entire story of the Trojan War at his disposal, but chooses to isolate the exemplary story of Achilles' wrath. He develops this exemplary narrative to the point where the wrath expires in the cathartic reconciliation—occasioned by Hector's death—with King Priam. The story produces and exemplifies a particular meaning: how the vain and meaningless wrath of one hero (Achilles) can be overcome when this hero becomes reconciled with his victim's father (Priam) at the funeral banquet. Here we have a powerful example of what it means to create meaning from a common mythic heritage, to receive a tradition and re-create it poetically to signify something new.

RK: And, of course, Chaucer and Shakespeare produced different "exemplary" reinterpretations of the *Iliad* myth in their respective versions of Troilus and Cressida, as did Joyce once again in *Ulysses*. Such reinterpretation would seem to typify the cultural history of our Hellenic heritage. Is this kind of historical reinterpretation also to be found in the biblical or Hebraic tradition?

PR: Yes, the biblical narratives of the Hebraic tradition also operate in this exemplary or exemplifying fashion. This is evident in the fact that the biblical stories or episodes are not simply added to each other, or juxtaposed with each other, but constitute a cumulative and organic development. For example, the promise made to Abraham that his people would have a salvific relation with God is an inexhaustible promise (unlike certain legal promises which can be immediately realized); as such it opens up a history in which this promise can be repeated and reinterpreted over and over again—with Moses, then with David, and so on. So that the biblical narrative of this "not yet realized" promise creates a cumulative history of repetition. The Christian message of Crucifixion and Resurrection then inserts itself into this biblical history, as a double rapport of reinterpretation and rupture. Christianity plays both a subversive and preservative role vis-à-vis the Judaic tradition. Saint Paul talks about the overcoming of the Law, and yet we find the synoptic authors continually affirming that the Christian event is a response to the prophetic promise, "according to the Scriptures." The Judaic and Christian reinterpretations of biblical history are in "loving combat," to borrow [Karl] Jaspers's phrase. The important point is that the biblical experience of faith is founded on stories and narratives—the story of the Exodus, the Crucifixion and Resurrection, etc.—*before* it expresses itself in abstract theologies which interpret these foundational narratives and provide religious tradition with its sense of enduring identity. The *future* projects of every religion are intimately related to the ways in which it remembers itself.

RK: Your work in hermeneutics always displays a particular sensitivity to this "conflict of interpretations"—even to the point of providing one of the titles of your books. Your hermeneutics has consistently refused the idea of an "absolute knowledge" which might reductively totalize the multiplicity of interpretations—phenomenological, theological, psychoanalytic, structuralist, scientific, literary, etc. Is there any sense in which this open-ended intellectual itinerary can be construed as a sort of odyssey which might ultimately return to a unifying center where the conflicting interpretations of human discourse could be gathered together and reconciled?

PR: When Odysseus completes the circle and returns to his island of Ithaca, there is slaughter and destruction. For me the philosophical task is not to close the circle, to centralize or totalize knowledge, but to keep open the irreducible plurality of discourse. It is essential to show how the different discourses may interrelate or intersect, but one must resist the temptation to make them identical, the same. My departure from Husserlian phenomenology was largely due to my disagreement with its theory of a controlling transcendental *cogito*. I advanced the notion of a wounded or split *cogito*, in opposition to the idealist claims for an inviolate absolute subjectivity. It was in fact Karl Barth who first taught me that the subject is not a centralizing master but rather a disciple or auditor of a language larger than itself. At a broader cultural level, we must also be wary of attending exclusively to Western traditions of thought, or becoming Europocentric. In emphasizing the important of the Greek or Judeo-Christian traditions, we often overlook the radically heterogeneous discourses of the Far East for example. One of my American colleagues recently suggested to me that Derrida's deconstruction of logocentrism bears striking resemblances to the Buddhist notion of nothingness. I think that there is a certain "degree zero" or emptiness which we may have to traverse in order to abandon our pretension to be the center, our tendency to reduce all other discourses to our own totalizing schemas of thought. If there is an ultimate unity, it resides elsewhere, in a sort of eschatological hope. But this is my "secret," if you wish, my personal wager, and not something that can be translated into a centralizing philosophy discourse.

RK: It appears that our modern secularized society has abandoned the symbolic representations or *imaginaire* of tradition. Can the creative process of reinterpretation operate if the narrative continuity with the past is broken?

PR: A society where narrative is dead is one where men are no longer capable of exchanging their experiences, of sharing a common experience. The contemporary search for some narrative continuity with the past is not just nostalgic escapism but a contestation of the legislative and planificatory discourse which tends to predominate in bureaucratic societies. To give people back a *memory* is also to give them back a *future*, to put them back in time and thus release them from the "instantaneous mind" *(mens instans)*, to borrow a term from Leibniz. The past is not *passé*, for our future is guaranteed precisely by our ability to possess a narrative identity, to recollect the past in historical or fictive form. This problem of narrative identity is particularly acute, for instance, in a country like France, where the Revolution represented a rupture with the patrimony of legend and folklore, etc. (I have always been struck, for example, by the fact that most of the so-called traditional songs the French still possess are drinking songs. Today the French are largely bereft of a shared *imaginaire*, a common symbolic heritage. Our task then is to reappropriate those resources of language which have resisted contamination and destruction. To rework language is to rediscover what we are. What is lost in experience is often salvaged in language, sedimented as a deposit of traces, as a thesaurus. There can be no pure or perfectly transparent model of language, as Wittgenstein reminds us in his *Philosophical Investigations;* and if there were it would be no more than a universalized *vide.* To rediscover meaning we must return to the multilayered sedimentations of language, to the complex plurality of its instances, which can preserve what is said from the destruction of oblivion.

RK: In *History and Truth,* you praise Emmanuel Mounier as someone who refused to separate the search for philosophical truth from a political pedagogy. What are the political implications, if any, of your own philosophical thinking?

PR: My work to date has been a hermeneutic reflection upon the mediation of meaning in language, and particularly in poetic or narrative language. What, you ask, can such hermeneutics contribute to our understanding of the rapport between the mediations of such symbolic discourses and the immediacy of political praxis? The fact that language is disclosed by hermeneutics (and also by the analytic philosophy of Wittgenstein) as a nontotalizable plurality of interpretations or "language-games" and so cannot pretend to the status of a universal science. Some recent exchanges I had with Czech philosophers and students in the Tomin seminar in Prague taught me that the problem of totalitarianism resides in the lie that there can be a universally true and scientific discourse of politics (in this instance, the communist discourse). Once one recognizes that political language is basically a rhetoric of persuasion and opinion, one can tolerate free discussion. An "open society," to use Popper's term, is one which acknowledges that political debate is infinitely open and is thus prepared to take the critical step back in order to continually interrogate and reconstitute the conditions of an authentic language.

RK: Can there be a positive rapport between language, as a political ideology, and utopia?

PR: Every society, as I mentioned earlier, possesses, or is part of, a socio-political *imaginaire*, that is, an ensemble of symbolic discourses. This *imaginaire* can function as a rupture or a reaffirmation. As reaffirmation, the *imaginaire* operates as an *ideology* which can positively repeat and represent the founding discourse of a society, what I call its "foundational symbols," thus preserving its sense of identity. After all, cultures create themselves by telling stories of their own past. The danger is of course that this reaffirmation can be perverted, usually by monopolistic elites, into a mystificatory discourse which serves to uncritically vindicate or glorify the established political powers. In such instances, the symbols of a community become fixed and fetishized; they serve as lies. Over against this, there exists the *imaginaire* of rupture, a discourse of *utopia* which remains critical of the powers that be out of fidelity to an "elsewhere," to a society that is "not yet." But this utopian discourse is not always positive either. For beside the authentic utopia of critical rupture there can also exist a dangerously schizophrenic utopian discourse which projects a static future without ever producing the conditions of its realization. This can happen with the Marxist-Leninist notion of utopia if one projects the final "withering away of the state" without undertaking genuine measures to ever achieve such a goal. Here utopia becomes a future cut off from the present and the past, a mere alibi for the consolidation of the repressive powers that be. The utopian discourse functions as a mystifactory ideology as soon as it justifies the oppression of today in the name of the liberation of tomorrow. In short, *ideology* as a symbolic confirmation of the past and *utopia* as a symbolic opening towards the future are complimentary; if cut off from each other, they can lead to a form of political pathology.

RK: Would you consider the Liberation Theology of Latin America to be an example of a positive utopian discourse insofar as it combines a Marxist utopianism with the political transformation of *present* reality?

PR: It also combines it with the *past,* with the memory of the archetypes of exodus and resurrection. This memorial dimension of Liberation Theology is essential, for it gives direction and continuity to the utopian projection of the future, thus functioning as a *garde-fou* against irresponsible or uncritical futurism. Here the political project of the future is inseparable from a continuous horizon of liberation, reaching back to the biblical notions of exile and promise. The promise remains unfulfilled until the utopia is historically realized; and it is precisely the not-yet-realized horizon of this promise which binds men together as a community, which prevents utopia detaching itself as an empty dream.

RK: How exactly does utopia relate to history?

PR: In his *History of the Concept of History*, Reinhart Koselleck argues that until the eighteenth century, the concept of history, in the West at any rate, was a plural one; one referred to "histories," not History with a capital "H." Our current notion of a single or unique history only emerged with the modern idea of progress. As soon as history is thus constituted as a single concept, the gap between our "horizon of expectancy" and our "field of experience" never ceases to widen. The unity of history is founded on the constitution of a common horizon of expectancy, but the projection of such a horizon into a distantly abstract future means that our present "field of experience" can become pathologically deprived of meaning and articulation. The universal ceases to be concrete. This dissociation of *expectancy* from *experience* enters a crisis as soon as we lack the intermediaries to pass from the one to the other. Up to the sixteenth century, the utopian horizon of expectancy was the eschatological notion of the Last Judgment, which had as mediating or intermediating factors the whole experience of the millennium of the Holy Roman and Germanic Empires. There was always some sort of articulated path leading from what one had to what one expected to have. The liberal ideology of Kant and Locke produced a certain discourse of democracy which served as a path for the citizen towards a better humanity, and Marxism also promoted mediating stages leading from capitalism through socialism to communism. But we don't seem to believe in these intermediaries any more. The problem today is the apparent impossibility of unifying world politics, of mediating between the polycentricity of our everyday political practices and the utopian horizon of a universally liberated humanity. It is not that *we* are without utopia, but that we are without *paths* to utopia. And without a path towards it, without concrete and practical mediation in our field of experience, utopia becomes a sickness. Perhaps the deflation of utopian expectancies is not entirely a bad thing. Politics can so easily be injected with too much utopia; perhaps it should become more modest and realistic in its claims, more committed to our practical and immediate needs.

RK: Is there any place in contemporary politics for a genuine utopian discourse?

PR: Maybe not in politics itself, but rather at the junction between politics and other cultural discourses. Our present disillusionment with the political stems from the fact that we invested it with the totality of our expectancies—until it became a bloated imposture of all utopia. We have tended to forget that beside the public realm of politics there also exists a more private cultural realm (which includes literature, philosophy, and religion, etc.) where the utopian horizon can express itself. Modern society seems hostile to this domain of private experience, but the suppression of the private entails the destruction of the public. The vanquishing of the private by the public is a pyrrhic victory.

RK: Are you advocating a return to the bourgeois romantic notion of private subjectivity removed from all political responsibility?

PR: Not at all. In my recent discussions with the Prague philosophers, I spoke about the crisis of the subject in contemporary Continental philosophy, particularly structuralism. I pointed out that if one does away with the idea of a subject who is responsible for his or her words, we are no longer in a position to talk of the freedom or the rights of man. To dispense with the classical notion of the subject as a transparent *cogito* does not mean that we have to dispense with all forms of subjectivity. My hermeneutical philosophy has attempted to demonstrate the existence of an opaque subjectivity which expresses itself through the detour of countless mediations—signs, symbols, texts, and human praxis itself. This hermeneutical idea of subjectivity as a dialectic between the self and mediated social meanings has deep moral and political implications. It shows that there is an *ethic of the word*, that language is not just the abstract concern of logic or semiotics, but entails the fundamental moral duty that people be responsible for what they say. A society which no longer possesses subjects ethically responsible for their words is a society which no longer possesses citizens. For the dissident philosophers in Prague, the primary philosophical question is the integrity and truthfulness of language. And this question becomes a moral and political act of resistance in a system based on lies and perversion. The Marxism of Eastern Europe has degenerated from dialectics to positivism. It has abandoned the Hegelian inspiration which preserved Marxism as a realization of the universal subject in history and has become instead a positivistic technology of mass manipulation.

RK: So the hermeneutical interrogation of the creation of meaning in language can have a political content?

PR: Perhaps the most promising example of a political hermeneutics is to be found in the Frankfurt school synthesis between Marxist dialectics and Heideggerean hermeneutics—best expressed in [Jürgen] Habermas's critique of ideologies. But here again one must be careful to resist the temptation to engage in an unmediated politics. It is necessary for hermeneutics to keep a certain distance so as to critically disclose the underlying mediating structures at work in political discourse. This hermeneutic distance is particularly important today with the post-1968 disillusionment, the demise of the Maoist ideology, and the exposure of Soviet totalitarianism by [Alexander] Solzhenitsyn and others.

RK: Is this disillusionment a worldwide phenomenon?

PR: It exists in varying degrees, but is most conspicuous in countries like France, where the essential distinction between state and society has been largely occluded. The French Revolution apportioned political sovereignty to all levels of the community, from the government at the top to the individuals at the bottom. But in this process, the state became omnipresent, the citizen being reduced to a mere fragment of the state. What was so striking in the Solidarity movement in Poland was their use of the term *society* in opposition to the term *state*. Even in the Anglo-Saxon countries, one finds certain national institutions—such as the media or universities—which are relatively independent of state politics. (It is difficult to find examples of this in France.) The weak ideologization of politics in America, for instance, means that it can at least serve as a sprawling laboratory where a multiplicity of discourses can be tried and tested. This phenomenon of the "melting-pot" is an example of what Montesquieu called the "separation of powers." It is interesting to remember that the state was originally conceived by the liberal thinkers as an agency of toleration, a way of protecting the plurality of beliefs and practices. The liberal state was to be a safeguard against religious and other forms of fanaticism. The fundamental perversion of the liberal state is that it came to function as a totalizing rather than a detotalizing agency. That is why it is urgent for us today to discover a political discourse which would not be governed by states, a new form of society guaranteeing universal rights yet dispensing with totalizing constraints. This is the enormous task of reconstituting a form of sociality not determined by the state.

RK: How does one go about discovering this new discourse of society?

PR: One of the first steps would be to analyze what exactly happened in the eighteenth century when the Judeo-Christian horizon of eschatology was replaced by the Enlightenment horizon of humanism with its liberal notions of autonomy, freedom, and human rights. We must see how this Enlightenment humanism developed through the Kantian notion of the autonomous will, the Hegelian notion of the universal class (of civil servants) to the Marxist universal class of workers, etc., until we reached a secularized version of utopia, which frequently degenerated into scientific positivism. We must ask: Can there be any sort of continuity between the religious eschatological projection of utopia and the modern humanist projection of a secularized utopia? The challenge today is to find alternative forms of social rationality beyond the positivistic extremes of both state socialism and utilitarian-liberal capitalism. Habermas's distinction between three forms of rationality is essential here: (1) *calculative rationality*, which operates as positivistic control and manipulation; (2) *interpretative rationality*, which tries to represent the cultural codes and norms in a creative way; (3) *critical rationality*, which opens up the utopian horizon of liberation. For a genuine social rationality to exist, we must refuse to allow the critical and interpretative functions to be reduced to the calculative. Habermas is here developing Adorno's and [Max] Horkheimer's critique *of positivist rationality*, which exists in both state communism and in the argument of liberal capitalism that once the society of abundance has been achieved, all can be distributed equally (the problem being, of course, that liberalism employs the means of an hierarchical and unequal society to achieve such an end of abundance—an end which never seems to be realized). So our task remains that of preserving a utopian horizon of liberty and equality—by means of interpretative and critical rationality—without resorting to a positivistic ideology of bad faith. I agree here with Raymond Aron's contention that we have not yet succeeded in developing a political model which could accommodate the simultaneous advancement of liberty and equality. Societies which have advocated liberty have generally suppressed equality and vice versa.

RK: Do you think that the critique of political power carried out by left-wing political philosophers in France, such as [Cornelius] Castoriadis and [Claude] Lefort, contributes to the hermeneutic search for a new discourse of sociality?

PR: Their contribution has been absolutely decisive. This critique has attempted to show that the error of Marxism resides not so much in its lack of a political horizon as in its reduction of the critique of power to the economic transfer of work to capital (that is, the critique of surplus value). Thus the Marxist critique tends to ignore that there can be more pernicious forms of power than capital—for example, the totalization of all the resources of a society (the resources of the workforce, of the means of discussion and information, education, research, etc.) by the central committee of the party or state. In this manner, the handing over of the private ownership of the means of production to the state can often mean a replacement of the alienation of society by the alienation of the state. The power of the totalitarian party is perhaps more nefarious than the dehumanizing power of capital insofar as it controls not only the economic means of production but also the political means of communications. Maybe the economic analysis of class struggle is but one of the many plots that make up the complex of history. Hence the need for a hermeneutics of sociality that could unravel the plurality of power plots which enmesh to form our history.

RK: In "Non-violent Man and his Presence in History" *(History and Truth)*, you asked: "Can the prophet or nonviolent man have an historical task which would obviate both the extreme inefficacity of the Yogi and the extreme efficacity of the Commissar? In other words, can one commit oneself to the efficacious transformation of political reality and still preserve the critical distance of transcendence?"

PR: This idea of transcendence is essential for any sort of nonviolent discourse. The pacifist ideal resists violence by attesting to values which transcend the arena of political efficacity, without becoming irrelevant dreams. Nonviolence is a form of genuine utopian vigil or hope, a way of refuting the system of violence and oppression in which we live.

RK: Is it possible to reconcile the exigency of an authentic social rationality with the eschatological hope of religion?

PR: This has never struck me as an insoluble problem for the basic cultural reason that our Western religiosity of Judeo-Christianity has always functioned in the philosophical climate of Greek and Latin rationality. I have always objected to the simplistic opposition of Jerusalem and Athens, to those thinkers who declare that true spirituality can only be found in monotheism or try to drive a wedge between Greek and Hebraic culture, defining the former as a thought of the cosmos and the latter as a thought of transcendence, etc. From the eleventh century onwards we find models for reconciling reason and religion—in Anselm, for example—and the Renaissance confirms this primary synthesis of rationality and spirituality. If it is true that the rationality of scientific positivism has divorced itself from spirituality, there are many signs today that we are searching for new forms of connection.

Paris, 1981

Myth as the Bearer of Possible Worlds

RK: One of your first attempts at hermeneutic analysis concentrated on the way in which human consciousness was mediated by mythic and symbolic expressions from the earliest times. In *The Symbolism of Evil* (1960), you demonstrated how mythic symbols played an important ideological and political role in the ancient cultures of the Babylonians, Hebrews, and Greeks. And in this same work you declared that "myth relates to events that happened at the beginning of time which have the purpose of providing grounds for the ritual actions of men of today." Are you suggesting that mythic symbols can play a relevant role in contemporary culture? And if so, could you elaborate on how this might do so?

PR: I don't think that we can approach this question directly, that is, in terms of a direct relationship between myth and action. We must first return to an analysis of what constitutes the *imaginary nucleus* of any culture. It is my conviction that one cannot reduce any culture to its explicit functions—political, economic, and legal, etc. No culture is wholly transparent in this way. There is invariably a hidden nucleus which determines and rules the *distribution* of these transparent functions and institutions. It is this matrix of distribution which assigns them different roles in relation to (1) each other, (2) other societies, (3) the individuals who participate in them, and (4) nature, which stands over against them.

RK: Does this ratio of distribution differ from one society to another?

PR: It certainly does. The particular relationship between political institutions, nature, and the individual is rarely, if ever, the same in any two cultures. The ratio of distribution between these different functions of a given society is determined by some *hidden* nucleus, and it is here that we must situate the specific identity of culture. Beyond or beneath the self-understanding of a society, there is an opaque kernel which cannot be reduced to empirical norms or laws. This kernel cannot be explained in terms of some transparent model, because it is constitutive *of* a culture *before* it can be expressed and reflected in specific representations or ideas. It is only if we try to grasp this kernel that we may discover the *foundational mytho-poetic* nucleus of a society. By analyzing itself in terms of such a foundational nucleus, a society comes to a truer understanding of itself; it begins to critically acknowledge its own symbolizing identity.

RK: How are we to recognize this mythical nucleus?

PR: The mythical nucleus of a society is only *indirectly* recognizable. But it is indirectly recognizable not only by what is said (discourse), but also by what and how one lives (praxis), and thirdly, as I suggested, by the distribution between different functional levels of a society. We cannot, for example, say that in all countries the economic layer is determining. This is true for our Western society. But as Lévi-Strauss has shown in his analysis of many primitive societies, this is not universally true. In several cultures the significance of economic and historical considerations would seem to be minor. In our culture the economic factor is indeed determining; but that does not mean that the predominance of economics is itself explicable purely in terms of economic science. This predominance is perhaps more correctly understood as but one constituent of the overall evaluation of what is primary and what is secondary. And it is only by the analysis of the hierarchical structuring and evaluation of the different constituents of a society (that is, the role of politics, nature, art, religion, etc.) that we may penetrate to its hidden *mytho-poetic nucleus.*

RK: You mentioned Lévi-Strauss. How would you situate your own hermeneutical analyses of symbol and myth in relation to his work in this area?

PR: I don't think that Lévi-Strauss makes any claim to speak of societies in general. He has focused on certain primitive and stable societies, leaving aside considerations of history. This is important to realize so as not to draw hasty conclusions from his analyses. Lévi-Strauss has deliberately chosen to speak of societies *without history*, whereas I think that there is something specifically historical about the societies to which we in the West belong, depending on the extent to which they are affected by Hebraic, Hellenic, Germanic, or Celtic cultures. The development of a society is both synchronic and diachronic. This means that the distribution of power-functions in any given society contains a definite *historical* dimension. We have to think of societies in terms of both a set of simultaneous institutions (synchronism) and a process of historical transformation (diachronism). Thus we arrive at the panchronic approach to societies, that is, both synchronic and diachronic, which characterizes the hermeneutical method. And we must also realize that the kinds of myth on which our societies are founded have themselves this twofold characteristic: on the one hand, they constitute a certain system of simultaneous symbols which can be approached through structuralist analysis, but, on the other hand, they have a history, because it is always through a process of interpretation and reinterpretation that they are kept alive. Myths have a historicity of their own. This difference of history typifies, for example, the development of the Semitic, pre-Hellenistic, and Celtic mythical nuclei. Therefore, just as societies are both structural and historical, so also are the mythical nuclei which ground them.

RK: In the conclusion to *The Symbolism of Evil,* you state that "a philosophy instructed by myths arises at a certain moment in reflection and wishes to answer to a certain situation in modern culture." What precisely do you mean by this "certain situation"? And how does myth answer to this problematic?

PR: I was thinking there of Jaspers's philosophy of "boundary situations," which influenced me so strongly just after the Second World War. There are certain boundary situations, such as war, suffering, guilt, death, etc., in which the individual or community experiences a fundamental existential crisis. At such moments, the whole community is put into question. For it is only when it is threatened with destruction from without or from within that a society is compelled to return to the very roots of its identity, to that mythical nucleus which ultimately grounds and determines it. The solution to the immediate crisis is no longer a purely political or technical matter but demands that we ask ourselves the ultimate questions concerning our origins and ends: Where do we come from? Where do we go? In this way, we become aware of our basic capacities and reasons for surviving, for being and continuing to be what we are.

RK: I am reminded here of Mircea Eliade's statement in *Myths, Dreams, Mysteries* that myth is something which always operates in a society regardless of whether this society reflectively acknowledges its existence. Eliade maintains that because modern man has lost his awareness of the important role that myth plays in his life, it often manifests itself in deviant ways. He gives as an example the emergence of fascist movements in Europe characterized by a mythic glorification of blood sacrifice and the hero-savior, together with the equally mythical revival of certain ancient rituals, symbols, and insignia. The suggestion is that if we do not explicitly recognize and reappropriate the mythic import of our existence, it will emerge in distorted and pernicious ways. Do you think this is a valid point?

PR: You have hit here on a very important and *difficult* problem: the possibilities of a perversion of myth. This means that we can no longer approach myth *at the level of naiveté.* We must rather always view it from a critical perspective. It is only by means of a selective reappropriation that we can become aware of myth. We are no longer primitive beings, living at the immediate level of myth. Myth for us is always mediated and opaque. This is so not only because it expresses itself primarily through a particular apportioning of power-functions, as mentioned earlier, but also because several of its recurrent forms have become deviant and dangerous, for example, the myth of absolute power (fascism) and the myth of the sacrificial scapegoat (anti-Semitism and racism). We are no longer justified in speaking of "myth in general." We must critically assess the content of each myth and the basic intentions which animate it. Modern man can neither get rid of myth nor take it at its face value. Myth will always be with us, but we must always approach it *critically.*

RK: It was with a similar scruple in mind that I tried to show in *Myth and Terror* (1978) that there are certain mythic structures operative in extreme Irish Republicanism—recurrence of blood sacrifice, apocalypse/renewal, etc.—which can become deviant manifestations of an original mythical nucleus. And I feel accordingly that any approach to myth should be as much a demythologization of deviant expressions as a resuscitation of genuine ones.

PR: Yes. And I think it is here that we could speak of the essential connection between the "critical instance" and the "mythical foundation." Only those myths are genuine which can be reinterpreted in terms of *liberation.* And I mean liberation as both a personal and collective phenomenon. We should perhaps sharpen this critical criterion to include only those myths which have as their horizon the liberation of humanity *as a whole.* Liberation cannot be exclusive. Here I think we come to recognize a fundamental convergence between the claims of myth and reason. In genuine reason as in genuine myth, we find a concern for the *universal* liberation of all. To the extent that myth is seen as the foundation of a particular community to the absolute exclusion of all others, the possibilities of perversion — chauvinistic nationalism, racism, etc. — are already present.

RK: So in fact you suggest that the foundational power of myth should always be in some sense chaperoned by critical reason?

PR: In our Western culture, the myth making of man has often been linked with the critical instance of reason. And this is because it has had to be constantly interpreted and reinterpreted in different historical epochs. In other words, it is because the survival of myth calls for perpetual historical interpretation that it involves a critical component. Myths are not unchanging and unchanged antiques which are simply delivered out of the past in some naked, original state. Their specific identity depends on the way in which each generation receives or interprets them according to their needs, conventions, and ideological motivations. Hence the necessity of critical discrimination between liberating and destructive modes of reinterpretation.

RK: Could you give an example of such reinterpretation?

PR: Well, if we take the relation of *mythos* and *logos* in the Greek experience, we could say that myth had been absorbed by the *logos*, but never completely so; for the claim of the *logos* to rule over *mythos* is itself a mythical claim. Myth is thereby reinjected into the logos and gives a mythical dimension to reason itself. Thus the rational appropriation of myth becomes also a revival of myth. Another example would be the reinterpretative overlap between the mythical paradigms of the Hebraic exodus and the prophetic dimension in Hebrew literature. And then at a second level, this Hebraic *mythos* came down to us through a Hellenization of its whole history. Even for us today, this Hellenization is an important mediation, because it was through the conjunction of the Jewish *Torah* and Greek logos that the notion of law could be incorporated into our culture.

RK: You would not agree then with those modern theologians, such as [Jürgen] Moltmann and [Rudolf] Bultmann, who suggest that the Hellenization of the Judeo-Christian culture is a perversion of its original richness?

PR: No. The tension between the Greek logos and the Semitic nucleus of exodus and revelation is fundamentally and positively constitutive of our culture.

RK: Several critics have described your hermeneutical approach to myth and symbol as an attempt, almost in the manner of psychoanalysis, to reduce myth to some hidden rational message. In *The Symbolism of Evil,* you say that the aim of your philosophy is to disclose through reflection and speculation the *rationality* of symbols. And again in *On Interpretation,* you state that "every mythos harbors a logos which requires to be exhibited." But is it possible to extract the logos and yet leave the mythos intact? Or is myth something essentially enigmatic and therefore irreducible to rational content?

PR: This criticism must be understood in the following way. There are two uses of the concept of myth. One is myth as the *extension* of a symbolic structure. In this sense it is pointless to speak of a demythologization for that would be tantamount to desymbolization—and this I deny completely. But there is a second sense in which myth serves as an *alienation* of this symbolic structure. Here it becomes reified and is misconstrued as an actual materialistic explanation of the world. If we interpret myth *literally,* we misinterpret it. For myth is essentially *symbolic.* It is only in instances of such misinterpretation that we may legitimately speak of demythologization; not concerning its symbolic content but concerning the hardening of its symbolic structures into dogmatic or reified ideologies.

RK: Do you think that Bultmann's use of the term *demythologization* had something to do with this confusion between two different types of myth (as creative symbol or reductive ideology)?

PR: Yes I do. Bultmann seems to ignore the complexity of myth. And so when he speaks, for example, of the necessity to demythologize the myth of the threefold division of the cosmos into Heaven, Earth, and Hell, he is treating this myth only in terms of its literal interpretation or rather misinterpretation. But Bultmann does not realize that there is a symbolic as well as a pseudosymbolic or literal dimension in myth, and that demythologization is only valid in relation to this second dimension.

RK: Are myths *universal,* in terms of their original symbolic structures, or do they originate from *particular* national cultures?

PR: This is a very difficult problem. We are caught here between the claims of two equally valid dimensions of myth. And it is the delicate balance between them that is difficult to find. On the one hand, we must say that mythical structures are not simply universal any more than are languages. Just as man is fragmented between different languages, so also he is fragmented between mythical cycles, each of which is typical of a living culture. We must acknowledge, then, that one of the primary functions of any myth is to found the specific identity of a community. On the other hand, however, we must say that just as languages are in principle translatable one into the other, so too myths have a horizon of universality which allows them to be understood by other cultures. The history of Western culture is made up of a confluence of different myths which have been expatriated from their original community, that is, Hebrew, Greek, Germanic, Celtic. The horizon of any genuine myth always exceeds the political and geographical boundaries of a specific national or tribal community. Even if we may say that mythical structures *founded* political institutions, they always go beyond the territorial limitations imposed by politics. Nothing travels more extensively and effectively than myth. Therefore we must conclude that while mythic symbols are rooted in a particular culture, they also have the capacity to emigrate and develop within new cultural frameworks.

RK: Is there not a sense in which perhaps the source and not only the historical transmission of symbols may be responsible for their universal dimension?

PR: It is quite possible that the supranational quality of myth or symbol may be ultimately traced back to a prehistorical layer from which all particular "mythical nuclei" might be said to emerge. But it is difficult to determine the nature of this prehistory, for all myths as we know them come down to us through history. Each particular myth has its own history of reinterpretation and emigration. But another possible explanation of the universally common dimension of myth might be that because the myth-making powers of the human imagination are finite, they ensure the frequent recurrence of similar archetypes and motifs.

RK: Certainly the myth of the Fall as you analyze it in *The Symbolism of Evil* would seem to be common to many different cultures.

PR: Yes. We could say that genuine myth goes beyond its claim to found a particular community and speaks to man as such. Several exegetes of Jewish literature, for example, have made a distinction between different layers of myth: those which are foundational for the Jewish culture — the "chronicle dimension" — and those which make up a body of truths valid for all mankind — the "wisdom dimension." This seems to me an important distinction and one applicable to other cultures.

RK: In Irish literature over the last fifty years or so, one finds a similar distinction between these dimensions. In the Fenian literature of the nineteenth century or the Celtic Twilight literature of Yeats, Lady Gregory, and others, myth seems to have been approached as a "chronicle" of the spiritual origins of the race. For this reason, it often strikes one as suffering from a certain hazy occultism and introversion. Joyce, on the other hand, used myth, and particularly the myth of Finn, in its "wisdom dimension"; that is, as àn Irish archetype open to, and capable of assimilating, the rich resources of entirely different cultures. *Finnegans Wake* or *Ulysses* seem to represent an exemplary synthesis of the particular and universal claims of myth.

PR: The important point here is that the original potential of any genuine myth will always transcend the confines of a particular community or nation. The *mythos* of any community is the bearer of something which exceeds its own frontiers; it is the bearer of other *possible* worlds. And I think it is in this horizon of the "possible" that we discover the *universal* dimensions of symbolic and poetic language.

RK: You have stated that what animates your philosophical research on symbolism and myth is not "regret for some sunken Atlantis" but "hope for a re-creation of language" *(The Symbolism of Evil)*. What precisely do you mean by this?

PR: Language has lost is original unity. Today it is fragmented not only geographically into different communities but functionally into different disciplines—mathematical, historical, scientific, legal, psychoanalytic, etc. It is the function of a philosophy of language to recognize the specific nature of these disciplines and thereby assign each "language-game" its due (as Wittgenstein would have it), limiting and correcting their mutual claims. Thus one of the main purposes of hermeneutics is to refer the different uses of language to different regions of being—natural, scientific, fictional, etc. But this is not all. Hermeneutics is also concerned with the permanent spirit of language. By *the spirit of language,* we intend not just some decorative excess or effusion of subjectivity, but *the capacity of language to open up new worlds.* Poetry and myth are not just nostalgia for some forgotten world. They constitute a disclosure of unprecedented worlds, an opening on to other *possible* worlds which transcend the established limits of our *actual* world.

RK: How then would you situate your philosophy of language in relation to analytic philosophy?

PR: I certainly share at least one common concern of analytic philosophy: the concern with ordinary language in contradistinction to the scientific language of documentation and verification. Scientific language has no real function of communication or interpersonal dialogue. It is important, therefore, that we preserve the rights of ordinary language where the communication of experience is of primary significance. But my criticism of ordinary language philosophy is that it does not take into account the fact that language itself is a place of prejudice and bias. Therefore, we need a third dimension of language, a critical and creative dimension, which is directed towards neither scientific verification nor ordinary communication but towards the disclosure of possible worlds. This third dimension of language I call the poetic. The adequate self-understanding of man is dependent on this third dimension of language as a disclosure of *possibility*.

RK: Is not this philosophy of language profoundly phenomenological in character?

PR: Yes it is. Because phenomenology as it emerged in the philosophies of Husserl and Heidegger raised the central question of "meaning." And it is here that we find the main dividing line between the structuralist analysis and phenomenological hermeneutics. Whereas the former is concerned with the immanent arrangement of texts and textual codes, hermeneutics looks to the "meaning" produced by these codes. It is my conviction that the decisive feature of hermeneutics is the capacity of world-disclosure yielded by texts. Hermeneutics is not confined to the *objective* structural analysis of texts nor to the *subjective* existential analysis of the authors of texts; its primary concern is with the worlds which these authors and texts open up. It is by an understanding of the worlds, actual and possible, opened by language that we may arrive at a better understanding of ourselves.

Paris, 1978

Stanislas Breton
Being, God, and the Poetics of Relation

RK: Your philosophical journey has been wide-ranging. You have published works on such diverse topics as Neoplatonism, Thomism, Marxism, phenomenology, logic, and poetics. What would you consider to be the unifying threads in this tapestry of intellectual interests?

SB: First, I would say that my philosophical journey is related to my biographical one. My early upbringing and education in a rural community in La Vendée certainly had a significant impact on my subsequent thinking; it determined my later leanings towards a certain philosophical *realism*. This perhaps accounts somewhat for the fact that in the doctorate I presented to the Sorbonne, *Approches phénoménologiques de l'idée d'être [Phenomenological Approaches to the Idea of Being]*, I tended to see the key metaphysical concept, "Being as Being," in terms of the four elements of the concretely experienced, real world — earth, fire, water, air. Strange as it may sound, the monastic experience of my early years in a Passionist seminary, which I entered at the age of fifteen, also corresponded in some way to my conceptualization of *Being as Being:* this decisive concept thus emerged as both a monastic desert and an all-englobing shelter of the four elements of nature. Philosophy begins, I believe, in the life-world. So it is not very surprising that our understanding of Being should be colored by our lived experience, by the formative *images* of our being in the world. This conviction predisposed me, of course, to *a phenomenological* approach to philosophy; it also confirmed my belief that a poetics of imagination is an indispensable dimension of genuine thinking.

RK: I think that your conviction would be shared by many of the phenomenologists. [Jean-Paul] Sartre, [Albert] Camus, and Merleau-Ponty all spoke of the decisive way in which their concretely lived experience affected their subsequent understanding of Being, which they saw as a "universal" reflection on their "particular," prereflective existence. But what philosophical or intellectual influences on your thinking would you consider to be of primary importance?

SB: The earliest intellectual influence I can recall was the Latin language—the way in which it was used in the seminary with a scholastic emphasis on professorial rigor and prepositional distinctions: *ex, in, ad, de* and so on. This language of *relations*, which Levinas calls "transitive language," greatly influenced my doctorate in Rome, entitled *L'Esse 'in' et l'esse 'ad' dans la métaphysique de la relation ['Esse In' and 'Esse Ad' in the Metaphysics of Relationship]*. This scholastic logic of relations was the second major influence on my philosophical imagination for it raised the fundamental question of how man can be *in* being (immanence) and still be said to be moving *towards* it (transcendence). Once applied to the work of St. Thomas, it opened up the whole problematic of the "operations" of ontological immanence with its crucial theological implications for our understanding of the Trinity: How does the Son belong to the Father and the Father to the Son through the agency of the Spirit? I would almost say that my mature interest in philosophy sprang from theological questions which theology itself could not answer. For example, the *being-in* relation provided an explanation of the unity of the Three Persons of the Trinity, while the distinction and difference between the Three could be understood in terms of the intentional or transitive relation of the *being-towards*. The Spirit could thus be interpreted as a twofold relation: (1) the perpetual attraction between the Father and the Son; and (2) the *power of* movement and carrying-beyond *(meta-pherein)*, which refuses the finite limits of proprietal possession and makes the Trinity an *infinite relation.*

This theology of operations also has important implications for our understanding of the Incarnation. The substantialist theology of the Councils, which spoke of the two natures in one, seemed to me insufficient insofar as it privileged the notion of *substance* over that of *function* or *relation.* The dynamic relation of the being-towards category struck me as being closer to the biblical language of transitivity. God as a being-in-itself, as an identical substance, cannot be thought by us;

we can only know or speak about God in terms of His relation to us, or ours to Him.

My interest in the theology of operations soon led to an interest in the philosophy of mathematical relations. When I was captured by the Germans during the war, I had three books in my bag: [Jozef] Bochenski's *Elements of Mathematical Logic*, [Leon] Brunschvicg's *Modality of Judgment*, and [Octave] Hamelin's *The Principal Elements of Representation.* Another work which deeply fascinated me at the time was Bertrand Russell's *Introduction á la philosophie mathématique [Introduction to Mathematical Philosophy]*, where he outlined a sophisticated philosophy of descriptive relations. In short, what I appreciated most in these thinkers was their analysis of the operative terms of relation-prepositions such as *in, towards*, and the conjunctions *for, as, as-if*, which I called "those little servants of the Lord." I believe they are not only the indispensable accompaniment of all thought but also the secret messengers of the philosophical future.

RK: Could you elaborate on your philosophical transition from the initial question of *being as being* (an ontology of the four elements of nature) to the correlative question of *being-in* and *being-towards* (a metaphysics of relation)?

SB: I was drawn towards the metaphysical problematic of relations in order to try to understand not just what being is, as such, but how it relates to man or accounts for the way in which the Three Divine Persons relate to each other. The relation of being-towards constitutes the element of metaphor or metamorphosis, that which assures the infinite movement of existence as a passing over from one phase to the next; it is that which compels us to continually alter our concepts, making each one of us a "being in transit."

The relation of being-in, by contrast, is that *élément neutre* which draws together and unifies existence; it is that which founds our notion of ontological self-identity. In the *Metaphysics*, Aristotle refers to this principle when he states that the addition of being or the One to something changes nothing. Being added to man adds nothing. For being is not a predicate but the most essential, necessary and universal function of existence, the function which allows each thing to be itself, to be one and the same. The principle of being-in is that which freely grants each thing the permission to *be*, to rest and recollect itself from the movement of becoming.

RK: Do you see this Greek metaphysics of relation as radicalizing our understanding of the Judeo-Christian tradition?

SB: I believe that both metaphysical relations—the being-towards and the being-in—are equally essential for an understanding of Judeo-Christian theology. At this level, I see no great opposition between Greek and biblical thought. What we call the historical "meaning" of Christianity or Judaism is the tradition of interpretations that have been historically ascribed to them, and in the history of Western thinking these interpretations are inextricably related to Hellenic concepts of ontology. Between the two traditions—the Greek and the biblical—there is a creative tension which ensures that we are never fully at our intellectual ease in either. We are inevitably committed to this philosophical exodus, this vacillation between two "homes" of thought. We have left the home of Israel just as we have left the home of Greece. We remain homesick for both. We cannot renounce the intellectual nostalgia of this double allegiance. The Western thinker is divided from *within.*

RK: Do you see Thomism as an attempt to bridge these two traditions in your own thought?

SB: I consider Thomism to be the paleoancephalus of my philosophical formation. There were three areas in the work of St. Thomas which particularly preoccupied me: (1) the attempt to think God and being together; (2) the theory of intentionality and formal objects— which I rediscovered later in [Franz] Brentano and Husserl (I was especially impressed by Thomas's statement that relation consists of a certain transit or transitivity; this implies that being is transitive and that our entire existence is a series of transitions towards the other, the loving potency which forever searches for its fulfillment in act); (3) the Thomistic definition of freedom or the free being as the being that is "cause of itself" *(causa sui).* This third concept occupied a very important place in my thought. For something to be free thus, meant that, as cause of itself, it can create something new, almost from nothing. For the thinker it offers the free possibility to open up new paths of enquiry not already charted or inscribed in the map of the world.

RK: How did you find your way from Thomism to phenomenology?

SB: Like most philosophers of my generation I was deeply influenced by the phenomenological movement inaugurated by Husserl and his disciples, [Roman] Ingarden, [Bernard] Häring, Heidegger, and so on. I saw the phenomenological emphasis on intentionality—the methodological investigation of how our consciousness is always intentionally directed towards something *beyond* itself—as a means of extending three of my primary intellectual concerns: (1) the logic of relations governing the activity of the human mind; (2) the dynamic teleological aspect of Thomistic metaphysics expressed in the notion of the *esse ad;* and (3) the biblical concept of Exodus. Of course, the original contribution of Husserlian phenomenology was to delineate and describe the relation of intentionality in terms of concrete experience—our everyday being-in-the-world—to ground our logical and metaphysical concepts in the lived experience of consciousness. Later, particularly in a work like *Être, monde, imaginaire* [Being, World, Imagination], I tried to combine these Husserlian insights into a philosophy of intentional relations invoking a more poetic language of metaphor and metamorphosis. My aim here was to suggest how our being-in-the-world, and our understanding of this being, unfolds as a creative interplay between the *logos* of reason, which unifies, regulates, structures, and the *mythos* of poetry, symbol, and myth, which is forever transcending and revising the order of *logos.* Both of these directions of consciousness—the positing power of *logos* and the differentiating power of *mythos*—are founded on an *imaginaire-rien,* which I define as the universal principle of language, a superabundant play which engenders all meanings.

RK: What would you describe as the specifically phenomenological characteristics of your work, given your early fascination for the Husserlian notion of intentionality?

SB: First, I would say it was through my interest in the "metaphysics of relation" that I became interested (via [Franz] Brentano, on whom I was working in my Rome lectures) in Husserlian phenomenology. In fact, the relation of intentionality, which Brentano had retrieved from medieval Scholasticism and reactivated for contemporary philosophical purposes, struck me as offering a very liberating understanding of meaning, irreducible both to the strictly logical notion of relations current in the forties and fifties and to the traditional ontological notion of the "transcendental" rapports between matter and form, essence and existence, and more generally between potency and act (rapports which I preferred to call "structural" and which were typically articulated in [Octave] Hamelin's *Éléments principaux de la réprésentation* [Principal Elements of Representation]). In my early work *Conscience et intentionalité [Consciousness and Intentionality],* I had already projected an enlarged notion of intentionality, and I well remember a discussion with Jean Beaufret (one of the first advocates of existentialist and Heideggerian phenomenology in France) in which I engaged him on the crucial question of the transition from intentionality to "existence," a question which, it seemed to me, represented a new and deeper understanding of the concept of the *esse ad* which was to pursue me all of my life. My initial interest in phenomenology, which corresponded, therefore, to my keenest philosophical preoccupations, also extended to my later works, in particular *Approches phénoménologiques de l'idée d'être* and *Être, monde, imaginaire.* Overall, I would say that the most inspiring aspect of phenomenology for me was its emphasis on the *predicative* and prereflective dimensions of experience. Indeed it was with this precise emphasis in mind that I distinguished in *Conscience et intentionalité* between several stratifications of consciousness: intentionality as a psychological act, intentionality as a "potency/power" (*puissance*) relating to formal objects, and a transcendental intentionality representing the opening of the soul to *being as being.* It is along similar lines that, in the first part of *Être, monde, imaginaire,* I proposed an analysis of what is meant by the "language of being" in a less rudimentary way than that proposed by Scholasticism or Thomism. I must admit, however, that in my early studies in phenomenology I paid little attention to the celebrated phenomenological reduction which, in the fifties, tormented those philosophers of my generation inspired by the Husserlian "discovery." (It was only later, by means of my reflections on freedom, that I came to appreciate somewhat what was involved in the reduction.) In summary, I would say that for me phenomenology was an extraordinary stimulant to my thinking, serving to crystallize some of my most formative philosophical concerns and ultimately providing me with an effective method of analyzing the key notions of "passage" and "transit" which the metaphysics of relation first impressed upon me.

RK: Another of your recent works, *Théorie des idéologies [Theory of Ideologies]*, also seems to be a variation on this theme of creative intentionality or transcendence. I'm thinking particularly of the key term of this work—the "operator of transcendence."

SB: This recent critique of ideology sprang from my fundamental preoccupation with the question of the "zero." The zero is a conceptual or mathematical way of formulating the metaphysical idea of the quasi-nothing (*rien*), or the Christian notion of the Cross—the emptiness of the crypt where Christian thinking as a critical thinking takes its source. A genuine questioning of ideology requires such a critical distance or dis-position. Without it, one can easily be misled by dogmatic ideologies—be they political or philosophical, or ecclesiastical.

The Neoplatonists also taught the importance of keeping a distance from all categories of facile objectivization. Their very definition of being as *Eidos* or Form expresses this critical reserve. They realized that our philosophical categories are really *figures* of thought and are thus capable of being critically altered or transcended towards the truth of the One, which is beyond all the forms and figures of established ontology. So that when the Neoplatonists spoke of the One or God, they spoke of it in terms of critical reserve or qualification: *hos* or *oion*, *quasi* or *quatenus* — God *as* this or that ontological form. In short, since the Divine One was considered to be "beyond being," He could only be thought of as being, or *as if* He were being. One could not say: God *is* being. The critical notion of the quasi-nothing, functioning as the "operator of transcendence," thus prevented God from being reduced to a simplified or idolatrous ontology.

This Neoplatonic notion of critical distance is confirmed by the Christian notion of mystery — and particularly the practice of mystical speculation advanced by Eckhart and other Christian mystics who remained very suspicious of all ontological objectivizations of God. The model of reason demanded by metaphysical thinking must, I believe, be accompanied by a mystical appreciation for that which remains beyond the reach of this metaphysical model. This is why I always felt the need to balance the Greek fidelity to being with a biblical fidelity to the Exodus — particularly as expressed in the Christian theology of the Passion and the Cross.

RK: Could you explain in more detail how your theological interpretation of the Passion as dispossession/disposition relates to the critique of contemporary ideologies? I think this is a crucial transition in your thinking and perhaps accounts for your occasional leanings towards the Marxist critique.

SB: I believe that the Christian doctrine of dispossession can be translated into modern socio-political terms as a critique of power. There is a certain correspondence between the mystical Neoplatonic critique of the divine attributes — as an attempt to *possess* God in terms of ontological properties which would reduce His transcendence to the immanence of Being — and the Marxist critique of private property. Christianity and authentic Marxism share a common call to dispossession and a critical detachment from the prevailing order. I was always struck by the similarities between the Christian doctrine of eschatological justice where Jesus identified with the poor — "I was naked. I was hungry. I was thirsty. I was imprisoned" (Matthew, 10:9) — and the Marxist ideal of universal justice for the dispossessed. I think that this universal "I" of Christ — not to be confused with a transcendental or absolute Ego — which is enigmatically present in every poor or outcast person who has not yet been allowed the full humanity of justice, can find common cause with what is best in genuine Marxism. I am not saying that the two are the same. For while Christianity sponsors a categorical imperative for human justice and liberation (which certain brands of Marxism also endorse), it is not simply reducible to this imperative. While both share what Ernst Bloch called a common "principle of hope" *(principe-espérance)*, pointing towards a utopian horizon in the future, Christianity transcends the limits of historical materialism in the name of a prophetic eschatology (that is, the coming of the kingdom).

The term *Christian-Marxist* is a loaded and ambiguous one: it may serve as a *question*—with all the creative, thought-provoking tensions that genuine questioning implies—but not as a *solution*. We should remain cautious about invoking such terms uncritically as yet another ideological authority.

RK: How would you react to those who construe your recent work as a "Christian atheism?"

SB: This is a dangerous term, and I would not like to be thus characterized. To refuse the attempts to possess God by reducing Him to an ontological substance or political power—that is, an ideological weapon—is not to disbelieve in God; on the contrary, I would argue that it is a way of remaining faithful to one's belief. The critical refusal of ideological theism is not a refusal of God. It implies, rather, that the secondary definitions of God in terms of proposition (I believe *that* God exists) or predication (God *is* this or that) must be continually brought back to their primary origin in existential belief (I believe *in* God). This existential belief involves the believer in an intentional relation with God which is perhaps best described in terms of trust and transition. The move to institutionalize this belief in an invariant corpus of dogmas, doctrines, and propositions was natural, perhaps even inevitable, if Christianity was to survive the vagaries and contingencies of history. But this movement of *conservatism* must always be accompanied by a *critical* countermovement which reminds us that God cannot ultimately be objectified or immobilized in ontological or institutional (that is, anthropomorphic) structures. In a recent study entitled *Théorie des idéologies et la réponse de la foi [Theory of Ideologies and the Response of Faith]*, I tried to reflect on this problem by discussing the central implications of the term *credo* in relation to the three major movements of belief—existential, propositional, and predicative—mentioned above. Religious faith begins with belief-in-God, which expresses itself as an intentional being-towards-God. It involves the primary existential idioms of desire, enchantment, and hope, etc. It is only subsequently that we return upon the existential level to appropriate the riches encountered in the immediacy of this original experience. Thus the second movement of faith takes place as an attempt to define and order the content and form of one's existential belief. It is as if one thus draws a golden circle around one's religious experience, which one calls "tradition" or "heritage" or "doctrine" and affirms *that* God exists and *that* God is good and almighty, etc. In this way, the vertical arrow of our primary intentional belief becomes a reflective or recollective circle — with those on the inside calling themselves Christian and those on the outside non-Christian. I think that this second move is indispensable in that every religion requires the form of a "society," and every society requires a specific identity and foundation. A religion that is content to be "anything at all" very easily becomes "nothing at all" — as indeterminate and all-inconclusive as the category of being-as-being. In the third movement, reflection goes beyond both the modalities of "I believe *in*" and "I believe *that*" to the definition of God as a *proposition in itself*, "God *is* this or that." Hence the intentional distance or commitment implied by the first two movements of "I believe" is transcended, and dogmatic theology instantiates itself as a historical institution or organization. It is the duty of the religious or theistic thinker to serve such institutional belief by reminding it that its doctrines are not autonomous or eternally guaranteed but intellectual sedimentation of the original "I believe," wherein God reveals Himself to man. This critical exigency of faithfulness to the irreducible mystery and radicality of divine revelation is beautifully expressed in a passage in Kings 1:2, where Elijah goes in search of God but discovers him not in the rocks, in the storm, in the shaking earth, nor in the fire, but in the voice of a gentle breeze as it passes through the mountain cave. God is passage not possession.

RK: Can this critique of theistic ideology also be applied to political ideologies which constitute the objectified or impersonalized institutions of contemporary society?

SB: I think so. But we must remember the natural and almost inevitable reasons for the emergence of ideologies. Ideology springs from the fact that there is an ontological rupture between existence and consciousness. We do not coincide with ourselves. We exist before we are conscious of our existence, and this means that our reflective consciousness is always to some extent out of joint with the existential conditions that fostered it. Freud realized this when he spoke about the gap between the conscious and the unconscious. I would say that every form of thought is ideology to the extent that it does not and cannot fully coincide with the being of which it is the thought. The existence of ideologies reminds us that there is a margin of obscurity which we can never completely recuperate or remove. The pure identification of being and thought—that is, the thought that thinks itself as being/being as the self-thinking-thought—is the Aristotelian-Thomistic definition of divine self-understanding that no ideology can legitimately pretend to emulate. Human thought can never be perfectly transparent or adequate to itself. It is the role of the philosopher to challenge all ideological claims to such absolute knowledge and, by implication, to absolute power.

RK: You once stated, "The cross of my faith, will it not remain this interrogation mark which ancient legend tells us is the firstborn of all Creation?" If your philosophy does remain this critical interrogation mark, can it ever serve as a creative affirmation? Is it not inevitably condemned to a *via negativa?*

SB: The two aspects of philosophy—as negation and affirmation—are for me by no means incompatible. Though the critical aspect is more in evidence in contemporary thinking, including my own, I would insist that the first step in philosophy—and therefore its *sine qua non*—is a fundamental experience of wonder, curiosity, or enchantment: in short, *affirmation.* My enthusiasm for philosophy began in the same way as my enthusiasm for poetry or the Bible, by responding to texts that sang to me. Writing retraces those paths that sing to us *(chantent)* and thus enchant *(enchantent)* us. In this sense, I see a close relationship between philosophy, theology, and poetics. Philosophy never speaks to us in the abstract with a capital P, but in the engaging terms of certain chosen texts *(morceaux choisis)* —in my own case, certain texts of the pre-Socratics, Aristotle, Plato, the Neoplatonists, or St. Thomas, [Friedrich] Schelling, Husserl, and Heidegger. The desire to know philosophy as a totality—the Hegelian temptation to absolute knowledge—is not only dangerous but impossible; one can never reduce the infinite richness of our existential experience to the totalizing limits of reason.

RK: But would you not acknowledge essential differences between philosophy and poetry as modes of this *affirmation enchantée?*

SB: The main difference between philosophy and poetry, as I see it, is that while both originate in an experience of enchantment which draws us and commits us to the world, philosophy is obliged, in a second movement, to critically transcend and interrogate the world, both as life-experience and poetic-experience. Philosophy thus leads a double life of residing within and without the world. Perhaps one of the greatest enigmas of philosophy is that a thinking being can serve as a chain in the historical world and yet also break free from this chain, rise above it (partially at least) in order to question its ultimate origin and meaning. Poetry celebrates that the world exists; philosophy asks *why* the world exists. Schelling and Husserl implicitly acknowledged this distinction when they spoke of the philosophical need to go beyond or suspend the natural attitude (which would include our primary poetic experience), in which all thinking begins, to a transcendental or questioning attitude: to be in the world and yet not *of* the world, to be *inside* and *outside* at once.

RK: How do you see this double fidelity to the philosophical and poetic attitudes operating in your own work?

SB: My work operates on the basis of two overriding impulses or passions. On the one hand, it strives for scientific rigor and form—a striving epitomized by my preoccupation with the mathematical logic of religions and the search for the principle of reason. On the other hand, I began to wonder if this search for rigor and reason might not ultimately lead to the sterile tautologies of a *mathesis universalis:* the pretentious claim to possess an absolutely certain principle-foundation through a synthesis of Aristotelian logic, Euclidean geometry, and the Scholastic doctrine of Transcendentals. And this doubt provided a space for the emergence of a second fundamental passion—what I might call my "poetic inclination." This second poetic passion challenged the speculative claim to absolute identity or totality and revived an attentiveness to the vibrant multiplicity of the life-world. I suppose this poetic inclination can be witnessed, in its modernist guise, in [Stéphane] Mallarmé's notion of *dissemination.* I chose the terms *metaphor* and *metamorphosis* to express this reality of movement, alteration, and diversification. And Derrida, Lyotard, [Gilles] Deleuze, and Levinas have developed their respective philosophies of "difference," repudiating the principle of identity for either the subject or the object. It is my own conviction that the classical metaphysics of identity and the modernist poetics of difference need each other, for both correspond to fundamental impulses in human thinking. This is what I tried to express in *Être, monde, imaginaire* when I analyzed how the speculative principle of the *logos* and the poetic principle of the *mythos* are committed to each other in a creative conflict which unfolds in the free space of the *imaginaire*. This act of faith in the "imaginary," in the open horizon of the possible, where oppositions confront and recreate each other, is where my initial reflections on the *esse-in* and the *esse-ad* have led me.

I might summarize this dual allegiance of my work as follows. To consider philosophy as an exclusively critical or speculative movement is to condemn it to an endless contestation which can easily slip into the nihilism of a *reductio ad absurdum*. Philosophy must continually remind itself of its origins in the bedrock of real experience. Only when one has experienced the opaque profundity of existential or religious reality can one legitimately take one's critical distance in order to question or reflect upon it. Similarly, it is only when one has been immersed in the social life-world that one can begin to interrogate the ideological structures which regulate it. Philosophy always presupposes the ability to say: *this* is what a tree is, *this* is how authority works, *this* is what a tribunal consists of, etc. The speculative instance is inextricably dependent upon the concrete immediacy of the person's lived experience. It cannot afford to ignore the existential conditions which precede it. I have always been struck by [Francisco] Suarez's principle of identity, which states that "every being has an essence which constitutes and determines it." Philosophy begins with a commitment to the determining world and only in an ulterior, reflexive moment proceeds to "objectify" or "formalize." Philosophy does not begin with Kant — though the "critical" turn is a crucial stage in its development. I think we should be grateful to Marx for having turned idealism on its head and for making it more humble towards reality; only by being engaged to the living body of history can critical thinking avoid becoming a corpse of solipsistic introspection. It is because philosophy is both critique and commitment that it can distance itself from the world precisely in order to transform it.

RK: This summary analysis of your philosophy reminds me of your theological interpretation of the ecumenical dialectic between Catholic, Protestant, and Orthodox thinking in *La Foi et raison logique* [*Faith and Logical Reason*].

SB: In this work, I tried to rethink ecumenism in terms of a group of metaphysical operations. In this schema, the Catholic tradition privileged the operation of transitivity and transformation, functioning as a process of historical realism bound to the preservation of Revelation in the temporal world. The Protestant Reform privileged the operation of a critical conversion (turning around) which returned to the fundamental origins of Christianity. And thirdly, the Orthodox church of oriental Christianity privileged the operation of "manence" *(esse-in)* or in-dwelling. I argued that all three movements—of historical transformation, critical return, and spiritual dwelling—are essential to the Christian reality, ensuring that it remains transitive and intransitive, transcendent and immanent. The history of Christianity is the drama of this divergence and belonging-together of Catholicism, Protestantism, and Orthodoxy as a fecund tension between complementary differences. I think that ecumenism is facile if it ignores the importance of this creative tension. It is only when one assumes the specificity of one's own religious tradition (in my case Catholic) that one can fully appreciate the *other*—the essential contribution which the other traditions make to one's own.

RK: France produced a considerable number of "Christian philosophers" in the first half of this century, including Marcel, [Emmanuel] Mounier, [Jacques] Maritain, and [Etienne] Gilson. Would you consider yourself a Christian philosopher?

SB: I am a Christian philosopher to the extent that the primary experience that fostered and colored much of my philosophical thinking was, as I explained at the outset, specifically Christian in certain respects—particularly as it determined my reflections on the Passion and the Cross. Such Christian reflection frequently dovetailed with my preoccupation with Greek and Neoplatonic thought. For example, my description of the Cross as the "seed of non-being" *(germen nihili)* bears an intimate correspondence to Proclus's notion of the *sperma meontos*. The Neoplatonic attempts to critically radicalize the Platonic philosophy of being *(On)* find common ground here with the theology of the Cross. If the theology of Glory—with its splendid doctrine of the superabundance of grace—is divorced from the critical theology of the Cross, it can degenerate into triumphalism. Grace is not power but dispossession, because it is given under the interrogative sign of the Cross. To the extent, therefore, that the theology of the Cross deeply affected my whole attitude to thought, I would be prepared to consider myself a Christian philosopher. But I would insist that philosophy and theology are separate, if equally valid, disciplines of thought. Whereas the theologian can presuppose the Christian tradition as a series of *revealed* doctrines, the philosopher—even the Christian philosopher—cannot. The theologian believes truth is given; the philosopher goes in search of it.

France, 1982

Jacques Derrida
Deconstruction and the Other

RK: The most characteristic feature of your work has been its determination to "deconstruct" the Western philosophy of presence. I think it would be helpful if you could situate your program of deconstruction in relation to the two major intellectual traditions of Western European culture — the Hebraic and the Hellenic. You conclude your seminal essay on the Jewish philosopher Emmanuel Levinas with the following quotation from James Joyce's *Ulysses:* "GreekJew is JewGreek." Do you agree with Levinas that Judaism offers an alternative to the Greek metaphysics of presence? Or do you believe with Joyce that the Jewish and Greek cultures are fundamentally intertwined?

JD: While I consider it essential to think through this copulative synthesis of Greek and Jew, I consider my own thought, paradoxically, as neither Greek nor Jewish. I often feel that the questions I attempt to formulate on the outskirts of the Greek philosophical tradition have as their *other* the model of the Jew, that is, the Jew-as-other. And yet the paradox is that I have never actually invoked the Jewish tradition in any "rooted" or direct manner. Though I was born a Jew, I do not work or think within a living Jewish tradition. So if there is a Judaic dimension to my thinking which may from time to time have spoken in or through me, this has never assumed the form of an explicit fidelity or debt to that culture. For short, the ultimate site *(lieu)* of my questioning discourse would be neither Hellenic nor Hebraic, if such were possible. It would be a nonsite beyond both the Jewish influence of my youth and the Greek philosophical heritage which I received during my academic education in the French universities.

RK: And yet you share a singular discourse with Levinas—including notions of the *other,* the *trace* and writing as *difference,* etc.—which might suggest a common Judaic heritage.

JD: Undoubtedly, I was fascinated and attracted by the intellectual journey of Levinas, but that was not because he was Jewish. It so happens that for Levinas there is a discrete continuity between his philosophical discourse qua phenomenologist and his religious language qua exegete of the Talmud. But this continuity is not immediately evident. The Levinas who most interested me at the outset was the philosopher working in phenomenology and posing the question of the *other* to phenomenology; the Judaic dimension remained at that stage a discrete rather than a decisive reference.

You ask if Judaism offers an alternative to the Greek philosophy of "presence." First we must ascertain what exactly we mean by "presence." The French or English words are, of course, neither Greek nor Jewish. So that when we use the word, we presuppose a vast history of translation, which leads from the Greek terms *ousia* and *on* to the Latin *substantia, actus,* etc., and culminates in our modern term "presence." I have no knowledge of what this term means in Judaism.

RK: So you would count yourself a philosopher above all else?

JD: I'm not happy with the term *philosopher.*

RK: Surely you are a philosopher in that your deconstruction is directed primarily to philosophical ideas and texts?

JD: It is true that "deconstruction" has focused on philosophical texts. And I am of course a philosopher in the institutional sense that I assume the responsibilities of a teacher of philosophy in an official philosophical institution—*l'Ecole Normale Supérieure.* But I am not sure that the site of my work, reading philosophical texts and posing philosophical questions, is itself properly philosophical. Indeed, I have attempted more and more systematically to find a nonsite, or a nonphilosophical site, from which to question philosophy. But the search for a nonphilosophical site does not bespeak an antiphilosophical attitude. My central question is: From what site or nonsite (*non-lieu*) can philosophy as such appear to itself as other than itself, so that it can interrogate and reflect upon itself in an original manner? Such a nonsite or alterity would be radically irreducible to philosophy. But the problem is that such a non-site cannot be defined or situated by means of philosophical language.

RK: The philosophy of deconstruction would seem, therefore, to be a deconstruction of philosophy. Is your interest in painting, psycho-analysis, and literature—particularly the literary texts of [Edmond] Jabès, [Georges] Bataille, [Maurice] Blanchot, [Antonin] Artaud, [Paul] Celan, and Mallarmé—not an attempt to establish this non-philosophical site of which you speak?

JD: Certainly, but one must remember that even though these sites are nonphilosophical, they still belong to our Western culture and so are never totally free from the marks of philosophical language. In literature, for example, philosophical language is still present in some sense, but it produces and presents itself as alienated from itself, at a remove, at a distance. This distance provides the necessary free space from which to interrogate philosophy anew, and it was my preoccupation with literary texts which enabled me to discern the problematic of writing as one of the key factors in the deconstruction of metaphysics.

RK: Accepting the fact that you are seeking a nonphilosophical site, you would, I presume, still acknowledge important philosophical influences on your thought. How, for example, would you situate your strategy of deconstruction in respect to the phenomenological movement?

JD: My philosophical formation owes much to the thought of Hegel, Husserl, and Heidegger. Heidegger is probably the most constant influence, and particularly his project of "overcoming" Greek metaphysics. Husserl, whom I studied in a more studious and painstaking fashion, taught me a certain methodical prudence and reserve, a rigorous technique of unraveling and formulating questions. But I never shared Husserl's pathos for, and commitment to, a phenomenology of presence. In fact, it was Husserl's method that helped me to suspect the very notion of presence and the fundamental role it has played in all philosophies. My relationship with Heidegger is much more enigmatic and extensive: here my interest was not just *methodological* but *existential.* The themes of Heidegger's questioning always struck me as necessary—especially the "ontological difference," the reading of Platonism, and the relationship between language and Being. My discovery of the genealogical and genetic critique of Nietzsche and Freud also helped me to take the step beyond phenomenology towards a more radical, nonphilosophical questioning, while never renouncing the discipline and methodological rigor of phenomenology.

RK: Although you share Heidegger's task of "overcoming" or "deconstructing" Western metaphysics, you could not, presumably, share his hope to rediscover the "original names" by means of which Being could be thought and said?

JD: I think that there is still in Heidegger, linked up with other things, a nostalgic desire to recover the proper name, the unique name of Being. To be fair, however, one can find several passages in which Heidegger is self-critical and renounces his nostalgia: his practice of canceling and erasing the term in his later texts is an example of such a critique. Heidegger's texts are still before us; they harbor a future of meaning which will ensure that they are read and reread for centuries. But while I owe a considerable debt to Heidegger's "path of thought" *(chemin de pensée)*, we differ in our employment of language, in our understanding of language. I write in another language—and I do not simply mean in French rather than in German—even though this *otherness* cannot be explained in terms of philosophy itself. The difference resides outside of philosophy, in the nonphilosophical site of language; it is what makes the poets and writers that interest me (Mallarmé, [Maurice] Blanchot, etc.) totally different from those that interest Heidegger ([Friedrich] Hölderlin and [Rainer Maria] Rilke). In this sense, my profound rapport with Heidegger is also and at the same time a nonrapport.

RK: Yes, I can see that your understanding of language as "difference" and "dissemination" is quite removed from Heidegger's notion of language as the "house of Being," that which "recalls and recollects" and "names the Holy." In addition, while Heidegger is still prepared to use such philosophical concepts as Being and existence to express his thought, you have made it clear that the operative terms in your language—for example, deconstruction, *différance,* dissemination, trace, and so on—are basically "nonconcepts," "undecidables." What exactly do you mean by "nonconcepts," and what role do they play in your attempt to deconstruct metaphysics?

JD: I will try to reconstitute the argument by means of which I advanced the notion of a nonconcept. First, it doesn't have the logical generality which a philosophical concept claims to have in its supposed independence from ordinary or literary language. The notion of *différance,* for example, is a nonconcept in that it cannot be defined in terms of oppositional predicates; it is neither this nor that, but rather this and that (for example, the act of differing and of deferring), without being reducible to a dialectical logic either. And yet the term *différance* emerges and develops as a determination of language from which it is insepa-rable. Hence the difficulty of translating the term. There is no concep-tual realm beyond language which would allow the term to have a uni-vocal semantic content over and above its inscription in language. Because it remains a trace of language, it remains nonconceptual; and because it has no oppositional or predicative generality, which would identify it as *this* rather than *that,* the term *différance* cannot be defined within a system of logic — Aristotelian or dialectical — that is, within the logocentric system of philosophy.

RK: But can we go beyond the logocentric system of metaphysics without employing the terminology of metaphysics? Is it not only *from the inside* that we can undo metaphysics by means of stratagems and strategies which expose the ambiguities and contradictions of the logo-centric system of presence? Does that not mean that we are condemned to metaphysics even while attempting to deconstruct its pretensions?

JD: In a certain sense it is true to say that deconstruction is still *in* metaphysics. But we must remember that if we are indeed *inside* metaphysics, we are not inside it as we might be *inside* a box or a milieu. We are still in metaphysics in the special sense that we are in a deter-minate language. Consequently, the idea that we might be able to get outside of metaphysics has always struck me as naive. So that when I refer to the closure *(clôture)* of metaphysics, I insist that it is not a question of considering metaphysics as a circle with a limit or simple boundary. The notion of the limit and boundary *(bord)* of metaphysics is itself highly problematic. My reflections on this problematic have always attempted to show that the limit or end of metaphysics is not linear or circular in any indivisible sense. And as soon as we acknowl-edge that the limit-boundary of metaphysics is divisible, the logical rapport between inside and outside is no longer simple. Accordingly, we cannot really say that we are "locked into" or "condemned to" meta-physics, for we are, strictly speaking, neither inside nor outside. In brief, the whole rapport between the inside and the outside of meta-physics is inseparable from the question of the finitude and reserve of metaphysics as language. But the idea of the finitude and exhaustion *(épuisement)* of metaphysics does not mean that we are incarcerated in it as prisoners or victims of some unhappy fatality. It is simply that our belonging to, and inherence in, the language of metaphysics is some-thing that can only be rigorously and adequately thought about from *another topos* or space where our problematic rapport with the bound-ary of metaphysics can be seen in a more radical light. Hence my attempt, to discover the nonplace or *non-lieu* which would be the *other* of philosophy. This is the task of deconstruction.

RK: Can literary and poetic language provide this *non-lieu* or *u-topos?*

JD: I think so, but when I speak of literature it is not with a capital L; it is rather an allusion to certain movements which have worked around the limits of our logical concepts, certain texts which make the limits of our language tremble, exposing them as divisible and questionable. This is what the works of Blanchot, Bataille, or Beckett are particularly sensitive to.

RK: What does this whole problematic of the closure of Western logocentric philosophy and of the limits of our language tell us about the modern age in which we live? Is there a rapport between deconstruction and modernity insofar as the latter bespeaks a crisis of scientific foundations and of values in general, a crisis occasioned by the discovery that the absolute origin that the Western tradition claimed to have identified in the "logos" is merely the trace of an absence, a nothingness?

JD: I have never been very happy with the term *modernity*. Of course, I feel that what is happening in the world today is something unique and singular. As soon, however, as we give it the label of "modernity," we inscribe it in a certain historical system of evolution or progress (a notion derived from Enlightenment rationalism), which tends to blind us to the fact that what confronts us today is also something ancient and hidden in history. I believe that what "happens" in our contemporary world and strikes us as particularly new has in fact an essential connection with something extremely old which has been covered over *(archi-dissimulé)*. So that the new is not so much that which occurs for the first time but that "very ancient" dimension which recurs in the "very modern," and which indeed has been signified repetitively throughout our historical tradition, in Greece and in Rome, in Plato and in Descartes and in Kant, etc. No matter how novel or unprecedented a modern meaning may appear, it is never exclusively *modernist* but is also and at the same time a phenomenon of *repetition*. And yet the relationship between the ancient and the modern is not simply that of the implicit and the explicit. We must avoid the temptation of supposing that what occurs today somehow preexisted in a latent form, merely waiting to be unfolded or explicated. Such thinking also conceives history as an evolutionary development and excludes the crucial notions of rupture and mutation in history. My own conviction is that we must maintain two contradictory affirmations at the same time. On the one hand, we affirm the existence of ruptures in history, and on the other, we affirm that these ruptures produce gaps or faults (*failles*) in which the most hidden and forgotten archives can emerge and constantly recur and work through history. One must surmount the categorical oppositions of philosophical logic out of fidelity to these conflicting positions of historical discontinuity (rupture) and continuity (repetition), which are neither a pure break with the past nor a pure unfolding or explication of it.

RK: How do you explain the way in which philosophy has altered and changed from one historical epoch to the next? How do you explain, for example, the difference between Plato's thought and your own?

JD: The difference between our modes of thought does not mean that I or other "modern" thinkers have gone beyond Plato, in the sense of having succeeded in exhausting all that is contained in his texts. Here I return to what I was describing as the "future" of a Heideggerian text. I believe that all of the great philosophical texts — of Plato, Parmenides, Hegel, or Heidegger, for example — are still *before* us. The future of the great philosophies remains obscure and enigmatic, still to be disclosed. Up to now, we have merely scratched the surface. This opaque and inexhaustible residue of philosophical texts, which I call their "future," is more predominant in Greek and German philosophy than in French. I have a profound respect for the great French thinkers, but I have always had the impression that a certain kind of rigorous analysis could render their texts accessible and exhaustible. Before a Platonic or Heideggerian text, by contrast, I feel that I am confronting an abyss, a bottomless pit in which I could lose myself. No matter how rigorous an analysis I bring to bear on such texts, I am always left with the impression that there is something *more* to be thought.

RK: What exactly is the inexhaustible richness which these great texts possess and which continues to fascinate us throughout the centuries?

JD: The temptation here is to offer a quick and simple response. But having taught philosophy for over twenty years, I must honestly say that now, less than ever, do I know what philosophy is. My knowledge of what it is that constitutes the essence of philosophy is at zero degree. All I know is that a Platonic or Heideggerian text always returns us to the beginning, enables us to begin to ask philosophical questions, including the question: What is philosophy?

RK: But surely it must be possible to say what philosophy is by way of distinguishing it from other scientific disciplines such as economics, sociology, the natural sciences, or even literature? Why learn philosophy at all, in schools, universities, or in the privacy of one's study, if it is impossible to say what it is or what function it serves? If deconstruction prevents us from asserting or stating or identifying anything, then surely one ends up, not with *différance,* but with indifference, where nothing is anything, and everything is everything else?

JD: It is as impossible to say what philosophy is *not* as it is to say what it *is.* In all the other disciplines you mention, there is philosophy. To say to oneself that one is going to study something that is *not* philosophy is to deceive oneself. It is not difficult to show that in political economy, for example, there is a philosophical discourse in operation. And the same applies to mathematics and the other sciences. Philosophy, as logocentrism, is present in every scientific discipline, and the only justification for transforming philosophy into a specialized discipline is the necessity to render explicit and thematic the philosophical subtext in every discourse. The principal function which the teaching of philosophy serves is to enable people to become "conscious," to become aware of what exactly they are saying, what kind of discourse they are engaged in when they do mathematics, physics, political economy, and so on. There is no system of teaching or transmitting knowledge which can retain its coherence or integrity without, at one moment or another, interrogating itself philosophically, that is, without acknowledging its subtextual premises, and this may even include an interrogation of unspoken political interests or traditional values. From such an interrogation, each society draws its own conclusions about the worth of philosophy.

RK: How, for example, can political economy interrogate itself philosophically?

JD: First, all of the major concepts which constitute the discourse of economics are philosophical, and particularly such concepts as "property," "work" or "value." These are all "philosophemes," concepts inaugurated by a philosophical discourse, which usually go back to Greece or Rome, and kept in operation by means of this discourse, which refers back at first, as does philosophy itself, to the "natural languages" of Greece and Rome. Consequently, the economic discourse is founded on a logocentric philosophical discourse and remains inseparable from it. The autonomy which economists might subsequently like to confer on their discipline can never succeed in masking its philosophical derivation. Science is never purely objective, nor is it merely reducible to an instrumental and utilitarian model of explanation. Philosophy can teach science that it is ultimately an element of language, that the limits of its formalization reveal its belonging to a language in which it continues to operate despite its attempts to justify itself as an exclusively objective or instrumental discourse.

RK: Is the logocentric character of science a singularly European phenomenon?

JD: Logocentrism, in its developed philosophical sense, is inextricably linked to the Greek and European tradition. As I have attempted to demonstrate elsewhere in some detail, logocentric philosophy is a specifically Western response to a much larger necessity which also occurs in the Far East and other cultures, that is, the phonocentric necessity: the privilege of the voice over writing. The priority of spoken language over written or silent language stems from the fact that when words are spoken, the speaker and the listener are supposed to be simultaneously present to one another; they are supposed to be the same, pure unmediated presence. This ideal of perfect self-presence, of the immediate possession of meaning, is what is expressed by the phonocentric necessity. Writing, on the other hand, is considered subversive insofar as it creates a spatial and temporal distance between the author and audience; writing presupposes the absence of the author, and so we can never be sure exactly what is meant by a written text; it can have many different meanings, as opposed to a single unifying one. But this phonocentric necessity did not develop into a systematic logocentric metaphysics in any non-European culture. Logocentrism is a uniquely European phenomenon.

RK: Does this mean that other cultures do not require deconstruction?

JD: Every culture and society requires an internal critique or deconstruction as an essential part of its development. A priori, we can presume that non-European cultures operate some sort of auto-critique of their own linguistic concepts and foundational institutions. Every culture needs an element of self-interrogation and of distance from itself, if it is to transform itself. No culture is closed in on itself, especially in our own times, when the impact of European civilization is so all-pervasive. Similarly, what we call the deconstruction of our own Western culture is aided and abetted by the fact that Europe has always registered the impact of heterogeneous, non-European influences. Because it has always been thus exposed to, and shadowed by, its *other*, it has been compelled to question itself. Every culture is haunted by its other.

RK: Did the arrival of Judeo-Christianity represent such a radicalizing "alterity" for the Greco-Roman civilization? Did it challenge the heterogeneity of the Western metaphysics of presence?

JD: I'd be wary of talking about Judeo-Christianity with a capital J and C. Judeo-Christianity is an extremely complex entity which, in large part, only constituted itself qua Judeo-Christianity by its assimilation into the schemas of Greek philosophy. Hence what we know as Christian and Jewish theology today is a cultural ensemble which has already been largely Hellenized.

RK: But did not Judaism and Christianity represent a heterogeneity, an *otherness*, before they were assimilated into Greek culture?

JD: Of course. And one can argue that these original, heterogeneous elements of Judaism and Christianity were never completely eradicated by Western metaphysics. They perdure throughout the centuries, threatening and unsettling the assured identities of Western philosophy. So that the surreptitious deconstruction of the Greek *Logos* is at work from the very origin of our Western culture. Already, the translation of Greek concepts into other languages — Latin, Arabic, German, French, English, etc. — or indeed the translation of Hebraic or Arabic ideas and structures into metaphysical terms, produces "fissures" in the presumed solidity of Greek philosophy by introducing alien and conflicting elements.

RK: The logocentrism of Greek metaphysics will always be haunted, therefore, by the absolutely Other to the extent that the *Logos* can never englobe everything. There is always something which escapes, something different, other, and opaque which refuses to be totalized into a homogeneous identity.

JD: Just so — and this otherness is not necessarily something which comes to Greek philosophy from the "outside," that is, from the non-Hellenic world. From the very beginnings of Greek philosophy the self-identity of the *Logos* is already fissured and divided. I think one can discern signs of such fissures of *différance* in every great philosopher: the "Good beyond Being" *(epekeina tes ousias)* of Plato's *Republic*, for example, or the confrontation with the "Stranger" in *The Sophist*, are already traces of an alterity which refuses to be totally domesticated. Moreover, the rapport of self-identity is itself always a rapport of violence with the other, so that the notions of property, appropriation, and self-presence, so central to logocentric metaphysics, are essentially dependent on an oppositional relation with otherness. In this sense, identity *presupposes* alterity.

RK: If deconstruction is a way of challenging the logocentric pretensions of Western European philosophy, and by implication of the sciences it has founded, can it ever surmount its role of iconoclastic negation and become a form of affirmation? Can your search for a non-site or *u-topos*, other than the *topos* of Western metaphysics, also be construed as a prophetic utopianism?

JD: I will take the terms *affirmation* and *prophetic utopianism* separately. Deconstruction certainly entails a moment of affirmation. Indeed, I cannot conceive of a radical critique which would not be ultimately motivated by some sort of affirmation, acknowledged or not. Deconstruction always presupposes affirmation, as I have frequently attempted to point out, sometimes employing a Nietzschean terminology. I do not mean that the deconstructing *subject* or *self* affirms. I mean that deconstruction is, in itself, a positive response to an alterity which necessarily calls, summons, or motivates it. Deconstruction is therefore vocation—a response to a call. The other, as the other than self, the other that opposes self-identity, is not something that can be detected and disclosed within a philosophical space and with the aid of a philosophical lamp. The other precedes philosophy and necessarily invokes and provokes the subject before any genuine questioning can begin. It is in this rapport with the other that affirmation expresses itself. As to the question of prophecy, this is a much more obscure area for me. There are certainly prophetic effects *(effets)*, but the language of prophecy alters continually. Today the prophets no longer speak with the same accents or scenography as the prophets in the Bible.

RK: Levinas has suggested that the contemporary deconstruction of philosophy and the sciences is symptomatic of a fundamental crisis of Western culture, which he chooses to interpret as a prophetic and ethical cry. Would you agree?

JD: Certainly prophets always flourish in times of socio-historical or philosophical crisis. Bad times for philosophy are good times for prophecy. Accordingly, when deconstructive themes begin to dominate the scene, as they do today, one is sure to find a proliferation of prophecies. And this proliferation is precisely a reason why we should be all the more wary and prudent, all the more discriminating.

RK: But here we have the whole problem of a criterion of evaluation. According to what criterion does one discriminate between prophecies? Is this not a problem for you, since you reject the idea of a transcendental *telos* or *eschaton* which could provide the critical subject with an objective or absolute yardstick of value?

JD: It is true that I interrogate the idea of an *eschaton* or *telos* in the absolute formulations of classical philosophy. But that does not mean I dismiss all forms of Messianic or prophetic eschatology. I think that all genuine questioning is summoned by a certain type of eschatology, though it is impossible to define this eschatology in philosophical terms. The search for objective or absolute criteria is, to be sure, an essentially philosophical gesture. Prophecy differs from philosophy insofar as it dispenses with such criteria. The prophetic word is its own criterion and refuses to submit to an external tribunal which would judge or evaluate it in an objective and neutral fashion. The prophetic word reveals its own eschatology and finds its index of truthfulness in its own inspiration and not in some transcendental or philosophical criteriology.

RK: Do you feel that your own work is prophetic in its attempt to deconstruct philosophy and philosophical criteria?

JD: Unfortunately, I do not feel inspired by any sort of hope which would permit me to presume that my work of deconstruction has a prophetic function. But I concede that the style of my questioning as an exodus and dissemination in the desert might produce certain prophetic resonances. It is possible to see deconstruction as being produced in a space where the prophets are not far away. But the prophetic resonances of my questioning reside at the level of a certain rhetorical discourse which is also shared by several other contemporary thinkers. The fact that I declare it "unfortunate" that I do not personally feel inspired may be a signal that deep down I still hope. It means that I am in fact still looking for something. So perhaps it is no mere accident of rhetoric that the search itself, the search without hope for hope, assumes a certain prophetic allure. Perhaps my search is a twentieth-century brand of prophecy? But it is difficult for me to believe it.

RK: Can the theoretical radicality of deconstruction be translated into a radical political praxis?

JD: This is a particularly difficult question. I must confess that I have never succeeded in directly relating deconstruction to existing political codes and programs. I have of course had occasion to take a specific political stand in certain codable situations, for example, in relation to the French university institution. But the available codes for taking such a political stance are not at all adequate to the radicality of deconstruction. And the absence of an adequate political code to translate or incorporate the radical implications of deconstruction has given many the impression that deconstruction is opposed to politics, or is at best apolitical. But this impression only prevails because all of our political codes and terminologies still remain fundamentally metaphysical, regardless of whether they originate from the right or the left.

RK: In *The Revolution of the Word*, Colin MacCabe employed your notions of deconstruction and dissemination to show how James Joyce recognized and revealed the inner workings of language as a refusal of identity, as a process of *différance* irreducible to all of our logocentic concepts and codes. In Ulysses, this process of *différance* is epitomized by Bloom, for instance, the vagrant or nomad who subverts the available codes of identity—religious, political, or national. And yet, MacCabe argues, the Joycean refutation of all dogmatic or totalizing forms of identity is itself a political stance—an anti-totalitarian or anarchic stance.

JD: This is the politics of exodus, of the émigré. As such, it can of course serve as a political ferment or anxiety, a subversion of fixed assumptions and a privileging of disorder.

RK: But does the politics of the émigré necessarily imply inaction and noncommitment?

JD: Not at all. But the difficulty is to gesture in opposite directions at the same time; on the one hand, to preserve a distance and suspicion with regard to the official political codes governing reality, and on the other, to intervene here and now in a practical and *engagé* manner whenever the necessity arises. This position of dual allegiance, in which I personally find myself, is one of perpetual uneasiness. I try where I can to act politically while recognizing that such action remains incommensurate with my intellectual project of deconstruction.

RK: Could one describe the political equivalent of deconstruction as a disposition, as opposed to a position, of responsible anarchy?

JD: If I had to describe my political disposition I would probably employ a formula of that kind while stressing, of course, the interminable obligation to work out and to deconstruct these two terms— "responsible" and "anarchy." If taken as assured certainties in themselves, such terms can also become reified and unthinking dogmas. But I also try to reevaluate the indispensable notion of "responsibility."

RK: I would now like to turn to another theme in your work: the deconstructive role of the feminine. If the logocentric domination of Western culture also expresses itself as a phallogocentrism, is there a sense in which the modern movement to liberate women represents a deconstructive gesture? Is this something which Nietzsche curiously recognized when he spoke of "truth becoming woman," or Joyce when he celebrated the "woman's reason" of Molly Bloom in Ulysses and Anna Livia Plurabelle in *Finnegans Wake?* Is the contemporary liberation of woman's reason and truth not an unveiling of the hitherto repressed resources of a nonlogocentric *topos?*

JD: While I would hesitate to use such terms as "liberation" or "unveiling," I think there can be little doubt that we are presently witnessing a radical mutation of our understanding of sexual difference. The discourses of Nietzsche, Joyce, and the women's movement which you have identified epitomize a profound and unprecedented transformation of the man-woman relationship. The deconstruction of phallogocentrism is carried by this transformation, as are also the rise of psychoanalysis and the modernist movement in literature. But we cannot objectify or thematize this mutation, even though it is bringing about such a radical change in our understanding of the world that a return to the former logocentric philosophies of mastery, possession, totalization, or certitude may soon be unthinkable. The philosophical and literary discoveries of the feminine which you mention—and even the political and legal recognition of the status of women—are all symptoms of a deeper mutation in our search for meaning which deconstruction attempts to register.

RK: Do you think then that this mutation can be seen and evaluated in terms of a historical progress towards the "good," towards a "better society"?

JD: This mutation is certainly experienced as better, insofar as it is what is desired by those who practically dispose of the greatest force in society. One could describe the transformation effected by the feminine as "good" without positing it as an *a priori* goal or *telos.* I hesitate to speak of "liberation" in this context, because I don't believe that women are liberated, any more than men are. They are, of course, no longer enslaved in many of the old socio-political respects, but even in the new situation woman will not ultimately be any freer than man.

One needs another language, besides that of political liberation, to characterize the enormous deconstructive import of the feminine as an uprooting of our phallogocentric culture. I prefer to speak of this muta-tion of the feminine as a "movement" rather than as an historical or political "progress." I always hesitate to talk of historical progress.

RK: What is the relationship between deconstruction and your use of poetic language, particularly in *Glas*? Do you consider *Glas* to be a work of philosophy or of poetry?

JD: It is neither philosophy nor poetry. It is in fact a reciprocal contamination of the one by the other, from which neither can emerge intact. This notion of contamination is, however, inadequate, for it is not simply a question of rendering both philosophy and poetry *impure*. One is trying to reach an additional or alternative dimension beyond philosophy and literature. In my project, philosophy and literature are two poles of an opposition and one cannot isolate one from the other or privilege one over the other. I consider that the limits of philosophy are also those of literature. In *Glas*, consequently, I try to compose a *writing* which would traverse, as rigorously as possible, both the philo-sophical and literary elements without being definable as either. Hence in *Glas* one finds classical philosophical analysis being juxtaposed with quasi-literary passages, each challenging, perverting, and exposing the impurities and contradictions in their neighbor; and at some point the philosophical and literary trajectories cross each other and give rise to something else, some *other* site.

RK: Is there not a sense in which philosophy for you is a form of literature? You have, for example, described metaphysics as a "white mythology," that is, a sort of palimpsest of metaphors *(eidos, telos, ousia)* and myths (of return, homecoming, transcendence towards the light, etc.), which are covered over and forgotten as soon as philosophical "concepts" are construed as pure and univocal abstractions, as total-izing universals devoid of myth and metaphor.

JD: I have always tried to expose the way in which philosophy is literary, not so much because it is *metaphor* but because it is *catachresis*. The term *metaphor* generally implies a relation to an original "property" of meaning, a "proper" sense to which it indirectly or equivocally refers, whereas *catachresis* is a violent production of meaning, an abuse which refers to no anterior or proper norm. The founding concepts of meta-physics —*logos, eidos, theoria,* etc. —are instances of *catachresis* rather than metaphors, as I attempted to demonstrate in "White Mythology" *(Marges de la philosophie [Margins of Philosophy]).* In a work such as *Glas,* or other recent ones like it, I am trying to produce new forms of catachresis, another kind of writing, a violent writing which stakes out the faults *(failles)* and deviations of language, so that the text produces a language of its own, in itself, which, while continuing to work through tradition, emerges at a given moment as a *monster;* a monstrous mutation without tradition or normative precedent.

RK: What then of the question of language as reference? Can language as mutation or violence or monstrosity refer to anything other than itself?

JD: There have been several misinterpretations of what I and other deconstructionists are trying to do. It is totally false to suggest that deconstruction is a suspension of reference. Deconstruction is always deeply concerned with the *other* of language. I never cease to be surprised by critics who see my work as a declaration that there is nothing beyond language, that we are imprisoned in language; it is, in fact, saying the exact opposite. The critique of logocentrism is above all else the search for the *other* and the *other of language.* Every week I receive critical commentaries and studies on deconstruction which operate on the assumption that what they call "poststructuralism" amounts to saying that there is nothing beyond language, that we are submerged in words — and other stupidities of that sort. Certainly, deconstruction tries to show that the question of reference is much more complex and problematic than traditional theories supposed. It even asks whether our term *reference* is entirely adequate for designating the *other.* The other, which is beyond language and which summons language, is perhaps not a "referent" in the normal sense which linguists have attached to this term. But to distance oneself thus from the habitual structure of reference, to challenge or complicate our common assumptions about it, does not amount to saying that there is nothing beyond language.

RK: This could also be seem as a reply to those critics who maintain that deconstruction is a strategy of nihilism, an orgy of non-sense, a relapse into the free play of the arbitrary.

JD: I regret that I have been misinterpreted in this way, particularly in the United States, but also in France. People who wish to avoid questioning and discussion present deconstruction as a sort of gratuitous chess game with a combination of signs *(combinatoire de signifiants),* closed up in language as in a cave. This misinterpretation is not just a simplification; it is symptomatic of certain political and institutional interests—interests which must also be deconstructed in their turn. I totally refuse the label of nihilism which has been ascribed to me and my American colleagues. Deconstruction is not an enclosure in nothingness, but an openness towards the other.

RK: Can deconstruction serve as a method of literary criticism which might contribute something positive to our appreciation of literature?

JD: I am not sure that deconstruction can function as a literary *method* as such. I am wary of the idea of methods of reading. The laws of reading are determined by the particular text that is being read. This does not mean that we should simply abandon ourselves to the text, or represent and repeat it in a purely passive manner. It means that we must remain faithful, even if it implies a certain violence, to the injunctions of the text. These injunctions will differ from one text to the next so that one cannot prescribe one general method of reading. In this sense, deconstruction is not a method. Nor do I feel that the principal function of deconstruction is to contribute something to literature. It does, of course, contribute to our epistemological appreciation of texts by exposing the philosophical and theoretical presuppositions that are at work in every critical methodology, be it formalism, New Criticism, socialist realism, or a historical critique. Deconstruction asks *why* we read a literary text in this particular manner rather than another. It shows, for example, that New Criticism is not the way of reading texts, however enshrined it may be in certain university institutions, but only one way among others. Thus deconstruction can also serve to question the presumption of certain university and cultural institutions to act as the sole or privileged guardians and transmitters of meaning. In short, deconstruction not only teaches us to read literature more thoroughly by attending to it *as language,* as the production of meaning through *différance* and dissemination, through a complex play of signifying traces; it also enables us to interrogate the covert philosophical and political presuppositions of institutionalized critical methods which generally govern our reading of a text. There is in deconstruction something which challenges every teaching institution. It is not a question of calling for the destruction of such institutions, but rather of making us aware of what we are in fact doing when we subscribe to this or that institutional way of reading literature. Nor must we forget that deconstruction is itself a form of literature, a literary text to be read like other texts, an interpretation open to several other interpretations. Accordingly, one can say that deconstruction is at once extremely *modest* and extremely *ambitious*. It is ambitious in that it puts itself on a par with literary texts, and modest in that it admits that it is only one textual interpretation among others, written in a language which has no centralizing power of mastery or domination, no privileged metalanguage over and above the language of literature.

RK: And what would you say to those critics who accuse you of annihilating the very idea of the human subject in your determination to dispense with all centralizing agencies of meaning, all "centrisms"?

JD: They need not worry. I have never said that the subject should be dispensed with. Only that it should be deconstructed. To deconstruct the subject does not mean to deny its existence. There are subjects, "operations" or "effects" *(effets)* of subjectivity. This is an incontrovertible fact. To acknowledge this does not mean, however, that the subject is what it says it is. The subject is not some metalinguistic substance or identity, some pure *cogito* of self-presence; it is always inscribed in language. My work does not, therefore, destroy the subject; it simply tries to resituate it.

RK: But can deconstruction, as the disclosure of language as *différance*, contribute to the pleasure of reading, to our appreciation of the living texture of a literary text? Or is it only an intellectual strategy of detection, of exposing our presuppositions and disabusing us of our habitual illusions about reading?

JD: Deconstruction gives pleasure in that it gives desire. To deconstruct a text is to disclose how it functions as desire, as a search for presence and fulfillment which is interminably deferred. One cannot read without opening oneself to the desire of language, to the search for that which remains absent and other than oneself. Without a certain love of the text, no reading would be possible. In every reading there is a *corps-à-corps* between reader and text, an incorporation of the reader's desire into the desire of the text. Here is pleasure, the very opposite of that arid intellectualism of which deconstruction has so often been accused.

Paris, 1981

PART III

From *States of Mind*, 1995

Julia Kristeva
Strangers to Ourselves: The Hope of the Singular

RK: How would you describe your identity as a European?

JK: I consider myself a cosmopolitan. I was lucky in my child-hood to learn French at an early stage. My parents sent me to a French preschool in Sofia run by Dominican nuns: it was an offshoot of the Jesuit college in Constantinople. So I started French before my Bulgarian studies. Then those ladies were accused of spying and expelled from Bulgaria. Their work was taken over by the French Alliance. So I learnt French at the same time as Bulgarian, and my entry into French culture was somehow a natural one. When I arrived in France to pursue my third-level education, I felt that I somehow belonged to the French culture, which is not the case seen from the French side for they still perceive me as a foreigner, although I was very warmly welcomed.

It is easier to consider oneself cosmopolitan—as I do—if one comes from a small country like Bulgaria, just as it is probably easier to be European when one is born, say, Dutch, than it would be if one is English. I insist on this point for I believe that the future of Europe lies in this idea of respect between nations, but also of conciliation between nations. I care very much for this cosmopolitan idea which is a heritage of the European culture of the ancient Stoics, later developed by French thinkers of the eighteenth century. I take this cosmopolitan idea of the Enlightenment very much to heart, and if there is hope for

Europe, beyond the recent ethnic divisions that have broken out in Yugoslavia, Czechoslovakia, and the Soviet Union, etc., it is in this spirit of universalism. We must move beyond nations, or archaisms, while also recognizing genuine particularities.

RK: To return to your own experience of so-called Eastern Europe. How do you now relate to this lost or amputated part of the continent?

JK: I don't experience this dichotomy of the two Europes in such a painful manner, for two reasons. First, for biographical reasons which I already mentioned, that is, my early entry into French culture, but also because I have made an intellectual choice which consists in thinking that the origin is not essential, that the origin is a reaction to pain and can become a condensed brew of hate. People who turn back to origins are people who don't know how to metabolize or sublimate their hate, they are wounded people, depressed people; and because they no longer have ideals—religion does not satisfy them, nor does Marxism, and no other providential ideology can come to their rescue—they turn towards the archaism of the origin. My entire intellectual education goes against this idea of origin.

RK: Is it feasible, or even fair, to dismiss the complex reality of nationalism in this way?

JK: I do recognize that we are going to live for a very long time in the frame of nations and nationalities. I am against that tendency of the Left to dismiss the idea of nation—I believe the idea of nation is going to have a long life. But it should be a *choice,* and not a reflex or return to the origin. When one lives it as a choice—that is to say, with clarity of vision, knowing the political, ideological, cultural reasons that make us adhere to France, Ireland, Great Britain, etc., and not because we are genetically linked to it—it can be a good choice.

So to come to the other aspect of your question: what can my experience of the East give me today? I believe two things: firstly, an ability to winter out, to acknowledge the importance of effort. We were children who suffered quite a lot of economic deprivations (although they weren't disastrous, especially at the age I was). So we were pushed into giving the maximum of ourselves; and those who weren't able to step over this threshold of discipline and endurance were swept away. This gave us a hard-learnt power to concentrate and be disciplined. Secondly, I learned from Bulgaria the importance of culture. Bulgaria is the country in which the Slavonic alphabet was created. It was two Bulgarian brothers, Cyril and Methodius, who gave the Slavonic alphabet to the world—it is now the alphabet that the Russians use. There is in Bulgaria a Feast of the Alphabet, probably the only one in the world. Every year on May 24, children parade through the streets of Sofia, each displaying a letter on their fronts, so we are identified with the alphabet.

RK: The Cyrillic script was originally Bulgarian?

JK: Yes, Saint Cyril gave his name to the alphabet. There are discussions still going on about whether he was Greek or Bulgarian; his mother was of Slavonic origin, he knew the Slavonic languages, and when the pope asked for the Gospels to be translated into Slavonic to evangelize the Eastern nations, it was the two brothers, Cyril and Methodius, who were sent on the mission.

So in Bulgaria there is this pull to identify oneself with culture which I experienced very vividly in my childhood as a positive element, and I believe that many people in the former "Eastern" Europe, especially students, have a cultural avidity and curiosity that Western youth has lost because it has a surfeit of culture (you can buy anything anywhere for your bookshelf) and because the mass media have destroyed the taste for classical culture and great modern culture. Europe is going to suffer the dissolution of culture for a long time to come.

I have just finished writing a novel called *The Old Man and the Wolves*, in which I tell the story of the brutality of the modern world, which one can find as much in Ireland, Great Britain, and France as in Eastern Europe. There is a crazed fashion—violence against people, lack of culture, lack of respect—and it is getting worse today with the collapse of the pseudoclassical culture; nothing is left. It is something we will find very hard to get through. There will be two big problems— the market economy, and the need to climb up the slope of fifty years of cultural and moral emptiness. We also have a lot of work to do as intellectuals, for example, in helping with cultural exchanges between the two parts of the continent at the level of the humanities.

RK: How do you combine your cosmopolitanism as a French citizen with the fidelity to your place of origin? Do you not think that some recognition of national or regional origins is necessary? You suggest that nationalism is a pathological phenomenon, but does it not only become that if we deny the basic human need for a certain national identity?

JK: Baltic, Serbian, Slovak, Croatian nationalism is, in my eyes, a regressive and a depressive attitude. If you'll allow me this little psychoanalytic excursion, these separatist nationalists are people who have long been humiliated in their identity. Soviet Marxism did not recognize this identity, so they have now an antidepressive reaction which takes manic forms, if I may put it like that. The exaltation of origins and of archaic folk values can take violent forms because one wants an enemy, and as the enemy is not communism any more—because it doesn't exist—the enemy will be the *other*: the other ethnic group, the other nation, the scapegoat and so on. This pathology can last for a long time and such archaic settling of accounts can prevent, or certainly handicap, the economic and cultural development which those countries need. One can try to accelerate the process, one can try to avoid sinking into stagnancy, to help it go a bit faster; and at that level, there is a huge amount of work that can be done, on one side by the churches and on the other by the intellectuals. It seems to me that in Eastern Europe the Catholic Church played a major role in the rebellion against communism. It has a great role to play today in helping to transcend nationalism and to give to those people ideals which would not be strictly ethnic or archaically national. Recently the church wrote an encyclical which shows it to be extremely interested in the moral struggle against totalitarianism but also against a certain Americanism. I am quite struck by this cosmopolitan and universalist idea of the Christian church as a remedy for those nationalisms that one shouldn't dispose of too promptly, but should try to transcend.

RK: If the crisis is not only political, but moral and spiritual as you suggest, does that mean that the solution must also be of a moral and spiritual order?

JK: Even economic problems cannot be solved without this moral renewal. Imagine people who must face a market economy based on the idea of individual competition while their sense of individuality is still extremely weak, wounded, frail. In order to consolidate this sense of one's individuality, of one's autonomy, of one's freedom, one needs a great moral support. That is why I think that those two aspects, the economic and the moral, are linked together. I would give priority to the moral revolution.

RK: Are you advocating therefore a return to nineteenth-century liberal humanism and individualism? I am thinking of the legacy of Locke, Hume, and Mill in particular, who advanced the idea of individual rights outside of a communal or social context. Or is what you're talking about something that goes beyond traditional individualism towards some new right to singularity compatible with social solidarity?

JK: In my view, it is a right to singularity. But it is not obvious that the ex-communist countries will be able to achieve this singularity, coming from an ideology of collectivism, unless they go through some form of individualism.

RK: Are you suggesting a necessary passage through liberalism?

JK: Not rampant or uncritical liberalism. This is why I insist on those better forms of individual identity that one can find in religion and in the Enlightenment. Here I quote a phrase that appears to me to express the aim of Christianity, even if it goes far beyond it. It is from [Charles de] Montesquieu's *Pensées [My Thoughts]*, and goes something like this: "If I knew something that would be useful to myself but detrimental to my family, I would cast it from my mind. If I knew something that was useful to my family but detrimental to my country, I would consider it criminal. If I knew something useful to Europe but detrimental to humankind, I would also consider it a crime." It is a very interesting idea because it recognizes the individual, the person, the family, the nation—but it also considers that the individual person can only find its development in a wider frame.

RK: Is this what you would call the cosmopolitan model?

JK: Yes, because the nation, the individual, the family are recognized as transitional objects, to speak like [D. W.] Winnicott, as moments of consolidation which are necessary but not sufficient. It is this transitional logic that Montesquieu develops in this saying. And I consider that it should be studied in all French schools, for example, because it is not clear that all French people apply this logic—far from it. There is difficulty in living as a foreigner in France. Above all, it is something we should try to share with our friends from the East, so that both their ethnic belonging and nationhood are recognized, while encouraging them to avoid fixations and limitations at that level, to move forward towards wider horizons.

RK: Are you suggesting that religion could play a positive role by going beyond particular denominations or sects and projecting some common universal vision?

JK: There is a homogeneity in particular religions which makes you into a stranger if you don't share their presuppositions. That said, our monotheistic religions have tried to develop a notion of *the other,* and it is this legacy of Western thinking that we should enrich and cultivate, that the Enlightenment tried to extrapolate, and that we need to redevelop today. What does that mean? When a stranger knocks at my door, for instance, I should, as the Bible says, consider that it might be God—a sign of the sacredness and singularity of others. It also means that, as the pilgrimages from the first centuries of Christianity until Saint Augustine taught us, the journey, the idea of carrying the message of Christ towards others and of receiving strangers coming as pilgrims, leads to a kind of osmosis between ethnic groups. The idea of *caritas*, Christian love, of which we know the degenerative form in the terrible history of Western colonialism, gives a strength today to the Christian churches. We can see it being developed, for instance, in *"le secours catholique,"* or other forms of action which Christians in France organize for foreigners: teaching migrant workers and their families how to read, providing material aid, etc. I believe it is important to focus on this aspect of religious culture insofar as it enjoys a popular audience and can respond to the dangers of narrow nationalism.

RK: Once religions have done that work, is there another kind of work that remains to be done?

JK: Yes. Alongside this work, there is much to be done at the level of the individual, developing the dimension of singularity. Our ideas don't fall from heaven; we have a heritage, and we must bank on it; otherwise we become abstract. There is a radical change which occurred in the eighteenth century in our understanding of human singularity, and there is also much to be done through psychoanalysis—something I am committed to in my daily work.

RK: Are you suggesting that this work on the private realm of the psyche cannot be properly exercised by politics or religion but only by psychoanalysis, a work of the soul?

JK: I am not going to preach psychoanalysis. For the analyst, the person who comes to analysis is a person who must express his or her own desire for it. So I am not going to suggest to your readers to start analysis. But I believe that psychoanalysis is a modern form which takes into account the Jewish and Christian monotheist heritage and the Enlightenment knowledge of the self and of our singularities. But it is possible to find other forms of learning more about this singularity, which range from personal meditation to art, reading, music, painting.

RK: Is it possible to achieve this through the relationship with another person?

JK: For me the relationship with another person is essential. As forms of sublimation, the arts are extremely important, but insufficient. Sometimes, indeed, they can lead someone to become complacent with singularity; they can induce closure rather than an overcoming of malaise. So, yes, relating to others is indispensable to the development of singularity.

RK: Finally I would like to ask what you feel is the role today of the European project of the Enlightenment? I am thinking Voltaire's and Montesquieu's dream of a great European cosmopolitan republic. Since they first expressed their vision, we have witnessed not only the breakup of Europe into rival nationalisms, but also two world wars in our century which were a direct result of such antagonisms. After those two world wars, and after Auschwitz in particular, what can we advocate today as a viable and legitimate project for a united Europe?

JK: We have to take seriously the violence of identity desires. For instance, when somebody recognizes him or herself in an X or Y origin, it can appear very laudable, a very appealing need for identity. But one mustn't forget the violence behind this desire, a violence that can be turned against oneself and others, giving rise to fratricidal wars. So we need to recognize not only the relativeness of human fraternity but the need, both pedagogical and therapeutic, to take account of the death wish, of the violence *within* us.

RK: How fraternity can become fratricide?

JK: Exactly. Therefore, along with the attention we should pay to the death wish, there is a need for finesse in the way we deal with individuals, and with their relationship to nations. After the Enlightenment, the idea of the nation was long considered a backward and redundant idea that one could brush aside, do without. I believe that, at least on an economic level, the nation is here to stay; we will have it with us for at least another century. But it is not enough to realize its economic dimension; we have to measure the psychic violence of the adherence to this idea. This is a violence that can also be carried by certain religions, for religions can be another form of originary adhesion. The shapes of fundamentalism that spring up nowadays on all sides cannot be dissipated simply by fraternal good will. One is going to encounter a lot of difficulties. We are faced with a death wish. I believe the closest we've got to it was after the fall of the Berlin Wall. When that happened, whatever screen hid us from this death wish fell. The screens of new Promethean ideologies, like Marxism, don't exist any more. The old religions, even if they are still solid and endure for a long while, are being put in question. Nothing can wipe out or hide this death wish. We are left face to face with it and the most adequate response to be found is, in my view, the sublimatory and clairvoyant forms that art and psychoanalysis offer.

The media propagate this death wish. Look at the films people like to watch after a long, tiring day: a thriller or a horror film; anything less is considered boring. We are attracted to this violence. So the great moral work which grapples with the problem of identity also grapples with this contemporary experience of death, violence, and hate. Nationalisms, like fundamentalisms, are screens in front of this violence, fragile screens, see-through screens, because they only displace that hatred, sending it to the other, to the neighbor, to the rival ethnic group. The big work of our civilization is to try to fight this hatred—without God.

Paris, 1991

Hans-Georg Gadamer
Text Matters

RK: What were the milestones on your own way to hermeneutics?

H-GG: My way to hermeneutics describes my initial experiences with the study of language as a young philologist in Marburg. I had already completed a dissertation on Plato for my first philosophical studies with [Richard] Hönigswald, [Paul] Natorp, and Nicolai Hartmann, and I had also met Heidegger. Only then did I actually begin my course of studies as a classical philologist with Paul Friedländer. It was at that point I had the opportunity to recognize the vital importance of a literary genre itself, especially when we are trying to correctly understand the produce of such a genre. For example, in a debate I had with Werner Jaeger at that time, I took issue with his use of Aristotle's *Protreptikos* as a significant measure of early Aristotelian thought. The genre of the "protreptikos" among the Greeks offered essentially nothing more than an advertisement for competing schools of rhetoric and philosophy seeking patronage. To expect that controversial questions in philosophy could be settled by appealing to such a genre, as Jaeger apparently did, seemed quite erroneous to me.

Or to take another example, I realized that the meaning of Plato's *Republic* could only be correctly understood after noting that we are dealing here with the literary genre of "utopia." To write in the utopian genre, especially under the political conditions of a Greek polis that afforded no separation of powers, was the only possible way to criticize the degeneration of a democracy through corruption, nepotism, etc., without suffering political consequences. The comedies of Aristophanes had a similar function. In more recent times, we also know what political censorship can mean for literary production. Goethe actually attributed the increase of the linguistic art of expression to this kind of censorship, and, in this respect, paid tribute to it. Leo Strauss pointed to Spinoza as an example of the difficult situation of "thinking" in the era of the European Enlightenment, and he showed how the worry about censorship influenced Spinzoa's *Ethics*. Strauss also indicated that similar concerns could be applied to Arabian repression in the case of the medieval Jewish thinker Moses Maimonides.

RK: What did you learn from these early observations?

H-GG: I learnt to attend more fully to the addressees of philosophical texts—to those for whom the writer writes. I thus encountered the twofold hermeneutic problem: (1) how we make ourselves understood to others through language, and (2) how we have to deal with writing to avoid misunderstanding, misuse, and distortion—as Plato had already warned us. In order to appreciate this, we have to acknowledge the central importance of *rhetoric*, which achieved its highest development in the blossoming of Greek culture in the city-state. At the time of the decline of the Greek polis, rhetoric turned into a literary genre that subsequently dominated the entire academic culture, only losing its leading role as a transmitter of culture in our era of modern science. I therefore constructed my studies with ancient rhetoric in mind, and, above all, on Plato's critique of rhetoric and his qualified recognition of rhetoric.

RK: Why did you choose hermeneutics as the best means of developing the phenomenology of Husserl and Heidegger?

H-GG: One doesn't really "choose" things like that. We always find ourselves in a tradition that is speaking to us. Therefore, there is an easy answer to your question. Philosophy only works by means of linguistic formulation, and for this to carry conviction it must include rhetoric. It is an error to think that mathematical formalism—whose clarity certainly constitutes its advantage—can be everywhere substituted for the use of natural language. In the mathematical and natural sciences, where it is a question of exact, measurable results, the apparatus of mathematics plays a decisive role. But in those sciences where one is *not* dealing with quantitatively measurable objects of research, the research is conducted and communicated to others by means of human language. In the course of time, philosophy has increasingly found that the elaborate conceptual language of Latin scholastics, a language that has penetrated into modern national languages, often introduces unrecognized and invisible prejudices. Even the philosophical reform movement, heralded by phenomenology and philosophical research at the beginning of our century, had to trust more and more in the power of living language to awaken insight. In particular, Husserl was a master of a highly discriminating art of description, exposing thoughtless professional constructions and jargon through the powerful language of phenomena.

RK: Was Husserl alone in this?

H-GG: By no means. The great thinkers in the history of this new philosophy, above all Kant and the German idealists, had modeled their conceptual art on the linguistic power of the German language. They used models like Meister Eckhart and Martin Luther, and finally, through the return to the Greco-Roman ancients, entered again into the teaching of their linguistic culture. Ever since the German romantic period, this attention to language also marks the work of those thinkers who came later, including such great thinkers as Bergson in France, as well as thinkers of the historical school in Germany, whose philosophical interpreter was [Wilhelm] Dilthey. Dilthey had a decisive influence on the continued growth of phenomenology, extending from Martin Heidegger to other newer tendencies in the phenomenological school. Since [Friedrich] Schleiermacher's modern development of hermeneutics, much of its older history has remained concealed in the background.

JC: But many people assume as self-evident that hermeneutics first begins with Schleiermacher.

H-GG: One ought not to present the case in quite that way, as if something like hermeneutics first appeared with German romanticism. *Hermeneutics* is actually a Greek term, and the conditions under which the art of understanding the other places its special demands are not first derived from the age of modern science. The genesis of the word *hermeneutics* itself shows an original connection with the god Hermes, the divine mediator between the will of the gods and the acts of mortals. It is clear that such a concept of hermeneutics comes very near to the concept of translation. The role played by the Delphic oracle in Greek history—namely, the interpretation of prophecies—rests especially on this concept of hermeneutics. The art of interpreting these prophecies through the committee of the Delphic priesthood truly made history in the political sense. One has to realize that the Greeks were the brilliant disciples of the high culture of the Near East. They were the first to develop a rational energy and thirst for knowledge that led them into inevitable tension with their own religious tradition, which, thanks to their poetic representation in the epics of Homer and Hesiod, deeply determined their own way of thinking. That goes right through the Greek educational movement in the narrow sense of the Sophists, and still distinguishes the lasting foundation of Greek philosophy for the history of the West going back to Plato and Aristotle.

RK: Could you say more about these "beginnings" with Plato and Aristotle?

H-GG: In Plato, we find a complex artistic incorporation of mythic-religious traditions into mathematical research and cosmological knowledge, and, in the end, into the constant question about "the good" posed by Socrates. In general, the expression *hermeneutics* is not used for this. Actually, the term *hermeneutics* is given a thematic treatment for the first time by Aristotle, but only in a very special and narrow sense. As the founder of ancient logic, Aristotle called "hermeneutics" the teaching of propositions of judgment, and it is upon this teaching that the secret of logical inference is based. Everyone recognized the importance of syllogistics—that is, the form of reaching valid logical conclusions—because Aristotle developed it with an eye towards supporting the new mathematical science, as well as defending rational thought against the rhetorical tricks of the Sophists.

JC: But isn't philosophy always afflicted with the art of understanding the unintelligible, if only in an unnamed way?

H-GG: Yes, indeed. We would like to know once-and-for-all what the Socratic question of the good really *is*, and it has in this way dominated all of Western thought. Particularly in late antiquity, this question proved to be the preparation for the debate with the Judeo-Christian religious heritage. In this respect, it is not surprising that Christian theology and especially Augustine, the great Latin scholar among the church fathers, developed the fundamental teaching of ancient and Greco-Christian hermeneutics in his *De Doctrina Christiana [On Christian Doctrine]*.

JC: Wasn't it necessary for theology to go its own way under the changing signs of the new secular science in the age of the Renaissance?

H-GG: That goes without saying. Especially Luther and the great Aristotelian [Philipp] Melanchthon played a decisive role amongst the reformers. Luther's textbook of interpretation has become one of the most important hermeneutic documents in world literature. And to Melanchton goes the unique merit of having defended the already-mentioned great heritage of ancient rhetoric, a heritage which he defended as the transmitter of cultural values of the entire ancient and medieval educational system, as opposed to the iconoclastic radicalism in the Protestant movement. Melanchton also deserves credit for having established it as hermeneutics. In his Latin lecture on rhetoric, Melanchton deals with the theory of rhetoric of the Greeks and Romans and the Latin Middle Ages, first as the art of making a speech or writing a speech. In truth, though, he diverted this ancient heritage of rhetoric into the art of *reading* speeches or texts. Ever since Melanchton made such a lasting imprint on the Central European educational system and on the entire academic culture of his era, an integrated line of hermeneutics runs through this culture, mainly due to the central place of the Holy Scriptures within the Protestant church system. Since the empirical sciences of the modern world challenge philosophy and metaphysics, hermeneutics directs itself to the task of seeking a scientific-theoretical way towards a universal art of interpretation based on the special domains of theology and jurisprudence. This task gained importance with the end of the age of metaphysics, or more precisely in the age of romanticism.

RK: Could you spell out the seminal relation of philosophical hermeneutics to theology and law?

H-GG: It was vital to implement a methodology of hermeneutics-as-philosophy in the theological and jurisprudential spheres that had already been cultivated. And that is what Schleiermacher achieved in his *Hermeneutics,* but even more so in his *Dialectic.* The spread of hermeneutic methodology into other content-areas lies not so much in this direction, but in the direction of common foundational questions (as in theology, in religious research, in historical research, in art, music, etc.), which call for philosophical work, as we see today particularly in the work of Paul Ricœur. However, the most important step taken by hermeneutics-as-philosophy was a new focus on the "life-world" as the major field of phenomenological research. Philosophy was no longer limited to the narrow program dictated by the "fact of science," as neo-Kantians or Logical Positivists would have maintained.

RK: Are you saying that the concept of method in modern science is not applicable to hermeneutics-as-philosophy?

H-GG: Philosophical hermeneutics doesn't mean a scientific method. All scientific methods are good only under the condition of their reasonable and judicious application. Here lies the boundary of all method and hypostasization. This state of affairs has been acknowledged since the development of historical consciousness, and it became increasingly important as scientific methods spread to the languages of modern civilization, which set the stage through their mutual influence on one another. Anyone who has used a translation where he himself knows and commands the original language has the undeniable experience that the translation is very much harder to understand than the original. The natural use of language is less a question of texts than the "matter" of experience itself.

Hermeneutics and the Greeks

RK: In what sense do you believe that the origins of hermeneutics are to be found in the Greek philosophers?

H-GG: Do you mean, why must Greek philosophy still be the actual point of departure for hermeneutic questioning?

RK: Yes.

H-GG: In the intellectual culture of Europe, the Greeks were the people who first developed science and the logic of proof. And for this they used their own living language, which the citizens of their cities spoke and their poets had elevated to literary language. They didn't have to struggle with a technical language of philosophy, which would have been for them a second and strange language, as it was for the Romans when the upper classes absorbed Greek culture.

The problem of molding the Greek language into Latin became more noticeable in late antiquity when the emerging Christian church began to formulate its teachings of faith in Latin, with the help of Greek philosophy. In the end, this led to the "forced" logical culture of the medieval Scholastics. Their language of concepts, in more or less refined or alienated forms, has informed the conceptual language of modern philosophy. Since then, the task has been to relearn what the Greeks showed us, namely, to summon up the imaginative power of living language for conceptual thinking. This doesn't mean that we should adopt Greek philosophy, but it does mean that we should learn from it how to think in concepts with the help of our own spoken language. Luther became a great translator because he paid attention to the language of the people.

JC: In this connection, can you explain to us what is involved in the idea of "eminent texts"?

H-GG: These are texts that we may refer to as literary or poetic texts, and the same distinction is also applicable to other art forms. The question that I especially pose to Derrida is the distinctive role which this kind of text plays. I call these "eminent texts" because in them the true nature of "textura," that is, the indissoluble interweaving of threads, is the appropriate description. We cannot extract information from literary works if we allow them to speak to us merely as literary works. But that's exactly it; they speak to us, and they are even tireless, with questions as well as answers, so that we don't simply consult them once and then know everything about them. Rather, we find ourselves questioned again and again, receiving answers that are always new. And this experience *stays* with us, so that we recognize ourselves when allowing ourselves to be affected by the great portrayals of human destiny and suffering in tragedies, novels, or poems.

It is no exaggeration to claim that a poetical text is a partner in conversation. Furthermore, the literary text speaks to us only so long as it is and remains such a partner, and not merely an object of objectifying research. These are things that we misunderstand and cover over if we speak of "fiction" only in order to emphasize a contrast with scientific knowledge. In that instance, a scientific concept of truth functions in an improper context.

JC: What are philosophical texts?

H-GG: These are naturally not "eminent texts," which is to say that they are not linguistic works of art. But while the "eminent text" is for the partner-in-dialogue, the "problem" is for the philosophical thinkers. We make it too easy for ourselves if a "problem" is seen simply as a "question to which there is an answer." Rather, a problem is precisely that which is thrown into our path and which cannot easily be avoided. Certainly we cannot get around it by alternative questions that require a mere "Yes" or "No" in response. Here I believe that the close intertwining of philosophy with literary language, which I have often described in this context, receives its own crucial priority. In philosophy, as in art, it's a matter of coaxing prereflective knowledge out of its depths. It is almost as if everybody basically knows it. Everybody who can think and speak a language lives in the totality of a world-orientation which is always already on-the-way-towards-understanding.

Faced with a question that we don't completely understand, it remains an open question. This invites the process of recognition that Plato called *"anamnesis."* He demonstrated it with mathematics, but we would do well to take the concept of *anamnesis* so that it broadly corresponds to its original Pythagorean idea of salvation from the circle of rebirth. Foreknowledge guides that which we ask—ourselves or another—and our answer is recognized as true. This confirms the religious tradition of *anamnesis*. We ourselves only truly "know" when we re-cognize or encounter something again. And we are sure that another has understood us when he or she has responded. This is the only, albeit relative, criterion of truth.

Hermeneutics and Dialogue

RK: Is it the concept of "dialogue" in particular that marks the difference between your philosophy and that of other hermeneutic thinkers in our century, such as Heidegger, Habermas, or Ricœur?

H-GG: It is well known that philosophy always had a basis in spoken language, which, prior to all science, constituted a guide in the unfolding of vocabulary, grammar, and syntax for human thought—a guide which helps to determine conceptual formation. Admittedly, with the advent of reading culture in the [Johannes] Gutenberg era and the rise of the mathematical sciences, this is not always as evident as it should be. The foundational concepts of philosophy originally stem from the Greek tradition, but at present these concepts just seem to exercise a purely instrumental function of ordering experience, which has become dominated by the language of mathematical symbols. As the reference to the original proximity of language to the philosophical thought of the Greeks has indicated, the concepts of philosophy were not a mere working tool for them. These concepts were rather formed in *spoken* language, drawing on all the raw materials that constituted the totality of world experience. Thus, Plato could say that all learning and knowledge is a remembering *(anamnesis)* which comes in the play between question and answer.

On this basis, the great turn of philosophical thought towards the primary concept of the "subject" and the modern idea of methodology took place. This turn has dominated all of modern German philosophy, and this is true even for the transcendental self-interpretation of the later Husserl of *Ideas*. It is also true, to some degree, for the transcendental framework Heidegger used for presenting his masterpiece, *Being and Time*, a work which exhibited a residual neo-Kantianism that eventually generated new critiques by thinkers like Martin Buber. Heidegger eliminated this transcendental framework in his search for the new way of the so-called turn or *Kehre*, by which he meant a path in the forest that makes a turn in ascending to the top. But what Heidegger described as a new way is, in fact, a return to his own beginnings in the reinterpretation of Aristotle.

In any case, whatever importance the hermeneutic approach has for philosophy only comes into general consciousness slowly. Otherwise, Derrida would hardly complain about "phonocentricity" in this regard. Phonocentricity is only another expression for the concept of presence-at-hand, introduced by Heidegger, or of *présence*, introduced by Derrida.

RK: How would you identify your own specific approach to hermeneutics on this issue?

H-GG: I think there is a decisive point here which distinguishes me from Habermas and Ricœur and others who appeal to hermeneutics. The crucial step is indicated in the title of my book *Truth and Method*, which marks a gap between "truth" and "method." Understanding, trying to comprehend others, seeking communication with others—all these are processes of the life-world. One should, of course, be able to take on tasks of communication where understanding is the issue, as it interacts with art and science. However, when human beings speak with one another and inhabit the communicative world, this complex interaction can't be fully captured by scientific method alone.

Since human experience goes far beyond the questioning attainable through knowledge of the quantitative sciences, it is pointless to create a false contrast between the objectivity of science and the alleged relativism of hermeneutic sciences—those sciences for which objectivity cannot be the final goal. It is a fatal error to assume that the incomplete nature of our world experience can ever be negotiated through the so-called empirical sciences. When we seek communication with others, we ourselves are no mere "objects" of science. The natural sciences aim at universal "knowledge," as Husserl correctly emphasized. That assures their success, but also marks their limit.

Incidentally, this difference between the natural and human sciences has nothing to do with the famous quarrel between the ancients and moderns. That was a literary dispute between the traditional humanists and modern poets that took place in France during the seventeenth and eighteenth centuries. One can extend the same quarrel to other areas, as Leo Strauss does in his Spinoza critique and his Maimonides studies, consciously taking the side of the ancients. But basically that is not a viable alternative. Ever since the work of C. P. Snow, we speak of science and the humanities as "two worlds," yet we also desire to overcome this difference between the natural and human sciences. For the twentieth century and the future, this European debate, which exists even in philosophy, will ultimately appear far too provincial. The hermeneutic art of understanding others, in spite of the otherness of the *other*, will have to tackle harder tasks, when, as at present, the large world cultures meet each other more often as real partners in conversation.

RK: In this respect, how would you defend yourself against Derrida's charge that you subscribe to the phonocentrism of traditional metaphysics?

H-GG: I especially want to say that there are a plurality of traditions, out of which human questioning arises. It cannot be denied that philosophy too must give an account of itself to people coming from other traditions. However, I do not believe that Derrida's choice of "writing" has achieved a higher universal validity, as he apparently believes. True, we can't deny the fact that the written evidence of human life in Chinese literature or Central African myths, Indian epics or the Koran certainly takes the form of written traditions. But while these texts derive from the most diverse origins and symbols, they all refer back to lived life and spoken language. In this respect, phonocentrism is a common *condition* for all human writing, and naturally also for the "deconstruction" demanded by Derrida and his friends. To me, Derrida appears to be the victim of a curious metaphysical remnant in Husserl's thought. What Derrida means by "phonocentrism" can be found in his debate with Husserl: the assumption that the "voice" is something "material." One can only be amazed. Voice, this fleeting breath of air that passes and which first allows the "written" to be conveyed as meaningful, is itself a text-to-be-understood. Whether as a text recited aloud or as a text read silently to myself, the articulation of meaning first fulfils itself by means of the sound formation. In any case, the one who speaks, hears; and the one who understands, answers — *not* to the particular voice that one recognizes on the telephone, but rather to that of which the talk is about.

RK: So there are different concepts of "voice"?

H-GG: Yes. Apparently, Derrida has in mind the narrow view of *"logos"* that he found in Husserl. However, this ancient concept was again put into a new light by Christianity as cited in the beginning of the Gospel According to St. John: "In the beginning was the Word . . ." Thus, if we focus only on sentential propositions and those sciences founded on such "true" propositions, we will indeed arrive at a very one-sided rendering of the meaning of *logos*. This is an artificial restriction, which Aristotle first made explicit when he talked about hermeneutics with logic in mind. I think that we must free ourselves from such theoretical burdens, precisely because the linguisticality of human beings doesn't produce structures made of propositions. It rather consists in a living exchange of question and answer, request and fulfillment, command and obedience, etc. To whatever degree one extends reciprocity, that alone allows communication to take place.

JC: Are hermeneutics and deconstruction capable of communicating with each other?

H-GG: I cannot accept that there is a *single* hermeneutic position that ought to agree with the position of deconstruction. But neither is the hermeneutic position at all a counter-position. Hermeneutics doesn't rely on *one* point of view; rather, it refers to *mutual* praxis. We both seek in dialogue to convince the other, or at least to share with the other what we mean. Both partners have the experience that this is only possible by going beyond what has been said *literally* to me, and by the other seeking to understand me. We may not succeed on the first or second attempt, especially when it is a question of partners speaking different languages. But, by the same token, it is certainly not being claimed that the hermeneutic effort of communicating with the other is always crowned with success. That's how I think matters stand between myself and Derrida, insofar as we could learn to understand one another, and then neither of us would remain the same as we were before our conversation. In short, we learn from one another.

Let me illustrate this with another example. I refer to the well-known debate between Habermas and myself. That debate was, at the time, a publicly argued, written dialogue that raised a great deal of interest. Now people want us to engage in such a conversation again, but conversations are not the kind of thing that one can program. This "written conversation" that occurred was an especially fortunate constellation, consisting of comprehensive common elements shared by many others, elements that could he brought into the written conversation from both sides. The conversation with Derrida in Paris didn't achieve such a fortunate literary organization of form, and what is more, was subjected to the mutilations that translation brings about between two foreign languages.

RK: What do you mean exactly?

H-GG: I mean that we hold no "opposed" positions, rather that we are all "on the way," even when we resort to writing. When one reads something written—whether it is something like a poem by Goethe, or lines of verse scribbled down in the moonlight or found in a book—the reader is not the one first addressed. Only personal correspondence in a private letter names and means *its* addressee, and nobody else. When we are dealing with texts, the reader is involved, and he or she is the *other*. Similarly, in a conversation, we need attention and cooperation to reach some understanding. I can see how someone could be overwhelmed by the silent stillness in which a sudden insight dawns and definite preconceptions collapse. But we should be able to agree that writing must be read, and that writing is only read when it is read-with-understanding. Only reading-with-understanding makes the signs of writing speak. Whether it is an inner voice or an audible voice that speaks makes no difference to the *différance*.

RK: How does this relate to your understanding of Derrida's critique of metaphysics?

H-GG: It isn't really clear to me that what I've been discussing ought to have something necessarily to do with "metaphysical thinking." This always seemed to me a weak point in Derrida's book on Husserl, *Speech and Phenomena*. I can't understand what metaphysical thinking is supposed to be. Certainly, I can imagine a *language* of metaphysics which has been marked by Aristotle's ontology of substance. And I can also imagine the role played in this context by the concept of "presence"—a role which, at least since the analysis of time in Aristotle's *Physics*, leads to the dead-end described by Augustine. On the other hand, I don't see how the issue of understanding is seriously affected by whether a text appears in the continuity and coherence of a book or in the discontinuity of aphorisms á la [Friedrich] Schlegel or Nietzsche. I find it quite incomprehensible to interrogate this discontinuity under the guise of a critical scrutiny of the unconscious hiding in a text. Naturally, we can do this at any time. But in my eyes, that's not conversation at all: the partner is merely "objectively" observed and doesn't sit there willing or able to respond.

Derrida loves to speak of a "break" in such a context. However, we know that Freud himself was able to make the ruptures of dream-events fruitful, and eventually even cure patients through interpretation and understanding. It should thus apply all the more to aphorisms or to the ambiguity of words that we are left with *something*, a significant remainder. It is not true that we simply play a game. Certainly, there are differences in the weight of interpretation, in the pregnancy, the amazement, the evidence, the thoughtfulness with which we move in conversation. But all these are "modes" of understanding. It is no different in actual conversation or in handling a text, especially when genuine communication doesn't occur. We may initially talk past the other, and then return to the other with clarification. Even if both partners in dialogue finally have something as a result of conversation, it may only be a superficial harmony of agreement that never quite escapes "distorted communication." Merely "understanding" the viewpoint of the other isn't enough. Understanding may be where the conversation actually stopped, and perhaps the other has already changed his or her standpoint in the process of presenting it. Nobody who takes the hermeneutic problem seriously imagines that we can ever entirely understand the other or know what the other is thinking. More important is the fact that we *seek* to understand one another at all, and that this is a thoughtful path.

RK: So you would repudiate Derrida's critique of metaphysics as logocentric?

H-GG: What the metaphysical concept of "presence" has to do with such a context is a complete mystery to me. A conversation worthy of the name remains with one over time and is not simply about the presence of a voice speaking to a listener. Again, I cannot understand how Derrida thinks that one can listen to one's own voice. We all have the experience of being startled by our own voice, for example on radio, as if by something entirely strange. Hearing our own voice is one of the strangest things that self-knowledge can experience. Perhaps it is exactly in this shock that unconscious familiarity is concealed. Derrida has himself developed the concept of *différance*, a concept that has an exact parallel in Heidegger's treatment, or whatever one may call the *"Da"* ("there") of being *(Da-Sein)*. This is a "being-there" which is like a reverse electrical current. In any case, Heidegger's *"Da"* is not *"Präsenz"* like the presence that dominates the Greek worldview and that is fixed by Derrida as the concept of *présence*.

RK: What do you believe Derrida actually means by deconstruction?

H-GG: When Derrida speaks of deconstruction, I understand it precisely in its concrete execution, specifically as a surprising radical upheaval that sheds new light. I won't venture to exemplify his French concept in quite this way, because connotations intrude in a foreign language. I prefer to look at Derrida's reflection, say, on Heidegger's "Nietzsche" and the quotation marks surrounding it. I understand that reflection very well, and would even maintain that Derrida understands Heidegger very well. The quotation marks indicate that Heidegger was here suggesting an "interpretation-unit" which he himself disagreed with. In Heidegger's view, for the will-to-power and eternal recurrence to be the same only means that both present a dwindling stage of being that has sunk into the forgetfulness-of-Being. And Heidegger did not think that this forgetfulness-of-Being can ever be definitive.

To look at another example, in *What Is Thinking?* Heidegger is playing with a double meaning. We may say that deconstruction alerts us to the fact that behind the apparent meaning, there is a secret call that suddenly breaks through. Wherever one meets such examples in Derrida's own work, the reader seeks to understand and to enter new horizons through them. Why would he write otherwise? In any case, such a break is not a breaking-off, but rather a beginning, and this beginning represents a going beyond everything said. Such is the hermeneutic experience that we create with each other constantly. Each of us would become a comedy figure if we took the other at his *literal* word, even though we have really understood him. I wouldn't want to say that deconstruction is incompatible with hermeneutics, rather the reverse. All of us rely firmly on hermeneutics, as soon as we open our mouths to speak.

JC: What role does the concept of intersubjectivity play in hermeneutics?

H-GG: If we describe conversation as an intersubjective "play" with language, we are already deeply immersed in the language of metaphysics. This immersion is so deep that we no longer believe ourselves able to say what we mean by a "conversation" without the concept of the "subject." The term *intersubjective* has become fashionable ever since the beginning of our century. At that time, [Martin] Buber, [Theodor] Haecker, and others, stimulated by Kierkegaard, began the critique of transcendental idealism. With Husserl, we can understand how he arrives at a concept like "intersubjectivity" because he is determined to remain in the Cartesian sphere of subjectivity. That leads to Husserl's tireless phenomenological investigations which now fill three thick volumes. It also leads to the utterly absurd consequence that we first intend the other as an object of perception constituted by aspects, etc., and then in a higher-level act, confer on this other the character of a "subject" through transcendental empathy. We can admire the consistency with which Husserl holds fast to the primacy of his approach. However, we notice that the narrowness and one-sidedness of the ontology of presence cannot be avoided by such an approach.

RK: Was Heidegger captive to a similar one-sidedness?

H-GG: In my opinion, Heidegger did not succeed in jumping over Husserl's shadow with his concept of *"Mitsein"* (being-with) in *Being and Time.* Heidegger's analyses were so pioneering because he disclosed the hermeneutic structure of *Dasein* and explored the possibility of *"Mitsein."* However, he diminished the truth of "conversation" when he got lost in the critique of idle talk *(Gerede).* I don't say this merely to criticize, but rather to reveal the flaws whereby Heidegger's attempt to connect with Husserl by deploying a transcendental framework in *Being and Time* led to a dead-end. The absence of the projected second volume of *Being and Time* is evidence of this dead-end. I would also characterize Habermas's "ideal-speech situation" in the same way. It is an "ideal-type" construction which collapses under the burden of what Habermas seeks to build on it. He attacks rhetoric as a means of illegitimate and forced persuasion. Such a view indicates the narrowness of a life-world that seems like a "detention pending trial," wherein an ongoing interrogation is artificially isolated and scientifically analyzed. Sometimes it seems the same with Ricœur, whose sensitive richness and attention to theoretical differences I certainly admire, in particular his teaching on metaphor. In a poem, it has been rightly said, every word is a metaphor. But I miss the fundamental ground of rhetoric—the art of wanting to convince others of what we are already convinced.

RK: In your opinion, what precise role does the language of rhetoric and metaphor play in hermeneutics?

H-GG: If we want to clarify the role of language in hermeneutics, we discover that Greek already gives us some indication—because it doesn't even have a specific word for *language!* That shows how much language is unconscious of itself. But that doesn't mean that it remains entirely hidden and concealed. Quite the opposite! Language is wherever it is, where conversation takes place. It is so omnipresent that nothing else is really present, not the speaker and not the one spoken to. In the hermeneutic analysis of *Truth and Method,* I hit upon the insight that language isn't exclusively a matter of spoken expression. The diversity of languages does not present the problem here. Language as a hermeneutic phenomenon is not an example among different languages. I have used the artificial expression *linguisticality (Sprachlichkeit)* to refer to interior speech. This concept is developed from the Stoics, and differs especially from the *"logos prophorikos,"* in that it is in no way found in any *one* of the many spoken languages. *Sprachlichkeit* rather indicates the inexpressible capacity that underlies and is actualized in all particular linguistic expression. From my studies of Augustine I have drawn analyses of the process-character of internal speech, analyses which show how a happening-of-being manifests itself for him in the mystery of the Trinity, for which presence *(Präsenz)* or other models of time are not at all appropriate.

Even the "while" or "duration," with which Bergson contrives to avoid the time of the moment, is admittedly not yet radical enough to successfully stand against the ontology of substance and presence. Neither is the concept of communication adequate for that purpose, because here, the particularity of *"Sprachlichkeit"* is not articulated along with it. Infectious laughter is perhaps one of the strongest forms of communication between human beings, but that is really not language, and even less *écriture.* Laughter also has nothing of the inner language which is put into words in the hundreds of different languages of mankind.

Hermeneutics and Politics

RK: What are the ethical and political implications of your hermeneutics? Is there a conservative agenda, as some suggest, behind your respect for tradition?

H-GG: When such questions are put to me, I always sense an expectation that I must leave unfulfilled. Even if one grants me that hermeneutics is not a method, in our thinking the schema of means-and-ends takes such priority that the question of what hermeneutics actually is *meant for* always intrudes. One would at least like to be told whether or not it overlaps with practical philosophy, thereby legitimating itself by its usefulness.

But even the idea of practical philosophy resonates strongly with the misunderstanding of modern utilitarianism. A practical philosophy is, of course, supposed to be practical, applicable like an instruction manual. In reality, that is a misreading of the concepts of "praxis" and "practical." These Greek ideas have no such petty connotation. One realizes particularly in this concept of "praxis" how, in much the same way, the concept of substance in Aristotle's ontology becomes misleading through its modern historical development.

RK: What precisely do you understand as "praxis" in this context?

H-GG: Praxis is not an "action" *(Handeln)* — a word which is very often incorrectly substituted for it in German. The concept of action *(Handeln)* is imbued with voluntarism and resonates with the calculations of profit and cost; it has no place really in the linguistic field of praxis. Praxis is a self-comportment, and we apply the word in entirely different domains: for example, the medical praxis of a doctor does not take place in his private apartment. And even when one uses the expression *behaving (sich-verhalten)* for praxis, the concept of *action (Handeln)* is still very much part of it. One is hardly able to overhear or discern that in all *behaving (sich-verhalten)*, there is also tucked away a *containing-oneself (an-sichhalten)*; or even a *holding-oneself-back (sich-zurückhalten)* and a *finding-oneself (sich-befinden)*. We ought to remember that the standard phrase concluding a letter in Greek was *"eu prattein,"* which in German would be *"Lass es dir gut gehen"* ("Let it go well with you"). In many regions in Germany, one still says *"machs gut"* ("do good"), without asking oneself what it actually is that one will or should do.

It is helpful to remember this lexical domain if we want to understand practical philosophy. We mustn't understand it as applied science, for example; something like applied mathematics that differs from pure mathematics. Obviously, in the expression *practical philosophy*, we have before us a peculiar creation of Aristotle. In its fine usual sense, philosophy is theory; indeed, it is the embodiment of a theoretical comportment. And now Aristotle asserts that there is also a "practical philosophy." We here find ourselves right in the middle of hermeneutic philosophy in our own day, and this demands something decisive from the return to Aristotle's concepts. This concerns the difference between theoretical and practical knowledge: the difference between the wisdom of the knower and the wakefulness of one who acts. The Aristotelian expression for the latter is *"phronēsis."*

By the way, this question presents itself independently of the linguistic observations we are making. The old Socratic pseudo-solution — that virtue is knowledge and lack of virtue is ignorance — tries to steer clear of the entire problem. Practical philosophy, which speaks of virtue, would then be akin to theoretical philosophy that speaks of nature. There is something unsatisfactory about that. Should one just talk about virtue in the same way that one speaks about mere occurrences? Should one neither lead nor educate towards virtue? Can the difference between the theoretical knowledge of celestial phenomena, on the one hand, and the foundations established in education, on the other hand, be dispensed with so easily? It becomes apparent that such a fusion of theoretical and practical philosophy is impossible, when one acknowledges that virtue or goodness (or whatever one calls it) has a political and social component. Practical philosophy doesn't just apply to the individual who acts in society: it applies to society itself, which can be constituted in its political condition for better or worse, and which can act for better or worse. Ethics and politics are both practical philosophies in their Greek genesis.

JC: But what is philosophical ethics, and what is political science in our own day?

H-GG: To approach this question we have to return once again to Aristotle, the founder of practical philosophy. At the beginning of the *Nicomachean Ethics*, Aristotle considers practical philosophy in relation to both ethics and politics. The two are not independent of each other. Ethics concerns the life of the individual in society, while politics, by comparison, concerns the proper constitution of society itself. For both, there is only one good: the life-happiness of the individual as well as the polis. However, the highest aim of politics is linked with the well-being of the individual. Politics concerns the legal regulation of our life-in-community *(Zusammenleben)* that in Greek was called "legislation," and it also includes the education of the young. Therein lies the difficult question: What does philosophy as philosophy have in both instances for its legitimation?

Obviously, it's not always a case of purely theoretical interests, just rather the highest practical ideal of human happiness. Just as the individual, who in every case must make his or her choice in a unique situation, wishes to serve this highest goal, the more holds true for the political office-holder in the polis. Expertise will be indispensable for both, what the Greeks called *"epistēmē"* or *"technē."* In his dialogue *The Statesman*, Plato makes a specific distinction between that which can be taken possession of with precise measurement and that which has its own measures within itself—for instance, the virtue of moderation. And he declares both necessary for politics. But the individual, like the politician, must also look towards the highest aim of all praxis— and this "looking" the Greeks called *"noos."* Both must internalize this highest goal. Useless beauty has priority over usefulness, unless necessity compels an insistence upon the useful.

RK: Is it misguided to look to philosophy for guidance in moral and political life?

H-GG: Philosophy itself is in no position to give an actual foundation for virtue or duty. That is what people have mistakenly sought in the Kantian approach to duty-ethics in Kant's *Foundations of the Metaphysics of Morals*. Philosophy can't give the foundation of right action for either the individual or society; rather, it helps keep us on course in the direction of the good (to which one is already open) and seeks to safeguard us from error. That is all. And it is already a great deal. This is the autonomy which Kant defends. One doesn't give oneself the law, but rather accepts the law, so that one will not sneak by it.

RK: Is hermeneutics "neutral" then?

H-GG: It is senseless to want to designate any political orientation to hermeneutics. Admittedly, a certain expertise may be required to comment concretely on the situation of the individual as well as of society as a whole. But in every case we must remember to keep in mind the well-being of the individual and the well-being of the whole. This is true especially in democracy, whose essential features Aristotle was the first to outline. We have political parties, all of which claim to have the correct proposals for ordering social matters. Naturally, this holds true for every political aberration as well, whose cause lies in a lack of expertise that oversimplifies utopian ways of thinking. All of us, as individuals and citizens, are capable of such reductionist thinking, and this lack of expertise makes itself felt through all judgments in individual and political life. Above all, this tendency to oversimplify means that every human being has his weaknesses. Our political world has its own problems. Even though a democracy need not be defined as a parliamentary democracy, it's still true that the formation of parties which repudiate the very foundation of political constitutions are not permitted. Whether one is more conservative or more innovative has nothing to do with it. Thus, we can already recognize, in the case of Heidegger, the portents of the terribly wrong decision of 1933, as well as a certain one-sidedness in his earlier development and thought. However, this doesn't at all affect the basic insight we owe him—that human *Dasein*, in all its domains, possesses a hermeneutic structure. Heidegger's error of political judgment regarding the "Being" of the Führer, or his own unsuitability for politics, is not due to his characterization of the hermeneutic structure of *Dasein* as understanding itself and things.

RK: Hermeneutics is not just a matter of interpreting texts, therefore?

H-GG: For me hermeneutics is more than the interpretation of texts. Hermeneutics is not only a Being-towards-text. Whoever thinks this annihilates the decisive step of Husserl and Heidegger that led to the life-world. One can only recommend today a reading of the chapters of Aristotle's *Politics*. What was at that time to be criticized is still to be criticized today: namely, the priority of the useful vis-á-vis the beautiful.

RK: Are you suggesting that hermeneutic philosophy can guide or direct us from interpretation to social commitment?

H-GG: There is a natural demand latent in that question: What does hermeneutics as philosophy have to offer for the solution of our problems today or in the future? I don't believe that we would ask this question of theologians or prophets. We know that worldly wisdom is not to be gotten from them. Why expect advice and instruction from philosophers in such a situation? Surely, it must have something to do with our reflections on the vital problems of human *Dasein;* for example, on beginning and end, birth and death, evil and good, right and wrong. However, all of these milestones lie on a path that doesn't lead to a goal that can be reached quickly. We can't expect that the mere power of thought, concentration, and dedication to thinking can become another kind of trailblazing.

My attempt to dampen this expectation, by specifically dealing with the paradox of practical philosophy, will hardly reach human beings who are oppressed by the worries of daily existence. But that is precisely what is so hard for human beings to grasp: that we all stand in such complicated life-circumstances that nobody is in a position to work out clear, final goals that are agreeable to everyone. According to Socrates, the question of the good is actually unanswerable; and yet for everyone a knowledge of the good is indispensable if we are to remain directed toward the future in what we do and don't do. We must take the Socratic question seriously. We know then that we ourselves are responsible for our actions. We have to admit that for a long time we've been ready to overestimate the capabilities of experts in this world. But the true expert knows the limits of his competence. Why do we expect the philosopher not to recognize the boundaries of his competence? That is the true situation. I have only this answer: like everyone else, we philosophers are not excused from the question of the good, nor do we have privileged access to it. We are not experts. Everyone must pose this question for himself.

Even the conscientious expert will hesitate and carefully maintain his limits when giving advice, so that the road towards "the good" won't be blocked by his advice. These are the inevitable features of our complicated delegation of knowledge to the expert, which apply to experts in politics as well. And yet it is not much different in every stage of human social development. We are never exempt from the question of whether we can justify what we do or don't do—before ourselves or before God. The issue of human weakness can't be ignored, and we should, moreover, remain aware of the limits of our ever attaining mastery in our present and future existence. Hermeneutics insists that we recognize these limits, both in general and in particular cases. Only then can a real coexistence of cultures and societies on this planet become possible. Only then can we discover solidarity through the exchange of our limited experiences. Hermeneutics isn't the invention of any particular thinker; it names what we all have known since human beings have organized their lives together. At best, philosophy has eased some of the burdens on us through its expertise.

Hermeneutics and Science

RK: Is hostility towards science implicit in your confrontation between truth and method, as it is in Heidegger?

H-GG: Let's change the formulation of the question a bit. It's not a case of a friendly or hostile relationship with science. This doesn't apply in the least to Heidegger. In his "Examen Rigorosum" [Rigorous Examination] Heidegger elected to take mathematics and physics as examination subjects, in addition to philosophy. He did not confine his examinations to the historical sciences, for example, church history or religious scholarship, in which he was certainly competent. Philosophy is not concerned with the methods of science: it is concerned with the foundations of all science and all other experience. Hermeneutic philosophy doesn't exclude the sciences; therefore, it frees us from a superficial conception of subjective and objective in order to properly grasp the foundations of science.

RK: Does this entail a reorientation of our understanding of truth?

H-GG: It certainly requires an enlargement of our concept of "truth," reaching beyond the ideal of precision in the quantitative sciences, an ideal which the natural sciences cannot completely fulfill. In the so-called human sciences *(Geisteswissenschaften)*, one operates for the most part in a sphere different from exactness. One is not in the domain of precise measurement, but rather in the domain of things that have measures in themselves, such as the virtues of moderation, courage, etc. Fundamentally, this problem concerns the relationship between rules and regulations. With his emphasis on judgment, Kant correctly said that for the correct application of rules, there is not just another rule. One cannot learn judgment as if it were a science made up of true propositions. One must practice it and develop it out of one's own experience.

RK: How can one reconcile the domains of understanding *(Verstehen)* and explanation *(Erklärung)*?

H-GG: The much-discussed opposition of understanding and explanation lags far behind the universality of hermeneutic experience. It is understood as an opposition of a scientific-theoretical kind. The debate of the nineteenth century in Germany was totally dominated by this question. "Value philosophy" was the theoretical expression of an alternate approach. As I have shown, however, judgment isn't a question of the correctness of rules, but rather a question of the appropriate application or non-application of rules. And so hermeneutics is that aspect of philosophy that includes the universal expanse of all problems of application, as well as of values and therefore of all technology. It can itself have no criteria. Take the example of a brain transplant or genetic cultivation of a robot. As these phenomena emerge, the first reaction of the public is strong and disturbed, pointing to a dimension that neither science as such, nor value philosophy, nor so-called ethics could claim for themselves.

This may all sound general, especially when conversational dialogue is here again placed in the foreground, in contrast to our educational institutions and universities where the fundamental style of teaching is the lecture. Indeed, it is an astounding atavism that we still use the lecture as a method of teaching, since it is based on the mere transmission of a general body of recognized knowledge. Even Kant had to give his lectures based on previously written textbooks in philosophy, and from these he had to work out his own revolutionary way of thinking. Today the universities can no longer support such a one-sided transmission of an unquestioned canon. Nor can the professors of philosophy.

However, we can demand what Kant demanded: to teach thinking, instead of passing on doctrine. This is what is called "ability" *(Können):* to practice an ability-to-question and an ability-to-think. Naturally, one uses this in all sciences, but these sciences have only developed their methods with it. Are there corresponding rules and customs in the praxis of life? We return once again to the fact that we need judgment in science as well as in the life-world.

Hermeneutics and Theology

RK: Is the hermeneutic question of Being compatible with the question of God?

H-GG: That sounds too much like a scientific-theoretical thematic! However, in formulating the question this way, we thereby underestimate both philosophy and theology. On the one hand, philosophy may have a universal hermeneutic basis, but it also deals with other problems. We likewise underestimate theology by treating theology as identical with religion. This is simply not the case. We can think of the special place of so-called Greek orthodoxy within Christianity which, despite its name, involved no theology at all, but rather the practical care and worship of the soul and its unassailable status in human life. However, we cannot ignore the fact that the idea of ecumenism in the present world situation concerns not only the Christian world, but the other great world religions as well, or perhaps even religious experiences that have almost no written tradition at all

We can, of course, ask ourselves how philosophy stands vis-á-vis religion. Heidegger's well-known methodological verdict—that there cannot be a Christian philosophy because philosophy in the methodical sense is atheistic—obviously accentuates the difference between philosophy and theology. We might ask whether there can be "theology" in other world religions or whether this is a specific development of the West. As we know, historically speaking, science itself has been a phenomenon of Western civilization.

It is incorrect, however, to suggest a special affinity for hermeneutics with the theology of nineteenth-century Germany and its exponent, Schleiermacher. The whole history of theology speaks against it, in particular the pedagogical tradition of the Catholic Church. Unlike the Reformation, Catholicism insisted there be something like a philosophical theology, that is, a science based on reason. The question of God had to be open to examination by everyone, without relying on revelation or faith. We can say, however, that with the advance of the Enlightenment in the modern era, the tension between philosophy and religion in the face of Luther's reformationist "By faith alone" came into sharpened conflict with the scientific mind. In earlier centuries, a universal science based on reason contained the concept of all science. In this respect, it is naturally true that with the rising self-consciousness of the Age of Science, the appeal to absolute faith turned into a hermeneutic mysticism. The modern Enlightenment thinker speaks then of *"sacrificium intellectus"*; and on the other side, the Christian speaks of the paradox of faith, or about how the limits of understanding faith become manifest to the believer.

Certainly, we can ask if the question of God, which belongs to theology, has grown together with the philosophical question of Being. Heidegger's dictum that a Christian philosophy is absurd is directed against such harmonizations. We must, after all, ask if the question of Being, which Parmenides was the first to ask, isn't closely related to all the wonders of *Dasein,* and whether it leads to Leibniz's foundational question: "Why is there something rather than nothing?" We call that the basic question of metaphysics. But is the "religious" thought of the Creation and the Creator included in this question? Would that not include the Greek concept of Being which has dominated both Greek philosophy, and the thought of the Christian Middle Ages? In the church history of the West, this has issued in a lasting debate with Platonic heresies. On the other hand, it applies equally to the Gnostic heresies which maintained that, in the end, human reason needed no divine revelation but would unite the self with the One.

The Future of Hermeneutics

RK: What do you see as the future of hermeneutics?

H-GG: When we ask about the future of hermeneutics we mean not only its own internal process, but also the claim that in a world organized more and more through regulation, an awareness of the limits of our world-system is emerging. It is not easy to imagine a future in which the robot thrives supreme. We see ourselves referring back to the fact that our mother tongue is an inviolable endowment for the course of our lives. The German word *(Muttersprache)* reminds us of the mother and, by extension, thereby of birth. At the same time, it reminds us of the way human life articulates itself in different language communities and how secondary all interlingual possibilities of understanding between speech communities are. This is essentially the problem of translation, of its desirability and its questionability.

We cannot blind ourselves to the fact that the peaceful coexistence of human beings on this earth depends, to a large extent, on the cultivation of interlingual exchanges between nations. The breathtaking expansion of the world economy that today embraces humanity cannot deceive us about the fact that such a competitive economy, in which human capacities are developed, simultaneously creates new controversies and contains the temptation to resort to violence. Nevertheless, we cannot easily convince ourselves that the elementary drives of will-to-power that permeate everything should have the last word. With due respect to economic competition and performance, to the self-discipline of human beings and to their energy for work, it seems inevitable that there will always be some object of conflict, if only because nobody can possess it without others claiming a share in it too.

RK: So what does this augur for the future in practical terms?

H-GG: Certainly, humanity today is still far removed from a unified ideal of world culture in which all human beings could have a part. Such an ideal would encompass a higher moral value, insofar as more human beings could gain a share in it. Sometimes it seems as if the world of music might announce such a world culture beyond all differences of language and culture. But then we remember and know the kind of incomparable intimacy possessed for its part by the mother tongue, nativeness, the care of ancestral memory, and all the other unconscious characteristics that form us from an early age. These are traditions in which all human beings stand and from which we look forward. It strikes me as a bit ridiculous to regard these traditions and formative experiences—which are forms of self-understanding for human beings—as atavisms to be overcome. Hermeneutics as philosophy demands a special awareness of these differences and their reconciliation as a task which has founded community among humans since time immemorial. And in any conceivable future it must continue to do the same. Can we really believe that a "correct speech" or analytically linguistic precision could replace the mother tongue and her world-disclosing power? We must think with language, not about it or against it.

Paris-Heidelberg, 1994

This exchange between Hans-Georg Gadamer, John Cleary and Richard Kearney took place in 1994 and was translated by Mara Rainwater.

Jean-François Lyotard
What Is Just?

RK: Today you are seen as the first philosopher of the postmodern condition. Yet one of your earliest works was entitled La phénoménologie [Phenomenology] (1954). How would you describe the development of your own thinking—from phenomenology to postmodernism? Is there a continuity between the two?

J-FL: *La phénoménologie* was a homage to the thought of Merleau-Ponty: a meditation on the body, on sensible experience and, therefore—in contradistinction to Hegel, Husserl, [John-Paul] Sartre—on the "aesthetic" dimension which unfolds beneath the phenomena of consciousness. I was also reading at this time what was available of Heidegger's work. The little book on phenomenology was motivated by a concern to address the absence in Marxism of any genuine thinking about ideology. I felt it was important to establish how the possibility, and success, of the revolution depended on the consciousness that workers could and should have of their situation and desire. The work done by both Tran Duc Thao and Claude Lefort in this direction was very useful. I was then a committed member of the *socialisme on barbarie* project (from 1952 to 1966), whose main objects of critique were dogmatic Marxism, Stalinist politics, the class structure of Soviet society, the inconsistencies of the Trotskyist position, and postwar capitalism (quite the opposite of "late" or declining capitalism). Our practical activities included cooperating with workers, wage earners, and students with a view to establishing self-management groups. I left this project in 1966 when I realized that the basis of both our practice and theory was lacking—the alternative figure of the proletariat (Marx's "spectre") as a laboring class conscious of its goals. I only began to formulate the idea of the "postmodern" in the late 1970s, after a long detour. The term, purposefully ambiguous, was borrowed from American criticism and Ihab Hassan. I used it to name the transformation of bourgeois capitalism and its contradictions into a global "system" ruling, for better or worse, its imbalances (including those in the "ideological" field, henceforth entitled "cultural") with the help of growth due to techno-scientific means. Several things were becoming clear: that a new dominant class—the managers—was replacing the private owners without capital, that the workforce was no longer of the nineteenth-century kind, that the redistribution of surplus value was done in a completely different way, and that a structural level of unemployment was emerging, even though we were still in a period of full employment. In these changing circumstances it was necessary to review radically the nature of history and politics.

RK: Given the multiple definitions of postmodernism which circulate in contemporary debate, do you believe your initial formulation of this term—in *The Postmodern Condition* and *The Postmodern Explained*—have been misinterpreted or altered? Could you describe the basic meaning of "postmodern" as something more than a historical period?

J-FL: There have been many misunderstandings indeed, including my own. The notion of periodization is one of them—a typically modern mania. The essential features of the postmodern as it manifests itself today seem to me numerous. They include the generalization of the constraint of exchangeability (the old "exchange value" of Marx) which traditionally weighs on the objects and "services" of capitalism, and its extension to include hitherto unexploited objects and activities: opinions, feelings, cultural pleasures, leisure, disease and death, sexuality, and so on. (Totalitarian systems took the lead here in a terrifying fashion and the message was heard and duly corrected.) One might also mention the constraint of "complexification" with respect to the relations of work, consummation, and communication, whose effect is to "optimize" the performance of the system; the concomitant collapse of traditional values (labor, disinterested knowledge, virtue, the sense of life-debt)—the crisis of education in all the developed countries is a direct witness to this collapse. Then there are the current phenomena of latent nihilism (in Nietzsche's "passive" sense) and "discontent" (in Freud's sense), not to mention chronic anxiety due to absence of symbols—which camouflage themselves as individualism, cynicism, the cult of play, the almost compulsory sense of celebratory conviviality, the obsession with participation and interaction, the return to roots. This "postmodern" situation discloses nothing new. On the contrary, in the name of the fulfillment of liberties, the Western will-to-knowledge (and by extension doubt) and will-to-power (and by extension mastery) has "secreted" *(secréte)* nihilism from its beginnings: death of the gods, death of God, death of man. The "system" functions simply as a very improbable type of organization—the living organism, and subsequently the human being and the brain, already functioned in this way—which draws the energy it needs in the energetic chaos which formerly went by the name of *nature* or *cosmos* (the immense fallout from an enigmatic explosion). But in response to your question, I would situate the "basic meaning" of the postmodern above all in the way the Western will discovers the "nothingness" *(néant)* of its objects and projects, thereby finding itself inhabited by something which it neither comprehends nor masters. Some "thing" crypted in itself, which resists us. Its name is irrelevant. It is "unnameable" because too rapidly named.

RK: How then can we say anything about it? What evidence do we have of its existence? How does "it" show itself?

J-FL: All the thinkers, writers, and artists of the West, including the great "rationalists," stumbled upon this thing, sought to name it, realized its inexpungeability, and recognized that no odyssey, no *grand narrative* could contain it.

RK: This brings us, of course, to your famous critique of the "grand narratives" of the Western tradition (Marxism, Judeo-Christianity, Enlightenment rationalism, etc.). But is it possible, or even desirable, to do away with every kind of narrative model? Is there a way in which *des petits récits* might serve an ethical-political task? Is the commitment to a pluralistic paradigm of little narratives compatible, for example, with a basic defense of a charter of universal rights? What I'm really asking is: Is it possible to avoid relativism in order to save what is best in the Enlightenment fidelity to shared human values that are non-culture-specific? In short, is it possible to reconcile your defense of the singularity of the event with a certain minimal universality of rights and duties—that is, of justice?

J-FL: I protest, first, against the expression *Judeo-Christian.* The hyphen signals the annexation of the Torah to the Good News of the Incarnation. This is a traditional usage, I know. But it is nevertheless unjust in the strongest sense of the term; and after the Shoah, it represents an insult to the "people" who were victims of extermination (when one recalls the role of Vatican politics at the time). That said, I do not know whether the defense of universal valid human rights is "compatible," as you say, with a proper attention to the event in its opacity (as mentioned above in relation to "the thing"). To tell the truth, this question of compatibility doesn't really bother me, being neither Leibnizean nor Hegelian. On the one hand, it is evident that rights must be defended by every citizen against the "cynical" effects of the efficiency demands of the system; and on the other hand, we are indebted to the "thing" irremediably. Why seek to reconcile these? That kind of fraternization is always to be feared.

RK: Why? Can you give me an example?

J-FL: A notorious example: Heidegger, the author of *Sein und Zeit,* construing the politics of *Mein Kampf* as pretext for the manifestation of Dasein's dread.

RK: Are you saying that we cannot use "little narratives" in the cause of universal rights?

J-FL: I am saying that it would be futile to consider using *des petites récits.* Always and everywhere, in Tibet, the Amazon, or Livry-Gargan, they use us to tell themselves. They mock illusions of grandeur. The kitchens and stables of Shakespeare laugh at the tragedies of court, just as in Rabelais the bad boys mock the knowing and the powerful. What is little is almost invariably comic. To laugh is to acknowledge that the thing is unsayable—that its tragic dramatization is pure vanity. [Samuel] Beckett is funny in this way also. But that doesn't make up a humanist party.

RK: Does your departure from the Enlightenment and Marxist projects necessarily condemn you to "neoconservatism" as Habermas and others claim? How do you now consider the political positions you adopted during the *Socialisme ou barbarie* period?

J-FL: It is logical to accuse "postmodernism" (a term I never use to describe my work) of neoconservatism if one holds to the modern project. Reciprocally, the modernist obstinacy, could be taxed with "archeoprogressivism." I never used these kinds of terms to differentiate myself from Habermas and his disciples. This rhetoric of political tribunals had some sense when conflicts of thought were immediately transcribable into public tragedy: one was obliged to solemnly denounce the Enemy in the adversary. Habermas has obviously mistaken his epoch. I never viewed his discourse ethics as an ideology of the enemy.

RK: How would you identify the ethical and political motivation implicit in the arguments of *The Postmodern Condition,* and subsequent works such as *The Inhuman?* What are the implications of [Guillaume] Apollinaire's claim that artists and intellectuals nowadays should make themselves "inhuman"? Does this mean that postmodernism is incompatible with "humanism"?

J-FL: I only use the term *postmodernism,* let me repeat, as a label of convenience for a certain movement or school (in literary criticism, in architecture). I personally prefer the expressions *the postmodern* and *postmodernity.* I quote Apollinaire's phrase—from the *Peintres Cubistes [The Cubist Painters]* and which applies to cubism as a whole—because it states that the inhuman in us is the unknown thing *(la chose meconnue),* the only genuine resource of art, of literature, and of meditation. *Les Essais, L'Eloge de la folie, Le Neveu de Rameau:* humanism has always been inhumanism.

RK: I'm interested in the political implications of this position, particularly as outlined in your *Political Writings.* Could you elaborate on the distinction between "specific intellectual" and "organic intellectual" in this work? Does the intellectual still have a role to play in the project of emancipation? And what critical function, if any, remains for the philosopher once one has declared the death of the "modern idea of a universal subject of knowledge"? Must the postmodern intellectual limit him/herself, as you suggest, to the "resolution of questions posed to a citizen of a particular country at a particular moment"?

J-FL: The organic intellectual has a role to play in countries more or less relegated to the margins of development. Here his work is itself the proof of both his emancipation and his belonging, and the basic problem confronting these countries is emancipation without betrayal of local culture. (One would have to locate the phenomenon of fundamentalism here and its strategy of assassination.) In the privileged developed countries, by contrast—and one knows how scandalously exclusive this privilege can be—great prosecution witnesses like Voltaire, [Emile] Zola, [Antonio] Gramsci, [Max] Horkheimer, [Bertrand] Russell, no longer seem to play a role. Formerly emancipation was under threat in Europe itself, with absolutism and totalitarianism, and the work of these already famous figures was in itself a demand for liberties. Today we face a different scenario, where critical works are rarely read, sparsely distributed except when the media latch onto them and serve them to a consumer public hungry for cultural commodities. In fact, the person who speaks for liberties on radio or television doesn't need to possess an *"oeuvre"*; it is sufficient that his/her eloquence and "presence" on the platform are better (more effective and credible) than those of other media professionals or even than other thinkers, writers, or artists. The only exceptions here are the scientists, and that by reason of the fact that the system idolizes techno-scientific performances.

RK: You speak in "Tomb of the Intellectual" of a "new responsibility" which renders intellectuals impossible — a "responsibility to distinguish intelligence from the paranoia that gave rise to 'modernity'" What do you mean by this "paranoia"? And how are we to differentiate between the new responsibility of postmodern "intelligence" and the irresponsibility of irrationalism?

J-FL: Some rationalism is the paranoia of discourse; I will say everything, know everything, possess everything, be everything. Nothing will escape the concept. On the other hand, literature must plead guilty because it is *authorized* by nothing, as Georges Bataille said (following Kafka). The "thing" that demands writing or art has no *right* to demand it. This "irresponsibility" is the greatest responsibility, that of remaining attentive to an Other, who is neither an interlocutor nor a party to contractual closure. It is essential to guard over this "secret existence," as Nina Berberova called it, to protect it against the *indiscretion* of the system which wants to see and know everything, have an answer for everything, exchange everything. We need to reread Orwell.

RK: What are the implications of your postmodern idea of "inhumanity" for our understanding of the "social bond"? Do you think traditional concepts of nation, state, and civil society are adequate to the analysis of these implications? Have universalist notions of social progress been altered by the transition to postmodernity?

J-FL: The implosion of the big totalitarian regimes engendered by the modern dream provokes a nostalgia for "natural" communities, defined by blood, land, language, custom. Fidelity to the demos takes priority here over respect for the republican ideal. The latter is nonetheless the only veneer of legitimacy for the system to require all countries in the world to remain open to the free circulation of goods, services, and communications. It is in fact essential for the republic to become universal. In its name, the "market" is permitted to assume world proportions. That is why, today, the privilege of sovereignty which nation states enjoyed for several centuries (at most), appears an obstacle to the furtherance of development in every domain: multinational transactions, immigrant populations, international security. . . . It may even be the case, despite appearances, that the unification of Europe is more easily achievable through the federation of "natural communities" ("regions" like Bavaria, Scotland, Flanders, Catalonia, etc.) than through sovereign states—with all the risks attendant upon the dominance of the *demos* in each of these communities.

RK: This scenario would seem to support your suggestion that the "modern" category of "universal thinker" will be replaced by the "symptomatologist" who responds to singular phenomena of irreducible difference *(le différend)*. But would this not imply the end of philosophy as an academic discipline? What do you believe is the function now of philosophy and the university, generally?

J-FL: Philosophy, we should remember, has only recently—1811, Berlin—been recognized as an academic discipline. The ancients and the medievals didn't teach philosophy, they taught how to philosophize. It was a question of "learning" rather than "teaching." To learn to find one's way in thinking, as Kant put it. Or to borrow Wittgenstein's formula—"I no longer know where I am" is the basic position of philosophical questioning. To philosophize is not to produce useful servants of the community, as Kant well knew, which is why philosophy faculties never have the same prestige as faculties of medicine, law, economics (not to mention the exact sciences). The philosopher always has a fundamental difficulty in presenting himself as an expert. This is not a recent phenomenon; in fact, it goes back to Socrates's struggle with the "experts." One could tolerate the presence (inexpensive) in pedagogical institutions of an *inexpert* discipline for as long as this aimed at forming "enlightened citizens," capable of coping with complex or unprecedented conjunctures. The contemporary system aims at forming the experts it requires. The capacity to meditate is not much use to it; even less so when the system has managed to produce more sophisticated automatons than digital computers. A considerable part of the academic discipline of philosophy is already geared to research (direct or indirect) into "artificial" languages. And an inevitable consequence of this is that those who continue to think about the unexploitable "thing" find themselves half inside the institution, half out. I think, I hope, that philosophy will manage to limp along like this for a long time, in spite of its growing loss of credibility (which also affords some prestige).

RK: Much of your work has focused on the relationship between aesthetics and politics. Why has the notion of the "sublime," particularly as enunciated by Kant in the Third Critique, come to occupy such a pivotal position in your thinking on this relationship?

J-FL: What, from Kant to [Theodor W.] Adorno, has often been called the "aesthetic" is that region where rational thinking encounters something in itself which violently resists it: this is "creation," the way of making that is art, the sentiment of the absolute. Kant elaborates on the latter in his *Analytic of the Sublime.* I believe we find there a form of recollection (*anamnesis* conducted in "critical" terms) of the relation of all thought—meditative, literary, pictural, musical—to the unknown thing which inhabits such thought. This relation is necessarily one of a *differend* internal to thought, at once capable and incapable of the absolute—"sentiment of spirit," not of nature, like the taste of the beautiful. Kant repeats the words: *Widerstreit, Widerstand, Unangemessenheit, differend,* resistance, incommensurability—the same terms used by [Vincent] Van Gogh, [James] Joyce, [Arnold] Schöenberg, [Søren] Kierkegaard, or Beckett (I cite at random) to signify the ordeal undergone by thought when it opens itself to desire for the absolute. One could even say that such thought engenders "symptoms." This is so for most of us, for whom the desire is no less pressing than for the writers and artists cited. But the enigma of the "aesthetic" is that they make of this *angoisse* a work.

RK: Given your readings of Kant, Heidegger, Adorno, and Derrida, would you be inclined to the view that the thinker/symptomatologist should take his/her lead more from art and literature than from the more traditional discourses of epistemology and ontology?

J-FL: I think so. But I also believe that if there is an ontology—perhaps negative—it would be found on the side of art and literature. Why? Because on that side, being (or nothing) is not situated or posited on principle as reference to cognitive discourse. It is not projected, or ejected, onto the place assigned to that about which one intends to speak, as in the case of the most serious epistemology. On the contrary, it is approached in a "poetically concrete" fashion, experienced and settled like something immediate to be resolved, something present but not presented. Which word here, which color there, which sound or melodic form? How can we *know?* It is not a matter of knowledge. Being (or nothing) doesn't wait at the door you identify. It lives in you, already waiting for whatever idiom you offer it to reside in momentarily.

RK: When you contrast "reading" to "theory" (or interpretation), do you believe this better enables us to engage in aesthetic and ethical judgment? If we abandon "meaning" out of fidelity to the irreducible singularity of the event, are we not eliminating the very basis of a judgment that could be shared by others in a socially committed way? How is your position compatible with solidarity—or what Hannah Arendt referred to (again in relation to Kant) as "representative thinking," which she believes is an indispensable tool for ethical judgment?

J-FL: Theory is a system of propositions formulated in explicitly defined terms according to a determined syntax. These propositions are supposed to explain all the phenomena which emerge in the field of reference to which the theory applies. (I am not discussing here the serious objections leveled against this axiomatic model by intuitionism or by the theorem of nonclosure of discursive systems.) No aesthetic or ethical judgment could ever satisfy the terms of this system. It is often a "passionate" business, often "accomplishing" an unconscious desire, as Freud said. And it is always dangerous. The task is to render such judgment "pure," free of interest, free of ends (conceptualized or not), free of all that subordinates it to something other than the appreciation of the just and the beautiful. It is at the price of such ascesis that judgment of this kind can claim to be shared with others. Everyone tries to argue, for or against, but in truth, one can only rely on the capacity of others to carry out for themselves the same kind of ascesis or "destitution" *(dénuement)*. Arendt unscrupulously transfers Kant's aesthetic category of *sensus communis* to the order of sociality and interpersonal solidarity, as if it were some kind of "shared feeling." But in Kant the *sensus communis* is laboriously deduced, in the name of a transcendental affinity between diverse faculties of thought, on the basis of the "experience" of a happiness which an "object" can unexpectedly procure. Moreover, Arendt seems to ignore the case—for me even more significant—where thinking profits not from its affinity but its disaffinity or dissent *(dissentiment)* from itself; this is the case of the sublime, which also demands to be shared by all. As regards *ethical* decisions, if it had to authorize itself by invoking theories of Goodness or Justice, it would forfeit its ethical character forthwith. Why? Because it would lose all responsibility for what it decides by submitting itself to the authority of theory. Decisions are ethical precisely when they are not authorized by a system (intelligible or otherwise), when they take upon themselves the responsibility for their "authority." An SS torturer is not ignoble because Miler's "theory" was false, but because he refuses his own responsibility and believes himself justified by obedience. Arendt refers to this as the "banality of evil"—the banalization of responsibility by "necessity." Necessity here is poverty, but it is also theory which is the poverty of morality.

RK: If existing politics is defined as a totalitarian model of Grand Narratives, is it ever possible to move from an ethics of the *différend* back to a politics of communal action? Do you think that hermeneutics, structuralism, and critical theory are necessarily condemned to totalizing paradigms of Grand Narrative? Is there a dialogue possible between these philosophical methods and your own?

J-FL: Such a dialogue is always possible. But the trust one places in dialogue is a hermeneutic prejudice. Can you imagine Antonin Artaud dialoguing with Bill Clinton? Dialogue is an ordinary passion. The true—the rapport with the real (with the thing)—escapes dialogue. My philosophical colleagues haven't read Freud. If they had, they'd have at least learnt that dialogue is shot through with unconscious demands, fed on unruly transfers and countertransfers. And they would have learned that a controlled transfer, which is the most difficult of all in relation to the other, has nothing to do with "dialogue." That said, there is nothing against a politics of common action, and we should lend ourselves to it, as long as we attribute to it a healthy *(salubre)* rather than salvific *(salutaire)* value. It is the minimum commitment to safeguarding elementary rights of humanity as it is.

RK: Do your claims for the "irrepresentable" and "incommensurable" not confine you to an endlessly deconstructive practice and thus prevent you from advancing to a rationally coherent model of the just and the good? How would you situate your own thinking here vis-à-vis Derrida or Levinas?

J-FL: I repeat: there is no "rationally coherent model" of justice and injustice. Such a model is the dream of the system, which someone like [John] Rawls proposes to realize innocently. Look at history, at least it has the force of nihilism: abortion, divorce, homosexuality, corporal punishment (guilt itself), child education, old age, death of course, but also birth, hospital care and hospitality, war and murder, the body and competition (the first Olympic Games and Atlanta 1996).

The Yes and the No have managed to accommodate each of these situations one by one, and they've always managed to rationalize them. Have my colleagues ever heard that "rationality" is related to "rationalization"? This can lead to skepticism. And to this I would oppose the difficult anamnesis which decision demands: "In my soul and my unconscious . . ." As for those who think, along with Spinoza and Hegel, that there is no room for judgment, I don't think they realize that God (including the *Natura naturans*) is dead. This is something Levinas clearly signals: the risk undertaken in understanding the *other (l'Autre)* in the other *(autrui)*. That isn't an everyday occurrence like the transactions of the Wall Street stock exchange, which a good Rawlsian reads in his evening newspaper. Finally, as regards "deconstructive" thought, which I respect and which is also the thought of the undecidable, it has problems of necessity with decision and judgment *(Urteil)*. This is as it should be; and I have reason to think it is concerned by this.

RK: Is the politics of the *différend* inevitably a politics of rhetorical dispute without finality—without solution or resolution? Paralogism and paradox as the last word? Anarchism as the last stance? Dissidence as the last cry?

J-FL: There is no "politics of the *différend.*" Definitely not. The *différend* can only give rise to a terrible melancholy, a practice of meditation, a poetics.

RK: Can a postmodern politics do anything more than problematize the political as an order of representation (the junction of the political in the West since Plato) from the inside? Is there any alternative, in your view, to the prevailing system of commodification and exchange, other than a defeatist internal critique which exposes our incarceration in the labyrinth but offers no paths leading beyond it?

J-FL: I honestly don't think there is anything "beyond" the system. There is something "beneath" it, the "thing" which Freud called infantile. Any work derived from it will itself be made into "cultural merchandise": mistaken, misappropriated, *méprisé,* as of no importance. Its quality as a work—wrestling with the absolute—will perhaps be acknowledged one day by a reader, listener, or spectator.

RK: And the charge of "defeatism"?

J-FL: Defeatism, as you understand it, has always been the fact of the serious, *le fait du sérieux.* Every true thought knows itself to be defeated. Aristotle's *epistēmē* knew itself to be incapable before the *pollakis* that Being opposes to it. The same goes for Platonic idealism before the *khōra*. Relieved of doctrinaire ornament, Western thought has always been a resistance. Resistance is the way of the defeated who does not acknowledge defeat. But the claim to triumph — in the Roman sense — is the worst kind of folly. The "beyond" does not allow itself to be approached without burning you up *(vous foudroyer)*. There is nothing "romantic" in this: it is "realist," if anything — the relation to the *res,* the thing. That is why it is so severe and so humble to "learn to philosophize" or to paint, to make music or a film. The apprenticeship is without end and without solution. One can make some progress, but how could one ever be satisfied? There is no defeatism in this recurrent disappointment, except for those who hold to the fantasy of full accomplishment which the system exhibits: you shall be *fulfilled.*

RK: Finally, if the politics of the *differend* offers no project of forward advance, would you claim that your notion of the *immemorial* (as that which is irrepresentable to memory yet will not be forgotten) provides us with a critical task of anamnesis, as you call it, motivating a resistant reading of our culture? Is there a certain postmodern strategy of looking back without representation, a strategy which might offer more effective potential for change than the Enlightenment obsession with *future progress?*

J-FL: This last question would appear generous. But the alternative *backward/forward* is, in fact, extremely miserly with regard to temporality. It reduces the latter to the opposition of before and after. By the term *immemorial,* I try to express another time, where what is past maintains the presence of the past, where the *forgotten* remains *unforgettable* precisely because it is forgotten. This is what I mean by anamnesis as opposed to memory. In the time set out by concept and will, the project is only the "projection" of present consequences on the future (as in "futurology"). This kind of projection forbids the event; it prepares, preconceives, controls it in advance. This is the time of the Pentagon, the FBI, security, the time of empire. By contrast, what I call anamnesis is the opposite of genealogy, understood as a return to "origins" (always projected *backward*). Anamnesis works over the remains that are still there, present, hidden near to us. And with regard to what is not *yet* there, the still to come *(l'à-venir),* it is not a matter of the future as such (which shares the Latin root, *fuit,* meaning "it has been") but that which is still awaited with incertitude: hoped for, feared, surprising, in any case *unexpected.* It will come; but the question is: what *will* come? One can't really talk therefore of a "postmodern *strategy."*

If there is an enemy (the obscure primitiveness of the thing, indifferent perhaps, a power both threatening and cherished), that enemy is inside each one of us. The labor of "working through" is to find the idiom that is least inappropriate to it. One is guided here only by an obscure sentiment of *rightness (justesse)*. But one is never satisfied with the idiom chosen and, more often than not, the other *(autrui)* doesn't understand anything. You only have to read the letters of Van Gogh, Artaud, or Kafka, Augustine's *Confessions* or [Michel de] Montaigne's *Essays*, the life of Angelo de Foligno or the studies of Henry James — you see how the "postmodern" is not confined to a single period — to witness the kind of resistance they encountered. One must not traduce, in the sense of translate *(traduit)*, what in itself remains ciphered *(crypté)*. Instead of making the ciphered common currency, we must try to do justice to its insignificance. That is what is right. That is *justesse*.

Atlanta, Georgia, 1994

This dialogue was completed in Atlanta, Georgia, in April 1994 and translated by Richard Kearney.

George Steiner
Culture: The Price You Pay

RK: Do you believe that there is such a thing as the "whole mind of Europe"?

GS: I believe that there is in the history of Europe a very strong central tradition, which is by no means an easy one to live with. It is that of the Roman Empire meeting Christianity. Our Europe is still to an astonishing degree, after all the crises and changes, that Christian Roman Empire. Virgil was taken to be, rightly or wrongly, the prophet of this empire, and Dante the great incarnation. It is very striking that when General de Gaulle, who really used to think hard about these things, was interviewed and asked, "Are there three or four authors who are Europe to you?" he said immediately, without hesitating, "Of course, Dante, Goethe, Chateaubriand." The astonished interviewer, having fallen like an elephant into the pit, said, "What, Monsieur? No Shakespeare?" And the icy smile came, "You asked me about 'Europe.'" In that joke there is a deep Roman Christian truth.

RK: Do you believe in de Gaulle's notion of a great Europe extending from the Atlantic to the Urals, as the slogan goes?

GS: Let me answer honestly, not to make a joke, but out of deep conviction: if you draw a line from Porto in western Portugal to Leningrad, but certainly *not* Moscow, you can go to something called a coffeehouse, with newspapers from all over Europe; you can play chess, play dominoes; you can sit all day for the price of a cup of coffee or a glass of wine; talk, read, work. Moscow, which is the beginning of Asia, has never had a coffeehouse. This peculiar space—of discourse, of shared leisure, of shared exchange of disagreements—by which I mean the coffeehouse, does define a very peculiar historical space roughly from western Portugal to that line which runs south from Leningrad to Kiev and Odessa. But not east of it and not very far north.

RK: This culture of the coffeehouse you speak of would appear to be located only in certain European cities?

GS: Yes. The shared culture we have is the culture of the *cities*. I mean, it strikes me that Europe is essentially a constellation of cities which no other place on earth, no other civilization, not even the United States, has ever known. When you come to think of the Muslim cities, for instance, they are all holy shrines. They are tied to religion, with the results we know. When you come to think of American cities, they look to me, except for a few of them, like settlements, just put there on the large wide expanses, plains and so on, with no heart, with no core in them, and everybody living in the suburbs and so on, and the city just being the sky line. But when you come to Europe, what strikes you immediately is the great diversity of all the cities, each one with its historical moment of grandeur, its historical past being engraved in stone, and there to be admired. And, therefore, this is our sharing; this is what we have in common. We all of us have developed and evolved from the cities, from the Italian cities and from the Flemish cities.

RK: But couldn't one object that it is precisely the European cities that are quintessentially national—Paris as the epitome of France, London the epitome of England, Dublin the epitome of Ireland, Rome the epitome of Italy, that these are expressions of nation states, not of some pan-European culture?

GS: Paris is the epitome of a national city. But I would say that Paris is an exception. My theory is that France, and Paris as representative of France, are exceptions in Europe, and the French will be a long time becoming aware of that; they will probably have to change their ambitions and to rethink their nation, their sense of nationality, in order to adjust to the new European demands. But as soon as you mention Rome, I start smiling, because immediately I think of Venice and Milan, which are as diverse as possible, as different as possible from Rome, and which opposed themselves in the first place to Rome.

What about Florence as well? What is now happening is that cities are reemerging, as it were, taking over from nations, and entering some sort of competition; I personally think this is good, quite sound and healthy, because it's going to displace national competition, which was so cruelly messy and bloody.

RK: So what do you make of all the recent talk about a "Europe of regions," of the argument that, as we enter a more united Europe — some would even go as far as to say a United States of Europe — we need a counterbalancing movement of devolution and a decentralization from the center back to the regions? Can a unified Europe also be a Europe of differences?

GS: Differences and diversities, yes. I love every dialect; I'm passionate. I eat languages like hors d'oeuvres. I just hate uniformity. In Switzerland, where I live and teach much of the year, blindfolded, you can say within ten kilometers where you are by the accent, the smell, almost the pace of the human beings you are hearing walking by you. But careful. Much of regionalism has a cruel, dark atavism. It lives by hatred: Fleming against Walloon, the Basque situation, the Irish — the bombs in the pocket of the local, small, agricultural, fanatical movement. Regions do tend too often to define themselves not by remembering in joy, but in hatred. And I think we have to be very, very careful, lest that come back and that flame burn again.

RK: It seems to one that the Europe you champion is a Europe of high literacy, which lasted for so many hundred years, by your definition. It seems to be, in fact, a rather elitist concept of Europe: confined to the coffeehouses where intellectuals talk to each other; confined to universities, to reading rooms. But one could argue that this is not something shared by the great majority of people, and indeed, that your elite notion of culture is now coming under threat. Do you see any way in which your Europe of high literacy can be preserved today?

GS: You are quite right about the threat to this notion, and I think we could define it in very honorable terms. There is very great anger and bitterness from human beings who have felt left out, who were never elected to the club, and that anger and bitterness is increasing all around us. There is, I hope, among those of us who have been privileged, and very lucky to be in the club, some severe self-questioning: we must ask ourselves what the price for this privilege of discourse was. It did not prevent the collapse of European civilization into ultimate barbarity; it did not prevent savagery. Instead, it may even have abetted it. We are really very vulnerable. And the question is, are we going to find something better than Disneyland? Twenty-eight or thirty miles from Paris, there is a Disneyland, the second largest in the world, and it will be followed by other amusement parks. Apparently, Russia is now equally eager to get in on this. I look on this with despair. And yet you may ask me, do I have something better to offer? What am I going to do for human beings who don't think that reading Kant, or Joyce, or Goethe, is the be-all and the end-all of their lives, and who, nevertheless, want more leisure, want more elbowroom for sensibility? That is probably the most difficult question of all, and in a funny way, people like us, privileged intellectuals, have almost disqualified ourselves from answering it.

RK: There is of course the opposing argument, which would hold that the electronic media of television and radio have actually made the cherished works of European culture — Shakespeare, the great operas, the great concertos — more accessible to people, because on their Saturday or Sunday nights, they now have an opportunity to tune into these classic works, and have access to them in a way they never could have had before.

GS: This would be the optimistic point of view. It would depend on whether, having enjoyed the television program, you might then like to buy the book, or read it to your children, or want to see the play you've liked in a living theatre. As you know better than I, this is one of the most vexed topics. Is it happening? Is there, what they call, carryover or spillover from the mass media? Some people argue that there is, without doubt, and indeed there have been classic books whose sales have rocketed after a television presentation. There is, unfortunately, a lot of evidence which goes the other way, indicating an inverse trend. The bad drives out the good gradually, and, if anything, it is the trash that is beginning to fascinate more and more. We have to guard against being both too pessimistic and too optimistic. [Marshall] McLuhan's idea that we knew what we were doing doesn't seem to be quite accurate. We've outguessed ourselves on some of it. I would not deny that certain human beings, who, because of distance, economics or leisure, cannot get to concert halls, let alone operas, have certainly been introduced to new possibilities. But can we follow this up? Can we convey these forms to them in a living mode? Unfortunately, as you know, in the British Isles, statistics show that an overwhelming number of theaters, music halls, and serious film houses are closing and becoming bingo halls. If anything, television has driven out the alternative live forms.

RK: This it what you call the "Culture of the Secondary"—parasitism, talk about talk, images of images, replacing the real presence of the works themselves. But is there any sense in which that real presence can survive in anything but a mystical, or sacramental, reverence for the unique work of art, something no longer really feasible today?

GS: Is it no longer feasible? Let's take the really ugly end of the stick. Historians will one day say that this culture went insane when it paid one hundred million pounds for a painting, when the whole world rivaled itself in auction for one Van Gogh, one [Pierre-Auguste] Renoir, one [Pablo] Picasso. And you will say, what a vulgar and mysterious way of honoring great art. Of course it is. But it comes very near to deification. Let's not forget that half the great churches of the Renaissance in Europe were built by rich patrons, trying to eclipse their neighbors—built, in fact, for conspicuous, ostentatious consumption. So there is a queer, philistine craziness about very great icons of art which continues, it's also true, in the building of new museums, of new emporia. It's not quite clear yet that in some kind of much crueler way, the worship is gone. There is some sort of complicated idolatry. But if I could do something about it, I would like to start at the most day-to-day level. Will mothers or fathers begin to read more again to their children? Sociologists give us some evidence on that. There seems to be a deep shock, particularly in the middle class, about the fact that the child has never heard its parents' voices reading to it, reading good books to it. We're beginning, perhaps, to go back to certain possibilities. I think we're in a stage of acute conflict and transition where on both sides of the ledger you can find evidence. But the picture is not all black. The most terrifying prospect would be that of the fragile structures of privacy and of leisure being broken down by starvation, by mass migration which could come from Eastern Europe, or by the breakdown of civil forms of organization, legalism, and economic exchange in some of the critical areas. If I had to choose some kind of insane dictatorship, it would be to try to bring back the little silence into our lives. The latest estimate is that about 87 percent of adolescents cannot read without hearing a radio, a record player, a cassette, a long-playing disc, or television in the background. That electronic noise has become the *sine qua non*, the condition, of any act of attempted attention. If that is true, then something is happening to the old cortex which we don't fully understand.

RK: This is what you call the Americanization of the planet, and indeed of Europe in particular, isn't it? And you do say, at one point in your recent book, *Real Presence,* that the American genius is the attempt to democratize eternity and domesticate excellence. Do you think we in Europe can face that kind of competition?

GS: The best of America, like the best of any culture, doesn't export very well. There are very great wines which spoil when you ship them to other countries. The best of America, which has a kind of largesse of generosity, of human experimental humor and relaxation, does not export well. What does export is McDonalds, Kentucky Fried Chicken, the comic book, and all the dreadful soap operas.

RK: So, you would say we get the worst.

GS: We are importing the worst. We have invested our passions in the worst.

RK: And would you support the German and French moves, particularly at a cultural level, to protect national languages and European culture from that onslaught by promoting native filmmaking and publishing?

GS: It does not work. Walk the streets of Germany, see the presence of "Franglais" in France, and you must recognize that the American language, as also in England, has been almost totally triumphant. With the exception of the Beatles, there has not been a major counterstatement with any kind of comparable explosive dynamic, in the English language. It's like Fairy Liquid—it comes over, it tides over, it deterges, it cleans, it purifies, it uniformizes. It might go away. I see one hopeful alternative in northern Italy. There, much of the best of America has been adopted—why should people not have laundromats, and proper clothes off the rack, and look better and feel better, and have decent shoes, and so on? —but the double presence of socialism and Catholicism in Italy, and the tension between them, has preserved an enormously powerful sense of national and linguistic identity. In other countries, however, we find hardly any national self-consciousness left. If it tides over, we may be in for a hundred years, two hundred years, during which human beings will say, "Oh, shut up with all your cultural talk, we want to live decently. We actually want to have an icebox." And for a while, that's what we're going to try—happiness is a new idea in Europe. Suppose we're on a new threshold of domestic comfort and elbowroom, in which intellectual passions are not only curiously luxurious, but positively the enemy. That's why I think we should be studying more about what is wrongly called the Dark Ages, when small groups, particularly Irish monks, scholars, wanderers, lovers of poetry and scripture and of the classics, began copying texts by hand again, began founding libraries. We've been through difficult stages like this. I'm not at all pessimistic. I see a pendulum motion between a certain elitist rapture of excellence and the ordinary passion for just having a better day and night of it. One must be a sadistic, arrogant fool ever to say to another human being, "You have no right to live a bit better." Of course they have that right.

RK: So, in defense of the American ideal, one could say that it did introduce a certain egalitarian hope for many human beings, and, indeed, perhaps also a culture of tolerance for diversity, for inclusion, for what we call the melting pot.

GS: Very much so. It has not worked all that well in America. Ethnic problems are obstinate, resistant, intractable, beyond our hopes. That very great observer, the greatest we've ever had in America, [Alexis] de Tocqueville, in the nineteenth century, wrote that wholly prophetic sentence: "Aristocracies create works in bronze, democracies in plaster." This was his dictum of the American situation, to which the answer is, perhaps, "that's the inevitable concomitant of an increase in humanity." That is a very strong defense. My reserve is, put not in that business. I've given my life to teaching, to trying to say to a very small number of human beings, "Let's read Homer, and Virgil, and Dante, together. That's what life is about." I may be wrong, but I can't fake it. And what horrifies me about the present climate is that some of my colleagues, some of those of the intellectual profession, want it both ways. That, I think, is a piece of cant which is becoming very expensive.

RK: Do you think in Europe we're much better? We have witnessed two world wars this century based on the worst kinds of tribal nationalism, intolerance for the other, intolerance for diversity, which at least America has been able to accommodate with its notion of a pluralistic society. Also, in recent times, we have witnessed the resurgence of ethnic nationalism in Europe, which, some would say, augurs very badly for our immediate future. And we cannot forget, indeed, that if we are a continent and a civilization that has produced great minds, many of those minds in our own century, such as Heidegger, [Ezra] Pound, [Paul] de Man, [Louis-Ferdinand] Céline, proved to be very immoral people in their support for fascism. How does one answer that charge?

GS: One cannot answer it on the factual level, it is true. But you and I have taken a kind of oath of clarity. Doctors take the Hippocratic oath—"if I'm going to sign that, I'm going to behave in a certain way for the rest of my life, whatever the circumstances." We have taken an oath, which is to try to transmit excellence, to try to transmit beauty, to try to transmit form. It often seems to come a little out of the corner of hell. That is a very central truth and enigma. But I can't fake it. A world without the figures you've mentioned, a world without the great classics, a world without the great paintings and music, would to me, if not to others, be an ash-heap. That is not to defend the Manichaean claim about the double, the blackness being a constant part of every great creation. Saints don't need to write poems. Illiterate people don't write poems, or very rarely. The cultivation of the highest powers of expression and thought does seem to go along very often with a real political inhumanity. It would be wonderful if these people were nice. They aren't. But you and I write books about them. We live by what they teach us. We live by the joy, the worry, the anguish they give us and, sorry, we're in a bit of a trap there. And I think one can be honest about the trap, not pretend that human love, egalitarian justice, liberal dispensations, are very great creators of absolutely first-class work. They aren't.

RK: This touches on one of the central concerns of your writing—the notion of answerability as an aesthetic openness to the text, to the otherness of the text, a certain mode of concentration, attention, vigilance; and there seems to be built into that word *answerability*, being responsible to the text, an element also of being responsible for the text, and by implication, for others. Now, this seems to me to be quite problematic—the claim that an aesthetic answerability, to great works of art will lead, logically and emotionally, to a sense of moral responsibility. Yet the facts are otherwise. Very answerable people, in terms of artistic work, have been very morally suspect. How do you explain that contradiction?

GS: Since we have so little time, let me try to answer you in two very simple ways. And the hardest thing in the world is to try to be simple on problems like this. Very roughly, Thomas Jefferson, Matthew Arnold (still a great teacher), F. R. Leavis, really believed that if you read better, you would vote better and treat other human beings better. I am simplifying, of course, but they made the link passionately, confidently—saying, you can't but be a finer human being, because your sensibility will be richer, more delicate, more apprehensive of the condition of others. In all my early work, when trying to show that people who could play Schubert like angels and read Goethe couldn't then torture other people in concentration camps, I came to the conviction that this was not demonstrable. On the contrary, as you've hinted before, sometimes, most awfully, the contrary prevails, and great readers are sadistic human beings or vote for fascism, and so on. Where is the bridge? In my more recent work, I've narrowed; I've tightened. That dubious figure and Titan among thinkers, Martin Heidegger, who will, I think, dominate much of culture in the future, as did Hegel and Plato — not politically very reassuring either, by the way — Heidegger said, look, the great poet, the great artist, he isn't *speaking*, he is being *spoken*. Something we can express by a little English pun, he's being "bespoken." Something is passing through him. Something much greater than any individual. The language is greater than the individual; it chooses certain vessels to contain its glory and its radiant pressure. I'm now speaking in opposition to what is the prevailing fashion, the prevailing way of teaching, which says that anybody can rearrange what he reads. I'm protesting desperately against the posters on every single wall, where the conductors' names are much larger than those of the composers. I'm protesting against the producer thinking he's greater than Shakespeare, or Moliére, or Aristophanes, when he has everybody naked, or in rubber masks, or on spaceships, doing classic plays. I'm pleading for a certain courtesy in the face of really great art. Put quite simply, the great poet doesn't need me. I need him. There is the picture of Pushkin in which he said, "Look, I'm Pushkin. I'll give you the mail to carry. See that it gets to the right delivery box." I love to do that. I'm not pushed when I can't do it, but I love to carry the letters, which is one way of teaching, one way of being, as you and I are, writers, critics, elucidators. It's a very modest function, but it has become a dangerous and, I think, essentially a difficult one — to get people to listen at all, to look at all. But if you were to ask me does this carry the liberal, confident hope that you will then behave a little better in the street or in your home, I could not say I really have that hope.

RK: If we could return to the notion of the European mind. You mentioned earlier that the Dark Ages of Europe was a misnomer, and you seemed to imply that pre-Enlightenment Europe was a time when people had a single culture, and that with the lingua franca of Latin, they could move across borders and boundaries, and enter some sort of social and political unity . . .

GS: You use the phrase *"lingua franca."* There is no more deeper witticism or irony of history, and history is much wittier and more ironic than we are. *Lingua,* Latin. *Franca,* French. The two great moments when Europe thought it had a single language. And what is the *lingua franca* now? Anglo-American or American Creole or commercial American, which organizes the computers from Vladivostok to Madrid, the language every young scientist has to publish in, and has to know. I see a terrific contradiction, almost a trap. Can there be this new Europe when it speaks American? I don't know the answer, and I don't know anybody who has even begun to think this one through, because it's such a fierce challenge to all past history. What could be the basis for an answer? Could it be a revival of religion? Tricky one, that. Fundamentalism is rampant again, not only in Islam, but also in Christianity. The Ukraine, which is one of the biggest nations on the globe, could again become a passionate Catholic wedge driven into the very heart of the Slavic world. Will we again have great religious wars? It's not excluded. One doesn't need to say this in Ireland. Is there another basis? I see only one. It is that of a shared body of active remembrance. When you visit Leningrad, whatever your feelings, you have twelve kilometers—it's scarcely imaginable—of cemeteries, of more than a million people who died of starvation and suffering in the siege. Right to the frontiers of Asia, which I tried to say are at Moscow, Europe shares a body of terror, of remembered sorrow, of unspeakable self-destruction to the brink of suicide, in which there is perhaps also some hope. History might become the passport of shared identity, an actively lived and known history—and history is in many ways at the moment the dominant discipline of sensibility. We have lived through something so unspeakable. We were so close to the possibility of there being no Europe at all. And there's the reentry of Spain—after forty years of France, we have one of the powerhouses of liberal thought, art, philosophy, and painting among us again, with its eagerness to join Europe: "we're one of you; we too have lived that hideous history, of inquisition, and civil war, and Napoleon, and fascism." There are shared memories which an American does not share, which an Asiatic and an African does not share. They have their own immensely rich empires and evidences of the past tense. Ours is probably the most urgent, and there is at least a chance the young today are crossing borders as even you and I never were able to do, that there is somewhere a decision that the past has to have borne some very fragile fruit. Otherwise, the darkness at the back of us becomes even less endurable.

RK: But the remembrance is of our collective errors as much as our collective achievements.

GS: There is a marvelous remark by the German poet [Rainer Maria] Rilke, that at the end of a good marriage one has to become the loving guardian of the other's solitude. I would say that at the end of an historic crisis one must become the loving guardian of one's own mistakes.

Dublin, 1991

Paul Ricœur
Universality and the Power of Difference

RK: Do you believe in the idea of a European identity?

PR: Europe has produced a series of cultural identities, which brought with themselves their own self-criticism, and I think that this is unique. Even Christianity encompassed its own critique.

RK: And how would you see this ability to criticize ourselves operating? In terms of Reformations and Renaissances?

PR: Yes. Plurality is within Europe itself. Europe has had different kinds of Renaissance — Carolingian, twelfth-century, Italian and French, fifteenth-century, and so on. The Enlightenment was another expression of this; and it is important that in the dialogue with other cultures we keep this element of self-criticism, which I think is the only specificity of Europe (along with, of course, the enhancement of science). Europe is unique in that it had to interweave several heritages — Jewish-Christian, Greek-Roman, then the Barbarian cultures which were encompassed within the Roman Empire, the heritage within Christianity of the Reformation, Renaissance Enlightenment, and also the three nineteenth-century components of this heritage, *nationalism, socialism,* and *romanticism* . . .

RK: How does this pluralist legacy fit with the European claim to universality?

PR: The kind of universality that Europe represents contains within itself a plurality of cultures, which have been merged and intertwined, and which provide a certain fragility, an ability to disclaim and interrogate itself.

RK: This of course opens the question, doesn't it, of how we in Europe relate not just to the differences within our borders, but also how we relate to the differences of other non-European continents and countries; and how the universalist project of Europe can engage in dialogue with their differences, their nationalisms, their fundamentalisms? I mean, can we preach to others if we haven't sorted out our own problems of national identity?

PR: I think we must be very cautious here in Europe when we speak of fundamentalism, because it is immediately a pejorative word, and this prevents good analysis. We have to look at the phenomenon because there are several kinds of fundamentalism. We put one word above a multiplicity of events. But there is, for instance, a difference between a return to a culture close to the practice of the people and a fundamentalism imposed from above.

RK: Well, if we take the example of the Baltic states, do you have a sympathy with what their nationalist claims for sovereignty and autonomy are trying to achieve?

PR: I must say that I am surprised by the extent of the phenomenon, but also the extremist dimension, because in my own philosophical culture, I had underestimated the capacity of language to reorganize a culture and to unify it. And secondly, I had also underestimated the fragility of each identity which feels threatened by another. People must be very unsure to feel threatened by the otherness of the other. I did not realize that people are so unsure when they claim so emphatically to be what they are.

RK: Wouldn't you agree that there are very good historical reasons for this insecurity, not only in the Baltic states, but also in Yugoslavia, in Czechoslovakia, or in Northern Ireland—hence the need to attach themselves to a separatist national identity?

PR: But there is also the fact that there is no political distribution of borders which is adequate to the distribution of languages and cultures, so there is no political solution at the level of the nation state. This is the real irritator of the nineteenth century, this dream of a perfect equation between state and nation.

RK: That clearly has failed.

PR: Yes, that has failed. So, we have to look for something else.

RK: There is much talk now in Europe about the necessity to go beyond the limitations of the nation state (while preserving it as an intermediary model) to a transnational federation of states on the one hand, and a devolution of power from the nation state to regions on the other hand—to regions that would be more self-governing, that would encourage the practice of local democracy, of participatory democracy. Do you think that might work?

PR: Yes, but there is a political problem here. Is the project of European federalism to be a confederation of regions, or of nations? I don't know the solution because it is something without a precedent. Modern history has been made by nation states. But there are problems of size. We have five or six nation states in Europe of major size, but we have micro-nations which cannot become microstates in the same way as nation states have done.

RK: One could argue that it's not unprecedented in what some call the "other Europe" of Canada and the United States, where they did develop a model of federation, and indeed a certain amount of local autonomy in government at the level of the town halls, particularly at the beginning of the American Revolution.

PR: In a sense, the United States is a different case because it is a melting pot of immigrants.

RK: But surely we've also got an opportunity here in Europe to accommodate the immigrants from those countries we colonized for two or three centuries.

PR: The United States has solved the problem due to its unit of language, English, to a certain extent. We have an opposite problem, with our multiplicity of languages and national dialects.

RK: I'd like to bring in the question of sovereignty here. At the moment we're pooling sovereignty in Europe. The notion of sovereignty, if I'm not mistaken, actually goes back to the idea, first of all, that God is the universal sovereign, later replaced by the king as sovereign, as the center of one indivisible power. Then, with the replacement of monarchy by republics, with the French Revolution, for example, the nation state becomes sovereign.

PR: In modern republics, the origin of sovereignty is in the people, but now we recognize that we have *many* peoples. And many peoples means many centers of sovereignty—we have to deal with that.

RK: Wasn't one of the problems of the French Revolution the definition of sovereignty as one and indivisible? That creates problems when you export the Revolution to other countries or continents.

PR: Take the Corsican people who are also a member of the French people. Here we have two meanings of the word *people*. On the one hand, "people" means to be a citizen in a state, so it's not an ethnic concept. But, on the other hand, Corsica is a people in an ethnic sense—within the French people which is not an ethnic concept. So, we are struggling with two concepts of people, and I think it's an example of what is happening throughout Europe now.

RK: Does this mean two different kinds of membership—ethnic membership and civic membership?

PR: Yes, because the notion of "people," according to the French constitution, is not ethnic. Its citizenship is defined by the fact that somebody is born on the territory of France. For example, the son or daughter of an immigrant is French because he or she was born on this territory. So, the rule of membership has nothing to do with ethnic origin. This is why it was impossible to define Corsican people, because we had to rely on criteria other than citizenship, on ethnic criteria, and to whom are we to apply these criteria?

RK: Does this not raise the problem of ethnic nationalism and racism?

PR: The criterion of citizenship is there to moderate the excess of the ethnic criterion.

RK: To enlarge the discussion somewhat, could one not say that there are in fact several Europes?

PR: The German thinker Karl Jaspers used to say that Europe extends from San Francisco to Vladivostok. This raises the issue of the cultural expansion of Europe.

RK: Perhaps the solution, if there is one, is not to be found within the limits of Europe. Maybe we need to extend those limits and go further to what some people have called a world republic, a cosmopolitan society which can harbor differences yet bind all peoples and continents together?

PR: Even in political terms, it may be impossible to solve the problem of the unification of Europe without solving the problem of some international institution which would provide the proper framework.

RK: This utopian vision of a cosmopolitan republic is one that goes back to the Enlightenment, to Kant and Montesquieu . . .

PR: We need now a plurality of utopias, utopias of different kinds. Surely, a basic utopia is a world economy which is not ruled by efficiency, by productivity, but based on needs. Maybe this will be the problem for the next century—how to move from an economy ruled by the laws of the market to a universal economy based on the real needs of people. We are now at the stage where the market is winning and provides the only source of productivity, but this productivity is not shared, because the success of productivity increases inequality. We'll have to address that. And then there's the political problem of resolving the hierarchy of sovereignties–global, Continental (European, American, African, etc.), national, and regional.

RK: Maybe we can take a step back from the immediate political implications of this problem and say a little about the cultural and philosophical presuppositions of this discussion.

PR: I would like to focus on the role of *memory* in this context. On the one hand, memory is a burden; if we keep repeating the story of wars won or lost, we keep reinforcing the old hostilities. Take the different states of Europe. In fact, we cannot find a pair who weren't at war at one time or another. The French and the British, the Poles and Germans, and so on. So, there is memory which is a prison, which is regressive. But, on the other hand, we cannot do without the cultivation of the memory of our cultural achievements, and also of our sufferings. This brings me to the second element. We need a memory of the second order which is based on forgiving. And we cannot forgive if we have forgotten. So, in fact we have to *cross* our memories, to *exchange* our memories with each other to the point that, for example, the crimes of the Germans become part of our own memory. Sharing the memory of cruelty of my neighbor is a part of this political dimension of forgiving. We have some examples. When the German chancellor went to Warsaw and knelt down and asked for pardon, I think that was very important for Europe, because, while we have to get rid of the memory of wars, of victory, and so on, we must keep the memory of the scars. Then we can proceed to this exchange of memories, to this mutual forgiveness.

RK: It's an unusual idea.

PR: I don't see how we can solve Europe's problems only in terms of a Common Market or a political institution. We need these, of course. We need the extension of a market which would be the basis of the unification for Europe and also a relationship between Europe and the rest of the world, the invention of new institutions to solve the problem of the multiplicity of nation states. But there is a *spiritual* problem underlying both the economic problem of a Common Market and the political problem of new institutions.

RK: What would be the role of narrative—one of the key concepts in your philosophy—in relation to this cultural crisis we are facing in Europe today? I mean narrative as storytelling, as remembrance or as projection.

PR: I would say three things concerning the role of narrative. First you have the narration of founding events, because most cultures have some original happening or act which gives some basis of unity to the diversity within the culture. Hence the need to commemorate founding events.

RK: Such as the French Revolution, the Soviet Revolution, 1916 in Ireland?

PR: Yes. We have to keep that because we have to retain some claims, some convictions that are rooted in these founding events. Secondly, I would say that one of the resources of the theory of narrativity is that now we may tell *different* stories about ourselves. So, we have to learn how to vary the stories that we are telling about ourselves. And thirdly, we have to enter this process of exchange, which the German philosophers called *Auseinandersetzung*. We are caught in the stories of others, so we are protagonists in the stories we are told by others, and we have to assume for ourselves the stories that the others tell about us, which have their own founding events, their own strategies, their own plots.

RK: So the crossing of memories involves the crossing of stories. But is there any sense in which in Europe today we can tell each other the same story, a common universal story? Is there anything to bind us together?

PR: I would say that this concept of universality may be used in different contexts. On the one hand, you may speak of universal rules of discourse—what Habermas says about rules of discussion; let us say the logic and ethics of argumentation. This is one level of universality, but it is too formal to be operative. Secondly, you have a universalist claim within our own culture. For example, we may claim that some rights to free speech are universal, in spite of the fact that for the time being they cannot be included within other cultures. But it's a claim, and remains only a claim as long as it is not recognized by the others. So we bring to the discussion not only procedures of universality but *claims* of universality. The project of universality is central to the whole debate about human rights. Take the example of the mutilation of women. I am sure that we are right to say that there is something universal in our assertion that women have a right to pleasure, to physical integrity, and so on, even if it is not recognized. But we have to bring that into the discussion. It's only discussion with the other which may finally convince the other that it's universal. And thirdly, I would say that you have a kind of eschatological universalism—the universal as an ultimate project or goal as in Kant's *Essay on Perpetual Peace*.

RK: The project of some kind of universal republic.

Recorded in Paris in 1991 and first published in *Visions of Europe*, 1992

Umberto Eco
Chaosmos: The Return of the Middle Ages

RK: You have argued that the Dark Ages is a much maligned period of European history. Why?

UE: We can speak of the Dark Ages in the sense that the population of Europe fell by twenty million. The situation was really horrible. The only flourishing civilization was the Irish one, and that's not by chance. Those Irish monks went to civilize the continent. But immediately after the millennium, we cannot speak any longer of Dark Ages. You know that, about the tenth century, they discovered a new cultivation of beans, all those vegetable proteins. One historian called the tenth century "the century full of beans"; it was an enormous revolution. Now, the whole of Europe started to be fed with vegetable proteins. A real, biological change. And the centuries immediately after the millennium were called the First Industrial Revolution, because in those three centuries, more or less before the Renaissance, there was a larger-scale application of the windmills and the invention of the new collar for horses and for cattle. With the old collar, they were practically strangled. With the new one, on the chest, the force of the animal was four, five, or six times greater. Then there was the invention of the posterior rudder. Until that time, ships had a lateral rudder and it was very difficult to move against the wind. With a back-moving rudder, the possibilities for shipping became enormous; the discovery of America by Columbus wouldn't have been possible without this

technological innovation. And we can list many other miracles of discovery. So, it means that European culture, European society, grew
with the new feudalism and the new bourgeoisie, the birth of Italian
and Flemish communes, the free cities, the invention of the bank, the
invention of the check, of credit.

RK: In one of your essays, you actually talk about the return of the
Middle Ages. Do you believe that there is some sort of cycle to history,
and that we are now reliving some of the traumas of the Middle Ages?

UE: Well, in that essay I wanted to stress certain common elements
in the sense in which our era is undoubtedly an era of transition, in a
very accelerated way. It's enough to think of what happened in the last
few years in Europe to understand the sense in which we are living in
a new era of revolution. This is, as the Middle Ages was, an era of transition in which new forms, new social, technological, philosophical forms
are invented. And at the time I wrote the essay I was also impressed by
certain common patterns in the rise of terrorism: I saw the rise of groups
like the Red Brigade and PLO, etc., as a return of medieval millenari-
anism, informed by a sense of apocalypse and breakdown. The Atomic
Age as a sort of reliving of the Middle Ages.

RK: If I could take an example from literature now—Joyce, somebody you have written much about, including your book, *James Joyce
and the Middle Ages*. You seem to argue that Joyce represents a balance
between a fidelity to the cosmic order of the Middle Ages (represented
in particular by his fascination for Thomist aesthetics), and an avant-
garde pioneering quality which you equate with the contingency and
experimentation of modernity. Is there not a sense in which for you Joyce
is an exemplar who combines a medieval aesthetic with a modern one?

UE: I think that Joyce is a paramount case of contrast and fusion,
an incredible cocktail between those two aspects. They are present in
his life in a Catholic milieu, the reading of St. Thomas Aquinas, a deep
understanding of it, and his interest in experimental literature, and this
sort of destruction of language that he called in *Finnegans Wake* the "abni-
hilation of the ethym." Joyce's work, as well as his life, was an oscilla-
tion, or dialectic, between opposites. Take *Ulysses*. In *Ulysses*, he destroys
all the existing forms of narrative, destroys all the existing forms of language. In doing that, he has built from the structure of the Odyssey, but
it could have been something else; it was this medieval idea of the cathe-
dral-like structure, and without this structure he would have been unable
to undertake his work of disruption, destruction, decomposition. I think

that this dialectic is present in every author, but in Joyce it was especially evident and openly confessed by the author himself—the nostalgia for order and taste for adventure, the necessity of using order as a disruptive machine. That's absolutely new and Joycean.

RK: So, you would argue that there is a dialectic between the nostalgia for a medieval order and a modern sense of chaos in Joyce?

UE: Well, I chose as a subtitle of my book, *Chaosmos*, a word invented by Joyce in which you have this sandwich between *cosmos*, which means organized structure, and chaos. Obviously, an author who has invented the word *chaosmos* was a little obsessed by this possibility of creative opposition.

RK: I'm reminded here of an example from your novel *The Name of the Rose*, where the hero, the monk, is wandering through the labyrinth of the library, and he comes across a forbidden section where books on comedy have been hidden away. The point seems to be that while the Western tradition, and the Western church in particular, allowed Aristotle's teachings on tragedy, it censored Aristotle's writings on comedy; and in this secret section of the library, you also have a series of commentaries by learned Gaelic monks full of the paraphernalia of the *The Book of Kells*—humor and mischief, contradiction and conflict. Are you making a point here about a certain Irish openness to contradiction and humor?

UE: You know, the Middle Ages was a serious age, because it was an age of faith and such things, so that the subject matter of every discourse was God. It had to be serious. But since it had also a great sense of humor, it was also an age of carnival and popular license. One only has to read Chaucer or Boccaccio to understand that they were not as virtuous as it seems. They tried to exploit this. The margins. There is a form of decorative art called marginalia. The texts were dealing with divine martyrs, and the margins were a sort of amusement, inventing, quoting from fairytales, from popular legends. What happened with the Irish medieval culture was that *marginalia* became *centralia*. *The Book of Kells* is made only of marginalia, and that is the way in which Irish culture was already Joycean at that medieval moment, trying to introduce extraneous elements to disturb the order of things, to find a different order.

RK: You've argued that *Finnegans Wake* recounts the quest for a universal language—or to be more accurate, a parody of the old traditional quest for an original tongue, some kind of alphabet that would preexist Babel and the division into multiple tongues that today make up our polyglot civilization. Now your point seems to be that there is no such thing as a return to a time before Babel, that we live in a post-Babellic age, to use your phrase, where it's the very multiplicity, plurality, confusedness, and complexity of languages that makes us what we are and is perhaps our greatest virtue.

UE: Well, the story is the following. For years I've been working on this extraordinary episode in the history of European civilization — the quest for a perfect language. Before the birth of Europe, there was not such a preoccupation, because the Greek civilization, or the Latin civilization, had their own language, which was considered the right one, and all the rest was considered barbarian. (The term *barbarian* originally meant stutterer, people unable to speak; without a language). As soon as Europe discovered the plurality of new languages, they started dreaming of some kind of universal language. There were two options. One, to go back before the confusion of the Tower of Babel where, according to Genesis 11, God confused language. Before, there was a single perfect language. And so there is in European history this effort to return to the purity of the original Hebrew, or another pre-Hebrew language, the one used by God to speak to Adam. And the other attempt was, on the contrary, to build up a new language that would allegedly follow the rules of universal reason — a language that could be spoken by everybody. Both were attempts to heal the wound of Babel. But there are, in this history, other such efforts. I discovered recently, probably one of the first texts about the story of Babel is an Irish drama of the seventh century in which it is told that the Gaelic language, invented by seventy-two wise men, instead of trying to go back before Babel or to eliminate the plurality of the other languages, tried to pick up the best from every language to create an alternative language — Gaelic. This mythical idea seems to be very similar to the idea of Joyce, who dreamed all his life of an alternative poetical language — *Finnegans Wake* is a proof of it. He did not try to invent a new one, or to rediscover an old one. *Finnegans Wake* is not written in English; it is a sort of polyglot construction in which every possible type of language is contributing to a new kind of discourse. What is the meaning of this metaphor — which is a metaphor, obviously, because it's impossible to think of a future Europe speaking in Finneganese? It is probably that the future of Europe is not to be seen as a development under the standard of a unique language, such as Esperanto, but as a sort of acceptance of a civilization made of various languages.

In Europe something different can happen, unlike what happened in the United States where the unification was made under the heading of a single language.

RK: You mean *English?*

UE: Yes. There were French-speaking people, German-speaking people, Dutch-speaking people, and all of that, but English became the unifying tongue in America. In Europe, we are facing more and more a fragmentation of languages. Look at what is happening in Yugoslavia. Or in the former Soviet empire. Lithuania, Estonia and Croatia are becoming again official entities. If today we could think of a Europe with three, four, five languages, the Europe of tomorrow would have tens of different languages, each of them recognized in their own autonomy and dignity. And so the future of Europe is probably to acquire a sort of polylingual attitude. And there is in the universities, at present, an interesting prefiguration of this. It is the Erasmus project. I have always said that the most important feature of the Erasmus project is the sexual one, because what does it mean if every student is supposed in the future to spend one year, at least, in another country? It means a lot of mixed marriages. It means that the next generation will be largely bilingual, with a father and mother from different countries. That's the best chance for Europe.

RK: So you're really talking about exchange, interchange, confusion in the best sense of the word. It reminds me of something that Brian Friel, one of our Irish playwrights, once said in his play *Translations*, that confusion is not an ignoble condition.

UE: No. It's the original condition of the cosmos. Before the Big Bang there was a great order, and a great peace. The Big Bang was the beginning of the confusion in which we live.

RK: But isn't there actually a stronger claim in what you're saying? I'm thinking of your argument that if God spoke to Adam, He spoke in Finneganese.

UE: It was again a metaphor. But yes, the idea of a perfect language is a utopia. If it is possible to think that evolution took place several times in the world in different places, it is also possible to think that language was born several times in several places. The idea of an ideal language is that there was first a speaking animal, then all the other languages derived from it. And so it was for centuries: they dreamt of Hebrew as the original one, and then of Indo-European, and so on. Humanity being a speaking species, it is probable that languages were plural from the beginning. And seeing that plurality is a natural condition, it would be artificial and inhuman to reduce this plurality to an impossible unity.

RK: To take this back again into the realm of Europe, aren't you really claiming that cultural contamination is a good thing, that we should be muddying the waters, mixing together different languages, different races, different nationalities, and that one of the great errors of Europe has been the attempt to fashion some kind of purity of culture or politics? Two indications of this might be, on the one hand, the tradition of the centralized nation state which suppresses its regional minorities and languages—in other words, refuses to acknowledge the existence of a plurality of cultures within—and on the other hand, the attempt to close the frontiers of Europe and see it as some kind of ethnocentric, privileged continent which seeks to deny all those influences from Asia, North Africa, or the Americas, which have shaped us as we now are. So could it be said that your basic argument is for a Europe of open frontiers which would see the confusion of different identities and languages as something positive?

UE: I dislike the use of terms like *should* or *would* that imply will and intention. It is irrelevant what Europe wants or doesn't want. We are facing a migration comparable to the early Indo-European migrations, East to West, or the invasion of the Roman Empire by the Barbarians and the birth of the Roman-German kingdoms. We are not just facing a small problem of immigration from the Third World; if that were so, it would be a problem for the police, for the customs, to control. The new migration will radically change the face of Europe. In one hundred years Europe could be a colored continent. That's another reason to be culturally, mentally ready to accept a multiplicity, to accept interbreeding, to accept this confusion. Otherwise, it will be a complete failure.

RK: One thing that comes through in nearly all of your work— your fiction and your critical writing—is a wonderful sense of humor.

UE: I think that a sense of humor is a healing quality in every culture. When there is a total absence of humor, we have Nazism. Hitler was unable to laugh. It's not only a European problem. I think that there is in humor, in a serious practice of humor, a religious effect. We are small creatures; we need not take ourselves too seriously.

Dublin, 1991

PART IV

Colloquies with Richard Kearney

Villanova Colloquy
Against Omnipotence: God Beyond Power

LIAM KAVANAGH: The very title of the conference series which has brought us together today, namely, "Religion and Postmodernism," raises the question of the possibility of a productive exchange between religious and philosophical narratives. What benefits do you think might follow for religious discourse from bringing philosophically orientated perspectives to bear on the reading of Scripture? Similarly, what benefits do you think might follow for philosophy from direct exposure to and engagement with religious texts?

RK: Well, I think it is crucial to maintain an exchange between the two disciplines. The whole rational, conceptual, metaphysical heritage of Greek philosophy meeting with the biblical monotheisms and revelation can be extremely creative. Indeed, I think our entire Western heritage consists of an intermingling of and between these two genres of thought, the philosophical and the religious or the philosophical and the biblical. But as you know, it is precisely the idea of a decisive *breach* between the two discourses, particularly since Kant and the Enlightenment, that has significantly determined much of the development of our philosophical tradition. In the twentieth century, this conviction was repeated in Husserl's and Heidegger's bracketing out of theology and revelation, as one of those presuppositions that we should suspend as we do phenomenological philosophy. So both in the Enlightenment separation of scientific reason from faith and in Heidegger's subsequent separation of phenomenology and theology (in his famous 1927 lecture), there is a very strong scruple in contemporary Continental thought about keeping the two disciplines apart.

Of course, there are those, like Levinas and Ricœur, who try to blur the boundaries a little bit, though it seems to me they usually do so apologetically. Levinas, for example, will claim no longer to be engaged in phenomenology but in Talmudic studies, when he raises questions about God. But I think it is evident that Judaism deeply informs his work, especially when he speaks of eschatology or messianism or the stranger in *Totality and Infinity* and other philosophical texts. Similarly, Ricœur, in *Thinking Biblically* and other religious works, will claim to be engaged in scriptural exegesis or biblical studies, rather than philosophy per se. Now I tend to be a little bit less scrupulous, less worried about the blurring. So, for instance, in *The God Who May Be*, I don't have a huge problem about saying, "Let's do a hermeneutics of religion." Now, it is a *hermeneutics* of religion, a philosophy that analyses — without theological pretensions or expertise — certain scriptural texts. In the case of *The God Who May Be*, these include Exodus 3:14, the transfiguration on Mt. Thabor, the Annunciation, the Song of Songs, etc.

I am, however, leaving aside the specifically historical context of these texts — questions of the historical Jesus, whether the Shulomite women ever did exist or not, whether the Song of Songs is a Babylonian or Jewish text, whether there are Greek influences, etc. These are fascinating questions, but they are not my questions. I am not an expert in the whole theological discourse about these passages, but I feel quite free to engage in a poetics and a hermeneutics of scriptural passages *as* texts, without necessarily saying that these have a privilege with regard to the revelation of truth. That question I am bracketing. So although I cannot claim theological expertise in this discourse, this tradition is nonetheless my tradition; it is my set of narratives. It is also my faith, my heritage, and therefore I know it better than, say, Hinduism or Buddhism or other religious traditions that talk about God. So it makes eminent sense for me to take that liberty. If I had more expertise in Sanskrit or Japanese, then maybe I would feel more competent to comment on other traditions, even if they are not mine. I would certainly be open to dialoguing with them.

Therefore, it seems to me that to cut off all dialogue between philosophy and these wisdom traditions, including the biblical, is actually cutting off your nose to spite your face. I think it's lopping off too much. I can fully understand how the Enlightenment, given the invasion of philosophical discourse by church authorities during Scholasticism and the medieval inquisitions (and the ensuing burnings and condemnations), would say, "Faith, take a step back" or "Theology, take a back seat." So whether it is the separation of faith and reason to preserve faith, as in the case of Kant—who set the limits of reason in order to make way for faith—or whether it is to preserve reason, as in the case of the philosophical Enlightenment, I understand where that is coming from. However, I think in so-called postmodern discourse, with which I have some concerns to which we can return, we have made some progress in this regard, namely, the ability to engage in interdisciplinary dialogue. I strongly advocate such interdisciplinary exchange, and not just between philosophy and religion, but also between philosophy, religion, science, literature, and other disciplines. I would call it a "creative confusion," to borrow from Edward Said—a creative confusion of disciplines, while also respecting the genre limits of each one. So it's a delicate balance.

LK: In a provocative reading of Exodus 3:14 from *The God Who May Be*, you identify a "seismic shift" occurring at the "chiasmus where *'ehyeh* meets *einai.*"[1] What constitutive roles do you think these formative readings have played in the philosophical and theological traditions of the West? And secondly, what significant similarities and differences do you think distinguish your position from that of Jacques Derrida's appeal to "Jewgreek is greekjew," in "Violence and Metaphysics"?

RK: The standard translation of the Exodus 3:14 passage "*'ehyeh, 'asher 'ehyeh*" is "I am who am"—"*Ego sum qui sum,*" in Latin—and there is a long history of interpretation of this text from Philo to Augustine to Aquinas and the Scholastics and so on. The most commonly agreed reading is that it is an ontological self-definition of God: I am who am. Now as a tautological pun, that is interesting. It could be a way of saying, "I'm *not* telling you who I am. I am who am." So the repetition could be seen as a rhetorical deflection of the answer, of any easy answer. "You are not going to get hold of me!" Well, if that is true, then it is even more fitting that we translate the phrase as Martin Buber and Rashi, the medieval Jewish commentator, and others have done, as "I am who shall be," or "I am who will be," or "I am who may be." In doing so, one restores the element of promissory note and also the conditional nature of God's manifestation in the world. "I am who may be," that is, "I am unconditionally the promise of the kingdom, I am unconditionally love, the call, invitation, and solicitation, but I can only be God, God in the flesh, God in history, God in matter, if you are my witnesses," to quote Isaiah.

Furthermore, Hebrew scholars like [Martin] Buber, [Franz] Rosenzweig, and Rashi point out that in the Hebrew the verb *"ehyeh 'asher"* actually has a conditional, subjunctive, futural mode. In German it is translated as *"werden."* So, on this reading, God says, "I am who becomes. I am who will be, may be, shall be. If you listen to what I am saying, you will go back and liberate your people, and you will lead them into a new relationship with Egypt and the Word. But if you don't do that, and you think that you possess Me, then you've only got an ontological formula of Me as totality, self-sameness, self-love, self-causing cause, self-loving love, self-thinking thought. You attach all that Greek metaphysical stuff to Me. That's being unfair to Me and unfair to Aristotle, because Aristotle wasn't talking about Me. He was talking about a certain notion of form and causality which, to his mind, was divine. But he is coming from a different tradition, a different way of thinking, a metaphysical way, and I respect that. But I, Yahweh, am giving you a different message. Maybe I can enter into dialogue with Aristotle's God and the God of the philosophers, but don't think you can easily collapse the two, one into the other."

So by not going with the standard orthodox translation of "I am who am," which can lead to the notion of a God of totality, and instead choosing the hermeneutic wager that "I am who may be," we open up that space for a different inflection in the biblical notion of deity.

With regard to the second part of your question, I don't see any great difference between myself and Derrida with regard to the Greek-Jew formula. The phrase originally comes from Molly's soliloquy in Joyce's *Ulysses*, of course: "Jewgreek is greekjew. Extremes meet. Woman's reason." So for Derrida and deconstruction, this exemplifies the movement beyond binary opposites to the necessary and mutual contamination of Jew with Greek, Greek with Jew. I am in agreement with Derrida on this point, though I perhaps would use the term *creative confusion* rather than *contamination* (but I know what Derrida means). Where I would differ from Derrida is that I think for him the "Jew" side of the equation does not necessarily entail a faith component. In other words, for Derrida, the messianic structure of existence does not necessarily need to be fleshed out in terms of a "messianism," be it Christianity, Judaism, or Islam. And there I would be of the view that we need to give the Jew some flesh back. It is not just a transcendent, unnameable, ineffable, unthinkable, unlocatable Other with a big "O." It is also the little people in the world who need cups of cold water and give cups of cold water. It is Isaiah and Joseph and Jesus, and it is that whole world of embodiment and enfleshment, which I think is sometimes lacking in Derrida's notion of the messianic, which for me is too formal, too quasi-transcendental, too abstract—although I have huge respect for what he is doing. So I would try to give the "Jew" back more body than Derrida, perhaps, who "rightly passes for an atheist," though he does call himself the "last of the Jews" (le dernier Juif) in Circumfession . . .

LK: Could you say you rightly pass for an atheist?

RK: No. I would say the opposite—that I rightly pass for a theist! Derrida admits in the phrase a certain ambiguity about "rightly passing for . . ." He seems to be saying, "That's how people understand me, and I understand that they understand me like that, because my work suggests as much." But he doesn't say, as Jack Caputo keeps coming back to, "I *am* an atheist," only "I rightly *pass* for an atheist." So, likewise, I would tend to say that I rightly pass for a theist. I don't really have a problem in saying that I am a theist—but in the way that I try to define that in the introduction to *The God Who May Be*, namely, that I am a theist in the sense of wagering on an eschatological God of the possible. The way I see God might be defined by many theists as atheistic. For many, what I am doing in *The God Who May Be* could be a form of atheism or agnosticism. It's not that for me, but people were burnt for less in the Middle Ages!

LK: In light of your exploration of the theme of transfiguration in terms of *persona/prosopon*, would you "subscribe to this infinitely ambiguous sentence from the *Book of Questions* by Edmond Jabès: 'All faces are His; this is why HE has no face'?"[2]

RK: I would say, He has no *one* face. In other words, God is not reducible to one person or to the unique. Now, when the one becomes the unique, and therefore the exclusive reserve of one person or church, then we're in trouble. This is one of the dangers of monotheism and, arguably, principally of Christian and Islamic monotheism, both of which appeal to one special face, to Jesus and Muhammad. It is particularly an issue for Christianity. Yahweh has no face, but all faces are Yahweh's face.

What I would try to do as a Christian is to reread the uniqueness of Christ in another way? I would argue that Kierkegaard is right. There was only one God-man, who embodied a unique, singular, special coming-together of the divine and the human. Furthermore, by reinvoking that whole prophetic biblical image and reidentifying with so much of the Jewish narratives, particularly Isaiah, Jesus is actually saying, "before Abraham was, I am." "I was there *before* Abraham, and also *with* Abraham. I was there when the three angels visited Abraham. That was Me! I was there every time someone asked for a cup of cold water, and I will be there in the future every time somebody asks for and gives one, even if they don't realize it's Me." Now, as I understand it, this refusal by Jesus as *prosōpon* to be reduced to a singular face/person is the refusal of possession. It is the refusal to be made into an idol or property of any particular church. This refusal by Jesus proclaims that as much as we may try, we cannot latch on to him as the unique *Noli me tangere.* He must go, so that the spirit may come. Now what is the spirit? Well, the spirit for me is other faces. As in that beautiful line by Gerald Manley Hopkins, "to the Father, through the features of men's faces," it is the possibility of lots of other faces, including every face that asks for a cup of cold water and receives it. So in a kind of *second* kenotic act, Jesus says, "Yes, I am called to be the unique one, and I assume that act here and now," and then goes through the drama of the Resurrection in order that everybody else can be called to that too. We have been called since the beginning of time—before Abraham was—and will continue to be called in the future.

So the second coming is not just a coming of the end of time, although it is that too. It is also a coming in every single moment of time. That is why I like to quote Walter Benjamin when he says that the future is made up of moments, which are portals through which the Messiah may enter at any moment. Then the face of Jesus becomes—potentially at least—every face. That is very different from saying there is only one Jesus. Such Christian exclusivism is something I'm trying to go beyond and open up. And I would want to go further and extend the Jewish-Christian dialogue to include interfaith dialogue with Buddhists and Hindus and so on, because the more I read of the Upanishads or the Bhagavad-Gita or the writings of Buddhist sages, the more I realize that the Word is there, too. There are faces there, too, though I think sometimes we in the West can get locked into the "Greekjew is jewgreek" equation. But just as the Jew is *prosopon*, so is the Greek in terms of other traditions. And sometimes deconstruction has not been sufficiently open to this. I think Derrida himself would be, but I'm not sure Levinas was. In fact, I think Levinas believed that the infinite face was the exclusive preserve of monotheism, and there is textual evidence to suggest that. I'm being a bit hard on Levinas, perhaps. Christian exclusivism can be even more brutal than anything you'd find in his work. But once I asked him, at the Cérisy-la-Salle colloquium in Normandy, "What do you think of when you think of the face?" (because Levinas never really describes the face), and he said, "I think of Christ." I found that very interesting. So, following a certain Levinas, the Jewish face is open to the Christian face, and I would like to think that the Christian face is open to non-Christian faces.

LK: In *The God Who May Be*, you stress the codependent relationship obtaining between God and humanity. You argue that we should read the formula *"ehyeh 'asher 'ehyeh"* in terms of "relation rather than abstraction. God's 'I shall be' appears to *need* Moses's response 'Here I am' in order to enter history and blaze the path toward the kingdom."[3] What distinctions and comparisons do you see between your position and Gianni Vattimo's claim that the narratives of Jesus's incarnation and crucifixion inaugurate a covenant or alliance between God and humanity, a covenant which serves to weaken hierarchical structures?

RK: Well, I think in both cases there is a definite opening of the religious to the moral and the political. Both of us in our different ways have been involved (he more centrally than I, of course) in politics (myself mainly in Ireland and Britain, and he in Italy) and we have both been described, rightly or wrongly, as politically engaged intellectuals. So yes, I think that these issues of how you translate the Word of God have big implications for ethical and political practice. God needs us to be enfleshed in the world—God as unconditional love, justice, invitation, call, solicitation, promise. But if we don't have ears to hear and eyes to see, if we don't respond to the call, as Mary and Isaiah might have chosen not to do, then God would not have been present in Mary or in Isaiah, and we would not have had the incarnation or the Book of Isaiah and the whole prophetic tradition. So I want to keep open the fact—over and against the metaphysics of omnipotence—that it is possible that God might *not* have been incarnated as Jesus, or rendered prophetically audible, visible, communicable, and transmissible as Isaiah, just to take those examples, and there are others.

So God needs us. Yes. God needed Moses to hear "I am, who am" and then to go off and implement that missionary statement of liberation, which he did. Not that it didn't get all mixed up and confused further down the line, but Moses did listen and hear. So yes, there is a need in God, a desire in God for us, to be made more and more fully incarnate in every moment. I think I share that with Vattimo. I'm not sure that he believes in a transcendent God, whereas I do. I'm not sure that he doesn't take Christianity as a story of nihilistic kenosis, implying that the covenant of self-abasement and friendship is good for us, because it makes us good people. This might serve for Vattimo like a pragmatic Humean fiction—let's stick with it, because if we don't, we're going to have a chaotic, selfish society. It is as if for Vattimo we need this narrative illusion, this story. It is not, of course, like the meta-narratives of the past, which claim to be objective and are therefore powerful, militaristic, imperial, coercive, and repressive. For Vattimo, it is purely subjective. So it is nihilistic in that it is nothing. Now, I don't personally ascribe to such a view. Not that I wouldn't find common cause with him—perhaps if we really got into what *nothing* means, the meaning of *nihil* and the God-beyond-being and all that. But I'm not sure he wants to go down the route of Meister Eckhardt and the mystics, as outlined by Stanislas Breton, for example, in *The Word and the Cross*. I don't think Vattimo really embraces the mystical *via negativa*. I suspect his position is closer to a moral and political pragmatism, hence his invocation of Habermas and [Richard] Rorty. He seems to be saying, "Look, this is a good story, and it is a story about charity and compassion and self-abnegation. It is subjective, and it serves to get rid of questions like 'Is it true?' 'Is there a *God out there?*'" These are all metaphysical questions for Vattimo, and I think he believes we should jettison them along with the question of transcendence.

So there is a kind of radical immanence of subjectivity in Vattimo that says, "Well, if the Christian story can make people behave with compassion and charity, then it works, and, following pragmatism, if it works then it is 'true.' Truth is what works for the good." So although I run parallel to him on many of the issues—promoting the kenotic God of compassion and charity, etc., against the God of omnipotence— I think I would hold out for a transcendent God. My notion of a hermeneutic narrative would have a reference *outside* of itself. It points towards something other, bigger than us, and I don't think Vattimo wants to go there. What we both share in common, however, is our notion of the Christian God as committed to love and justice. On the issue of whether the God of *posse/possest* exists unconditionally as call, as promise, and as transcendence—that is an area where I think we may disagree.

LK: Would religious narratives play a more central role in your work than philosophical or literary narratives for example?

RK: Well, I think there is a difference, from the point of view of ethics. Now, I've no doubt that all kinds of literary books have made people do good things, and the same goes for certain philosophies. Some people read Levinas, Kant, or [Leo] Tolstoy and then go out and become good people because of that. But there is a truth claim in religious discourse which is different from the literary and philosophical. Now, I'm not saying it is necessarily more powerful, but it is different. It claims that this narrative has a reference outside of itself. Literary narratives do not claim to be referring to anything outside of themselves. And philosophical discourse tends to "bracket" the truth claims of faith and revelation. At least since Kant and Husserl.

LK: Could this be the case for all nonreligious narratives?

RK: No. Historical narratives also claim to refer to things outside of themselves, that is, "the way it actually happened," even though we can never get back to it and tell it objectively or adequately. Here there is a claim to be saying something beyond the narrative, something *about* reality. There is the crucial question of reference. Something *did* happen; Auschwitz *did* happen, for example. Now revisionists would say, "No, that's just a story, and I have a counterstory, and whoever wins will decide whether Auschwitz existed or not." But I hold that historical narratives, as opposed to literary ones, do refer to something outside of themselves, and religious narratives, I would hope, also refer to something outside of themselves (that is, God—however you define God, whether as *posse*, promise, or love, etc.). That is a central debate in the philosophy of religion, in the hermeneutics of religion, in theology. Religious narratives are not in that sense the same as literary discourse. Again, I differ from Derrida here in that I don't think he wants to entertain the truth claims about whether messianic expectation is referring to an *other* that does exist. I don't think he wants to get into that, and that's why he "rightly passes for an atheist." And I think Rorty and Vattimo take a similar line. I totally respect that. But I think a hermeneutics of religion can also take a theistic turn. It is a *wager,* of course, but one I would take with Ricœur and [Karl] Jaspers, and [Gabriel] Marcel and [David] Tracy. It may be right and it may be wrong, but let's entertain the possibility, let's bet on the possibility that the *posse* does exist and is more than a figment of our imagination or a good story in itself. I think it *is* a good story, but I think it is also more than that. It refers to Good News that goes beyond even our most ingenious supreme fictions. It claims to speak of something other than us, greater than us, and indeed transcendent of us.

LK: Richard Rorty has recently accused certain postmodernist thinkers of engaging in a "rationalization of hopelessness" and a "gothicizing" tendency to cast allegedly ubiquitous and irreducible structures in terms of the inescapability of original sin.[4] Given that in your recent work you have also charged certain postmodernists of engaging in a "cult of apocalyptic traumatism," do you agree with Rorty's assessment?

RK: You know, I would, almost! I think he is onto something quite important. I think there is a cult of traumatism in a lot of postmodernism. Even the Impossible can be pushed too far. Now, if you were to reinterpret it as a possibility beyond the impossible, then that's fine, and I think Jack Caputo is very open to that, even though he starts with and stays with the Impossible for 99 percent of the time. But I don't think he is closed to the possibility of a possibilizing God beyond the impossible. I think Marion is potentially open to it, particularly in his "God: The Impossible" paper, though prior to this I don't think he would have been. Derrida, I'm not so sure. There are passages in "As If It Were Possible" where he picks up some of my arguments from the *Poetics of the Possible,* so it's an ongoing dialogue. But I still find in Derrida—and he is by no means the main culprit here—an emphasis on the Impossible over the possible, an overemphasis which can lead to a certain sense of disorientation and dismay. There is the *other* out there, there is Justice out there, there is Pardon out there, and there is the Gift out there, but they are all impossible. Now, I know he doesn't mean that they never happen, but even by using the word *impossible,* even if it is hyperbole or pedagogical rhetoric, there is a certain tone and style of thinking imparted. It is not an accident to talk of the God of *Impossibility* or the God of *Possibility.* Each has a certain inflection, and one, it seems to me, invites more hope than the other.

I think that there is also a certain movement in deconstruction and in postmodernism generally that finds *hope* and *memory* almost dirty words. Why? Probably because they seem to suggest narrative and continuity, reconciliation and recapitulation. All of which are considered nonkosher because they appear to imply metanarratives and the retrieval of totality, etc. But I would define these terms differently. To be fair, I think there are definite grounds for hope, indeed, a messianic hope in Derrida. All I would say is that I wish he would be more emphatic and more audible in giving voice to that strain in his thought, because the one that has been heard more often, rightly or wrongly, is the one that has not been the clarion call to social action and political transformation, but rather the one that goes into very minute qualifications and disqualifications about the possible meanings of gift, justice, forgiveness, and so on. I do not want to fault Derrida here, because I do believe, particularly in his recent work, that there is a real movement towards ethical hope and political commitment. I remember very well, for example, how he replied to Mark Taylor here at Villanova at the first Religion and Postmodernism conference. He said, "You cannot just say that everything is a text, and America is a casino, and prison is a casino, etc. Not fifty miles from here there is a prisoner, Mummia Abu Jamal, on death row, and that is not a metaphorical or a textual prison; it is a *real* prison. There is a real person there, and he will really die if we do not do something about it." So Derrida certainly has this sense of moral and political urgency. It's just that sometimes his texts are so decontextualized, so formal, so quasi-transcendental, and so verbal that one can get lost in labyrinths of deferred meanings and slippery signifiers and not get to the point. I remember Ricœur once saying that the thing about Derrida (whom he greatly respects) is that he is always beginning but he never begins. It's all about how to begin; it is all preamble. I think there is a certain truth in that, though it would be a little unfair to dwell on it. There are other postmodernists in whom the sense of hope seems to be lacking altogether—[Jean] Baudrillard and [Slavoj] Zizek, for example.

LK: In *Strangers, Gods and Monsters,* you mention Zizek in particular.

RK: I find Zizek is full of iconoclastic, rhetorical, self-undermining positions. There is dialectical dexterity, irony, and humor on every page. I find all that hilarious. I think he is so entertaining, and his combination of Marxism and Lacanianism is brilliant. And such political incorrectness! It's a riot; he's a real entertainer. But I do find that when you put down his book you say, "Well, what the heck! Nothing means anything! Let's have a good laugh and get drunk in the bar, rather than join the revolution, to juggle with [Jean-Paul] Sartre's conclusion to *Being and Nothingness!*" It becomes verbal game playing and intellectual confidence trickery after a while. Not that every philosopher has to be joining the barricades and sending us out to action. But I am committed to the hermeneutic formula, "From action to text to action," and I think the return of the text to action is very important. I don't think either Baudrillard or Zizek leave us many paths to travel back from text to action. I think Derrida is certainly trying, and, without a doubt, Caputo is swinging out all kinds of little bridges here, there, and everywhere to cross over the abyss, but it's almost in spite of the language of his deconstructive position. Jack Caputo, like Jacques Derrida, wants justice. They want God—certainly Jack Caputo does, and I think Derrida does too. They desire these things. Derrida says that God is the name of the "desire beyond desire," and they want "hospitality" and "pardon" and all these things. But the difficulty is how do you get there? They want to get there, they desire it, and that is the messianic expectation. But what I don't see in their work, particularly in Derrida's, are the hermeneutic paths and narratives and examples that get us there.

If somebody says to me, "What does *posse* mean?" we can do some hermeneutic work by looking at various texts and traditions — scriptural, philosophical, literary, etc. We can go back and say, "This is what the Greeks say about *dunamis,* and this is what Aquinas says, and this is what Leibniz says, and this is what Heidegger says." That gets us somewhere. But where it really comes to life in philosophy, it seems to me, is where those intraphilosophical references go on to also invoke testimonial examples, which you then can analyze philosophically. If you leave out flesh and blood people, or even literary examples of flesh and blood, then you've got something desolate. It's too desertlike. That is a problem for me with deconstruction. I admire the feat, but I don't know how anyone can live in deconstruction. It is an-khorite, as Jack Caputo says. There is nothing in Derrida's text to prevent commitment, but there is nothing in his texts, I find, that helps you get there either. It seems all we have to do is close our textual shop and go into action, but the inter-action between the two is not clear to me. So it is the step out of philosophical deconstruction and into action that I find problematic. That said, as a detour, I think deconstruction is more or less indispensable for all disciplines. We should all have our day in the desert, our retreat in the deconstructive *klinger.* But I think that once we have fasted for forty days without food, water, or shelter, there is somewhere else to go afterwards. That's important. You have got to come down from the mountain and in from the desert. We may have to go back there again, but for me it is a detour rather than an end in itself.

LK: Throughout your work, you have advocated the role of narrative in facilitating the possibility of mutual translation and understanding between diverse cultures and communities. Do you think that scriptural narratives also have the potential to foster and enhance understanding of this kind, or might they serve only to reinforce alienation and division?

RK: Well, there is no doubt that for centuries, millennia in fact, religious narratives have been abused by those in power who declare themselves to be on the side of the good and others to be on the side of evil. There is nothing new about that. I suppose that what is astonishing is that so many people continue to believe it. What I would offer as a defense of religious language against its abuses by certain people in power are the counter examples of the powerless who evoke religious language, not to divide the world into good and evil and to engage in apocalyptic scenarios of Armageddon, but to actually struggle for love and justice. There are all kinds of examples of this, maybe numerically far more examples than the former. But even if there were not, it would still be valid. Even if there was only one person — Ettie Hillesum or Bishop Romero in El Salvador or Maximillian Colbe or St. Francis or whoever. Take the examples of Gandhi and Martin Luther King. Millions were inspired by them, and aspired to be like them. They resisted power structures of repression and coercion and injustice in the name of the God of liberation, in the name of the God of *posse*, the promise of the kingdom of justice.

So I think we have got to measure up the abuses and good uses of our invocations of the Gospel message when we come to citing history as abusing and not abusing. Now, where that becomes a bit problematic is in a place like France, where politicians would never use the name God. It would be unthinkable to invoke "God on our side," and so on, as American presidents have done. This has something to do with secular republics, and the memory of religious wars that devastated Europe throughout the centuries, and the Enlightenment, of course. But when you consider that over 90 percent of Americans believe in immortality and personal salvation, that they will meet their friends and loved ones when they go there, etc., that's a hugely believing population; and therefore religious discourse requires more of a hermeneutics of suspicion in America than it does, say, in Europe and certain other parts of the world, because in America it is still a majority discourse, the majority way of thinking. Given the fact that almost everyone in the most powerful country in the world is a believer and that their president invokes God — a certain omnipotent God — as being on his side, that is where we have to be critical, perhaps.

I think scriptural narratives can play a negative role in hegemonic discourses, but in counterhegemonic discourses it can have very important revolutionary and subversive potential. Isaiah and the Gospels are still, when invoked by the right people in the right context, incredibly emancipatory for millions of people throughout the world. You only have to look at the Philippines, Latin America, and Africa to see how this is so. The Gospel can be used by people for good or evil. I have heard people invoke "peace with a sword" to justify Vietnam or Iraq. The just war arguments are very delicate ones, very problematic. Personally, I'm for nonviolence, *Satyagraha*, Gandhi's principle of nonviolence, nonviolent resistance. But resistance doesn't mean doing nothing. If a psychotic or a Nazi intends to enter my home and shoot my children or cut them into little bits, I'm going to stop him if I can. I'll try nonviolently, but if that doesn't work, if persuasion doesn't work, if argumentative communicative action, as Habermas would say, is just not doing the trick, then I'm going to stop him by physical force—and if that means wounding him in the knees, I will try and do that, and if it means shooting him in the head eventually, I will do that. Now, I won't deny that that is an unjust thing to do to a living being, but it would be more unjust not to do anything and to allow innocent children to be slaughtered. So we try in such instances to do the least unjust thing possible.

These are delicate matters. What I am saying is that basically the Gospel can be invoked for evil or for good, and it is a constant drama. From this point of view, hermeneutics plays a central role in discerning in each situation whether this is a loving and just thing to do or whether it's not a just thing to do. I say that acknowledging that I have little doubt that when Blair and Bush went into Iraq, they probably thought they were doing the just thing and that it was a just war. I don't agree with them, but there are grounds for hermeneutic debate. And in such an instance, you cannot leave religion out of the realm of philosophical discourse, because it is one of the most mobilizing discourses still operative in the world. It's all very well to say, "Well, after the Enlightenment, we live in a post-Christian, postreligious age." We don't actually. Probably the vast majority of the world are believers in one kind of deity or another, and sometimes it is the secular humanists in the universities who think that because they don't believe in God anymore, nobody else does, when in fact about 90 percent of the world does. At best, a postreligious age means that we don't take it for granted, that it's not the hegemonic discourse it used to be. Happily. But I don't think religion has gone away, and I don't think it should.

LK: So how does one deal with the abuses?

RK: The abuses are terribly hurtful for any believer who thinks there is something liberating in Isaiah or the Gospels. It's hurtful because there is a sense of betrayal, that the real message is being perverted, diverted, deflected from its original message of love and justice. But here philosophy can play a crucial role in helping to sort out some of the distinctions, to discriminate and discern and judge in a way that's very difficult to do if you only rely on the Bible or the Gospels. That is what fundamentalists do. They try not to engage in hermeneutics, because for them there is only one way of reading the Bible, and that is The Truth. That kind of literalism is disastrous. And that is why, going back to your first question, the separation of religion and philosophy is on one level ruinous, because religion needs philosophy to keep it critically investigating its own intentions, presuppositions, motivations, and translations into action. Similarly, I think philosophy needs religion because religion remains one of our most, I repeat, motivating forces, and I think it will always be, even if religion is secularized. To expel all religion from the domain of phenomenological investigations is incredibly foolish and irresponsible. It is inverted dogmatism. After all, how come we can talk about every thing in the phenomenological order of experience except religion? It just doesn't make sense. So I say, Long live the hermeneutics of religion! God too deserves to be questioned!

This conversation was recorded at the *Religion and Postmodernism* conference, Villanova, September 2003, and first published in the *Journal of Philosophy and Scripture*.

Athens Colloquy
Between Selves and Others

DEMETRIUS TEIGAS: I would like to put some critical questions to you, not in order to oppose your views, but to welcome your fresh thoughts on the topic of alterity, and also to invite you to elaborate on the diacritical hermeneutics you propose in your recent trilogy. Such an effort, in my opinion, could fill in a gap felt daily in our present historical conditions, where we witness countless exclusions of the *other* in terror and suffering. Although you distinguish clearly your proposal for a diacritical hermeneutics from both Gadamerian and radical hermeneutics, it is not evident what exactly you propose so that one could see "oneself as another." For this purpose, could other past philosophical attempts—for example, the Hegelian model showing the logical necessity of the Master-Slave engagement (both dependence and conflict)—be of help? Could they provide bridges of explication in the relationship between *eauton* and *heteron?* Is your diacritical hermeneutics *open* to other past philosophical endeavors, or does it *exclude* them because they do not sufficiently comprehend "oneself as another"?

RK: I think there are several significant prefigurations of the dia- critical model in the history of modern philosophy—I say *modern* because I am assuming that most agree that the crisis of selfhood was not a radical problem up until Descartes and the Enlightenment. Hegel, you are right, is one of the most cogent cases in point, though almost all the German idealists and romantics address the issue in some form or other. The difficulty for me with Hegel and his followers is not so much the use of dialectical inversion between self and other—this can actually be quite salutary as an exercise in imagining oneself in terms of one's adversary or opponent—but in the idealist tendency to reduce the other to various categories of sameness. In Hegel, this takes the form of dissolving distinct, contingent, singular others into the totality of Absolute Spirit. In the final analysis, the "truth is the whole." Totality wins out over infinity, to use Levinas's terms. The other as concrete face, standing before me here and now, is subsumed into the onward march of history. The deep enigmas and long shadows of the neighbor—not to mention the unfathomable mysteries of the stranger!—are all ultimately resolved and decoded by the Ruse of Reason. Napoleon riding through the streets of Jena is no more (nor less) than the "world soul on horseback," a puppet of the dialectic, a mere pretext for the text of Absolute Spirit. Napoleon's poor valet doesn't even feature! So while we can learn a lot from the Hegelian dialectic of self and other—look at the marvelous analyses that thinkers like [Søren] Kierkegaard, [Alexandre] Kojeve, or Sartre were able to extrapolate from it—we must be wary, in the heel of the hunt, about embracing its totalizing conclusions. This is why I prefer the post-Hegelian hermeneutics of Ricœur and others, for whom the paradigm of "oneself-as-another" (*soi-même comme un autre*) is much more nuanced in its diacritical balancing of selfhood and alterity. Such an approach gives each its due. For if someone like Hegel errs towards the Triumph of the Self, Levinas and the postmoderns can often veer off too much in the other direction, sacrificing the self altogether, out of deference to the absolute claims of the other. I'm against absolutizing either self or other. And here I would endorse Ricœur's critique of Hegel in volume three, chapter 9 of *Time and Narrative* (1985) (entitled "Should We Renounce Hegel?") as well as his later critique of Levinas in the concluding chapter of *Oneself as Another* (1990) and *Autrement* (1997). This is also, may I add, the main thrust of my critical reservations about deconstruction—and especially its cult of the sublime *other*—in *Strangers, Gods and Monsters* (2003), especially the third study, "Others and Aliens." What I am looking for is a third way, between the Scylla of self-sameness and the Charybdis of alienation: what I call a *juste milieu* of self-as-other and other-as-self. Not easy. I admit that. But I am not alone here. There are many others, in my view, working to clear a similar track—from Ricœur and Taylor to Tracy, [Jean] Greisch, [Peter] Kemp, [Dominico] Jervolino, and others . . . the list goes on. Diacritical hermeneutics is not a one-man show. It is, like its immediate intellectual ancestor phenomenology, very much an ongoing project involving a diverse and growing community of minds. Long live the democratic conflict of interpretations! Philosophy would be dead without it.

DT: I would like to stress the fact that in trying to assimilate the relationships between ourselves and the *other*, one encounters not only the *invisibility* of the other (resulting in our inability to understand this other), but also certain *constraints* built within us, which hinder and effect our proximity to the other. If this is so, could [Michel] Foucault's analysis of the concept of "self-formation," or the "subjectivation of the self" offer itself as a significant bridge in our efforts to concretize and historicize our relationship to the other? Could we, with the help of a Foucauldian hermeneutics, discover within ourselves obstacles and structures responsible for distancing the other and also show that they have been formed during the subjectivization of ourselves? In this respect, might we not think of forms of alterity as basic ingredients in the constitution of ourselves?

RK: I think this could be very useful indeed. My one reservation here would be, however, that in concentrating on how the logics of the same—structural epistemologies of self-formation, psychoanalytic disclosures of unconscious desire, genealogies of will-to-power, dialectical models of self-consciousness and self-realization, etc.—constitute our relationship to the other, we risk giving too much away. In other words, by focusing on the shaping and determining powers of subjectivity and subjectivization (even if they be impersonally and structurally generated as thinkers like [Louis] Althusser, [Jacques] Lacan, and Foucault argue), we open up the danger of ignoring the radically transcendent dimensions of alterity. And here I have some sympathy with Derrida's critique of the structuralist reduction, as well as with Ricœur's more hermeneutic objections to the triumph of system (the machine of signifiers) over signification (the more referential model of someone saying something to someone about something). I am wary of all attempts to subordinate the irreducible alterity of the other to an immanence of self or system. Such approaches take the enigma out of otherness and give too much power to the social and psychological functions of *subjectivity* (however one understands the term). We need to give each its due—*both* self *and* other.

DT: Moving away from the individual and his/her inability to understand the other, could we register further obstacles which restrict or forbid the dialogue with the other? In concrete historical examples of alterity, we often encounter obstacles of this kind, such as the state, ideologies, or other particular social practices (a theme to which you have referred in your recent trilogy, *Philosophy at the Limits*). However, could we examine such obstacles under Foucault's categories of "power" and "power relations"? Could a diacritical hermeneutics utilize some of Foucault's views on "power" in order to comprehend real historical contingencies? Or do you finally see the hermeneutics you propose as working at some distance from Foucault? Do we need a "hermeneutics of power" to accompany your diacritical hermeneutics? Or to put it another way, can diacritical hermeneutics incorporate such an analysis if one considers that the critical interrogation of power is important for approaching real, pragmatic cases?

RK: It can and it does incorporate such analysis. This is, in fact, a central part of what "dia-critical" interpretation is all about. If you consider what the term actually says—*dia-crinein* or *dia-crisis* in Greek—the critical implications of this term are already evident. Originally, the term referred to a process of discerning or discriminating between signs. These signs were originally understood as medical symptoms of fevers or secretions, but they later accrued an additional, more technical meaning as linguistic marks. This second meaning referred to how certain signs distinguish different sounds or values of the same letter or character. One example is the letter "e" with its four different kinds of accents in French—grave, acute, circumflex and diaeresis (è, é, ê, ë). Another example would be the difference between the French terms "ou" and "a" with and without accents. With a grave accent over the "u," the sign "où" means "where," but without, it means "or." With a grave accent on the "à," it functions as a preposition, "towards," but without it, the "a" serves as an indefinite article, and so on. Here we see how small graphic signs—points or accents—can be deployed to prevent confusion between otherwise identical terms. So such diacritical signs can be said, in this context, to preserve the "difference" between distinct meanings. They resist the collapse of the *other* into the *same*. One might say, accordingly, that "diacritics" is all about critical sounding, listening, reading, fine-tuning, with an attendant dimension (which I choose to emphasize) of diagnosing and healing. In short, while the term *diacritical* can have a quite technical meaning in contemporary linguistics and semiotics—namely, the process of making differential demarcations in units of language (signifiers, phonemes, graphemes, accents)—it also has an additional and much older resonance as a act of therapeutic discrimination and understanding, which, in my view, should underlie our political and ethical judgments. And it is just this kind of hermeneutic discernment between different kinds of others and different kinds of selves which I believe is lacking in certain extreme positions of both romanticism and postmodernism: the former because it reduces all strangeness to the "egotistical sublime," the latter because it subsumes selfhood and subjectivity into "absolute otherness." Neither, in my view, contributes much to the diacritical vocation to help us to live better with others, to read and reveal our respective symptoms, to heal our wounds, to face our monsters, to welcome each other's differences.

But to come to the more specific aspect of your question—the relationship between my diacritical hermeneutics and the Foucauldian critique of power relations. In fact, I do cite Foucault at crucial moments in both *On Stories* and *Strangers, Gods and Monsters*. "There are monsters on the prowl whose form changes with the history of knowledge." And I quote his brilliant analysis of how covert alliances between knowledge and power in different ages have served to marginalize and criminalize so-called fools, strangers, madmen. Foucault's *Madness and Civilisation* (1965) greatly informs my various studies on scapegoating and alienation in part 1 of *Strangers, Gods and Monsters*. But I also part company with Foucault at certain key points—when he jettisons, for example, the responsible, choosing subject; when he demonizes the System—be it science, religion, government, medicine, psychoanalysis, or metaphysics—as some omnipresent, all-pervasive structure; when he too rapidly embraces an anarchy-versus-absolute scenario that foments apocalyptic anxieties; when he celebrates the sublimity of madness and transgression (for transgression's sake). On these points, I take issue with Foucault's overly alarmist and pessimistic tone. I think his enthusiasm for structuralism was an over-determined reaction to existentialism—he was so desperate to break from Sartre and make his own mark. He went to the other extreme. That said, I find his last writings on "parhesia" (which Tom Flynn and Jim Bernauer develop so wonderfully) and the aesthetics of "self-caring" *(le souci de soi)* quite remarkable and very inspiring.

DT: Although you attempt to offer a philosophical analysis of diacritical hermeneutics, is there some danger in creating a gap between the logical categories a theory wishes to use and the real concrete historical contingencies of life? For example, we talk of "alterity," but there are concrete historical alterities; we talk of "power," but real concrete exercises of power are visible. This has always been a main problem for philosophical thinking—the gap between the logical and the historical. We know that the real is not rational, as Hegel would wish. I think that the Gadamerian notions of the "historicality of understanding" and of "effective history" attempt to mediate this gap. How would your diacritical hermeneutics address concrete historical cases of monstrosity and alterity, when applying its theoretical (logical) conceptions? How can it avoid misunderstanding, or avoid hypostatizing (by forcing under its general concepts), concrete historical alterities?

RK: Well, I do address a number of "concrete historical cases" in my trilogy—genocide, pogroms, Vietnam, and September 11 in *Strangers, Gods and Monsters* (chapters 1–5 and 8); the Holocaust and the exploits of colonial and imperial regimes (Rome, Britain, America) in parts 2 and 3 of *On Stories*. These are all attempts at a critical "applied hermeneutics," and they would certainly be consonant with Gadamer's notions of "effective history" and the "historicality of understanding." Perhaps I should have mentioned Gadamer more often in the trilogy. Maybe this omission is due to the fact that my frequent invocations of Ricœur's hermeneutics took for granted all the decisive work done by [Wilhelm] Dilthey, Heidegger, and Gadamer in blazing the path of contemporary hermeneutics. In other words, maybe it is because I presupposed so much of what Ricœur presupposed! There is no doubt that of all the precursors of diacritical hermeneutics, Gadamer is the most open to thinking about historical cases in moral and political terms; but he could be more open still. And on this last point, I do think that Ricœur manages to negotiate an appropriate middle course between the Habermasian and Gadamerian positions in "Hermeneutics and the Critique of Ideology." I believe he charts a judicious path between the need for critical distance (Habermas's hermeneutics of suspicion) and the need for ontological appropriation (Gadamer's hermenutics of affirmation). I would like to think I am following in Ricœur's footsteps, pursuing that diacritical itinerary.

DT: It seems to me that you rightly understand the two poles of a possible hermeneutic approach to alterity, asking for both a "critique of the self" and a "critique of the other." Nevertheless, your main position, if I understand you well, is that this double critique is essential for two reasons—neither to totally distance the other from us, nor to make the other a mere extension of ourselves. This bipolar criticism must, it seems, constitute *an essential part* of your diacritical hermeneutics. But there are times when you appear to be less than even in your critical judgments, casting greater suspicion on the operations of the

self than on those of the *other* or neglecting the importance of the legitimate suspicions that the other may have of oneself. You often speak,
for example, of your goal "to make us *hospitable* to strangers, gods, and
monsters" [italics mine]. But do we not also need to be susceptible to
the other's criticisms and disruptions of ourselves? Would you accept
that *criticism* of the other is *as important* as understanding of the other?
And would you accept that criticism of oneself by the other is a crucial part of the equation?

RK: Yes, I would certainly accept that the criticism must work
bilaterally, in both directions at once. If we are too suspicious of ourselves and too unsuspecting of others, we can end up with various sorts
of naive sentimentalism (the other is always on the side of the angels)
or mystical masochism (the other is irreducibly ethical even when he
is persecuting me, holding me hostage, tearing the bread from my
mouth). You find this in certain notions of Christian self-abnegation
(rightly exposed by Nietzsche and [Max] Scheler in my view) but also,
in more sophisticated postmodern guise, in the later Levinas or in Derrida's formula that "every other is every other." That is going too far.
That is indiscriminate hospitality. That is (almost) indifferent justice,
precluding the possibility of discerning judgments. On the other hand,
if we go around denouncing the other at every turn, we lapse back into
the logocentrism of mainstream Western ideology, or just good old
Margaret Thatcher individualism: Every Self for Itself, The Self Is
Always Right, Ego Is Empire, Beware of Strangers, Trespassers Will
Be Prosecuted, No Irish (Blacks, Jews, Women, Gays, Atheists, Arabs,
whatever) Need Apply! Who wants to go back there? There has to be
another way, a middle way. The alternatives are acquiescent passivism
or war, postmodern paralysis or modern voluntarism. Neither is acceptable. Diacritical hermeneutics seeks a way between.

Recorded at the *Philosophy of Otherness* conference at The American College of Greece,
Athens, June 2002

Halifax Colloquy
Between Being and God

FELIX O'MURCHADHA: Two of your most recent books deal explicitly and thematically with the question of God. That is not to say that this issue has been absent from your earlier work. Could you please trace the development of this theme in your philosophical journey from *Poétique du Possible* [The Poetics of the Possible] to *The God Who May Be* and *Strangers, Gods and Monsters?*

RK: My first sortie into the God debate was during my time as a doctoral student with Paul Ricœur in Paris in the late 1970s. I was participating in Ricœur's seminar on hermeneutics and phenomenology, along with Levinas, Derrida, Greisch, [Jean-François] Courtine, [Françoise] Dastur, and others. It was a tremendously exciting time, and the relationship between phenomenology and theology was very much in the air just then. That was when I and an Irish colleague of mine, the theologian Joseph O'Leary, got together and decided to organize a public colloquium in the Irish College in Paris on "Heidegger and the Question of God." This was held in 1980 and subsequently published in 1981 by Grasset, under the same title. Along with Ricœur and others mentioned above, we also invited the more orthodox Heideggerians — [Jean] Beaufret, [François] Fédier, and [François] Vezin, those officially charged by Gallimard and the Heidegger estate with the dissemination and publication of Heidegger's writings in France. It was an explosive cocktail as it happened; indeed, we unsuspecting Irish were told, after the event, that it was something of a miracle that such a diverse group of philosophers actually sat around the same table to discuss the relationship between phenomenology and God. But they did. And that debate lit all kinds of bonfires in my own mind. My doctoral thesis at the time, *Poétique du Possible*, was an exploration of the hermeneutic dialogue between what I called "ontology" (broadly based on a Heideggerian/Husserlian approach) and "eschatology" (inspired by Levinas and Ricœur). The basic argument was that there were two fundamental hermeneutics underlying the different regional (ontic) disciplines — the ontological guided by questions of "being" and the eschatological by questions of "God" or the "Good." While I argued that these ran in parallel, and worked with distinct methods and presuppositions, I also wanted to suggest that there were possibilities of overlap and exchange. That at least was my wager in that inaugural work. There followed a long period, I have to admit, between the publication of *Poétique du Possible* in 1984 and the publication of *The God Who May Be* in 2001 — almost twenty years, if you consider that the first book was actually completed in 1980. During that time I worked mainly at University College Dublin, where the question of God was almost unmentionable in a country where people were still killing each other over religion (at least in the north of the island). I taught and wrote mainly on questions of imagination, myth, symbolism, literature, and art. It was really only when I moved to Boston College on a permanent footing at the end of the 1990s that I came back to the God question and picked up the debate about Being and the eschaton that I had left behind me in Paris.

FOM: Any discourse on God will have a personal element — an element of testimony and an element of declaration (of faith or unbelief, of theism or atheism, etc.). Your testimony and declaration are to love and justice,[5] against which you will judge the Catholic, Judeo-Christian tradition from which you hail. Are these "values" higher than God for you? To put the question otherwise, could there ever be an incompatibility between seeking love and justice and seeking God?

RK: Yes, there is almost always a certain personal commitment or conviction involved in any discourse on God. Since the Enlightenment's ban on bringing presuppositions to bear on the "facts" themselves (something we see, albeit in revised form, in the phenomenological reductions and bracketings of Husserl and Heidegger), there is an assumption that matters of faith and value must somehow be placed beyond the Pale. Now, I have no difficulty with this if it is merely a methodical strategy for focusing on the "things themselves." As a temporary and provisional suspension of our presuppositions, that's fine. In fact, it may even help us to acknowledge our tacit presuppositions all the more clearly. After all, it is a good thing to bring covert assumptions that work behind our heads before our eyes! But if we go on to presume that the suspension of our basic interests and preunderstandings can serve as an *end in itself*, leading us to some pure domain of transcendental subjectivity (Husserl) or empirical positivity (Carnap and the logical positivists), then I blow the whistle. That, as Gadamer rightly pointed out, is "prejudice against prejudice"—with the added disadvantage that it thinks it is *above* all prejudice! So, yes, I have no real difficulty conceding that descriptions of phenomena always involve some kind of interpretation, implicit or explicit, bracketed or foregrounded, oblique or avowed. And if this is true of our ordinary value convictions, it is even more true of our religious convictions.

But to come back to the second part of your question: Would I choose Love and Justice over God? That reminds me of the famous Dostoyevskian dilemma about choosing between truth and God. We shouldn't have to choose, of course, if what we call God is really true, loving, and just—as the God of Isaiah and Jesus, for example, claims to be. But that is not always the case. All too often, we have cases of unjust, unloving, and untrue acts being made in the name of God. Think of all the wars and inquisitions and pogroms and witch-hunts carried out for religious reasons. It's terrible, but has to be faced. That's why if it came to it, I'd chose love and justice any day over God. But so would God—if God were a God of love and justice. And if not, then such a God is not worth believing in. To take a concrete example from the Gospels, I think the person who gives a cup of cold water to the thirsting stranger is far closer to God than the person who claims to believe in God but passes the neighbor by. So if and when a deity identifies itself as love and justice, I am prepared to follow that God. But there are, alas, many "Gods," and many "believers," who don't.

FOM: Although you take most of your discussions of God from the Judeo-Christian tradition, you refer also to other religions. Indeed the plural "Gods" in the title of *Strangers, Gods and Monsters* suggests this. Is the "God who may be," however, thinkable outside the messianic religions? Does the attempt to think philosophically a god other than the god of the philosophers lead inevitably back to the Hebrew and Christian Scriptures?

RK: I don't think it does. But I can certainly understand why you might think so from a reading of *The God Who May Be*. In that book, I was concentrating my hermeneutic investigations on biblical and scriptural texts; not because I believe they enjoy some exclusive access to the absolute—I don't—but because they are the ones I know best. They are my tradition. And just as the great Buddhist master Thich Nhat Hahn advises many of those who want to convert to Buddhism that they should return to their own traditions and find there the truth that Buddhists find in Buddhism, I would be inclined to say the same thing to those who might wish to convert to say Christianity or Judaism. There is, I believe, no absolute way to the absolute. There are different ways, and each way has something incredibly valuable and distinctive, and they may indeed all be pointing to the same absolute (we cannot "know" that, of course; we can only "believe")—such that each can learn a huge amount from the others through dialogue and interfaith exchanges. These diverse ways are not, in my opinion, mutually exclusive. Christ says that he is "the way, the truth, and the life." Granted. But he never says he is the "*only* way, truth, and life." In fact, he seems to spend half his time saying how much he owes to Abraham and Jacob and Isaiah and the prophets—not to mention those two other "persons," the Father and the Paraclete. I'm sure Jesus would have been similarly generous towards Buddhists and Hindus and Taoists had he encountered them. Just look how loving he was towards Samaritans and sinners and other strangers. It is inconceivable to me that such a Jesus could say that it is only if you give a cup of cold water to a Christian person in the name of an exclusively Christian God that you find salvation! So without wishing to endorse some kind of Californian New Ageism, I firmly believe that "God speaks in many ways" (to juggle with Aristotle's phrase about Being, which so influenced Heidegger). There are many mansions in the Father's kingdom, we are told, and we must therefore assume that there are many doors into them, too. As I moved from *The God Who May Be* to *Strangers, Gods and Monsters*, I found myself becoming more and more sympathetic to so-called heretics, pagans, nonmonotheistic believers, and so on. The important thing, in the final analysis, is to be actively and lovingly in search of God, not to have found him. God finds us; we don't find God. The moment we think we possess the divine, we have lost it. We are, in that instance, possessed by *ourselves* alone. I have become increasingly intolerant of intolerance—increasingly suspicious of narrowly monotheistic claims to be able to identify the "One" with the "one and only," "Unity" with the exclusively "unique." That way leads to triumphalism, persecution, fundamentalism, war. We even need to remind ourselves, if we are to be really generous and honest, that the so-called

New Age religions themselves—that we monotheists sometimes consider so superficial—are often (as in the case of Hinduism and Taoism) older than the Christian religion. If we were to be more accurate, we would call them Old Age religions. But in any case, I would be inclined to say, "let a thousand blossoms bloom."

FOM: To think philosophically a god beyond the god of the philosophers is itself a paradoxical undertaking, indeed, it lands us in the possibly aporetic discourse of the "end of metaphysics." How would you situate your latest thinking, that of the trilogy, in relation to the "end of metaphysics"?

RK: I am very partial to the idea of a postmetaphysical God, as is obvious in the last two parts of the trilogy. Here I am very much in dialogue with thinkers like Caputo, Derrida, Marion, and the various contemporary "negative theologians" involved in the "postmodernism and religion" debates. But I also recognize with Heidegger that you cannot attempt to go beyond metaphysics without using the language of metaphysics. So no matter how much I seek to save God from such metaphysical terms as cause, substance, sufficient reason, ground, system, etc., I acknowledge that I am still using language, ideas, and concepts to do so. And, of course, this implies a metaphysical heritage of some sort. It's the old one about pulling oneself up by the bootstraps. At best, we have a sort of hermeneutical circle where we enter with all kinds of metaphysical notions and assumptions and hope, as we "pyrne in the gyre" (Yeats), that we might reach a higher level of understanding in the next turn of the circle, and so on. But we never exit from the hermeneutic circle altogether. Paradoxes and aporias abound. That is inevitable. But one hopes that these might be productive paradoxes and affirmative aporias, inviting us to think more and more deeply, rather than paralyzing us with hopelessness. Speaking about the unspeakable (God) is indeed a performative contradiction of sorts. But it is the best we've got. And I prefer here the response of [Samuel] Beckett's unnamable narrator—"I can't go on, I'll go on"—to Wittgenstein's "whereof I cannot speak, thereof I must be silent." There is a proper time for silence, of course, but also a proper time to speak and think and imagine God, however tentatively and figuratively. Otherwise we could not engage in a hermeneutics of religion. Or any philosophy of religion for that matter.

FOM: Polemical terms such as "paganism" and "idolatry" slip into your texts from time to time. Firstly, do you accept that these are polemical terms? Secondly, what is it about the discourse on God in contemporary thinking which reflects almost unconsciously Judeo-Christian polemics?

RK: To return to what I said above, I am much slower to use such terms now than in my early work, especially *Poétique du Possible*. When I wrote that first book in the late seventies I was very much under the influence of Levinas and Marion—the latter's *L'idole et la distance: Cinq études [The Idol and Distance: Five Studies]* had just been published in Paris, and I was attending Levinas's final lectures at the Sorbonne. So the whole debate between the "holy" and the "sacred," between biblical infinity and pagan totality, was very much alive—aided by the revival of the mystical tradition of "negative theology" (Eckhart, Dionysius, Silesius, Gregory of Nyssa) and abetted by the deconstructive critiques of "logocentrism" and "onto-theology." I bought into all that and was perhaps too quick in my endorsement of somewhat simplistic reactions to so-called idolatrous thought—which usually meant some form or other of the "metaphysics of presence." I would be much more cautious about that now. I hope this is evident from my more inclusive approach to the God question in *Strangers, Gods and Monsters* and my growing interest in interreligious dialogue, especially concerning the opening up of biblical discourse to Buddhist, Hindu, or Taoist wisdom traditions. I can hardly believe, for example, that it took me almost forty-eight years to get around to reading the *Uphanishads!* Talk about Eurocentrism!

FOM: What is the place of faith in philosophy? Can we think God or the divine without faith or unbelief, and, if not, does this say something about us, about our particular Judeo-Christian heritage, or about thinking itself? In other words, how does the Heideggerian project of thinking God beyond faith—beyond, one might say, theism and atheism—relate to your project of thinking the God who is to come?

RK: This is a very difficult question. I have a lot of sympathy with a certain version of the phenomenological move to raise all fundamental or "essential" questions in an open space beyond doctrinal positions of theism or atheism. But I wouldn't be as extreme as Heidegger in his *Introduction to Metaphysics* or in *Phenomenology and Theology,* where he sees the being-question and the faith-question as mutually exclusive. For me, the hermeneutic realm of "eschatology" opens a place of phenomenological thinking which is reducible to neither Greek ontology nor Biblical theology, though both can enter into conversation here.

As dealing with the other who may be, the other to come, with messianic peace and justice (Levinas/Derrida), or the advent of the kingdom (Ricœur/[Franz] Rosenzweig/[Walter] Benjamin), I think that the eschatological can operate in a transconfessional or even postconfessional domain, where atheists and theists can explore questions of ultimacy and can do so—this is all-important—without having to confine the "eschaton" to a particular name (Yahweh, Jesus, Allah, Apollo, Zeus, Krishna) or to a particular religious tradition. So to try to answer you question: I do not, I repeat, believe that thinking about God needs to be confined to the specific biblical tradition of monotheistic revelation (here I differ from Levinas, Marion, or [John] Milbank, for example). It is certainly very manifest and vocal in this tradition but is, in my view, present in other nonbiblical traditions also. Simone Weil offers some powerful examples of this in her *Letter to a Priest*, though she goes too far, I think, in her critique of Old Testament exclusivism. And one finds very persuasive arguments for opening up monotheism to its *others* in Stanlislas Breton's work, especially *Unicité et monothéisme*. When one considers just how arrogant we in the West have been in our condescending attitudes to non-Western ways of thinking and talking about God! And I would include here not only monotheistic intolerance of so-called pagan and heretical religions, but also Heidegger's embrace of a Greek-German paganism to the exclusion of Eastern, African, or Native American spiritualities. I am not sure that Heidegger's "gods" are really beyond all kinds of faith or religion. They often seem to me to have their own brand of numinous charge and sacramental allure—even at the ostensibly neutral level of "thought." So if Heidegger's thought may be considered *god-less* with respect to biblical revelation, it has its own kinds of gods—one of whom is, as you know, dramatically invoked by Heidegger as our only hope of salvation in his final *Der Spiegel* interview. Talk about the ontological pot calling the eschatological kettle black! So to come back to the first part of your question, I would be inclined to say that most philosophies dealing with fundamental questions involve some version of faith or conviction (religious or otherwise). I have never believed in the idea of the philosopher as some disembodied and disengaged transcendental spectator. Almost all our thinking is informed and motivated—however prereflectively—by some set of deep hermeneutic presuppositions. I am *moved* to think, therefore I think.

FOM: You pose Ricœur's question to Heideggerians, as to why Heidegger thinks only of [Friedrich] Hölderlin and not of the Psalms.

May I pose a question to you which reverses this one, namely, can you—or anyone—think of the gods of the Greeks, the gods of Homer, and the God of the Hebrew Scriptures together, or is a choice between the Olympus and Calvary (or in Nietzschean terms Dionysius and the Crucified) inevitable?

RK: Not only do I think that we *can* think them together, I would go further and say that we *should* think them together. And to be fair, I think that many philosophers and theologians, prior to the Levinas-Heidegger quarrel in contemporary Continental thought, were doing just that—for centuries. The dialogue between Athens and Jerusalem has a long and impressive heritage—from Paul, Philo, and the early Church Fathers, up to Augustine and Aquinas and beyond. The fact that this lapsed into reductive and totalizing forms of "Christian metaphysics" on occasion, especially in late Scholasticism, doesn't mean that there wasn't really important work going on for almost two thousand years on the Athens-Jerusalem nexus. All too often, blanket critiques of the entire tradition of Western metaphysics as "onto-theological" and (by extension) "idolatrous" do a grave injustice to the complexity of the texts themselves. You can throw out too many babies with the bath waters of logocentrism! And, in fairness, both Heidegger and Derrida acknowledge this (too long after the damage is done, some might say, but no matter). What is certain is that the dialogue between Olympus and Calvary, as you put it, not only needs to be revived and rethought in our age of global closure; it also needs to be opened up to include other poles of world spirituality—we need to get Tibet in there and the Ganges and Kyoto, other holy spaces of wisdom—so that rather than speaking of opening monologue to dialogue, we should more accurately be speaking of a polylogue: different lines of faith and thought crisscrossing in a flourishing tapestry of conversations. That is not, I would insist, a lapse into New Age relativism or postmodern perspectivism. Nor is it necessarily a rejection of monotheism (everything depends on how one interprets oneness—"in the beginning was hermeneutics!") in favor of polytheism. For me, it is rather a way of growing deeper and further in one's own tradition by opening one's imagination to others.

First conducted at the *Annual Conference of the Canadian Society for Hermeneutics and Postmodern Thought* at Dalhousie University, Halifax, May 2003

Stony Brook Colloquy
Confronting Imagination

Q: I would like to begin by asking when and how you became interested in philosophy and literature. Was there a moment when you realized you would make these fields a lifelong investigation?

RK: I think it was probably when I was at secondary school in Ireland. I had a very good French teacher who had just come back from Paris and had read a lot of Heidegger, Sartre, Ricœur, and Derrida. This would have been in the early seventies. So I got my philosophy mainly through the literature of Sartre, [Simone] de Beauvoir, and [Albert] Camus. It was existential phenomenology through a literary detour. When I went to university, I did a joint degree in philosophy and literature. I was going to go to the Abbey Theatre in Dublin to become a professional actor. In my application to the Abbey, I submitted a philosophical dissertation as to why I wanted to study acting. The director of the Abbey at the time said I was welcome to study acting, but he recommended that I should go and study philosophy first. I never got back to the Abbey. After my undergraduate work, I did my MA with Charles Taylor in McGill University (Montreal), which was on the philosophy of art, and then my Ph.D. with Paul Ricœur in Paris on the phenomenology of imagination. Over the last few years, I have been writing more poetry and fiction. I have just finished my second novel; the first one came out two years ago. Philosophy and literature were always my two interests, my Janus-face as it were. My literature is contaminated by philosophy, and my philosophy is contaminated by literature. The English critics didn't really like my novels—they thought they were too Francophile and philosophical. But the Continentals liked them. The first novel sold about 3,000 copies in England and 30,000 copies in German, French, and Czech translations. As one of the English reviewers pointed out, the Germans have been mistaken in their judgment before!

Q: Philosophy and literature as a joint venture for you is very much displayed in your book *The Poetics of Modernity* (1996). I would like to specifically ask how you came to focus on the relationship between poetics and ethics.

RK: I would say it was when I was doing the doctorate with Paul Ricœur in Paris in the late seventies. Two of my main interlocutors at the time were Derrida and Levinas. It was before Derrida started to talk about law, justice, ethics, and so on. Although he would say the ethical dimension was already in his work, it just wasn't visible for me or most other people at the time. In 1977, when I was writing my *Poétique du Possible,* Derrida was very much on the literary side of things, moving more and more towards an aesthetic Nietzscheanism. That's how it was understood, at any rate. Derrida's "Violence and Metaphysics" essay on Levinas was seen as a farewell to ethics, as a challenge to a phenomenological relationship with the other. There seemed to be a tension between Derrida the poeticizer and Levinas the ethicizer. And there I was with Ricœur, trying to do a hermeneutic mediation between these two extremes. Subsequently I found a poetics at work within Levinas, which I tried to tease out in my essay on "Levinas and the Ethics of Imagining" in *The Poetics of Modernity.* And of course, there is an ethics at work in Derrida, as he now constantly points out.

Q: You say in *Poetics of Modernity* that Kierkegaard criticizes Kant for segregating poetics and ethics. Do you find yourself trying to do something similar, that is, criticizing this segregatory practice?

RK: I try to conjugate the two. But I think that Kant, in the Third Critique, actually provides us with a very good pretext for this. When he says, for instance, that "beauty is the symbol for morality," he is, in effect, saying that reflective aesthetic judgment has a huge contribution to make to morality. In fact, I would say it is a discreet corrective within Kant to his own morality. The categorical imperative in the Second Critique, *The Critique of Practical Reason,* is actually an impractical morality. Because the categorical imperative is so rationalistic and abstract, it ignores the attempt in certain sections of the Third Critique to counterbalance the Second Critique. I think Hannah Arendt has actually brought this out well when she talks about reflective judgment as a common basis for a dialogue between ethics and poetics. Derrida and Lyotard have also been fascinated by the Third Critique and I think for similar reasons.

Take this example: when Kant talks about *exemplary judgment,* or "representative thinking," and says we really can't have a proper judgment unless we can put ourselves in a position where we can imagine what it's like for as many other people as possible to think in the way that we're thinking, this is a mode of universalizability, but it's also a phenomenological experience. It's Kant being true to the phenomenologist in himself, to the transcendental imagination in himself (which Heidegger rightly identifies with *Dasein* in his *Kant and the Problem of Metaphysics*). When it comes to describing "exemplary judgment" in the Third Critique, Kant is actually talking about an "exemplary imagination." One must put oneself into other people's shoes—and that requires a certain exercise of "free variation," extending empathically from your limited self to other selves.

Q: A phenomenological relationship.

RK: A phenomenological relationship of imagining what it is like to be another and only making your universal judgment on the basis of having (as it were) traversed these other minds. Husserl makes much of this in the fifth of his *Cartesian Meditations*. But Kant already foresees it in the Third Critique when he talks about "representative judgment"; that is, one cannot make a representative universal judgment without making appeal to the multiplicity of different individuals. One can only construct a universal out of a multiplication of singularities through imagination. The beauty of the power of imagination is that it can combine the intelligible with the sensible, the mental with the physical, the general with the particular. That was its standard role from Aristotle through Aquinas down to Kant. To bring together these opposites.

Q: Aristotle calls it *phronēsis*.

RK: I think "aesthetic reflective judgment" is Kant's term for *phronēsis*. It's actually a matter of negotiating the relationship of the universal and the singular, but with attribution to the singular. You're not moving from the universal to the singular; you're actually moving *between* them. And so the categorical imperative that says one must act as everybody else acts is in itself sterile, cheerless, and unworkable, unless it

is bodied forth by imagination. Even Kant, the most desiccated of rationalists, realized this and conceded, *mirabile dictu,* that "beauty is the
symbol of morality." This is an extraordinary statement for the author
of the Second Critique, at last acknowledging a role for inclinations,
feelings, affections—and thereby, by extension—for imagination.

Q: Could you expound on your reading of Sartre's notion of the
imaginary as the "negation of the negation" in chapter 4 of your *Poetics of Imagining* and then try to clarify Merleau-Ponty's reasons for
rejecting Sartre's notion?

RK: The particular phrase "negation of negation" comes from
Sartre's text *The Psychology of Imagination,* which was published in
1940. In French, it is called *L'Imaginaire*—which is a better title—
meaning "The Imaginary." The subtitle was *Une Psychologie
Phénoménologique de L'Imagination,* a phenomenological psychology of
imagination. It's primarily a phenomenological work. In it, Sartre
actually does a Heideggerian reading of Husserl's thesis on imagination in the "Sixth Logical Investigation." Husserl there separates out
perception, imagination, and signification. What Sartre does in the
Postscript to *The Psychology of Imagination* is take Heidegger's notion
of being-in-the-world, *In-der-Welt-Sein,* and basically say that this is
the same thing as imagination. Curiously, Sartre at that stage hadn't
read the *Kantbuch [Kant and the Problem of Metaphysics],* where Heidegger says that *Dasein* is another name for "transcendental imagination." But Heidegger couldn't use the term "imagination," because
he was a German writing in 1927 and wanted to get away from the
romantic baggage of Kant, [Friedrich] Schelling, [Johann Gottlieb]
Fichte, and Hegel. He mentions this in a long footnote. He says that
what the romantics meant by *Produktiv Einbildungskraft*—the productive imagination—prefigures what he means by *Dasein.* He didn't
want to be thought of as just another German idealist (which is probably not too far from the truth). He admitted that the temporalizing,
schematizing power of imagination is another word for *Dasein,* but
he renounced the term "imagination."

Sartre, without alluding to this particular analysis, nonetheless also
had the instinct to realize that being-in-the-world, *Dasein,* has the same
temporalizing, schematizing structure as imagination.

Now the "negation of the negation" goes something like this: we can
only be in the world (*In-der-Welt-sein*) by already understanding the
world in terms of the projection of our possibilities. *Dasein* is the projection of possibilities. But *Dasein* only has possibilities and can only

construe possibilities, read possibilities off its world, if it has already in some sense *negated* the world, that is, if it is not *in* the world—in the sense of being spatially located like a thing in a box.

So being-in-the-world is actually an intentional relationship that presupposes—and here Sartre is true to Husserl—a relationship of distance as well as proximity, of transcendence as well as of belonging. And that is, of course, true to the basic Husserlian principle that "all consciousness is consciousness *of* something," an "of" that is both conjunctive and disjunctive.

It is the *distance* that is the negation. In other words, I cannot see a world, I cannot read a world, I cannot understand a world unless I am in some sense *not of the world*, unless I am surpassing the world towards my possibilities—and therefore construing the world in terms of my possibilities. So everything in the world becomes *zuhanden*, becomes a thing for me. I'm going up a hill, and there is a rock. I interpret the rock as a building brick if I happen to be a mason looking for stones, as a weapon of defense if I happen to be chased by an enemy army, as an obstacle if I happen to be a mountaineer trying to get to the top of the hill, as a sculpting block if I happen to be Michelangelo and it's the hill. My imagination sees the rock *as* an instrument. So whatever my existential project in the world is, I interpret things of the world (that is, a rock on my way) as a *possibility* for me. But I can only symbolize and signify the things of the world if I am somehow *not* of the world. This negating is the act of "primary negation." Sartre says that since imagination is the power of annihilating or unrealizing the world, without negating we cannot be free beings in the world, we cannot be *Dasein* in the first place. So, we are *always* negating.

Now that's the primary negation which all of us carry out in order to be in the world. If we didn't do that, we would be a mere "thing among things," we would be simply a part of the world. As Sartre puts it in the conclusion to *The Psychology of Imagination*, we would be beings in the "midst of the world" if we did not carry out the primary negation.

In other words, we do that no matter what we are doing—receiving, touching, feeling, hearing, signifying, dreaming, hoping, dreading, deriving, eating, sleeping—it doesn't matter; we're negating. If we didn't, we couldn't *signify* things in the world. And as we know from Lévi-Strauss, "things are not only good to eat, they're good to *symboliser*)." So everything presupposes the primary act of negation which Sartre says we do not have unless, implicitly, we are deploying our imagination. Imagination is an invisible act; it is the "art hidden in the depths of nature," as Kant called it. It's the blind spot that we can't see but that lets us see everything. We don't see it; we don't see ourselves seeing. But it's at work all the time.

Now the "negation of the negation," — to come back to your point — is imagination doing a *double* take. Not only does *(a)* one negate the things of the world in order to make of it what Sartre calls a "synthetic totality," a meaningful ensemble (in other words, our imaginations always *schematize* the world), but *(b)* I can negate *that* world too in turn.

So there is no such thing as a nonschematized given. The given is *already* synthetically totalized by the primary negation, and that gives us what we call our "actual world." Then we can choose to negate that actual world as a synthetic totality, to operate a double-negation, thereby providing the unreal world — what we call the *imaginary*. Let me repeat: our perceptual *world* is already a negation. And in that sense, Sartre joins company with Merleau-Ponty when Merleau-Ponty says "perception already stylizes"; it is already a mode of negation and interpretation. The primary reason is (both Merleau-Ponty and Sartre would share this with Kant) that the transcendental imagination — even in its operative, prereflective, ordinary, average way of being-in-the-world — is already interpreting everything in the world in terms of temporary horizons, past and future. I can only interpret this piece of white paper as a piece of white paper because I am phenomenologically retaining the horizons of past memory that allow me to interpret this thing as white — a color, a word in English — and as paper, a thing to write on. I make sense of it; I see it *as* paper, as I see everything in the world *as* something. I *presuppose* my temporal horizons of the past, and at the same time I *project* and surpass myself toward the possibility of that paper as something that I can now write on. The paper only makes sense to me in terms of a "retention" and a "protention," to use Husserl's terms. That is what Sartre means by the primary negation of imagination. The secondary is the negation of the real world in order to constitute what we properly call the "imaginary" world.

Now, that is a long way around to the first part of your question. Let me be a little quicker with the second part. Basically, where Merleau-Ponty differs most from Sartre is in his claim that one *cannot* make a neat distinction in that way, between a primary act of apprehending the world, which is perception, and a secondary act, which is imagination. In other words, for Sartre imagination is always a negation of perception because it's a double negation. Sartre says if one wants to imagine Pierre in Berlin, one must negate this room, the "actual world" in which I find myself. I must negate my present perceptual world in order to "presentify" the absent world, the world of imagination —

Pierre in Berlin. Merleau-Ponty says that's too dualistic. Basically, when we're perceiving, he claims, we are *also* imagining, and when we're imagining we're *also* perceiving. Mealeau-Ponty has a much more chiasmic, intertwined relationship between the two modes of intentionality. For Sartre, as for Husserl (in *Logical Investigations*), the two modes of imagination and perceiving are sui generis and separate. There is also a third mode of intentionality called "empty signification" that doesn't have any intuitive component of presencing or presentification, because signification, unlike perception, gives us the thing *emptily (à vide)*. Husserl made much of those three modes of intentionality, and Sartre still remained faithful to that. Merleau-Ponty, by contrast, wants to say that those three modes of intentionality—language, imagination, and perception—are always *overlapping*. Perception for Sartre is dangerous, because he feels it leads one into a meaningless and absurd existence; it is our imagination that projects meanings and values onto the world, and carves it up and gives it shape. Whereas for Merleau-Ponty that kind of Cartesian voluntarism is an "addiction to magic," to changing everything into a subjective image—"We create the world into our own image." In politics, Mereleau-Ponty claims that Sartre's voluntarism of imperial imagination leads to"ultra-Bolshevism"—the imposition of the will of the subject on other people. That is something that Merleau-Ponty clearly doesn't go along with in Sartre. In so doing, he is trying to get away from the idealist, Cartesian residues in Sartre's phenomenology and to take a more a postsubjectivist dialectical turn.

Q: He does this especially with embodied consciousness.

RK: Yes, and that is why, for instance, Merleau-Ponty can say that every sense and every bodily organ has its "imaginary." This would be unthinkable for Sartre. For Merleau-Ponty, when you are eating, sleeping, breathing, running, when you are relating to other people, etc., there is already imagination at work.

Q: It's like [Marcel] Proust . . . explosive characters, a central motion that opens up a past, present, and future in a single moment in their imagination. It's all built into the ever-most-present moment. At that same point, you're still carrying all that external world's retentions, being fired off with every turn of the eye.

RK: Exactly. And it's actually more than just retentions (the past *and* the future are implicated in the present moment). Derrida makes much of this in *Speech and Phenomena,* suggesting that the present is already shot through with the nonpresent past and future. There is also another sense in which Proust is important to Merleau-Ponty. What happens in the Madeleine incident is a form of involuntary memory. It is another aspect of imagination that is totally un-Sartrean, because it is not at all an act of consciousness imposed upon the world (in terms of a primary or a secondary negation). It is a *dehiscence,* an upsurge of sensation and meaning through involuntary memory. It is not *voluntary* imagination. It comes upon you, overtakes you. That is the Proustian moment. Imagination is not just something that one does to the world. It is not a voluntarist act of consciousness; it is something that the world does to you—something one undergoes.

Q: There is a quote in the working notes of Merleau-Ponty's *The Visible and the Invisible,* when he's talking at the end about how it is that things have us and we have the things, how language has us and we have it, how it is being that speaks through us and not just we who speak of being. In that little quote he speaks of "the memory of the world." And now that you have shed this insight, I can see better what he means . . . it's not just you grasping your own memories; the memories grasp you, or are giving you, so to speak.

RK: In any case the two are inseparable—the self and the world. The self is simply a fold in the coiling and uncoiling of the world, so you are talking about an unconscious of the world that is imagining itself through you. I often think here about the *Noos Poïetikos* of Aristotle or the *Anima mundi* of the Neoplatonists.

Q: I would like to make a detour and focus some questions in relation to current events. Two weeks ago, I was watching a news program about a shootout in Los Angeles. I actually saw a man get shot, live, on my television screen. There were two thieves shooting it out with the cops, just like in the John Wayne movies. The next day the media swarms over the event, and we are bombarded with more pictures, media, stories, theories, etc. Tomorrow I'll switch to a channel and find a similar motive portrayed in a John Wayne movie, or Rambo. Where do we set up these boundaries between the real and the imaginary, or the "irreal" (like "Cops")? We watch all these movies and then we watch things "live." Reality becomes blurred and we are numbed. Taking this theme as an example, where does postmodernity stand? I guess I'm thinking of [Jean] Baudrillard's *Simulations,* when he says that we live in a hyperreal world of simulacrum upon simulacrum and that it is all one reading upon another in a multiverse of meaning.

RK: This is the great "undecidable" of postmodern media culture. In one sense, you see, the imagination is now everywhere. And this is not just a poetical but also an *ethical* crisis. Let me try and tease out this double crisis. I think poetically we've reached a point where it's very difficult for us to distinguish between the imaginary world and the real world. For the romantics, for example, the distinction was evident. Sartre also makes the distinction clear by saying we negate the real in order to conjure up the imaginary. As Coleridge observes, you "suspend your disbelief" to enter a poetic world. When we go into the theater and we see Polonius being stabbed by Hamlet, we don't call for the police, because we know it's "only pretend." When you are playing, you enter the world of recreation. The difficulty is with what [Roland] Barthes calls our dominant "civilization of the image" where "we" now abide. Here we are not quite sure any more when exactly we are transiting from the so-called real world into the un-real world. Then we have Baudrillard stepping in and saying, "The Gulf War was a TV war." So the epistemological state of affairs is that we are living in a hall of mirrors and the so-called real world is itself a fabrication of the media-world. News reporting is not reporting anymore—it is already prefabricated. The press release is already written before the event takes place. The news headline today says, for example, that the president will open the new wing of the J. F. K. library or whatever, even though the headline was printed *yesterday*. The headline was written *before* he even went to Boston. But sometimes the news gets it wrong and announces something in the past tense that doesn't actually happen at all because the train breaks down on the way! The newspapers are usually pretty good at making reality-checks, but they have to because they are so often in a simulated world. It's life imitating art, in some sense. We've reached a point where we're not sure of the language games anymore as distinct genres, so we think we are watching John Wayne "live" or Gulf War GIs as if in the movies. It's like Disneyland writ large. It's like the Palace of Living Arts in California, where you are told you will see a life represented as *larger than life* in and through an image. The imitation is more authentic than the original—that's the claim. I think the best example of all, cited by Umberto Eco in his *Faith in Fakes,* is the Venus de Milo reconstructed with pink skin pigment and her arm back in place. The label is then placed on it, saying it was made by real Florentine artists, and through the latest modes of digital and holographic technology, you now have the reconstruction of the original here in California that is better than the one in the Louvre. They can give you the actual *model* upon which the sculpture was based. This creates a poetic crisis insofar as there is an undecidability between the real and the imaginary. Today popular art imitates high culture and high culture imitates popular culture (for example, [Andy] Warhol). Our lived consumer culture and our so-called sanctuary of art that was meant to be confined to museums, theaters, etc., are no long separate. TV, DVDs, and the internet have brought art into our lives. Is news reporting reality? Or is reality, as Baudrillard says, somehow mediatized into the imagination? So there's this pervasive crisis in culture which postmodernism can play with in all sorts of interesting ways, asking whether we are seeing something real or something imaginary.

Q: But aren't those distinctions between the real world and the imaginary world too crude to cope with the multiplicity of possibilities?

RK: Yes and no. It is certainly true that postmodernism opens us up to these multiple takes on being, whereas before we were too dualist. Being and nonbeing. Visible and invisible. Mind and body. Real and imaginary. Our postmodern culture (from an epistemological point of view) could actually be seen as a richness. That's a possible response. But you could also argue that postmodernism is the collapsing of the real, with all its multiple differences, into the imaginary—so we end up with, as [Fredric] Jameson says, the "logic of late capitalism," where everything enters the exchange-value of simulation. If that's the case, then we are talking about a virtualizing of the world into pure surface. Baudrillard comes close to saying that, but he doesn't really attach any value judgments to it. I think postmodernism—if Derrida is to be called a postmodernist (though he's wary of the term)—would go in your direction, that is, realizing a multiplicity of singularities. I suspect, though, that consumer, late-capitalist postmodernism, which, perhaps, it's the duty of philosophical postmodernism to come to terms with, is far less beneficent. I think we have to make a distinction between a sociological postmodernity—namely, the description of the world in which we live—and the philosophical reflection upon that world. However, I want to issue a caveat here, and then come back to the question of crisis. I think that even if you give a positive reading of the postmodern undecidability of the real and the imaginary, you still have an ethical problem. Let me give two examples. First, if one buys into postmodern undecidability wholesale, there is no answer to the revisionists or the negationists who claim Auschwitz never happened. This kind of postmodern relativism would say, "That's just your narrative; that's just the Jewish version of what happened." But if we can no longer distinguish the real from the imaginary, then we have no way of knowing what happened. You have no response. Under these circumstances, there is no such thing as a fact. Everything is an interpretation of a fact, like Nietzsche says. So a radical postmodernism of undecidability could be construed by some to mean, "Well, you've got your view and I've got mine, so let's not worry about it; I'm not going to put you in prison; you don't annoy us, and we won't annoy you. We're in a world of language games; we're in a world of competing narratives, so what's the problem? Let's live in a pluralist world of multiple views!" But I argue we *do* have a duty to decide between these competing narratives. We must know which is true (or truer) and which is false (or falser) because of the significant moral implications of the answer. Politically and ethically, we do have a certain "debt to the dead," as Ricœur puts it. We have a fidelity to the singular truth of Auschwitz existing or not existing. So it does matter if what is said at the Nuremberg trials is true or not. I mean, if you tell a survivor of Auschwitz that Auschwitz never happened, I think you'll receive a rapid reproach, and rightly so! The epistemological question of "What actually happened?" raises a very real ethical problem.

The second example I want to give is the issue of recovered memory. I'm thinking especially of the "long-term-recovered-memory syndrome," where people have forgotten instances of abuse and then remember them under certain psychotherapeutic circumstances (for example, trance work). There have been several books written about this. In most cases, the abuse recovered in memory actually did happen. But in some instances, apparently, it didn't. One person—I believe his name was David Ingram—was accused by his daughter (who had read a book on Satanic rituals) of child abuse. Mr. Ingram reasoned, "I must have done something; my child could never lie; if she says I abused her, then I must have done so." Mr. Ingram went through trancework with a therapist who said it would all become clearer as he got back to the feeling of his guilt. And sure enough, he eventually confessed; he said, "Yes, it happened," even though it subsequently transpired that it hadn't. In terms of the abuse story, I would argue therefore that there must be some distinction between the real and imaginary. The whole problem goes back to Freud's child seduction theory. Freud vacillated. Sometimes he said, "Yes, it did happen," and then he reasoned not every child in Vienna could have been abused by their parents! So it must be fantasy, a suppressed fantasy—wish fulfillment. But it *does* matter whether the narrative told by the abused who recalls the memory, or interpreted by the analyst, is real. For example, when

Freud interpreted Dora's case and said, "Well, you are neurotic because you want to marry Herr K., and you have repressed this"—instead of being cured by the "talking cure," Dora got worse. Freud eventually discovered *countertransference,* that he himself was identifying with Herr K. and with fantasies of fellatio he was attributing to Dora, and then suggesting this to Dora. So he ended up calling it a "fragment" of a case of hysteria, which was an acknowledgment that he was wrong, but also an acknowledgment that it does matter whether or not abuse occurred. One must be very sensitive and discerning when someone who has a repressed memory of abuse gives a narrative version of it merely through trance work or free association. It matters *legally;* it matters *judicially* and *ethically* whether the account is true or false. It matters both to the person being accused, and to the person who has (or has not) been abused, because if they have been abused they should be taken very seriously. This is another area where, ultimately, although we may never possibly get back to a pure, uninterpreted "fact," we nonetheless have a duty to distinguish as best we can between something that is *real* and something that is *not real.* To say that it doesn't matter, to say, like Baudrillard did, that the Gulf War was a TV war, is doing a profound disservice to those who died in the deserts of Iraq, on both sides. It wasn't a TV war for them. The images we saw on television *refer* to people who died, just as the girl running covered in napalm in Vietnam referred to someone who really suffered; and it was because viewers felt the moral force of such images on their television screens that the United States eventually pulled out of Vietnam.

Q: That is the hazard of narrative you discuss in *The Poetics of Modernity.* Narrative, you argue, is crucial to the narrative self, to the poetic imagination. But at what point does the narrative self become a hazard? Is it when the continual writing of the self becomes a fantasy? When does it become a representation of power over others? At what point does it become an obligation for us *ethically* to interrupt or interrogate a purely *poetic* narrative?

RK: I would say it is when you are being accused by the other, who says, "I am being murdered—where are you?" and you say, following Levinas, "Here I am, *me voici.*" At such moments, you exist in the accusative. Then you have to say, "Well, a person is accusing me, a person is saying 'do not kill and do not let me be killed' on the roads of Vietnam, in the deserts of Iraq, the famine fields of Ethiopia, the streets of Northern Ireland, or wherever it happens to be. When the person makes the summons to me (which I may not want to hear), even if the summons is made through television images, that is the moment that I am challenged. I am called directly or through an image or narrative; I am summoned to respond. That is the ethical moment: when we ask, what or who is it? Does that image refer to something or does it not? And I think at this moment Baudrillard's cult of "sublime irreference" (where we never know if the call refers to something or not) is simply not accurate.

Q: Is that a form or representation of power? Can it be construed as such?

RK: The ethical call of the other is the power of the powerless, but not ideological power. Maybe for certain big news channels, it is about holding ideological power. Most TV networks are probably more interested in money, power, communications, networking, and so on, than in the moral situations of the people depicted on their screens. They may be quite happy that viewers can get off on their images, feel and share the suffering of others, voyeuristically and vicariously suffer with others, and get some kind of emotive kick. I don't know. Maybe media moguls are very cynical; maybe they don't think at all about these issues. But either way, the medium is morally neutral in itself. The images either speak or don't speak, regardless of the intentions of the author. So, what we need to do is apply two forms of hermeneutics. On the one hand, we need a *hermeneutics of suspicion* to apply to narratives in order to explore the "hidden interests" of those who give us the representation or image. This also applies to the story of victims. A victim who says, "Look, I've been abused," could be telling a lie. There are stories of harassment, child abuse, and other abuse stories that are not true. There are all kinds of stories people tell about themselves. It may be rare, but it can happen. So we have to exercise our means of suspicion, on every representation. We have got to let Marx, Freud, and Nietzsche loose on our various narratives—and especially those of the dominant class or regime. But we also have to keep in mind the *hermeneutics of affirmation*, which comes afterwards and which basically is a wager that once you have done your critical purging of the imaginary, once you have been critical and autocritical about it, you still remain open to the possibility that there may be a "surplus meaning" left. In other words, an image—like any mode of signification or communication—is *someone saying something to someone about something*. The ethical moment supplements the epistemological moment. I think, epistemologically, Baudrillard and Derrida are probably right. You reach a point of radical undecidability. But that is where the debt to the dead, the debt to the other, the *response to the call*, does make a difference. So you can talk with Baudrillard about "sublime irreference" all you want, you still have to make ethical decisions about "real" and "unreal" stories. You can say that the notion of reference has to be rethought, resituated, relocated, as Derrida quite rightly does, but one cannot deny that there is a self who speaks and an other who calls (and Derrida himself concedes this). There is always someone who speaks, something that is spoken, someone to whom you are speaking, and there is something about which you are speaking . . .

Q: There isn't an endless chain of signification . . .

RK: No, and Derrida makes clear in our 1982 dialogue that he never suggested there was and that people misunderstood what he meant by the phrase, "There is nothing outside of the text." Derrida does not mean that we live in a world of hyperreality, information superhighways, and pure simulation. Of course we live in that world, too, but that is not *all* we have, because there is a reference, no matter how difficult and how undecidable that reference is. Every narrative refers to *something outside of itself*, be it real or unreal. In the case of the napalmed girl in Vietnam, it happened to be real. In other cases, as we know, it happens to be simulated. When we go to the movies, it is simulated. We need to learn the various rules of "reading" images and of making those distinctions. We have to be *epistemologically* faithful to the multiple layers of reference, but we should also be faithful to the truth for *ethical* reasons. Derrida's recent work on lying is basically saying that you have to make a distinction between what is a lie and what is not a lie. He gives his own first person singular narrative as to why this is important to him. He was accused by the *New York Times* of somehow condoning (after the event) the Vichy government's disappropriation of Jewish property during the war. Chirac apologized for that, and the *New York Times* columnist said, "Well, Chirac is doing it now, but the French intellectuals were silent for forty years." Derrida replied and said, "No," that he along with Levinas and Foucault and others had written countless petitions to the last three French governments, pleading with them to make this acknowledgment and this apology. To Derrida, it matters *hugely* that the *truth* be reestablished. He refuses the purely relativist view that says, "Well, maybe the *New York Times* critic is right: that is his *read* on it, his narrative, and it doesn't matter." Well it does matter. And to come back to the question, at what moment does it matter? One such moment is when the other appeals to you, and a second moment is when you yourself experience injustice because someone tells a lie. Then you know the distinction between reality and unreality. There may be a hundred ways of reading reality, a hundred ways of reading unreality, and two hundred ways in which reality and unreality overlap. So we will go on doing deconstructive readings forever, and so we should, in the name of the richness of textual experience. But truth still *matters*. We cannot dispense with the distinction between the real and unreal, however complex the relation between them.

Q: In *The Wake of Imagination*, you raise the issue of being confronted by the other in and through images. You bring up the image of starving Ethiopians. This image, along with other images of victims, are constantly used for ideological or economic purposes, and they are juxtaposed in flyers, brochures, and elsewhere. After seeing these images hundreds of times, we become desensitized. If they run another marathon special trying to get food to Africa, like they did ten years ago, it will not be as successful. At what point are we no longer confronted by the other, because we have been so numbed and desensitized? Ten years ago, there would not be a broadcast of someone getting shot live on television; now they are showing Bill Cosby's son lying dead with blood all over the place. We have become anaesthetized, and it has almost become unreal. It has become a movie. When you say that it matters to the people fighting in Iraq . . .

RK: And it *should* matter to us, too . . .

Q: Right, it should matter to us. But these images seep into the imagination, and they are a precursor. There are situations where you feel like you are in a movie, where the people in the street are imagining they are John Wayne. And if they die, it's like the TV tuning out. There is a whole generation of people who watch talk shows—where the biggest thing is to go on the talk show and become the victim—so that they can confront others with their victimhood. For them, even if they have been in a horrible situation, it becomes a way of getting on television; it isn't anything that challenges even themselves.

RK: We all live in this *société du spectacle*. Warhol said everyone can have fifteen minutes of fame. And Walter Benjamin surmised that we may well reach an age where humanity will be able to contemplate its own self-destruction with an aesthetic frisson—where we all become part of a television game, where we can all sit back, eat chips, and watch ourselves destroying ourselves. But there is often a kind of apocalyptic logic that takes over when we talk like this; it can become a self-fulfilling prophecy. And that's a danger in the fatalist discourse of certain "prophets of extremity."

Q: The more you say we are just part of the spectacle, the more it seems to occur.

RK: Yes.

Q: So then we apply the role of the witness.

RK: The roles of witness and performer become very blurred. I think that is part of the doomsday scenario, and a lot of films bring this out—[Frederico] Fellini, [Robert] Altman, David Lynch, [Quentin] Tarantino. They are right to look at it, but they sometimes push it to apocalyptic extremes. The person who needs to go on a talk show and tell either a true or untrue story often needs to do that because life outside of the talk show is considered boring. People who go on television to do that know that most of their lives are *not* TV lives. When people watch murders taking place on television, one of the reasons that it causes such a sensation is that people *do* realize that it is "live" and that it is real, and that gives them an extra kick. The real, the live, the contemporaneous, is now being served up through a broadcast image so that one can witness the event as if one were on the scene. But from a safe distance. Now, if there was a report to go out tomorrow declaring this was a joke, an April Fools' Day prank staged by CNN to get more viewers—I am thinking here of Orson Welles's famous radio hoax about aliens landing in New York—people would be very annoyed. In a sense, they would be right. People would feel cheated in some way, because we still operate according to certain rules; for example, when we watch the news, we know that we are watching something that is an image but *refers to a reality,* unlike a soap opera or a commercial. When we switch from the news to commercials or a sitcom, we know that we are going from one mode of truth claim, albeit through images, to another. Of course, this becomes blurred at times. There are all kinds of ways of packaging the news and putting narratives into the news. You begin with a preview, then you go into the big news stories, then you go into the domestic violence story, and then you end with a folksy piece on the Queen Mother or the president playing golf. It is all nicely packaged. We are not getting uninterpreted, unallied truth by any means; nonetheless, we live with what Merleau-Ponty called *perceptual faith,* which applies both to the natural world and to the communications world, where we still operate prereflectively according to certain rules. This image *does* refer to reality; this *doesn't*. I think if we didn't do that, we would be in serious trouble. To come back to *The Satanic Verses* and *Ulysses*, two books that were banned. When Joyce's book was censored in New York, the defense council said, "Your Honor, no one was ever raped by a book." (He was replying to the prosecutor who argued that the novel would lead to heinous acts.) Likewise, Salman Rushdie has a right to imagine whatever he wants in the order of the imaginary, particularly when he says that this is a work of fiction, and these are the genre rules. Rushdie is not a theologian saying, "Muhammed *did* really frolic with prostitutes." He is a fiction-writer making this up. Just as [Nikos] Kazanzakis has a right to imagine the "last temptation of Christ"—having a family and marrying Mary Magdalene, as any Jew on a cross might have imagined as his life was disappearing. There is Christ, in the prime of his youth, surrounded by three women, one of whom was no doubt physically attractive, so he has a last temptation; he says, "God! I've even got to give *this* up!" It is a radical exercise in narrative fantasy. But some people took it upon themselves to put bombs in cinemas in Paris when [Martin] Scorcese's film of the book was screened. Others assassinated the translators of Salman Rushdie and put a fatwa on his head. Now I think that most of us would agree that this is not right, that people are mistaking the real for the imaginary and vice versa. I think that either collapse has very serious ethical implications. That is why in the heel of the hunt, no matter how much we conjugate the real and the imaginary and show that there are inflections and echoes, one in the other, we must remember that a chiasm can only be formed because there are *two* lines and the two lines are *different;* they intertwine and overlap, but they are not the same thing. Merleau-Ponty's philosophy is not a monism. The difficulty of a certain kind of postmodernism, which says that everything is simulation and there is no reality . . . the danger with this "hysterical sublime" of pure nonreference is that it *is* a monism. And fundamentalism is also a monism. That is the irony: the fundamentalism of the so-called East meets up with the postmodernism of the so-called West. The cult of kitsch actually joins forces in a strange way with the cult of fact. So the extreme of the figural slips over into the extreme of the literal. If you have nothing but the figural, then the figural disappears, because the figural is only figural by opposition to the literal. The same with the literal. You may upset the difference, but you do *not* completely eliminate the difference. The real contaminates the imaginary, and the imaginary contaminates the real, yes, but that does not mean they are the *same* thing. If they were, there would be no *différance*.

There is a final point I would like to mention. When Andy Warhol said that in contemporary culture we all have a right to be famous for five minutes, I think that was actually quite a democratic statement. Why shouldn't someone go to a talk show and tell their story, real or imaginary, and be recognized? As Ricœur says, "Every life is in quest of narrative." Everybody wants to tell their story: some people spend sixty dollars a session telling it to a psychotherapist; others can't afford that so they go to the Oprah Winfrey show. And there are, of course, lots of other ways of recounting one's life to others.

Q: In Freudian terms, it is projection of the ego.

RK: It may be more than that. In order to have a sense of identity, people need to recognize that this involves a *narrative* of identity, that they are the tapestry of the stories they tell about themselves and other people tell about them and that they inherit from tradition. And given the fact that they are being bombarded with so many different narratives, coming at them from all angles, from billboards, media, advertising, news, documentaries, TV, etc., they need to try and make a coherent little story out of this vast concordance of stories. There is quite a legitimate need for someone to stand up and tell their life story. Maybe if people no longer felt the need to tell their story, and everyone was content to passively, vicariously, and voyeuristically identify with others who live their lives for them, that would be worse.

Q: You have to draw the line when someone goes up to the Empire State Building and starts shooting everyone just to get onto the news.

RK: Agreed. I think you don't have any right to tell whatever story you want if it has a direct impact on action. That is where I would draw the line. I agree with Ricœur that *l' imaginaire me connaît pas de censure,* the imagination knows no censorship, but I would draw the line at snuff movies, for example, where there is a real production of violence, sometimes involving real sadism. And then there are propaganda movies where viewers actually mistake the simulated action for reality and then reproduce it in reality. I remember having a conversation with Noam Chomsky once, where I asked if he would allow anyone to say *anything* on television? Supposing someone from some terrorist group or fascist group were to stand up in a TV studio, point to the camera, and say: "Go out and kill Jews." Or kill Blacks, or Protestants or Catholics. Would we not blow the whistle there? There comes a point when the text leads into action and feeds into action. I think that is where the ethical has to resort to the legal to protect people from the threat of actual violence. Chomsky agreed; he said that free speech at that stage cannot be free anymore, because it is actually an incitement to violence.

Q: It is like yelling fire in a movie theater. The general theory is that you have a right to say anything so long as you don't incite people to action.

RK: And you can say, "I didn't really mean it; I thought it was a good joke," but if people get trampled, then it has moral consequences. An example where the line tends to get fuzzy is in Stanley Kubrick's *A Clockwork Orange*. Eventually he decided to withdraw the film because people were imitating it and forming these groups called Drooges in London and going out and killing emigrants. Kubrick's point was (and this applies also to Oliver Stone's *Natural Born Killers* and some of Tarantino's films) these were imitation killings. Kubrick had a very different response to this than Stone. Kubrick's response was that even though he put everything he could into the film to estrange the viewer from the violence—wide camera angles, curved lenses, Beethoven score—it was actually counterproductive, because when people saw a woman getting raped in slow motion and ripped apart to Beethoven music, some thought this was *terrific* and went out and imitated that behavior. Kubrick made it clear that he was not responsible intentionally for the impact that it had, but, given the fact that it had that impact, no film was worth a human life. So he withdrew the film. Actually, the distribution company protested, but he said that he was making a moral judgment even though it meant sacrificing his aesthetic freedom. On the other hand, I heard Oliver Stone interviewed on British television, and his argument was a curious self-contradiction. It went something like this: "My film doesn't incite people to murder because art has no relation to reality. If people go see my movie and don't realize that it is mere fiction, then that is not my problem; it is their problem. They have to be educated to make the distinction between what is film and what is reality." But then in the same interview, when asked about the violence, he said "Well, I'm not making anything up. This happens all the time in reality. I'm simply holding a mirror up to society." So he was having it both ways—on one hand, saying that there was no distinction between his film and reality and, on the other hand, that they are worlds apart.

Q: But in making that statement, Stone is implicitly saying that there are no copycat killings, that imitation killings never existed. If reality never imitated art, then how could you explain what happened with Kubrick's film? You can't.

Q: I think Stone's movie was to show the implications of desensitization. But unfortunately, because of his movie, further desensitization occurred. He missed his goal by a long shot.

RK: I think the film was too brilliantly made to be quite as naive as Stone pretended. He was naive about its impact. We could also cite *JFK* here as another interesting fictional recreation of "facts" that will never be known to us. There is a blurring of fiction and history. Just as when we read Simon Schama's or [Jules] Michelet's history of the French Revolution, we are getting narrativized versions of history. When we read Tolstoy's *War and Peace*, we are getting historical fiction. There are modes of crisscrossing. We know that there are two genres coming together; we call it a historical novel or novelistic history. We make a distinction between history, historical novels, and novels.

Q: Some people don't. The current trend is to have "made-for-TV movies" or "docudramas." One of the problems with *JFK* is that people go to see the movie and come out thinking that is the true history. That changes things; paranoia develops. In terms of paranoia, one could cite D. W. Griffith's *Birth of a Nation*, where you have a nation of illiterates going to the movies for the first time to see a feature-length film in 1915; the images that are projected by that movie had very serious political implications.

RK: Yes it served to promote a certain racist propaganda, glorifying the Klu-Klux-Klan. There was also *Triumph of the Will*, Leni Riefenstahl's propaganda film for Hitler, which is extraordinarily powerful. And then there are counterexamples, such as Richard Attenborough's *Gandhi* or Neil Jordan's *Michael Collins*, biopics which can actually recapture forgotten moments of political history. I think that certain films should be clear about what they are doing. If they are fictional recreations of history, they should say so. While Jordan admitted that his film was not accurate in every detail, he said he was making a feature film, and he had a right to exercise a certain poetic license. It is a film, a bio-epic, not a documentary, but it has a certain claim to represent historical reality. So that blurs the boundaries. But what you have to do there is have clearer help signals, or interpretation cues, where people say (and they generally do for legal reasons) that this is fiction or this is reality or this is fiction based on reality. For the most part, people understand those rules—both the filmmakers and the film viewers—even though there are some very interesting examples where the lines get crossed. If, for example, *Birth of a Nation* was shown with the claim that "this is your history as it actually happened," then it would be a deceitful film, because it would be presenting itself as a historical documentary when it is in fact narrativized—to the point of farce and propaganda at times. I think that even though we never get to absolute distinctions, we accept that we should have some kind of ratings on films. Kids shouldn't see *Natural Born Killers*. Why not, if it is all imaginary? Because children aren't always able to discriminate between narrative genres. You know that because of common sense. Then you discuss *why* it is not right. The *sensus communus*, as Arendt and Kant realized, actually carries a lot of practical wisdom. But young kids haven't had much time to develop that.

Q: You cite the ethical claim in one of your books that killing children is evil. In any philosophical argument, we always have to presuppose each other. You put an emphasis on ethics; I think rightfully so. Referring back to Baudrillard, I think he continually says that the abstraction of the media is that it is intransitive; there is no opportunity for learning or real communication. Instead, there is a blurring of the real and a proliferation of images to validate behavior, and this reconditions our possibilities for action—in reality and with regard to the imaginative. There is an awareness on the part of the media that they are doing that, that they are being intransitive, and that is the whole point of the media. Chomsky takes it further and implicates other political influences.

RK: Yes, that is what Chomsky calls the "manufacturing of consent." Can you clarify your argument?

Q: The media is intransitive; it does not offer an exchange for communication. Mass-media images constitute neither real nor unreal versions of events, but rather function in order to maintain the illusion that the world outside of the media is real. On the other hand, the mass media dominate our imagination and, to a certain extent, control our desires. The basic structure of mass media today is one that conceals the fact that our society as a whole is itself hyperreal and entirely based on simulation.

RK: But it is power driven. Chomsky would say ideologically driven. I'm not sure that Baudrillard has as much of a conspiracy theory as Chomsky does.

Q: I once read an article where Chomsky posed the idea that we don't know if men actually landed on the moon, that it could have been done in any soundstage in Hollywood. It is a demonstration of mass media's esoteric power, that we are capable of such things.

RK: Did Chomsky seriously entertain that as a possibility do you think? Or was it hyperbole?

Q: I think it was hyperbole. I think that he was just trying to show the power and the intransitivity of the media in terms of how images can be regulated in a centralized media industry. We can, however, always maintain critical practices that may counter the power centers. Everyone now has access to a certain kind of technology; for instance, people can film themselves with a camcorder and broadcast it on public-access channels. Then there's the internet. In this respect, there is a decentralization of power. In any case, I think Chomsky is just focusing on the abuses of centralized media power.

RK: It is a very curious combination: Baudrillard and Chomsky. Some of our most sophisticated intellects give so much power to the media—which of course they deeply suspect and want to criticize—that they say that everything we watch must be suspected, that even the moon landing could be a hoax! That is one level of incredulity. A critical, skeptical, radical level. The other is the fundamentalist who says we never landed on the moon because he didn't *see* it—so it didn't happen. Here there is such an addiction to the literal that you believe it couldn't be true if you weren't actually there! It is a funny convergence of extremes—of the fundamentalists and postmodernists.

Q: I really appreciate having been introduced to Merleau-Ponty, because every time I have extreme thoughts, I always consider that I can negotiate.

RK: That's right. And it's a curious thing, because there has been a tendency in philosophy—maybe since the media age, since philosophers became "famous"—to go for a strong punch line, to say one thing. Generally, those who say one thing catch the public attention. For example, Derrida and Chomsky, whom I have huge admiration and affection for, are always saying the same strong thing. Heidegger also always said the same strong thing. I think he had a single thought. I think Levinas had a single thought. They are extraordinary thoughts. But that suits the public, in a way. The "grand public" often ignores the huge complexities underneath the summit. Heidegger is the thinker of Being, Levinas is the thinker of the other, Derrida is the thinker of deconstruction, Chomsky is the thinker of dissent, and so on. People want a quick fix on someone. These thinkers spend most of their lives going around saying that they have been misunderstood. Derrida, for example, says that he never *actually* meant that there is nothing outside of the text. But everyone has to admit, it *was* a great line. In politics or popular culture, this is even more so. There's a need for a sound bite. The badies often get the good lines. The terrorists. The cowboys. The orators. The powerful ones. It is different, of course, with philosophy. But even here the thinkers who get the good lines are usually the philosophers of a single thought, albeit a great thought. Whereas those who don't—and I think Merleau-Ponty is one of them, and Paul Ricœur, Charles Taylor, Hannah Arendt are others—those who negotiate, mediate, complicate, are not media-friendly people. These thinkers are almost untranslatable into the media because they are too complicated; they are too faithful to the multiple folds of being.

Q: They are faithful to a sort of truth which is nascent but, at the same time, always a little late. You are in the moment, trying to get there, always in that dynamic, configurational world of intentionality that remains incomplete and open-ended.

RK: This philosophy is dialogical, diacritical, always on the move. The sort I strive for but don't always achieve.

This exchange took place on March 18, 1997, at the State University of New York at Stony Brook. Questioners included Arthur Bangs, Won Choi, Sean Connolly, Felix Fermin, Peter Gratton, Lawrence Kalinov, James Sanderson, Patricia Sousa, and Leandro Gimenez Vega. The exchange was organized by Professor Hugh Silverman of the Philosophy Department.

Boston Colloquy
Theorizing the Gift

MARK MANOLOPOULOS: In the Derrida/Marion debate "On the Gift"(Villanova, 1997), you ask the question, "Is there a Christian philosophy of the gift?"[6] Do you think either Derrida or Marion or both provide handy directions? Could you summarize or interpret their insights? And whose argument do you find more persuasive?

RK: They did avoid the question. In Derrida's case, that is logical, because he will always—reasonably for a deconstructionist—try to avoid tying the messianicity of the gift to any messianism as such, be it Christian, Jewish, Islamic, or any other kind. So it makes sense for him not to engage in that debate per se, because he would say, "That's beyond my competence. I'm not a Christian. 'I rightly pass for an atheist.'[7] I respect Christianity. I'm fascinated by their theological and philosophical expressions of the notion of the gift—I learn from it—but it's not my thing." Marion I find a little bit more perplexing in this regard because he *is* a Christian philosopher. He has talked about "eucharistic hermeneutics" in *God Without Being*.[8] Christ is a "saturated phenomenon" for Marion.[9] But Marion is going through a phase—and this was evident at the Villanova conference—where he doesn't want to be labeled as a "Christian philosopher" and certainly *not* as a Christian *theologian*. He wants to be a phenomenologist. So, being true—at least to some extent—to Husserl's phenomenology as a universal science, he wants to be independent of presuppositions regarding this or that particular theological revelation: Christian, Jewish, or otherwise. I think that's why in his essays on "the saturated phenomenon," Marion goes back to Kant. The Kantian sublime offers a way into the saturated phenomenon, as does the notion of the gift or donation, which—like Husserlian phenomenology—precedes the question of theological confessions and denominations. And I think Marion wants to retreat to that position so that he won't be labeled a Christian apologist—which I think he is. I think he's a Christian theologian who's trying not to be one. Personally, my own response here would be to say that there's two ways of doing phenomenology—and both are equally valid. One is to begin with certain theological and religious presuppositions. The other is to operate a theological reduction, where you say, "We're not going to raise theological issues here." That's following the basic Husserlian and Heideggerian line. In the *Introduction to Metaphysics*, Heidegger says something like, "The answer to the question, 'Why is there something rather than nothing?'—if you fail to bracket out theology—is: Because God created the world."[10] But if you bracket it out, you don't begin with theological presuppositions. And that is what Husserl does, what Heidegger does, and what Derrida does. I think Marion mixes the two, although in the exchange with Derrida I think he's trying to get back to that kind of *pure* phenomenology. He keeps saying, "I'm a phenomenologist! I'm doing phenomenology!" But the lady doth protest too much. Then there is the other way of doing phenomenology *in dialogue with* theology, which doesn't bracket it out but *half*-suspends it. We might call this a quasi-theological phenomenology or a quasi-phenomenological theology. In other words, one acknowledges that there's a certain hybridity, but one doesn't want to presuppose straight off which comes *first:* the giving of the gift as a phenomenological event or the divine Creation of the world as source of all gifts. This allows for a certain ambiguous intermeshing, intermixing, crossweaving—what Merleau-Ponty described as a chiasmic interlacing. And it seems to me that that's perfectly legitimate. Even though it is methodologically more complex and more ambivalent than the Husserlian move of saying, "Bracket out all political, theological, ideological, cultural presuppositions," it is actually truer to life because life *is* the natural attitude. And the natural attitude *is* infused with presuppositions. And it includes *both (a)* experiences of the gift as pure gift and *(b)* experiences of the gift for believers as coming from Yahweh or Christ or Allah or the Sun God/dess. And it seems to me that the phenomenology of unbracketed experience, the phenomenology of the natural attitude—which I think

Merleau-Ponty gets pretty close to—is what I am practicing in *The God Who May Be*.[11] I'm not writing as a theologian because I don't have the theological competence. I'm writing as a philosopher, but one who, as a philosopher, feels quite entitled to draw from religious scriptures as sources, just as theologians do, and to draw from phenomenology as a method. I'll draw from anything that will help me clarify the question. And I think by drawing ambidextrously from both, it can open a middle path into some interesting questions, even though the Husserlians and the Heideggerians can shout, "Foul! You're bringing religion into this!" and the theologians can say, "Oh, well, you're not a theologian! Did you pass your doctoral exam in dogmatic theology?!" And I just say, "No. I'm just doing hermeneutic readings of texts—some phenomenological, some religious—and I'm going to mix them. If there be interference, let it be a creative interference. If there be contamination, let it be a fruitful contamination."

Q: In the Villanova exchange, Derrida wouldn't provide a theology of the gift, and Marion doesn't. If you provided a theology of the gift, what would be some characteristics or axioms?

RK: Well, I repeat, what I'm doing in *The God Who May Be* is not theology as such but a "hermeneutics of religion." It is, I hope, a contribution to the phenomenology of the gift. I usually call "the gift" by other names: (1) the "transfiguring" God; (2) the "desiring" God; (3) the "possibilizing" God; (4) the "poeticizing" God—the creating God (qua *poēsis*). They would be my four categories of gifting. *Poïēsis,* or the poeticizing God, engages in a cocreation with us. God can't create the kingdom unless we create the space for the kingdom to come.

Q: That's interesting in light of Catherine Keller's thesis that Creation *ex nihilo* is too one-way.[12]

RK: What I like about the *creatio ex nihilo*—though I can see that it's nonreciprocal—is that it's an unconditional giving. It's not a giving because there's some problem to be solved that precedes the giving. To use Derrida's language, it comes before economy, although it cannot continue without economy. As soon as there's history and finitude and humanity, there's economy, there's negotiation. And there is, to my mind, reciprocity. Here I disagree with Caputo, Derrida, Lyotard, and the postmodern deconstructionists who repudiate the notion of reciprocity or equity or reconciliation. They see it as going back to Hegel or conceding to some kind of economy. I don't think it is as simple as that. I am wary of the polarity between the absolutely-unconditional-gift *versus* the gift-as-compromised-by-the-economy (which gets rid of the gift as pure gift). I just think that's an unhelpful dichotomy, as I think messianicity *versus* messianism is an unhelpful dichotomy. It's an interesting idea; it's good for an argument. But I think it's ultimately unworkable because I don't think you can investigate messianicity without messianism; and I don't think you can have genuine messianism without messianicity. Now maybe Derrida would agree with that. But there's still a difference of emphasis. I don't see anything wrong with the mix. Whereas Derrida seems to think it is all that is *possible* for us human, mortal beings, what he's really interested in is the *impossible*. I leave the impossible to God and get on with the possible. Because that's where I find myself: I'm in the economic order. I look to something called "God"— what Derrida calls the Impossible—to guarantee that the economy doesn't close in on itself. But I don't hold out God as something that we should even entertain as an option for us because God is not an option for us: God is an option for God. Humanity is an option for us. If we can be more human, that's our business. Our business is not to become God. It's God's vocation to become more fully God, ours to become more fully human. We answer to the other without ever *fusing* in some kind of metaphysical unity or identity. When I say, "I'm for reciprocity, equity, and reconciliation," I'm not for premature Hegelian synthesis. I'm not for metaphysical appropriation or some ineluctable evolving "process" of integration. I'm not for reducing the otherness of God to being as such. But, on the other hand, and this may sound paradoxical, I'm all for *traversings* of one by the other—anything that muddies the waters and makes the borders between God and us porous. I don't believe there's an absolute God out there and then a completely compromised humanity here. I think there are constant *to-ings* and *fro-ings*. So the phenomenology of the gift that I'm trying to articulate in terms of poeticizing, is a cocreation of history by humanity and God, leading to the kingdom. A new heaven and a new earth. We don't know what that will be, because we haven't reached it. We can imagine, but we can't pronounce. It goes beyond the sphere of the phenomenology of history, because it involves a posthistorical situation. It's an *eschaton*. We can imagine it as an eschatology, but it's really something that God knows more about than we do.

Q: What do you mean when you say, "Giving is desiring"?

RK: I argue that giving is desiring because desire is not just the movement from lack to fulfillment or from potency to act or from the insufficient to the sufficient—these are metaphysical notions of desire.

I'm taking the idea of desire as coming from a fullness towards an absence as much as coming from an absence to a fullness. For example, *kenosis* is a form of desire. And it doesn't come from God being empty and wanting to become full. It comes from God being full and wanting to empty His divinity in order to be more fully in dialogue with the human, because, as Levinas says, *On s'amuse mieux à deux.* "It's better to be two than one."[13] And it's better in the sense of being *more* good, *more* just, *more* loving. It's Eckhart's idea of *ebullitio,* this "bubbling over," this excess or surplus of desire. Not a surplus of being but of desire. Desire is always the desire of more desire. And also the desire for an answer: What's the point in God desiring and having nobody to answer the divine desire? That's why Song of Songs says it all: the desire of the Shulamite woman—representing humanity—for the Lord (Solomon the lover) is a desire that actually expresses itself not just as frustration, emptiness, lack, looking for her lover, but as a desire that sings its encounter with the lover that celebrates its *being found.* In the Song of Songs, the lover *finds* the Shulamite woman and that is the inaugural moment, as it were, of the song of desire. It's a desire based not on *fine amor* and romantic passion—which is frustration, prohibition, or absence. It's a desire of plenitude, not of presence, because that's fusional. It's a desire of excess, not of deficiency. A desire that stems from being taken by God. A response to the desire of the absolute. So that's another form of giving. In other words, the desire of the Shulamite woman is a gift. It's not a subjective hankering. It's a gift; it's a response to a gift. And what's the gift? The gift is desire. So you've got two desires at work. The traditional view has been to consider the human as desiring the fullness of God because the human is full of lack, insufficiency, and finitude. But what I'm trying to do is to see it as much more complex than that. It's a question of both lack *and* fullness in God and humanity. There's a lack in God and there's a lack in humanity. What's the lack in humanity? It's that humanity is not divine. What's the lack in God? God is *not* human. So, in a way, the kingdom as a second coming or incarnation is what we're looking for. But as soon as you have that meeting of the finite and the infinite, you've left history behind— not to return to some kind of fusion or "oceanic oneness" à la Freud. Let's imagine it hermeneutically, poetically: What would the kingdom be if the desire of the Shulamite woman and the desire of the Lover Lord were to meet and mesh in a posthistorical fashion? The first answer is: we don't know. But if we were to imagine it—as various religions have done—it would be a dance; it would be a *perichōrēsis.* It would be the dance-around of the three persons or of the two lovers, and, arguably, where there are two, there is always a third. So the *perichōrēsis* is the refusal—even in *parousia* and *pleroma* and eschatology and even in the kingdom—to compromise in terms of a closed economy. It never closes. The economy is still bubbling, is still flowering, is still bursting into life and being—by virtue of this dance-around, which, as *perichōrēsis*, is something I explore in *The God Who May Be*. The *perichōrēsis* is the dance around the *khōra*. *Peri-chōra*. The dance-around is each person of the Trinity—whether you interpret that as Father-Son-Holy Ghost, or God-humanity-kingdom (one doesn't have to be patriarchal and gender-exclusive on this)—in dialogue with each other. We're just fantasizing here, which, of course, most theologians wouldn't allow us to do. They would say, "Well now, is that according to Saint Thomas or Saint Augustine?" At certain points in history, if you said something like Bruno of Nola, or even Eckhart, you could be burnt for it. But let's assume we're not going to be burnt in this day and age for imagining what might go on in the kingdom. Now, in terms of this desiring relationship with the three persons, there's a double movement that I'm arguing will or *could* continue—let's imagine—in the kingdom when history has ended as we know it and when the Shulamite woman who desires God has come face-to-face with her lover. The double movement is this: it's a movement of approach and of distance. The term *perichōrēsis* is translated into Latin as *circum-in-cessio*, which is taken from two phonetically similar verbs, *(a) cedo*, "to leave place," "to absent yourself," and *(b) sedo*, meaning "to sit," "to assume or take up a position." So there is a double movement of immanence and transcendence, of distantiation and approximation, of moving *towards* each other and then moving *away* from each other—as in a dance. It's a dance-around where each person cedes his/her place to the other, and then that other to its other, and so on. So it's not just two persons. There's a third person in this divine dance who you're always acknowledging and invoking. This third person is very important in Levinas, and I think it's very important in certain Christian notions of the Trinity. Because the danger of two is that two can become one: face-to-face can become a candlelit dinner, where romantic lovers look into each other's eyes and see themselves reflected in the other. Whereas the third introduces a little bit of symbolic castration that safeguards a certain distance and therefore allows for desire. If desire were to reach its end, it would end. And a God who is not desiring is a God who's not giving. And a God who is not giving is not God.

Q: What about the "transfiguring God"?

RK: The transfiguring God is the God who transfigures us; we transfigure God. The other example I use is Mount Tabor. Basically, God transfigures us through Creation, through interventions in history, whether it's the burning bush or Christ or the saints or the epiphanies that Joyce and Proust talk about: *that*, to me, is the divine transfiguring the everyday. So presumably if God is giving, God is giving as a constant process and practice of transfiguring. We may not see it. We may not know that it's there. And we may refuse to acknowledge it, in which case it doesn't affect our lives. In a way, that's God's loss, too, because if God's transfiguring goes unheeded and unheard, we're going to have wars, evil, and so on. I'm Augustinian in that regard: evil is the *absence* of God as transfiguring, desiring, poeticizing, and possibilizing—I'll come back to this fourth category in a moment. But transfiguring is not just something God does to us; it's also something that we do to God. We transfigure God to the extent that we create art, we create justice, we create love. We bring into being, through our actions— poetical and ethical—a transfiguration of the world. It's a human task as much as a divine gift. God gives to us a transfiguring promise; we give back to God a transfigured world—and we can transfigure it in ways that God can't. We can author a poem like a Shakespearean sonnet. God can't do that. But we can coauthor with God a poem called *poesis*, Creation, the so-called real world. That's a different kind of poem, where God and the human meet each other, complement each other. But either can withdraw from the dance, in which case the other just falls on his or her face. That's the end of it. We can destroy God. That's why I speak of a God who *may be*, which is an interpretation of the Hebrew "I am the God who will be, who may be."[14] If I am the God who simply *is*, I am already accomplished, already there, whereas the God who *may be* is *also* a God of promise, of potential, of the kingdom. At any point, we can pull the plug on God. As one of the victims of the Holocaust, Etty Hillesum, says, "We must help God to be God."[15] And that's where we can make a link with people like Eckhart and Cusanus and some of the other Church Fathers and biblical prophets.

Q: At first glance, the notion that "We must help God to be God" sounds arrogant.

RK: Yes, but what it's accepting is that *God is not arrogant*, that God does not presume to be able to stop evil. God can't stop evil. Why? Because evil is the absence of God. God has no power over what God is not—namely evil. God can only be good—unconditionally good in a gifting, loving, creating way. That is where the Gnostics and theodicists were wrong: God is not *both* good *and* evil. Even Hegel and Jung made that mistake. God is *not* omnipotent when it comes to evil. God is utterly powerless. And that's terribly important. You find that in the Christian story—Jesus before Pilate, the Crucifixion—he couldn't do anything. It's "the power of the powerless," as Vaclav Havel calls it—and he is right. God helps us to be more fully human; we help God to be more fully God—or we don't. If we don't, we can blow up the world and that's the end of humanity, and that's the end of God as the promise of the kingdom, because there's nobody there anymore to fulfill the promise. In that instance, God remains as pure *desiring*, of course, as pure *poeticizing*—except God's world has just been broken up by God's own creature. And to revisit the terms of *The God Who May Be*, God remains *transfiguring;* but there's nothing left to transfigure any more because we've destroyed it.

Q: You also mention the "possibilizing God."

RK: Basically, that means that divinity is a constant offer of the possibility of the kingdom, which can be interpreted in two ways (and you find this in the Scriptures). One is the kingdom as eschatological promise after history, at the *end* of history. The other is the kingdom *now:* in the mustard seed, in the little, everyday, most insignificant of acts. The kingdom is present in the "feast of these," just as Christ is present in the giving of a cup of cold water. That means that in every moment, there is the possibility of good and there is the possibility of nongood. There's the possibility of love; there's the possibility of hate, violence, aggression. We're choosing constantly. And every moment we are actualizing the kingdom or not-actualizing the kingdom. As Benjamin says so beautifully, "Every moment is a portal through which the Messiah might come." Now what we've got to get away from is thinking that the Messiah comes, and then it's all over. If you're a Christian—and I am up to a point; I am a Christian up to the point where the love of "Christians" offends justice, and then I'm not "Christian" any more—you draw from the Christian story and testimony the notion that *each little act* makes a difference. For example, the woman with the hemorrhage: you help her. You don't want to, but you help her.[16] There's no wine: okay, we reluctantly change the wine.[17] And so on and so forth. You do all of these little things—most of them almost imperceptible—and you don't make a big fuss about it. And when the Messiah comes—even if this happens to be a pretty extraordinary, exemplary instance of the divine in the human, as I believe Christ is—you don't say, "Now it's all over." You *can* say, "Now it's all over for me."

But history isn't over. The coming of Christ *wasn't* the end of the world: the Messiah always comes again in history. And the Messiah is always— including the Christian Messiah—a God who is *still* to come (even when the Messiah has already come). The Messiah is one who has already come and is always still to come. And that's why I see the Christian story as exemplary. (But it's not the only story in town, and, in my view, it has no absolute prerogative vis-à-vis other world religions. God speaks in many voices and in many traditions.) But to return to the Bible, I could take the Mosaic story as well: in the burning bush, God came. With Elijah in the cave, the Messiah came. But that wasn't the end of it. The Messiah came to John the Baptist, too, the voice crying in the wilderness. It always comes *and* goes. And that's the nature of the Messiah: it's already here—the kingdom is already here—but it is also not yet fully here. And it's this double moment that's terribly important, because the possible is not just *the Possible*, the *telos* of universal history coming to an end at the end of time. That's Hegel. That's triumphalism. That's the kind of monotheistic tyranny that leads to religious wars: "We own The Promised Land"; "*This* and only *this* is the absolute"; all or nothing. In contrast to such triumphalist teleologies and ideologies of power, the divine possible I am speaking of comes in tiny, almost imperceptible acts of love or poetic justice. It is in "the music of what happens," as Seamus Heaney says, or in what Joyce called "epiphanies," [Charles] Baudelaire "correspondences," Proust "reminiscences." These are all poetic testimonies to the possible that become incarnate in all these little moments of eschatological enfleshment.

Q: What does "eschatology" mean for you?

RK: If and when the kingdom comes, I believe it will be a great kind of "recollection" or "retrieval" (*anakephalaiōsis* is the term used by Paul) of all those special moments of love; but you can't even see it in terms of past, present, and future, because the eternal or emblematic is outside time, even though it comes *into* time all the time. Christ is just an exemplary figure of it. What does Christ say at the end? He says: "Time for me to go. Don't touch me. *Noli me tangere.* Don't possess me. I cannot be an idol that you possess." The Messiah is deferred. And here I always draw great sustenance from [Maurice] Blanchot's tale of the beggar waiting for the Messiah at the gates of Rome. The Messiah comes and the beggar goes up to him and says: "Are you the Messiah?" And the Messiah responds: "Yes." And the beggar asks: "When will you come?" because the Messiah is always still to come. The Messiah is *still to come* even as the Messiah is *there*. Because we're temporal, we're confronted with this unsolvable paradox or *aporia*—namely that the kingdom has already come and yet is not here. That's the way it is for our finite phenomenological minds. And no metaphysics and no theology or philosophy can resolve that one. To the extent that deconstruction is a reminder of the *impossibility* of ever having the total take on God as absolute, then I'm for deconstruction. But as an endless kind of "soft shoe shuffle" of infinite qualifications and refinements, forever declining any kind of incarnation, I find deconstruction too deserted, too *désertique*, too desert-like, too hard. Derrida's deconstruction is too inconsolable. It's overly uncompromising. Too puritanical in a way, strangely. It's all about the impossible. But for me, God is the possibilizing of the impossible. "What is impossible to us is possible to God."[18] We actualize what God possibilizes and God possibilizes what remains impossible for us. To sum up: *God is giving* means *God is poeticizing, possibilizing, transfiguring, and desiring.* That's my *religious* phenomenology of the gift. I also did a *prereligious* phenomenology of the gift in the first part of *Poétique du Possible*, published in 1984.[19] And if I were to do that again, I would certainly include readings of Proust and Joyce or just everyday testimonies to people's kindness, the small ways in which love and creativity works in the world—irrespective of whether people are religious or not. You can go either way.

Q: You've answered the question of a "theology of gift," in terms of thinking God as gift. To think *Creation* as gift: briefly, what would that entail for you?

RK: If we're talking about divine Creation—because I think there's two Creations going on: divine and human—I don't want to repeat myself, but I would probably go back to the idea of *poēsis:* God as *poēsis,* the *noos poiētikos* as Aristotle calls it, and the *possest* as Cusanus says. Poeticizing is the act of constantly opening horizons of possibility, gifts of possibility, for human beings to realize. The divine gift as Creation is powerless to impose that gift on somebody who doesn't want it because that would not be good: that would be evil. If you say to somebody, "I love you" and they say, "I don't want your love," and you say, "Sorry, I love you, and whether you like it or not, you are going to be transfigured by my love," that's coercion, violence, tyranny. That's what so-called benevolent dictators do. That's the imposition of the good on somebody who doesn't want it. Sadism in the name of God. How many times has religion done that? The Taliban were doing it. The Inquisition was doing it. The New England Puritans were doing it to the so-called witches down in Salem. "For your good, we are going to impose the good!" "But thank you very much, I don't want your good." That's why God loves rebels: God loves the Steven Daedeluses of this world who say, "I will not serve that in which I no longer believe," whether it call itself religion, language, or homeland. (It's at the beginning of Joyce's *Portrait of the Artist*.) I suspect that God would prefer people not to serve that in which they do not believe. God prefers honest people who rebel rather than the lackeys, the "creeping Jesuses who would do anything to please us" (Blake). I don't want to get into a cult of the rebel here. But God admires people like Job and David—who argue with God. God admires Jesus on the cross who says, "Why have you forsaken me? Come on, give me an answer to this." God likes that.

Q: In "Desiring God," you mention, quite prophetically, "there is a growing problem of closure to the other. I am sure, if it has not already become a problem here in the United States, it will become one—the problem of how one can relate openly and hospitably and justly to the other, without demonization."[20] These words obviously resonate in light of the current wave of terrorism. However, let's ask this question from an ecocentric perspective: Do you have any thoughts on how one can or should relate openly and hospitably and justly to the non-human other—animate and inanimate? We demonize the non-human. . . .

RK: We demonize all the time. When people want to show what the devil is, they usually take an animal. Just look at medieval and Renaissance portraits of demons. The iconography of *The Last Judgment* is full of this, goats, bats, snakes, dragons, griffins, dogs, gargoyles. I think that's a real question. I think it's something we in Western philosophy and in our excessive anthropocentrism have sometimes ignored, that is, the *alterity* of nature, of trees and of animals and so on. One thing I've taken great courage and guidance from is my own children's sensitivity in this regard. They are vegetarians and very opposed to wearing fur coats or buying factory-produced food. I think there's a growing awareness in the new generation which is very important as long as it's kept in balance with being good to your neighbor who's starving down the street (and perhaps can only afford factory food). I find there are many young people in Boston or New York who go down to protest against Bush or the death penalty as much as they will concern themselves with cruelty to animals and the pollution of nature. That's good. The balance is important. There's no point ignoring social and human issues out of some kind of obsession with eating "natural" food. That's just taking food as a surrogate symbol that can be "purified" as the world disintegrates before the ravages of global poverty and capitalism. There can sometimes be, for example, a certain New England obsession with health and the natural—a demonization of smoke, a demonization of alcohol, a demonization of sex (although it often goes hand-in-hand with fantasy sex or sub-world sex in Las Vegas and Hollywood, so it can be very ambiguous). There is a residual *Puritanism* in American culture, I think, and a certain demonization of the pagan earthiness of things. That may include food prohibitions against eating fish or "killing" tomatoes, etc., as well as the stringent laws against smoking, drinking, or sexual language. But that's only *half* the story—the *official* version as it were. The other half is very different and leads to all kinds of perversions, doublethink and doubletalk. It's a messy world, full of double messages. I'm not saying, therefore, that you should tolerate cruelty to animals and indiscriminately chop down trees. I'm saying you do your best, wherever possible and within the limits of the possible, to remain human while doing the *least* amount of harm to nature or to animals or to your fellow human being. But to pretend that you can enter into some realm of pure consumption where everything is as "organic" as in *Bread and Circuses* food markets is to ignore the fact that *Bread and Circuses* can only exist for the wealthy, who pay twice as much for their fish and vegetables while the poor have to go to *Star Market* (a bottom-end supermarket chain) and buy factory-produced food. I approve of going to *Bread and Circuses*—I just wish it were available to everybody. Somewhere along the line, the refusal of smoke, sex, alcohol, and meat in an *absolutist* fashion can, to my mind, smack of residual Puritanism. It can slip into demonization even with the very best of intentions—and I'm always wary of that. So I would say, "Be vegetarian. Fine. But when you find yourself in a situation where you go to another country and there's only meat on the table, have some meat." If I go to a tribe in Africa, and they give me goats' eyeballs, I may not particularly like it, but I'm not going to offend my host by saying, "I don't eat goats' eyeballs!" I'll eat it—raw or cooked. That's the kind thing to do. That's accepting the hospitality of the other as other. As the Dalai Lama advised his monks, "Eat whatever is dropped into your begging bowl."

Q: In *The God Who May Be,* you open up the question of discernment, whether we're facing saturation or the desert. You claim that "For the theist Marion, no less than for the atheist Derrida, we are left with the dilemma of 'holy madness,' how to judge between true and false prophets, between good and evil ghosts, between holy and unholy messiahs."[21] Even though Caputo and Derrida are suspicious of criteria—I guess we all are a little suspicious—how should we nevertheless judge between the true and the false, the good and the evil? After Derrida, how do you treat criteria?

RK: You do so by trying to discern and judge more carefully, more cautiously, more critically, and, I would say, more hermeneutically. You don't have to get rid of criteria altogether. Derrida would say, "Well, of course we have to make decisions all the time. We judge and we use criteria. We have to do that: we couldn't not do it." Strictly speaking, that's already a compromise. That's already entering into the economy of things. And I just find the gap between our decisions and undecidability too polar. That's my problem: it's too antithetical, too aporetical, too impossible. Decisions are "too difficult" in the deconstructive scenario. They are all made in "fear and trembling" because we're "in the dark!" At the 1999 Villanova exchange, I asked Derrida, "How can you read in the dark?" He said, "We can *only* read in the dark." But I want to turn the light on! Even if it's only a flashlight that will remove a little of the darkness and confusion. I don't believe in *absolute* light or total enlightenment for us ordinary mortals. It doesn't have to be either absolute light or total darkness. It doesn't have to be that hard. We're not all desperate Desert Fathers waiting for Godot as the apocalyptic dusk descends! It doesn't have to be that angst-ridden or melodramatic. The world is a place of light and dark: we always have a bit of both.

Q: Derrida might say that the world is in such a mess because we assume we can read in the light and that all decisions are easy.

RK: I can understand what he's saying in terms of an excessive *hubris* and arrogance on behalf of a certain Enlightenment, on behalf of rationalism, on behalf of science and technology. There I agree with him. But I'm not sure that's the way most people in the world today actually think or live. Most people are confused and bewildered. They're not cocksure *cogitos* in need of deconstruction but wounded, insecure, fragile subjects in search of meaning.

Q: What about religious dogmatism?

RK: Oh, before the Enlightenment, it was worse. What I'm saying is: to think you possess the light and everybody else is in darkness is a recipe for imperialism, colonization, injustice, holy war, *jihad*, "Good versus Evil." We're witnessing it again today. Nobody has a prerogative on light or the good. But that doesn't mean we're all condemned to a kind of total darkness, *khōra*, undecidability. I think everything should be deconstructed, but the question for me is: What's it like *after* deconstruction? That's why I still believe in hermeneutics. Derrida doesn't. I believe in reminiscences, resurrections, reconciliations. They're all temporary, they're all provisional, they're all muddling through. Granted—but they do happen. I believe in paths. Not massive metaphysical viaducts or Golden Gate Bridges between the contingent and the absolute, but I do believe in little footbridges—the kind you get in Harrison Ford movies. Hermeneutic bridges, connections, ladders. I find that deconstruction follows the template of the Lazarus parable, the implacable metaphor of the gulf that *(a)* separates paradise, the absolute, the impossible from *(b)* the land of the living—our finite, everyday, contingent, mortal world. The deconstructive gulf radically segregates the two. There's an unbridgeable gap between the divine and the human, the impossible and the possible. The deconstructionist Abraham won't allow Lazarus to send a message back to his brothers to warn and instruct them. It is too late. The kind of hermeneutics of religion that I'm talking about, by contrast, would be much more guided by the paradigm of Jacob's ladder, where there's *to-ing* and *fro-ing*, lots of people going up and down, in both directions. No *absolute* descent or *absolute* ascent. It's little people going up and down ladders. And that, to me, is how you work towards the kingdom. "Every step you take . . ." (as the song goes). Each step counts. Messianic incursion, incarnation, epiphany is a possibility for every moment of our lives. But because we are finite and temporal, the infinite can pass through time, but it can never remain or take up residence in some absolute or permanent present. That's the difference between the eternal and time. They can crisscross back and forth, up and down, like the angels on Jacob's ladder. But they are never identical, never the same. That's what a hermeneutic affirmation of *difference* is all about, as opposed to deconstructive *différance*, which, in my view, gives up hope in the *real possibility* of mediation and transition.

Q: One more question generated by "Desiring God." Whereas someone like Marion may turn to mystical theology and a phenomenology of saturation, I concur with you in your affirmation of "hermeneutical retrievals and reimaginings of biblical narratives and stories."[22] Could you briefly comment on the possible nature or direction of these retrievals and reimaginings? And could you perhaps suggest how such retrievals could inform—and be informed by—a philosophical theology of gift/ing? Kevin Hart and Jean-Luc Marion and others draw from mystical theology, but they seem to be turning away from biblical resources.

RK: That's why I'm into the hermeneutics of narrative imagination, whereas they're into a more deconstructionist position (yes, even Marion in my view), and there *is* a difference in that regard. So while I learn from deconstruction, I really am closer to hermeneutics—I try to negotiate between the two, but I'm closer to hermeneutics—what I call a "diacritical hermeneutics." It's not the romantic hermeneutics of Gadamer and Heidegger and [Friedrich] Schleiermacher: getting back to the original event and reappropriating the inaugural moment. I don't believe in that kind of hermeneutic retrieval of the original and the originary—some primal unity. Nor would I uncritically endorse what Jack Caputo calls "radical hermeneutics"—which is really another word for deconstruction—because it doesn't sufficiently allow, in my view, for valid retrievals, recognitions, or reconciliations. In *Strangers, Gods and Monsters*, I propose a diacritical hermeneutics which is a third way.[23] I propose mediations, connections, interlinks, and passages back and forth. So it's neither reappropriation and fusion of horizons à la Gadamer, nor is it a complete gulf, separation, or rupture à la Caputo, Lyotard, and Derrida. Diacritical hermeneutics holds that faith is helped by narratives. Now, I don't privilege in any exclusivist sense the Christian narratives over the Jewish or the Islamic or indeed the nonmonotheistic. I just say, "They're the ones I know best." If I with a Muslim, I'd work with Muslim narratives. If I were Jewish, I'd work were Jewish texts. (Indeed, as a Christian, I generally work with both Christian *and* Jewish narratives.) My niece has become a Buddhist: I learn from Buddhist stories and I try to include them in my work. I still do it from a Christian perspective because that's what I'm most familiar with. But if I'd grown up in Kyoto, I would invoke the Buddhist texts first. I don't believe that any religion has an absolute right to the absolute. There is no one, royal route. There should be no proprietal prerogatives here. They're all narrative paths towards the absolute. And if you happen to be born on this particular road or highway rather than another one, and you've walked it for twenty or thirty years, then you know it better than another one, and you can help other people walk it. And from your knowledge of it, when you come to a crossroads, you may have more interesting and intelligent dialogue with the person who has come along the other highway. You know where you've come from, and you can talk to them about it. They can learn from you, and you can learn from them. Whereas if you say immediately, "Oh well, to hell with my highway! I'm only interested in yours," they might well respond, "Well, I'll tell you about mine, but do you have anything to add to the conversation?" And you'll say, "No, no! I hate everything about my road! I've learnt nothing. That's only a load of baloney!" I'm always a bit suspicious of zealous converts who repudiate everything in their own traditions and look to some New Age trendy alternative for a solution—and that can be a Buddhist becoming a Christian as much as a Christian becoming a Buddhist. I'm all for dialogue between the two. Some people have to change their religions to shake off the tyranny of their tradition. Their experience may be *so* negative that they *need* to do that. And here you can have a kind of religious or cultural transvestism that is very helpful: you wear the clothes of another religion, and through it you can see the spiritual in a way which you couldn't have done previously. I'm not against conversion as such, unless it's from one absolutist disposition to another absolutist disposition. I don't think any religion should be absolutist. I think it should be *searching for* the absolute, but the *search itself* should not be absolutist because that's to presume we can own the absolute. Where I am wary of a certain mystical New Ageism or deconstructionism is their tendency to repudiate historical narratives and memories as invariably compromising and totalizing. I see narratives and memories as necessary mediations. If you don't go down the route of hermeneutic reinterpretation—which is, as Ricœur says, a long route, an arduous labor of reading and rereading—then you must go towards the desert like Derrida and Caputo and their ana-khorites, which is hard. Or else you go towards the opposite, mystical extreme—not towards *khōra* this time (with Derrida and Caputo) but towards the "saturated phenomenon" or hyperessential divinity (with Marion or Michel Henri). But then it's another kind of "holy terror," because you're completely *blinded* by it. You embrace another kind of "dark" (from overexposure to the absolute in the dark night of the soul). Here, too, it seems to me, there is no interpretation possible. It's immediate, nonmediated presence. In both cases—whether you're going into the emptiness and undecidability of the *khōra* or whether you're going into the blinding overexposed splendor of divine saturation—you are subjected to an experience of "holy madness." Now, I'm not against that *as a moment*. But you can't live with the moment: you've got to interpret it after the event. Otherwise, what's the difference between Moses and the burning bush and Peter Sutcliffe in his pickup truck claiming he's illuminated and hearing a so-called divine voice that says, "Go and kill prostitutes, and do my will, and clear the world of this evil scourge"?[24] What's the difference? There *must* be a difference. And we must try to discern as best we can between *(a)* psychopaths like Charlie Manson or Peter Sutcliffe, who think they're on a *divine* mission to kill in the name of God and *(b)* prophets like Moses or Isaiah, who go out to liberate and comfort their enslaved people. You have to be able to *even vaguely* and *approximately* tell the difference. No?

Q: So we return to the problem of Abraham sacrificing his son?

RK: Yes, but my reading of this episode is very different to Kierkegaard's and closer to Levinas's. The way to read that, I suggest, involves a critical hermeneutic retrieval. The story illustrates how monotheistic revelation is anti-sacrifice; it marks a move away from human sacrifice. This may be read, accordingly, as a story about the transition from pre-revelation to revelation monotheism. The first voice that Abraham hears — "Kill your son" — is, by this account, his *own voice.* It's the voice of his ancestral, tribal, sacrificial religion. But the second voice that says, "Do *not* kill your son," is the voice of the kingdom. That's how I read it. I think we should read every story in the Gospel according to this principle: "Where is justice being preached here, and where is injustice?" Where there's evil, you have to say no to it. You can find other passages in the Bible that say, "Go out and kill all Gentiles or Canaanites." If you take that literally, you're into the Palestinian/Israeli situation. You are into Holy War. Ditto for the Christian invocation of a "blood libel" against Jews. We should read such texts hermeneutically, critically, and say, "No! That was an interpolation by certain zealous scribes during a certain century . . ." We need historical research on this. We need to demythologize it and say, "They were trying to justify the occupation of their neighbors' lands. So ignore that mispresentation of divine revelation and look rather to the Psalms where God calls for the protection of the widow, the stranger, and the orphan. The stranger is your neighbor — *that's* God speaking. 'Go out and kill Canaanites' is *not* God speaking — that's *us* speaking." Knowing the difference is a matter of hermeneutic discernment. And it's a matter which concerns every believer, every reader of Scripture.

Q: Nietzsche asks, "Can there be a God beyond good and evil?"[25] Maybe we're just projecting our idea that God is "simply good," that God can only do "purely good things"?

RK: Everyone makes their choice, but the God of love and justice is the only God I'm interested in. I'm not interested in the God of evil, torture, and sadism. I'm just not interested in those Gnostic (or neo-Gnostic) notions that see the dark side of God — destruction and holocaust — as an indispensable counterpart to the good side. Such theories or theodicies can justify *anything.*

Q: But there is that possibility?

RK: There *isn't* that possibility—for me, or, at least, it is one I refuse. It's how you interpret it. You can, of course, interpret divinity in terms of a moralizing God where you say, "Oh, homosexuality, masturbation, divorce, sex outside of marriage, etc., is evil." That's the Christian Coalition, Pat Buchanan, and Ian Paisley. They seem to know what's good for all of us! I'm against such a *moralizing* God, but I'm not against an *ethical* God. There's a big difference. I *don't know* what the absolutely good is. How could anyone know? But I do *believe*— precisely because I can't know—that good exists, and I will do everything to try to differentiate and discern (according to what Ignatius calls "the discernment of spirits") as best I can between the God of love and the pseudo-God of hate. I do believe that the divine is the good. In fact, for me, "God" is another name for "the good," rather than "the good" being another name for God. We don't know what the good is. We don't know what God is either. But they *must* be the same, because otherwise there's no way to avoid theodicy and its ruinous logic: "This war was necessary. It's all part of the will of God. It's the necessary dark side to God." Jung's answer to Job. Pangloss's answer to the Lisbon earthquake. Hegel's answer to the Terror. The rise of Divine Reason run amok. As humans, I agree, we have to confront the *thanatos*, the shadow in ourselves, the sadistic instincts, the perversions, the hate, the evil, the aggression. *We* have to confront the shadow in ourselves. But divinity doesn't have to confront the shadow in itself, because if it has evil in itself, it is not God. If you say, "The shadow in God—the sacrifice of innocent children, the torture of victims—is part of God's will," well, frankly, I'd prefer to burn in Hell than believe in a God who justifies the torture of innocent children. And I'm not ambiguous about that. That said, I take a very dramatic example here that very few people would say is good, because on many occasions it's very hard to tell what's absolutely good or evil. It is very hard for people to justify the torture of an innocent child. Should the Americans have dropped the atomic bomb in Hiroshima? I would say no, but I'm not going to be too moralistic about that, because I know there's an argument. You can negotiate that. Should a woman have an abortion? I would say, "Ideally not, but it's her right, and if she believes she is doing what is right, on balance, it may be the right thing for her to do." So I think a law that says, "You can never have an abortion" is wrong. Abortion is very complex. It can be right in some respects and wrong in others—*at the same time*. It may be right *and* wrong. Morality is often gray on gray; it's not black and white. Let's just say it is morally difficult. And everyone—for or against—has a right to discuss it. That's what human morality is. It's not about absolutes. But when it comes to God, who is absolute, either God is good, or I'm not interested in God. This mixing evil with God is Gnosticism. I wrote my second novel, *Walking at Sea Level,* as an argument against that.

Q: There are all these other metaphysical characteristics ascribed to God: God is one, God is pure, and so on, and to say, "God is purely good" . . .

RK: Well, I'm not sure I would use the word *purely* here because then you're back into Puritanism. But I do insist on the claim that God is unconditionally and absolutely good, or God is not God. I would not claim that I know what the good is. I would simply *try* to discern better between what is good and what is evil, or what is better and what is worse, what is more or less just, in a *given* situation. I can recognize many instances of good acts where people put others before themselves and give up their life or give up their wealth—that, to me, is a good thing to do. I want to reserve the right to say that. Whereas, when somebody chops a child's head off, I want to be able to say, "That's *not* a good thing." I think most people would agree. That's not an absolutist disposition: it is common sense, practical wisdom, what the Greeks called *phronēsis,* the Latins *prudentia.* Whenever someone does a good act—gives a cup of cold water to a parched neighbor—he or she is making God that little bit *more* real and actual and incarnate in the world. When someone does evil—torturing innocent children or simply stealing the cup of cold water from the parched neighbor who needs it more—he or she is refusing the possibilizing, desiring, transfiguring promise of God. In that sense evil is the refusal to let God exist.

Q: In your legendary 1984 interview with Derrida, he explains that there have always been "heterogeneous elements" in Christianity.[26] Was he referring to scriptural motifs or mystical theology or both?

RK: I don't know. You'd have to ask him. But I suspect that what he means by that is probably similar to what I've just been saying. There's no one pure religion. Christianity is heterogeneous. It draws from pagan elements, Jewish elements, Greek elements, etc.

Q: The context was Greek philosophy or metaphysics, mainstream Christianity, and you referred to the official dogmas of the dominant churches, and then Derrida said, "Oh, no, I can see that there are heterogeneous elements." But I didn't know if he meant biblical theology and some of the mystical texts . . .

RK: Generally speaking, when Derrida says, "There are heterogeneous elements," that's good news from his point of view. So I think he just wants to say, "Look, as I would interpret it, Christianity isn't just this triumphalist, totalizing, dogmatic, absolutist, intolerant body of beliefs. It's actually quite porous and permeable to dialogue with its other." And I would agree wholeheartedly with him here.

Q: And there are marginal voices.

RK: Exactly.

Q: Having cited that line, do you think Derrida prefers the biblical over the mystical?

RK: It depends how you define "the biblical" and "the mystical." There are elements of the mystical in Derrida. He is very taken, for example, by pseudo-Dionysius, Eckhart, Silesius, Cusanus. But I think there are other forms of mysticism that Derrida would not have much time for, particularly the fusional and somewhat hysterical claim to be "one with God."

Q: I haven't read many mystical theologians, but most of them say we can't speak about God and then . . .

RK: They go and speak about God.

Q: Yes, and affirm all the dogmas and say, "God is definitely Trinitarian," "God is this" and "God is that," and they just seem to slide back into this totalizing discourse.

RK: Then they're not really good mystics, I would say.

Q: Wouldn't mystical theology—taken to its logical or a-logical conclusion—have to say, "I'm going to suspend my beliefs on, say, the creeds of the churches, because the creeds are as positive as you can get"? I was just wondering how the mystics can balance their mysticism with their denominational affirmations. Dionysius wasn't considered a heretic.

RK: Most of them were. Eckhart was. John Scotus Eriugena was. Bruno and Vico were. They were in favor one moment, out the next. These thinkers were trying to make sense to their fellow believers. They had had these deep, spiritual experiences and were profoundly touched and were trying to reconcile these experiences with the doctrine of the virgin birth or the Filioque or something like that. They were mucking along. They were trying to be loved and accepted by their brethren in the monastery. Otherwise they were out in the rain with no food. We compromise and we muddle through. I would say here, again, that Derrida often discriminates: he picks and chooses—and rightly so. He's an à la carte rabbinical interpreter. Just think of his reflections on biblical passages in *Schibboleth—pour Paul Celan [Shibboleth: For Paul Celan]*[27] or "Circumfession,"[28] for example, or again in *Donner la mort [The Gift of Death]*, [29] where he goes back to the Abraham story. He takes what inspires him and rejects the kind of Zionist triumphalism which says, "Death to all Arabs." So he discriminates. You might say, "Well, *how* do you discriminate, Mr. Derrida, since there are no criteria, and we can only read in the dark?" But that's another day's work. Maybe it's a performative contradiction, but, happily, he does exercise it. He discriminates. He differentiates. He discerns. He's on the side of the good. Deconstruction is not a justification for evil. It's not an apologia for an "anything goes" relativism—as some of its critics unconditionally suggest.

Q: In the end, deconstruction is just trying to affirm that whatever is going on in the world . . .

RK: No, that's Heidegger. Derrida, as I understand him, is saying, "I'm for justice. I'm for the gift. I'm for the good. I'm for the democracy to come." He's not saying, "It doesn't matter whether it's democracy or totalitarianism. It doesn't matter whether it's justice or injustice. It doesn't matter whether it's gift or selfishness." He's not saying that at all. Derrida is on the side of the good. All his thinking, politically and ethically, is emancipatory. The differences I have with Derrida are not in terms of his values, his ethics, his politics—but how one gets there. That's a practical question, a pragmatic question. I think hermeneutics, *informed by* a certain deconstructive caution, vigilance, and scrupulosity, is a better way of getting there than deconstruction on its own (without hermeneutics). That's where I part company with Caputo, Derrida, and Lyotard. But they're all on the side of the good as I see it. I'm not saying, "We're all morally pure." I'm saying that the good is something we aspire to, something that is impossible, something that is "impossible" in its *absolute* sense but possible in all kinds of different, tiny practical ways. The messianic is potentially present in every moment, even though we can never be sure whether it comes or goes.

This exchange took place in the Philosophy Department of Boston College, Spring 2001.

Dublin Colloquy
Thinking Is Dangerous

STEPHEN J. COSTELLO: What attracted you to philosophy in the first place? Did you ever want to do anything else, such as medicine, like other members of your family?

RK: No, I never wanted to do medicine because I had a terrible fear of blood and was very squeamish when it came to human pain, inflicted or endured. So I wasn't a good potential doctor or, indeed, sportsman, except sport that did not involve painful physical contact. As a player on the rugby team in Glenstal Abbey (Limerick, Ireland), I was scrum-half but that consisted of avoiding forwards rushing in at you and getting the ball out to someone else who would get crushed instead of you. Medicine and pain were something I couldn't deal with very well, although my brothers and father and uncles and grandfather were all involved in that profession. I would like to think philosophy is another kind of healing, which involves the psyche. Medicine, of course, involves the body and the soul. But I have always thought of philosophy as a therapy of the soul, beginning with the Greeks. Socrates saw it as that, as you know yourself — the whole idea of midwifery. My uncles were obstetricians and gynecologists. In a way, philosophy is another kind of midwifery but, this time, of questions and answers and allowing the birth of answers by putting questions to somebody. It's a kind of psychic obstetrics. In a way, maybe medicine and philosophy aren't completely removed. Certainly, my family's approach to medicine always involved the person as much as the anatomy. My grandfather, for example, who was a professor of medicine in Cork and a doctor in Cork, always shook people's hands. They thought he was French initially. There was a recognition that medicine involved the mind as well as the body. But in philosophy, there is also a recognition that the mind involves the body, even though we are focusing on the mind—it's a therapy of the mind, as Wittgenstein put it. Philosophy is a form of therapy and asking questions and discovering which questions can be answered appropriately and which can't. At times, when you reach the mystical, as Wittgenstein says, which is God or beauty or the sublime, there is no answer, and you have to accept the limits of what knowledge can do. So that's another kind of therapy. Some questions don't have answers. Sometimes there is no definitive answer, and if you try to find one and say, "This is the only God," or "This is the only government" or "This is the only definition of the Good," what you end up with is tyranny or totalitarianism or dogmatism or ideology of the most constraining type. So what attracted me to philosophy? It was the possibility of finding healing and maybe, in time, helping to give healing through the profession of philosophy by helping people to ask questions about their lives and try to answer them and if there were no answers, to go the way of faith or acceptance or letting go—endurance, patience, abandonment. So that was one reason.

SJC: At a more biographical level, what first got you interested in philosophy?

RK: I suppose it was through studying French literature and theology in Glenstal Abbey. I had Mark Patrick Hederman and Andrew Nugent as teachers, two brilliant Benedictine monks who had done their doctoral studies in France—in Paris and Strasbourg respectively—and had come back to the monastery. It was while reading Sartre and Camus and Bergson to prepare for French A-levels that I became particularly hooked on philosophy. The Christian doctrine that was taught there was very enlightened in that Andrew Nugent used to come in with what the philosophers say about why God *doesn't* exist, so we would have Marx's refutation of religion, [Ludwig] Feuerbach's, Nietzsche's, Sartre's, and so on; and if we survived all the arguments against the existence of God, then maybe our faith was authentic. That was the challenge, and it got us thinking, and I became very interested in the philosophy of religion for that reason, being faced with the question of atheism. It was a very brave thing for a Benedictine monk to do—giving us all the reasons for *not* believing in God and then saying, "You give me a good reason for believing in God!" So it was really through the philosophy of literature and through the philosophy of religion that I came to philosophy, and I would say that I am still primarily interested in those two areas of philosophy. One of my recent books is called *The God Who May Be,* and that is still the philosophy of religion, with readings of Exodus 3:15 and the Song of Songs and the whole question of desire, but taken from the perspective of philosophy—Plato and Hegel, Heidegger and Levinas and Ricœur. And as you know, my work for the past twenty years has largely been in the philosophy of imagination, narrative, myth, and symbolism—so that is all the literary influence. I suppose I could say that I have always worked on the borderlines of philosophy, and that's where I like to be. I wouldn't consider myself a pure philosopher— I'm an impure philosopher! But I believe in the interdisciplinary challenge of putting philosophical questions to literature, to imagination, to desire, to the question of the unconscious (as you know I'm interested in psychoanalysis—Lacan and Freud in particular), to religion. These interest me more than the pure questions of abstract logic or cognition, which I always found a little boring. Kant formulated four important questions: "What can I know?" (the epistemological question), "What can I hope for?" (the religious question), "How should I act?" (the ethical question), and "What does it mean to be?" (the ontological question). I try to invite my students and readers to willingly suspend their belief or disbelief, their presumptions and assumptions, and to embark on a process of interrogation with the great thinkers. After this process of open questioning, one is, I think, in a better position to act. I believe that you must ultimately align yourself philosophically, politically, and religiously. Philosophy comes from and culminates in action.

SJC: And presumably that kind of self-questioning can end on an analyst's couch or in a therapist's chair? It might begin with philosophy and end elsewhere.

RK: Well you know what Julia Kristeva says: We all suffer from the malady of being, from the pain and pathology of existence. We start from hurt and confusion. As the Irish poet Paul Durcan says, "Is there one of us who is not confused?" Or as Brian Friel, another Irish writer, adds, "Confusion is not an ignoble condition." Freud calls it neurosis. We're all neurotic animals to a greater or lesser degree. Hitherto and traditionally, there were answers for questions, but nowadays it's not obvious. We're living in a postdogmatic, posttotalitarian, and post-ideological age, we're told. There are no ready answers for people. But Kristeva, who is a philosophical psychoanalyst, maintains that there are three main ways of dealing with the pain and separation of our "melancholic imagination,"—namely, *art, psychoanalysis,* and *religion.*

Ultimately, philosophy does not provide the answers. Philosophy gets you to question and then leads you to the limits of what can and cannot be answered. But when you reach that limit, art, psychoanalysis, or religion take over—psychoanalysis at the level of the unconscious, art at the level of aesthetic experience, and religion at the level of faith. Some choose one of these, others a combination of all three, and others again none at all—they just remain neurotic. She might have added friendship, but we're not talking about that; friendship is obviously the cure for all ills, but we're talking about professional areas of help. So I suppose that's where I would see my interest in philosophy, residing in the gap *between* these three and at the borderlines between the question of God, the question of imagination, and the question of the unconscious desire.

SJC: Whom have you been most influenced by philosophically, and how would you describe your philosophic position?

RK: The people who influenced me the most would have been two French philosophers—Paul Ricœur and Emmanuel Levinas—with whom I worked in Paris as a doctoral student in the late seventies. I consider myself a Continental philosopher (a hermeneutic phenomenologist to be more technically precise), who believes that philosophy is first and foremost a radical interrogation and interpretation of our existence in the world—political, personal, and metaphysical. Western philosophy originates with the Socratic doctrine of ignorance; that is, it begins with an admission that we do not possess knowledge, that we must doubt what we have hitherto taken for granted. Only then can we really begin to question and interpret.

SJC: Nietzsche ended his life in an asylum for the mentally insane; Camus refers to the absurdity of existence; Sartre says, "Hell is other people." Is it not frustrating to be dealing with a subject that questions everything and yet possesses few answers, if any, to the problems posed by existence?

RK: That's the risk you run when you do philosophy. Dostoyevsky said that "true faith comes from the crucible of doubt." It is better to doubt than to believe blindly from birth to death. Everyone in life, whether they do philosophy or not, should question their existence, and I don't see that as being incompatible with faith. There must be room for doubting and questioning. If you run the risk of committing suicide, then that's the risk you run. Looking at the statistics of my own students, the suicide rates haven't been particularly high! I believe that the majority of philosophers affirm and enjoy life. Some of them end up mad and commit suicide, but so do other people. I think it's a wager.

SJC: Does the philosopher have a role to play in politics?

RK: I think many philosophers do. Thomas Paine was extraordinarily influential in the American Revolution, and Rousseau and Voltaire in the French Revolution. Hegel and Marx influenced the socialist ones of our century. Even our own 1916 Rising was deeply informed by men of ideas. [Padraig] Pearse, [James] Connolly, and [Arthur] Griffith were all intellectuals. They all edited journals: Pearse edited *An Claidheamh Solais*, Connolly the *Irish Worker*, and Griffith was editor of the *Irish Statesman*. They were people of political action, and they were thinkers, not mindless Celts, dreamers of dreams, as the colonial stereotype would have it. Of course, that is not to say that academics should run the country! I believe in local democracy. I believe that everybody is potentially an intellectual.

SJC: You have written over a dozen books on philosophy and culture, a volume of poetry *(Angel of Patrick's Hill)*, and two novels *(Sam's Fall* and *Walking at Sea Level)*. You are a professor of philosophy, have been a television presenter, chairman of the Film Studies Board in University College Dublin, a member of the Irish Arts Council and Higher Education Authority. And you have made political presentations to the Forum for a New Ireland (on the joint-sovereignty model), the Opsahl Commission in Belfast, and the Forum for Peace and Reconciliation (on the British-Irish Council). You have also involved yourself as a speechwriter in Mary Robinson's presidential campaign. Where do you get your energy? Where does your passion and consummate conviction stem from? What keeps you going?

RK: I cannot really answer these questions, but I can say that in trying to make some contribution to public intellectual life I was personally very excited by the submission which Simon Partridge and I made to the Forum for Peace and Reconciliation (an idea which was ultimately included in the Good Friday Agreement of 1988). I had been working on the proposal for a transnational Council of Isles—with Partridge,

Robin Wilson, and others—for a number of years, and originally it was treated with total scorn, as totally utopian. We were exploring not just the idea of joint sovereignty but of postsovereignty—saying that we belong to a more federal and regional tradition in the British Isles and in Europe. If I have made a small contribution as a political thinker in Ireland, it would probably be, I suspect, in helping to challenge the old fetish of *absolutist sovereignty*, something which had a ruinous impact on both Britain and Ireland. In various submissions to national and international forums—as well as in books like *Postnationalist Ireland* and *Rethinking Ireland*—I was trying to imagine various ways of going beyond sovereignty to another kind of relationship where you give power to people regionally and transnationally (as well as nationally). It's very close to John Hume, in some respects, though he couldn't say it too explicitly for electoral reasons. It is a postnationalist vision, which doesn't mean it's antinationalist. And it involves a Europe of regions. That's where I would be most passionate in terms of my political commitments and as a critic of British nationalism, which has never been called nationalism. It's called "rationality." We Irish are the ones labeled "nationalist," and the Bretons and Scots—never the British.

SJC: You're juggling a number of balls. But where do the commitment, conviction, and enduring energy come from?

RK: I have no real idea where it comes from. Maybe (and I say this cautiously) it's about seeing division and wanting to see healing. Maybe it is something I have inherited from my medical ancestors, though, I repeat, it is more about psychic than physical healing. It's an attempt through ideas, images, and metaphors to come up some alternative possibilities, to bring reconciliation where there is conflict, though that might sound somewhat banal.

SJC: It's an act of synthesis.

RK: Yes. I remember Colm Toibin, a contemporary of mine at University College Dublin, saying in a review of one of my books (I think *Transitions*) that if Richard Kearney played in a band, he would play the synthesizer! I didn't know whether that was a compliment at the time. I knew what Colm meant. There was something of that— the desire to bring things together. And philosophy has two functions: to analyze and divide, to split things up and make distinctions; but also to try to synthesize. As Kant says, there is the analytic dimension of reason, and there is a synthetic function, and maybe I've been more into the synthetic than the analytic. Ireland, as you know, is a place of cleavage and fissure—class divisions, political divisions in the North, economic and religious divisions. So I suppose there was a passion to do something about that, to try to bridge some of the many divides.

SJC: Could all this active and outside involvement be a defense against going inward?

RK: Maybe. Occasionally I would burn out after all this activity. I experienced a series of depressions (there is no other word for it in our language; the Greeks call it *melancholia*). I would find myself exhausted and realize that things couldn't be solved as I'd imagined, that things were "impossible." But then I would get out of the depression, and the "impossible" sometimes became that bit more possible. Like the idea for the British-Irish Council. It ran up against so many obstacles initially, and you're called a utopian and idealist, someone who hasn't got his two feet on the ground. I even remember Minister Ray McSharry and Prime Minister Charlie Haughey telling me that the project of shared sovereignty was totally unrealistic at the New Ireland Forum in the early eighties. Most people then said, "This is impossible! Such crazy ideas could only come from philosophers!" As Haughey used to say, "Richard Kearney is my favorite philosopher, and I don't understand a word he says!" That sort of discrepancy between the possible and the impossible can lead to burnout, to depression and disillusionment, to the feeling that your ideas don't translate into reality. But one can also realize at such moments that philosophy is not just a philosophy of *action* but also of *contemplation*. The *vita activa* needs to be complemented by, and perhaps even founded upon, the *vita contemplativa*. That is one of the lessons I brought with me from my time at Glenstal Abbey and also from my religious upbringing as a child. My mother was very religious—not in a dogmatic way (she was never doctrinaire); she was very spiritual. From an early age, I learnt that there is a deep, inner part of the soul or psyche that needs to be catered for, that it is important at times to slow down. During one of my depressions, I did some work at Eckhart House in Dublin with a wonderful Dominican, Miceal O'Reagan, which was hugely helpful. The first time I went to see him, I said, "This is my theory of why I'm not feeling very well," and I quoted Freud and Jung and Lacan and [Bruno] Bettelheim and Kristeva. And Miceal calmly replied, "I think what you need to do is not analyze anything but just sit and breathe for thirty minutes every day." So I used to go and breathe and say little. It was very difficult for me at the time. But the point was to try to quieten the mind and "go gently," as Miceal used to say, to attend to the interior dimension of oneself. As it happened, I was having a well built in our house in West Cork, and I was very taken by the image of *going down* to the bottom of the well. The diviner and driller who sank the well said it was one of the deepest wells they had dug in fifty years. It was over four hundred feet down! I wrote a poem about it. It is very much in the Eckhart mode; the last sequence is called *Bridget's Island,* where we now have a little house:

> I will rest, now,
> at the bottom of Bridget's well.
> I will follow the crow's way
> footprint by footprint
> in the mud down here.
> I won't come up until I am calmed down
> and the earth dries beneath me
> and I have paced the caked ground
> until smooth all over
> it can echo a deeper voice,
> mirror a longer shadow.

Then the water image in the poem gives way to one of fire. . . .

> Then the fire may come again
> Beneath me, this time,
> rising beyond me.
> No narcissus-flinted spark
> behind closed eyes
> but a burning bush.
> A fire that always burns away
> but never is burnt out.

That's when you reach the inner point of nothing, stillness, emptiness. The mud in the dark. Then, the poem suggests, something else fills you with energy. You ask, "Where does the energy come from?" I like to think it comes from the burning bush, but there's always an ambiguity as to whether it's coming from the burning bush—therefore from a source deeper and greater than you, like water that wells up—or whether it's coming from your own fantasy. That's something that needs discernment. And for discernment, you need (well, I needed) to meditate and contemplate and try to keep things still and quiet. That didn't come naturally to me at all—it was a big effort.

SJC: You mean that the image could be ego-driven or could come from the grace or gift of Being, from God?

RK: Exactly. The question is discerning where the fire comes from. It could come from both. It's not easy telling the difference. If it's not coming from deep down, from the bottom of the well—and you have to go down there and stay there to ensure you are in contact with that— then the chances are it's what Kierkegaard calls the "aesthetic eros" of the ego, constructing and reconstructing itself endlessly, and that leads to *tedium vitae*—namely, burnout and melancholy. Not that burnout is always a result of egoism (that's not what I'm saying). It's just the body and the psyche reminding you that you can only do so much, that you have to acknowledge limits, boundaries, borders.

SJC: And a breakdown can lead to a breakthrough.

RK: Absolutely. I believe that completely. And it's not only the Meister Eckhart and John of the Cross image of the "dark night of the soul"—*das Nichts* (the nothing), the very seed of the Godhead, "God beyond God" as Eckhart says; it is also the existentialist notion, which I am very partial to, in Kierkegaard and Heidegger, of the *being towards nothingness*, of the *being towards death*, as being a breakthrough to authenticity, where you let go of the ego-driven desire to impose power and calculate and compute and possess and control. You let things *be in their being*. We don't do that naturally. We sometimes have to be brought down into the mud. Eckhart called it "letting go" *(Abgeshiedenheit)*. Heidegger called it "releasement" *(Gelassenheit)*—the abandonment of the self, which actually leads to a deeper self. It's not that it leads to *nothing*. Unless you mean that "nothing is more real than nothing," as Samuel Beckett said. Letting go doesn't come naturally to us; it sometimes has to be beaten into us by existence. It's a black hand that comes up from the bottom of the lake and pulls us under.

SJC: You've mentioned Eckhart House and these moments and moods, in the Heideggerian sense, of anguish and despair. What then is your view of psychoanalysis and psychotherapy?

RK: I use it a lot in my teaching and in my writing, and I have undergone it, both in Eckhart House and also for a time in Boston, and I found it tremendously helpful. I also have reservations about the potential abuses of it. It is such a deep area, and the whole process of transference is so delicate. It can, on occasion, flip into infatuation or obsession, where analysands become overdependent on analysts; and sometimes it can be very difficult for analysts, as Freud knew with Dora, not to engage in countertransference, particularly if the analysis reverts to some infantile neurosis or repressed memory. I think there is a danger with some kinds of "wild analysis" *(analyse sauvage)* that certain people regress to their childhood and become identified with a victim role, and they blame everybody else for their problems, starting with their parents, then their teachers, etc. That's not to say people aren't hurt when they're young and don't feel huge fear and anxiety. And there is lots of real abuse out there, as we know. Sometimes it is very important to revisit traumas of the past and come through them and "repeat them forward" by working them through, by turning melancholy into mourning (to use Freud's terms). But this is not easy. It is the old question of "analysis terminable or interminable." I think that, at worst, analysis can become a surrogate religion, where the analyst becomes God for certain clients who cannot live without their weekly (or more frequent) fix. And it is, of course, also a huge investment of time, energy, and money (the latter being a symbol of what you attach importance to). That said, the psychotherapists and psychoanalysts I've been fortunate enough to work with are people who have avoided such dangers. They helped me greatly and I am very grateful.

SJC: If you had to choose, though, between Lacanian psychoanalysis and psychosynthesis psychotherapy . . .

RK: They both have strengths. It depends on the person. Some people need the more Lacanian approach, some the more Eckhartian or interpersonal. But, I repeat, one can also get to the place of freedom and letting go through certain kinds of art (Dostoyevsky and Tolstoy, for example) or through religion (Meister Eckhart and the great mystical and spiritual traditions, East and West). It doesn't much matter in the long run. The important thing is to find that freedom of being. I think that every great religion and every small religion has a certain wisdom about attachment and detachment. It's a very hard thing for us Westerners to learn. When I travel to Africa or Latin America, I see people sitting on their doorsteps for hours and hours. How can they do that? Be at peace doing *nothing*. They seem to have a calm within. I'm not romanticizing it—they might not have enough to eat either.

SJC: Something has seriously changed in you, it seems to me. You're writing more fiction and reflecting more on spiritual topics in your academic articles. Are you consciously aware of a different orientation and perspective in your life?

RK: Looking for wisdom through philosophy is like trying to move from ego to self or, as Ricœur put it, from *le moi* to *le soi*. I don't regret any of the cultural and political commitments that I had here in Ireland.

The only thing is, if you are not a political animal, which I'm not (I was very ambitious, of course, and I thought nothing was impossible), it can be difficult. There is a prisoner deep down inside, discovering that poverty within can become a huge enrichment. For me to do that, I had to let go of the ego, which was overinvolved, overactive, although hopefully I was doing some good too. But I needed to go on retreat. Going to Boston was that in a way—not exile, so much as a step back from the compulsion to overinvolve or overcommit. A "leave of absence" says it all. It was important to be absent from the hectic world of activity for a while.

SJC: A sabbatical of space.

RK: Exactly. A psychic sabbatical. I am working on more spiritual, religious, and literary things at the moment, and that requires a different rhythm. I've just come back from West Cork where we're getting a cottage together, and I spent the last month digging a well, painting walls, and putting down trees. It was wonderful. I didn't read or write for one minute in the last month. I don't regret doing that. There's a house there to live in, which is great and real, but it requires labor and activity, transforming matter into a house; but now, as I speak to you, I need time out to read and write and think and imagine and pray and meditate and walk. If I had to keep building houses, I would collapse under the rubble. It's an act of balance. Like riding the wave. You can do the work of action and transformation (on the crest of the water) and then go down into the hollow of the wave and remain steady and still. That's the challenge. I haven't always been successful at that. The old mystics' adage was that you had to drown three times. I had three bad depressions, and I probably needed the three. The monks used to say you had to knock three times on the door before you were let into a monastery. There's something about the three. The Trinity and dialectics, too. I think I needed those three to do something that wasn't natural for me, to descend to the bottom of Brigid's well. I had to be brought there, and I went screaming and howling! But I didn't actually choose to go there. It was involuntary, against all my natural instincts. But you can learn a lot if you accept that you are in that space and don't try to escape through alcohol, drugs, or other kinds of distraction (not that I am against using medication for depression, of course). The most important thing, it seems to me, is knowing that there is work to be done that can be intellectually and spiritually transforming. Religion, art, and psychotherapy are, in a way, all disciplines that go against our nature, that is, our everyday instinct to escape interiority and flee the challenge of freedom. They are "unnatural" in that sense and require a lot of effort.

SJC: You have mentioned that philosophy and faith aren't incompatible. How would you describe your own religious views?

RK: I would describe myself as a seeker for God first, as a Christian second, and as an ecumenical Catholic third. I disagree strongly with the present pope's teaching on women and on sexuality, particularly in the areas of divorce and contraception, and with his insistence on a celibate male clergy. I think it's a very patriarchal system with the nonordination of women to the priesthood. Women are 50 percent of the church, of the real church, the church of the people. I am sitting out the present papacy, hoping that the next pope will be more like John XXIII. But if not, I'll remain a Catholic, because I don't believe that the church belongs to the hierarchy. It belongs to the people, to people like Sister Stan and Jean Vanier, and to the people who are actively thinking and working through their faith on a day-to-day basis. Catholicism for me is not just a doctrinal issue. The reason I don't call myself a Protestant or a Jew is because Catholicism is my tradition, and I still think that there are very valuable things within that tradition, which I am not prepared to abandon. The Catholicism I profess is one of radical ecumenism.

SJC: Philosophically, you have taught on and written about the imagination a lot, publishing books with titles such as *The Wake of Imagination* and *Poetics of Imagining*. Why are you so preoccupied with imagining? Is it because certain essential things can't be spoken, only imagined, that when words fail and fade away, only images remain?

RK: Well, that is well put. Imagination takes over where reason falters, stammers, and finds its limits. The most important thing with imagination is to know that it *is* imagination and not mistake it for reality, because if it does, then it can slip into pathological fantasy. Then one can no longer tell the difference between what's real and what's not. We see daily how people become addicted to movie stars or crazy fads and ideologies. We read about stalkers, psychotics, or just ordinary fantasists who have difficulty separating out fact from fiction. Healthy imagination is imagination that knows it's dealing with images and that images are not giving us the "real thing" (whatever about the Coca-Cola commercial!) Imagination is necessary for our survival, in order to think more, live more, and exist more fully. There's a thin line between fantasy as narcissism, where you think you have everything (mania or megalomania), and a more humble imagination, which knows the limits between the real and the imaginary. I have a genuine worry, for example, about our contemporary "culture of complaint," in which we're all victims (which is not to deny for a moment that there are many real victims amongst us). Our culture of compulsory consumerism (manic fantasy) and complaint (depressive fantasy) collapses the crucial distinction between truth and fabrication. The border between real and imaginary dissolves. And we find ourselves exposed to a zone of indiscriminate confusion, of radical indistinction and indetermination (not bad, perhaps, if we are in a seminar on deconstruction, but not great if we are trying to live out our lives reasonably and responsibly). In our civilization of spectacle and simulation, the real is being increasingly reduced to the order of the reproducible, the copy, the simulacrum, the fake. Again, this is fine if we are dealing with a critical art culture of pastiche and parody—say, Andy Warhol or Roy Lichtenstein—but when the zone of indiscrimination is amplified in popular culture, advertising, the global internet, etc., to cover a huge part of our everyday lived experience, then we may well have a problem on our hands.

SJC: Could you expand a little on this point?

RK: Let me put it like this: I think an avant-garde artist like Andy Warhol is doing something incredibly challenging with his famous seriographs of stars—Marilyn Monroe, Liz Taylor, Jackie Kennedy, etc. And I greatly admire the attempts made by several more recent postmodern artists and philosophers to think through the whole dilemma of the "undecidability" of image/reality. The pervasive pathologies of our contemporary imagination need to be faced and exposed if a more salutary kind of imagining is ever to survive. And, curiously, the primary pathology of our Western society—indiscriminate consumerism—could be said to coincide here ironically with a major pathology of the so-called East or Middle East, namely, fundamentalism. Let me explain. There was, I think, a certain terrible logic about Al Qaeda and the Twin Towers. Here the extremes of Western consumerism and anti-Western fundamentalism met in a tragic collision and convergence. For while one could say that consumerism sacrifices the complexity of experience to the one-dimensional order of the *figural* (for example, credit, simulation, fantasy, consumer confidence, and so on), fundamentalism does so in the name of an exclusive attention to the *literal*— there is only one truth, and that is the "reality" of Islamic revelation (as Al Qaeda see it, of course). In both these scenarios, the complex dialectical and pluridimensional relationship between reality and imagination is abandoned, and we can no longer tell which is which. Fundamentalism is about refusing the possibility of the imaginary—hence the fatwah against Salman Rushdie. There can be no hermeneutics here. Interpretation is outlawed. The work of semantic innovation is taboo. Texts are "facts" for fundamentalists—above all, the sacred text of the Koran. No discussion or discernment necessary. But at the other extreme, namely, that of a certain postmodern consumerism, there is another kind of tyranny, where there are no facts, only "texts." And here the real is reduced to the imaginary without residue or reference. I am thinking here, for example, of Jean Baudrillard's comments on our culture of "sublime irreference" or what Fred Jameson calls the "cultural logic of late capitalism," where all experience is dissolved into a pervasive "depthless present." In both cases, one witnesses a curious triumph of one-dimensional thinking. That's why I argue in *The Wake of Imagination,* and again in *Poetics of Imagining,* that it is essential to keep the dialectic going between the real and the imaginary—avoiding both dualism and monism. And that's why I call for a "diacritical hermeneutics" in *Strangers, Gods and Monsters,* so that we can remain open and critical before this contemporary dilemma, acknowledging the distinctions and differences between the figural and the literal, while equally recognizing how they overlap, interweave, and crisscross in all kinds of ways, positive and negative.

SJC: Are images in the mind enough to stave off the loneliness of memory? In other words, if I am alone in my room with images of my lover who left me, is that enough? I'm thinking of Sartre's example of Pierre.

RK: I don't think it is, and I don't think it should be, because if that were the case, we could replace a real person with an image. Art is about producing surrogate substitute objects for things that can't be thought, felt or experienced—for what Lacan called the "Real." In stories, writers are saying things that can compensate for loss and lack. It can be therapeutic. The danger is when aesthetic fiction is taken literally and we think that the image can replace the real person. Then you get people becoming addicted to Madonna, thinking that Madonna is the Virgin Mary, their lost object, their commodity muse.

SJC: So we should transform the image into something more symbolic?

RK: Yes, and also recognize that no image can replace a real person. As Freud said, we must go through the mourning, otherwise it becomes melancholy. Melancholy is the refusal to mourn. If we interiorize our lost objects as images that become part of us, we think we haven't lost them. We deny separation and absence; we refuse the truth of loss and lack. Then we discover that the internalized image of the "lost" person, that surrogate we have incorporated inside us to fill the gap, cannot do the work of really filling the lack, because the person is dead or gone or has left us or is not there; and then what we often do is turn our desire for that idealized lost object into hatred, as Freud says in "Mourning and Melancholy." We hate ourselves and it leads to depression. It's a wonderful essay by Freud. So we have to remember the melancholy of memory, even as we play with images that can help us overcome it.

SJC: And not be too quick to go through the mourning.

RK: No, you can't rush it. There's no quick fix. Alcohol or drugs can give you a temporary respite for a couple of hours, and certain forms of fantasy can alleviate the pain a little; but ultimately it comes back. It's like a sleeping pill. You get six hours sleep, but you are more tired when you wake up.

SJC: Your novel *Sam's Fall* tells a tale of two brothers who grow up in Cork and board at Columbanus Abbey. Sam stays on to become a Cistercian monk, and Jack leaves to fall in love and pursue his thesis on Toland. The book warns of the dangers of playing God and living out someone else's desires and dreams. The message I picked up is that we need to break free from the passionate prison of other peoples' desire and find our own place in the sun. What were you trying to work out in the book?

RK: Wasn't it Joyce who said that Dublin is a city of "doubling," existing "between twotwinsome minds"? This cleft mind is something I've been very struck by in Ireland. There's an almost compulsory and exaggerated politeness between people: "You're so welcome!," "It's such a wonderful day!," "She's so gorgeous!" etc. The addiction to hyperbole. An interesting take on this need to inflate reality is to be found in J. M. Synge's *The Playboy*. Christy Mahon, the protagonist, declares at one point that he has been "made a man by the power of a lie." We have to invent stories that we killed our father, that we did something we didn't do to prove that we are a man. It is a question of using words and images to compensate for something we've never had. You could call it power, in terms of a colonial explanation once again. But I think it's deeper than that. It's as if we haven't found the missing "fifth province" that our mythology speaks of (which will supplement and complete the other four existing provinces). So we *reinvent* it in words. I think the Irish are a people who fantasize and fabulate a lot. Everybody does this, of course, but there's that old cliché about the Irish being feckless Celts: "We are the music makers; we are the dreamers of dreams." All that stuff. It's part of the Celtic twilight and folklore; but there's often a grain of truth in clichés, and our addiction to fantasy is certainly something I was trying to explore in both *Sam's Fall* and *Walking at Sea Level.* I wanted to show how excessive fantasy can lead to doubleness, to that cleft existence that Irish writers have so often observed. The cleft in imagination is critical. The fact that Jack and Sam are the central characters and that Raphaelle is trying to negotiate and navigate this doubling is not an accident. Where the third part of the trilogy goes, I'm not quite sure. I call it *Writing for Nothing,* and it might be published or it might not. It's important for me to finish it, whether or not it sees the light of day. Balzac said that you should never talk your novels away! I think a lot of novels are talked away in Ireland, because we're talkers by instinct. We're not good at holding things in. We're not great containers. I think Heaney puts his finger on this deep tendency towards indiscretion in the Irish when he counsels us, "Whatever you say, say nothing." We tend to let things spill out, and I'm sure that may also have something to do with our long colonial history of disinheritance and dislocation. As Brien Friel says, "Words are the armory of the dispossessed." Fantasy compensates for a pervasive sense of lack, as evidenced in our recurring crises of authority and identity. But the fact that we don't know who we are can also be a positive thing. Captain McMorris (who was the first Irishman to speak in English literature) says "What is my nation?" It's in Shakespeare's *Henry V.* That's the positive side: to be asking questions. We're a very philosophical nation in that regard, despite the old colonial stereotype that the Anglo-Saxons are the philosophers and thinkers, while the Irish are all poets and dreamers. I think we're both. I think all peoples are both. I have tried to write about this in *The Irish Mind* and *Postnationalist Ireland.* We need to reclaim our great thinkers and scientists—[George] Berkeley, [John] Toland, [John] Tyndall, [William] Molyneux, [Edmund] Burke, etc.—along with our poets and playwrights. And this is particularly important for us as we attempt to retell the story of who we are.

SJC: Would you say, to use Hannah Arendt's famous distinction, that the private sphere in Ireland is becoming increasingly eroded, that everything is being exposed in the public sphere?

RK: In a way, yes. We don't need Oprah Winfrey or Jerry Springer because we're doing that kind of confessional stuff all the time, on the streets, in the pubs, everywhere. Gossip and "sca" (as it is called in Cork) are omnipresent. We're acting out our interior psychodramas with great gusto. I remember a Canadian telling me that he had a pain in the jaw from just answering questions after he'd moved to Ireland. He couldn't get over how much people talked. He was positively *ill.* Silence just doesn't exist in our culture! (This is why Joyce said that if he was to survive, he would have to practice "silence, exile and cunning.") We're terrified of silence. It's not just privacy—the invasive glare of the "valley of squinting windows"—but that whole place of interiority. We seem to have lost that capacity for inwardness somewhere along the line. (The old saints certainly seemed to have had it, but that is going back a long time—over 1,000 years!) That's why I think it is very important to retrieve and revere that inner place at the bottom of the well and spend more time there. Meditation practice and personal prayer are very important here. And we should be able to rediscover that in our own very rich spiritual traditions—Catholic and Protestant—no matter how much these have been abused and betrayed. One can find it in religion as readily as in art or psychotherapy— perhaps even more so. People like John O'Donohue, Patrick Hederman, Nuala Ni Dhomhnaill, Willie Desmond, and John Moriarity have been tapping these rich resources in our heritage recently. And committed religious figures like Sister Stan and Miceal O'Regan have also been extremely important in helping us to revisit this forfeited seam of deep spirituality. The official church has more or less lost it, I feel. It was so repressed in the unconscious. We have all those cases of child abuse and the hatred of erotic pleasure, the exclusion of women and fear of the body. Sexuality was talked about, but it was empty speech; and full speech was a rarity, except in our great poets and writers. The official religions in our country were too often used to hide the truth, rather than to express it. So the truth was repressed and then returned as a monster. The church has a lot to answer for. It's part of the solution (potentially), but it's also part of the problem. I think a revolution in the Irish church is necessary to retrieve what is genuinely spiritual and mystical and healing. But that also means acknowledging the sins that have been committed in the name of God, and there have been many. Practicing religion for me goes with thinking about religion philosophically, which I have been trying to do in recent books like *The God Who May Be* and *Strangers, Gods and Monsters,* books I've written since I moved to Boston in the late nineties. I'm not sure I could have written these books about God in Ireland. New England America and France, where I did most of my writing on religion, are basically secular modern republics. In the United States, Catholicism is a minority religion, because it's basically a secular republic, and even more so in France. You have to fight for the right to believe. I think we should have more secular spaces in Ireland. Then religion can become something you choose. I am all for the separation between church and state. The idea of a compulsory God or state religion is abhorrent to me.

SJC: Talking of religion and spirituality, in one of your poems in *Angel of St. Patrick's Hill,* you write: "O angel of the last days, where are you?" What I see in the poems is both a spiritual and sensual quest for a vanished face, for the burning bush, for the fire. It's also an odyssey of the imagination, and you are again resisting the dichotomy between the spirit and the senses. There is that same drive towards synthesis. The theme echoes again and again throughout your poems, novels, and philosophical works.

RK: Well, I would agree with that, and, philosophically, the closest parallel for me would be Merleau-Ponty and the phenomenology of the body. In other words, returning to the body-subject. The body and soul exist like two sides of the same sleeve or one's two hands touching each other. They are not two completely *separate* things. (That was the error of Platonic and Cartesian dualism, which my phenomenological work has always opposed). Or to take another analogy, we have one skin which faces both inside and outside. One face is immanence, the other transcendence. One spiritual, the other carnal. But they are constantly in touch, interweaving, overlapping. Like the figure of a chiasmus, as Merleau-Ponty puts it. The inside is your soul; the outside is your body. We need to retrieve this basic insight into the radically embodied and incarnate soul which was so central to certain kinds of early Christianity and to early Celtic spirituality in particular. If you go back to the Brehon laws in ancient Christian Ireland, you find a very liberal, celebratory—almost Rabellaisian!—attitude towards sexuality and carnality, for example. St. Brigid was said to have been wont to "down two partridges in one bite" and refused to "fast on an empty stomach." She had a huge appetite—physical and metaphysical! In other words, one witnesses a religious celebration of the sensual and terrestrial that goes hand in hand with a concelebration of the spirit. But then came Jansenism and the ultra-Montane Puritanism of the counterreformation. Catholicism ended up trying to outdo Protestantism in dour purism—and succeeded alas! Hence the appalling legacy of dualistic living that we witness even today in stories of child abuse, clerical cover-up, misogyny, etc. What a waste. What a shame.

SJC: That's a perversion.

RK: Yes. It's not the true spiritual heritage which can be something healing and liberating. That said, I'm not saying we can reverse the clock and go back to "Celtic spirituality." There can be a certain sentimental nostalgia about that. One needs to be wary of facile New Age pseudomysticism—something I try to warn about in my second novel, *Walking at Sea Level*. It's what I identify as the "Gnostic temptation." But that is not to deny that there is something very authentic and salutary about the various recent attempts by Irish thinkers and writers (mentioned above) to emancipate tradition into new forms of living and life-affirming spirituality.

SJC: Speaking of *Walking at Sea Level*, you deal in this book with the themes of duality—corporeality versus spirituality and the search for unity. The book is also a type of monastic meditation on life and religion, and in it Jack Toland is running from his past and has a profound metamorphosis. The pedophile pornographer, Klaus, at one point says, "Children aren't innocent. They're born with darkness in them. The darkness that's in all of us, Jack. The same lust to possess and be possessed. The same desire to fall. Remember Augustine's Confessions—the siblings wrestling at their mother's breast, eyes full of envy?" Klaus tells Jack that salvation is excess. It's either asceticism or libertinism; either extreme will do. Both Klaus and the abbot are Gnostics, believing, like Jung, that God has a shadow-side, that He dwells in thick darkness as much as light. Again, to what extent was writing the book an act of therapy or exorcism for you personally? Would you describe yourself as a Gnostic? Do hidden Gnostic ghosts haunt Christianity? Have we all a dark double?

RK: Perhaps the fiction was therapeutic in a way. The two betrayals of Christian spirituality I was exploring in the novels were dogmatism and Gnosticism. The biggest danger for Christianity today is still, I think, dogmatism—the slide towards authoritarian, paternalistic, intolerant self-righteousness. Just think of the Christian Coalition in the United States or the Vatican Curia. There is nothing particularly new about this. It started when Constantine brought the pioneering spirit of early Christianity to heel in Empire. Kierkegaard called this betrayal of Christianity "Christendom"—and I endorse his trenchant critique. The other betrayal is more subtle and less visible. It is what I identify as a certain postmodern Gnosticism—usually laced with a dash of the neo-Nietzschean, relativism, or hip New Ageism. This latter move suggests that ethical notions of good and evil, or political notions of justice and injustice, are purely relative. So why not just experiment with everything, since everything is the same as everything else anyway! Religion becomes a supermarket, and spiritual values become commodities to be tasted, consumed, and discarded. I personally am suspicious of this kind of anything-goes relativism; but I would defend a robust pluralism to the last. I am very much for the ecumenical: I would consider myself an ecumenist but not an eclecticist. I think there's a difference. And while I am wary of the consumer patchwork approach in certain forms of Californian New Ageism—all these ephemeral fads, cults, sects, trends, cliques, etc.—I fully respect the desire in people to look for spirituality. (I am not here supporting the Vatican denunciation of New Age religions as such, which often means warning Christians away from dialogue with Buddhism, Hinduism, Taoism, etc.—ironically, some of the *oldest* religions in the world! If the Vatican really wants to denounce that, they should call it *Old Ageism!*) I'm just chary of gurus who play God, trendy high priests of whatever religious persuasion who set themselves up as having all the answers. Sellers of snake oil for the soul. There's a sense in which the character of Abbot Anselm in *Sam's Fall* also tries to play God. He is named after the famous medieval theologian St. Anselm, who had an argument for the existence of God from the idea of perfection. It's this fatal obsession with perfection. If you're not perfect, you are *nobody*. It easily leads to Puritanism and dualism. Absolute good versus everything else (the body, the other, sex, desire, women, imagination, etc.), now condemned as evil. It's the flip side of the postmodern tendency to relativize good and evil. And it's equally ruinous in my view. The relativist extreme was represented in the second novel, *Walking at Sea Level,* by Klaus, advocate of the Carpocratian heresy, which claimed that the best way to absolute knowledge is to experiment with every form of crime, brutality, and perversion. The Nazis practiced a version of this Gnostic doctrine, believing that cruelty and destruction are part of God. And one finds it in some odd passages in Hegel, and Jung too in *Answer to Job.* The idea that we don't really know God until we experience God's "dark side." I am very cautious about that. It is a recipe for the worst kinds of theodicy, justifying the idea that the most egregious atrocities are part of God's design. Evil is necessary for good. By this account, there is no reason to say that anything is right or wrong. Klaus is Klaus Stavrogan (Russian for "cross"), called after a character in Dostoyevsky's *The Devils* — Dostoevsky's point being that even though his protagonist is revered as a savior, he is in fact a sadist, rapist, and child abuser. The question then arises: How can God exist if there are innocent children being tortured? That is one of the key dilemmas I am revisiting in my fiction. In short, what I am saying is that the purist dualism of good and evil (Anselm) can be as damaging to the soul as the relativist equation of both (Klaus). Absolutism is as bad for your health as amoralism. And what I am suggesting, in my novels and philosophical works, is that we need an aesthetic imagination *and* an ethical imagination. Any poetics of imagining worthy of its name needs these two aspects — an aesthetic imagination to keep our minds open to ever new possibilities and perspectives and an ethical imagination to remind us that, no matter how innovative and daring our dreams may be, we are always, in the first and last analysis, responsible towards others. We need both.

Recorded in University College Dublin in 2000; edited and updated in September 2003.

Appendix
Philosophy as Dialogue

For speculation turns not to itself
Till it hath travell'd, and is mirror'd there
Where it may see itself

[Shakespeare, *Troilus and Cressida*, Act III, Scene III]

The logical order of clear and distinct ideas presupposes a "saying" *(Sprechen)* which involves one in a historical community of speakers. Our being-in-the-world is revealed historically in and through language as a dialogical being-in-the-world-with-others.

Hölderlin states this primacy of dialogical, saying in the following lines of an unfinished poem:

Viel hat erfahren der Mensch . . .
Seit ein Gesprich wit sind
Und hören konnen voneinander

(Much has man experienced . . .
Since we are a dialogue
And can listen to one another)

Heidegger offers a gloss on these lines in a passage from his *Commentaries on Hölderlin's Poetry:*

The being of man is grounded in language; but this really happens only in dialogue (that is, in speaking and hearing). . . . From the time man places himself in the presence of something enduring, only from then can he expose himself to the changeable, the coming and the going. . . . We have been a dialogue since the time that 'time is.' Since time has arisen and has been brought to standing, since then we have been historical. Both—being-in-dialogue and being-historical—are equally old, belong together, and are the same.[1]

Inheriting and developing this hermeneutic model of dialogue, Gadamer and Ricœur point out that human consciousness can never know itself in terms of an intuitive immediacy (as Descartes or the early Husserl believed). Consciousness must undergo a hermeneutic detour in which it comes to know itself through the mediation of signs, symbols, and texts. In other words, consciousness cannot intuit *(anschauen)* its meaning in and from itself, but must interpret *(hermeneuein)* itself by entering into dialogue with the texts of historical community or tradition to which it belongs *(zuhören)*.

History, as the communal becoming and preservation of meaning, is a dialogue precisely because I cannot live by my own subjectivity alone. I derive my meaning through my relationship with the other (be it the individual, communal, or ontological other). To say, accordingly, that truth is dialogue does not necessitate a return to the romantic model, advanced by [Friedrich] Schleiermacher and others, which construes dialogue in terms of a perfect intersubjective correspondence between one speaker and another. On the contrary, the dialogical model variously developed by Heidegger, Gadamer, Ricœur, and Levinas insists that meaning always originates in some source other than the intuitive immediacies of subjectivity or even intersubjectivity. Meaning always remains irreducible to the immediacy of speaking subjects coexisting in a homogeneous time or space. The romantic model of dialogue as a mutually intuitive correspondence between two human presences is no more than one possible and derived expression of the more fundamental model of a "hermeneutic circle" in which meaning always remains prior to the contemporaneous copresence of subjectivities. We do not and cannot miraculously create meaning out of ourselves. We inherit meaning from others who have thought, spoken, or written before us. And wherever possible, we *recreate* this meaning according to our own projects and interpretations. But we are always obliged to listen to *(hören)* what has already been spoken, in other times and places, before we can in turn speak for ourselves in the here and now.

This is a crucial distinction, particularly as it pertains to the dialogues contained in this book. We are concerned here with "dialogue" in the sense of a spoken communication between two subjects, recorded and inscribed as a written text. This passage from *speaking* to *writing,* is vitally important. When a discourse passes from speaking to writing, the entire set of coordinates in the dialogue—*subject, word,* and *world*—undergo a significant change. What is involved is more than a mere external fixation of the spoken words which would preserve them from temporal obliteration. The inscription of a dialogue in writing grants the text an autonomy with respect to the subjective intentions of the authors. Otherwise stated, textual meaning, even in the case of a written conversation, can no longer be deemed to coincide completely with the original intentions of the speakers. While it presupposes and expresses these intentions, it also manages to exceed them. Once committed to writing, the meaning of the speakers is distanced or "distanciated" in some fundamental respect. And in the process, the text transcends the finite intentional horizons of the two interlocutors and opens up new horizons of meaning—the possible worlds of the text which lend themselves to the multiplicity of the reader's own interpretations. We thus discover that the original overlapping of the two speakers' horizons *(Horizontverschmelzung[2]),* is subjected to the additional overlapping of these same horizons with the reader's own infinitely extending horizons. Put in another way, the speakers' original intentions are doubly distanced in the textual process of inscription and reading.

The written dialogue is in itself an open invitation to the reader to fill in the gaps between the original speakers' words. It summons the reader to recreate and reinterpret the authors' original meanings according to his or her own hermeneutic and experiential presuppositions. In this sense, we might say that once the reader has entered the dialogue, it becomes a dialogue that never ends. Laurence Sterne expressed this point succinctly, albeit mischievously, when he addressed his readers in *Tristram Shandy:*

> Writing when properly managed . . . is but a different name for conversation: as no one, who knows what he is about in good company, would venture to think all—so no author, who understands the just boundaries of decorum and good breeding, would presume to think all: The truest respect which you can pay your readers' understanding, is to halve this matter amicably, and leave him something to imagine, in his turn, as well as yourself.[3]

Sterne offers here a fine blueprint for hermeneutic dialogue. I would only add that the reader will always have something to imagine or interpret, whether the author has the good grace to allow for it or not! The imaginative reinterpretation of meaning is not a luxury of literary etiquette but a necessity of textual understanding.

In contrast to the situation of spoken dialogue, limited by the particular contextualization of a synchronic discourse between speaking subjects, the textualization of dialogue emancipates meaning from the strict intentions of the authors and creates a new audience which extends diachronically to anyone who can read. As Ricœur observes in *Hermeneutics and the Human Sciences,* "An essential characteristic of a literary (i.e., written) work ... is that it transcends its own psychosociological conditions of production and thereby opens itself to an unlimited series of readings, themselves situated in a different sociocultural condition. In short, the text must be able, from the sociological as well as the psychological point of view, to "decontextualise" itself in such a way that it can be "recontextualized" in a new situation—as accomplished, precisely, by the act of reading."[4] Consequently, in the transition from the spoken to the written word, we find that the romantic model of dialogue as a preestablished harmony of mutual subjectivities is quite inadequate. The "textualized" dialogue reveals that language is never purely and simply our own (in the sense of a contemporaneous immediacy), but always involves the traces and anticipations of *other* language-users, existing in other places and in other times, past and future.

If the hermeneutic potencies of the word undergo such alteration in the transcription of speech into text, what of the world about which the authors speak? All discourse, spoken or written, presupposes "someone saying something to someone about something." The problem of reference can never be dispensed with altogether. But what happens to reference, we may ask, when spoken discourse becomes a text? In a written dialogue, the reference can no longer be limited to the spatio-temporal context of a "here and now," shared by the interlocutors of a spoken dialogue. All writing, fictional or otherwise, is in some degree a reinscription of an original context of experience, and to that extent it would seem to eliminate the question of reference. But the matter is not so simple. Written discourse certainly abolishes the *first-order reference* to the actual world of experience "here and now," but this abolition serves in turn to open up a *second-order reference* to the possible worlds proposed by the text. Ricœur aptly describes this shifting of referential order as follows:

> The unique referential dimension of the work (as written) ... raises, in my view, the most fundamental hermeneutical problem. If we can no longer define hermeneutics in terms of the search

for the psychological intentions of another person which are concealed behind the text, and if we do not want to reduce interpretation to the dismantling of structures, then what remains to be interpreted? I shall say: to interpret is to explicate the type of being-in-the-world unfolded in front of the text. . . . For what must be interpreted in a text is a proposed world which I could inhabit and wherein I could project one of my own-most possibilities. . . . The world of the text is therefore not the world of everyday language.[5]

We may ask finally what becomes of the subject (that is, the author or the reader) in the transition of both *word* and *world* from speech to writing? Each reader of these dialogues will be attempting to reappropriate in some dialectical way the authors' words and worlds expropriated by the very process of textual inscription. Because, however, writing is not some reversible process of first-order referential correspondence, the hermeneutic reappropriation *(Aneignung)* of the reader can never claim to achieve an exact correlation (temporal or intellectual) with the intentional reference of the author. In other words, when one enters into genuine dialogue with these texts, one in principle experiences some change in one's own understanding of oneself and one's world.

We might speak accordingly of the reading process as a "metamorphosis of the ego," which requires a process of distanciation in the relation of the reader's self to itself. The reader's self-understanding must be seen as a disappropriation quite as much as an appropriation. And this calls for a dialectical realignment of hermeneutics with critical theory: "A critique of the illusions of the subject, can and must be incorporated into self-understanding. . . . We can no longer oppose hermeneutics and the critique of ideology. The critique of ideology is the necessary detour which self-understanding must take, if the latter is to be formed by the matter of the text and not by the prejudices of the reader."[6] This is the decisive juncture at which Ricœur's hermeneutic analysis overlaps with the ethical critique of Levinas, the deconstructive analysis of Derrida, and the Marxist-Freudian critique of Marcuse and the Frankfurt school. While the subject-readers undergo a certain transformation in the reading of these dialogues, so too do the subject-interlocutors who have authored them. For example, my own self-understanding as a dialogical questioner (conditioned by my particular set of cultural, national, religious, philosophical, and affective discourses) has had to submit itself to a metamorphosis in the exchange of question-and-answer with the thinkers featured here (each with his/her own specific discourses). And it is probable that these thinkers themselves have undergone a certain transformation of their respective self-understanding—even if this entails no more than an alternative reformulation of their previously formulated *words* and *worlds*. In short, these texts of dialogue bespeak the transmigration of each author into new horizons of *possible* meaning, horizons which remain open in turn to the *possible* reinterpretations of each reader.

Notes

Part One: Recent Debates

1. Jacques Derrida and Gianni Vattimo, eds., *Religion* (Stanford: Stanford University Press, 1996), 11.

2. Richard Kearney, *The God Who May Be* (Bloomington: Indiana University Press, 2001), 6.

Part Four: Colloquies

1. Richard Kearney, *The God Who May Be* (Bloomington: Indiana University Press, 2001), 34.

2. Jacques Derrida, "Violence and Metaphysics," in *Writing and Difference,* trans. Alan Bass (London: Routledge, 1978), 109.

3. Richard Kearney, *The God Who May Be* (Bloomington: Indiana University Press, 2001), 26 (my italics).

4. Richard Rorty, *Achieving Our Country* (Cambridge: Harvard University Press, 1998), 38.

5. Richard Kearney, *The God Who May Be* (Bloomington: Indiana University Press, 2001), 6.

6. Richard Kearney, "On the Gift: A Discussion between Jacques Derrida and Jean-Luc Marion, Moderated by Richard Kearney" in *God, the Gift, and Postmodernism,* ed. John D. Caputo and Michael J. Scanlon (Bloomington: Indiana University Press, 1999), 54–78.

7. Geoffrey Bennington and Jacques Derrida, *Jacques Derrida,* trans. Geoffrey Bennington, (Chicago: University of Chicago Press, 1993), 154.

8. Jean-Luc Marion, *God Without Being,* trans. Thomas A. Carlson (Chicago: University of Chicago Press, 1991).

9. Jean-Luc Marion, "Le phénomène saturé" in *Phénoménologie et théologie,* ed. Jean-François Courtine (Paris: Criterion, 1992), 79–128 and "The Saturated Phenomenon," trans. Thomas A. Carlson, *Philosophy Today* 40 (1996), 103–124. See also Dominique Janicaud et al, *Phenomenology and the "Theological Turn,"* (New York: Fordham University Press, 2000).

10. Martin Heidegger, *Introduction to Metaphysics,* trans. Gregory Fried and Richard Polt (New Haven: Yale University Press, 1959).

11. Richard Kearney, *The God Who May Be* (Bloomington: Indiana University Press, 2001).

12. See Catherine Keller's *The Face of the Deep: A Theology of Becoming,* (London: Routledge, 2002).

13. Emmanuel Levinas, "Ethics of the Infinite" in *States of Mind: Dialogues with Contemporary Thinkers,* Richard Kearney (New York: New York University Press, 1995), 177–99.

14. Exod. 3:14.

15. Etty Hillesum, *An Interrupted Life* (New York: Owl Books, 1991).

16. Matt. 9:19–23; Luke 8:43–48.

17. John 2:1–11.

18. Matt. 10:27, 19:26; Luke 18:27.

19. Richard Kearney, *Poétique du Possible: Phénoménologie Herméneutique de la Figuration* (Paris: Beauchesne, 1984).

20. "Desire of God," in *God, the Gift, and Postmodernism,* ed. John D. Caputo and Michael J. Scanlon (Bloomington: Indiana University Press, 1999), 112–45.

21. *Ibid.,* 140.

22. *Ibid.,* 139.

23. Richard Kearney, Introduction to *Strangers, Gods and Monsters* (London/New York: Routledge, 2002).

24. Peter Sutcliffe is the serial killer known as the "Yorkshire Ripper." He claimed that his killing spree was a divine mission.

25. Nietzsche asks in Section 55 of the *Will to Power* (ed. Walter Kaufmann, trans. Walter Kaufmann and R. J. Hollingdale [New York: Vintage Books, 1968]): "Does it make sense to conceive a god 'beyond good and evil'?"

26. Richard Kearney asks Derrida the following question in his interview with him in *Dialogues with Contemporary Continental Thinkers* (Manchester: Manchester University Press, 1984): "But did not Judaism and Christianity represent a heterogeneity, an 'otherness' before they were assimilated into Greek culture?" Derrida replied: "Of course. And one can argue that these original, heterogeneous elements of Judaism and Christianity were never completely eradicated by Western metaphysics. They perdure throughout the

centuries, threatening and unsettling the assured 'identities' of Western philosophy" (116–17).

27. Jacques Derrida, *Schibboleth—pour Paul Celan* (Paris: Galilée, 1986)

28. Jacques Derrida, "Circumfession: Fifty-nine Periods and Periphrases," trans. Geoffrey Bennington, in Jacques Derrida and Geoffrey Bennington, *Jacques Derrida*, (Chicago: University of Chicago Press, 1993).

29. Jacques Derrida, "Donner la mort" in *L'ethique du don: Jacques Derrida et la pensée du don* [Ethics of the Gift: Jacques Derrida and the Thinking of the Gift], ed. Jean-Michel Rabaté and Michael Wetzel (Paris: Métailié-Transition, 1992). The English version of the essay is *The Gift of Death*, trans. David Wills (Chicago: University of Chicago Press, 1995).

Appendix: Philosophy as Dialogue

1. Martin Heidegger, *Erläuterungen zu Hölderlins Dichtung*, 4th ed. (Frankfurt: Klostermann, 1971), 38–40.

2. Hans-Georg Gadamer, *Wahrheit und Methode* (Tübingen: Paul Siebeck, 1960), 289 *et seg.*

3. Laurence Sterne, *The Life and Opinions of Tristram Shandy* (Harmondsworth: Penguin, 1967), 127.

4. Paul Ricœur, "The Hermeneutical Function of Distanciation" in *Hermeneutics and the Human Sciences*, ed. and trans. J. B. Thompson (Cambridge: Cambridge University Press, 1981), 139.

5. *Ibid.*, 141–42. In respect to the dialogue in this book, we might even speak of a *third-order reference*, insofar as these dialogues involve authors producing dialogical texts *about* their own second-order philosophical texts, which are themselves in some sense *about* a first-order reference to lived experience. (And one might even argue, as Derrida does, that this first-order reference is itself already a text: a pattern of infinitely self-erasing traces or *archi-écriture*.) We may conclude, therefore, that the dialogues contained between these covers are not in fact attempts to retrace the texts of these thinkers back to some original discourse of everyday language or experience. They are texts about texts about texts. This self-confessed parasitism is not, however, intended in the negative sense of alienating or obscuring the meaning of the philosophies at issue. It is not meant in the mimetic sense of being a copy of a copy, invoked by Plato in the *Republic* to denounce literary artifacts as "poor children of poor parents" (i.e., the text as a mere imitation of natural experience, itself construed as a mere imitation of some otherworldly, transcendental truth). Our aim is to deploy the textural rendering of reference as a means of communicating the interpretive horizons of the author's world to the interpretive horizons of the reader's world. Such, at any rate, is our intention. The ultimate proof of the hermeneutic pudding is, of course, in the eating—the response of the reader.

6. *Ibid.*, 144.

Index

theology/Christianity, 127–34, 137–38; *Théorie des idéologies [Theory of Ideologies]* by, 131, 133

The Brothers Karamazov (Dostoevsky), 82

Buber, Martin, 82, 175, 180, 233, 234

Büchner, Georg, 89

Buddhism, 9, 18–20, 109, 232, 236, 256, 298, 299, 324

Bulgaria, 159, 160–61

Bultmann, Rudolf, 31, 122

Cage, John, 91

Camus, Albert, 261, 308; on Being, 126; *L'Etranger [The Stranger]* by, 103

Capitalism: corporate, 37; global monopoly, 92; Islam and, 8–9; Marxism and, 112; post-war, 192

Caputo, John D., 12; Kearney on, 235, 240, 241–42, 257, 286, 295–96, 298, 299, 304

Castoriadis, Cornelius, 115; *L'Institution imaginaire de la société [The Imaginary Institution of Society]* by, 106

Catharsis, 34, 35

Catholic Church: crisis in, 37; in Eastern Europe, 214; ecumenism and, 137, 316; Jesuit spirituality in, 18; Joyce and, 224; Kearney on, 316, 321, 322; Kristeva on, 162; pedagogical tradition in, 189; Roman Empire rescued by, 48; in United States, 322

Celan, Paul, 141

Céline, Louis-Ferdinand, 211

Celtic culture/mythology, 118, 119, 124; paganism in, 59, 60

Censorship, 278–79

Chaucer, Geoffrey, 107–8, 225

Chénu, Bruno, 102–3

Chile, 39

Chomsky, Noam: Kearney on, 278–79, 281–83; on rogue states, 5

Christianity: atheism and, 133; biblical interpretation in, 108; Breton on, 127–34, 137–38; Christian narratives and, 298; Christian philosophy and, 138, 189, 190, 284; European, 11; Gadamer on, 172, 177, 189–90; gift in,

284–87, 293, 312; historical meaning of, 129; Judeo-Christian-Islamic monotheism and, 8–9; Judeo-Christian monotheism and, 59–60; Judeo-Christian revelation and, 16, 17–18, 20; Kearney on, 233–38, 242–44, 252, 254–56, 258–60, 284–304, 306–307, 316, 321–24; Kristeva on, 162, 163, 164; Marxism and, 132–33, 306; metaphysics, 260; moralizing in, 301, 323; mysticism in, 132; paganism in early, 59–60; Passion in, 132, 138; polemics, 258; self-criticism of, 216, 252; Steiner on, 205, 214; theology of Cross in, 131, 138; Trinity in, 127, 128, 289, 303; tripartite ideology in, 59–60. *See also* Jesus Christ; Judeo-Christian tradition

Cinema. *See* Film

Cities, 38; European, 206; Greek, 48

Cleary, John, 191

Clinton, Bill, 201

A Clockwork Orange, 279

Cold war, 8

Coleridge, Samuel Taylor, 269

Colloquies: Athens, 246–52; Boston, 284–304; Dublin, 305–25; Hallifax, 253–60; Stony Brook, 261–83; Villanova, 231–45

Colonialism, Western, 164

Comedy. *See* Humor

Communism, 92, 112

Community: bishops in, 21; Derrida on European, 9–10; hermeneutics of text and, 21–22; Lyotard on, 197–98

Conatus essendi (Spinoza), 43, 44, 45, 75

The Confessions of Saint Augustine (Augustine), 76–77, 102, 204

Connolly, James, 309

Connolly, Sean, 283

Conscience et intentionalité [Consciousness and Intentionality] (Breton), 130, 131

Corsica, 219

Cosmopolitanism, 12, 14; Kristeva on, 159, 161, 162; Ricoeur on, 219–20; utopianism and, 220

Costello, Stephen J., Dublin colloquy with, 305–25

De surcroît [In Excess: Studies of Saturated
 Phenomena] (Marion), 17
The Devils (Dostoevsky), 325
Dialogue: hermeneutics and, 174–82,
 201, 328–32; history as, 328; philoso-
 phy as, 327–32; religion and inter-
 faith, 236–37; romantic model of,
 328; text and, 330–32
Dickens, Charles, 89
Difference, 178, 221, 277; deconstruc-
 tion of, 3, 146, 179; language as,
 142–43, 155–56; Lyotard on, 198,
 201–3; philosophy of, 136
Dilthey, Wilhelm, 169, 251
Dinesen, Isak, 33
Dionysius, 303
Disappointment, 24
Dostoevsky, Fyodor, 308; The Brothers
 Karamazov by, 82; The Devils by, 325
Dreams/dreaming, 58, 61
Dumézi, Georges, 53–61; on Eliade,
 54–55; on Indo-European civiliza-
 tion, 53–56, 59–61; on Lévi-Strauss,
 54–56; Mythe et epopée by, 58; on
 mythology, 54, 56–59; on tripartite
 ideology, 53–60
Durcan, Paul, 307
Dylan, Bob, 91, 93

East, Far, 109
Eckhart House, 311, 313
Eckhart, Meister, 21, 23, 24, 25, 169;
 Abgescheidenheit of, 25, 27; hermeneu-
 tics of revelation and, 21, 23, 24, 25;
 Kearney, on, 238, 288, 289, 303, 312,
 313, 314
Economics: discourse of, 146; Euro-
 pean, 220–21; morals and, 162;
 world, 220
Eco, Umberto, 269; on Europe, 223–28;
 on humor, 225, 228; on Joyce,
 224–26; on language, 225–28; The
 Name of the Rose by, 225; on religion,
 225–26; on terrorism, 224
Ecstasy, 25, 27
Eliade, Mircea, 18; Dumézi on, 54–55;
 Myths, Dreams, Mysteries by, 119–20
Empiricists, 30

En décovrant l'existence avec Husserl et Hei-
 degger [Discovering Existence with
 Husserl] (Levinas), 67
Enlightenment, 48, 115, 216, 220;
 Habermas and, 48, 115; humanism,
 115; Kearney on, 231–32, 233, 243,
 246, 254, 296; Kristeva on, 159,
 163–64, 165; Lyotard and, 194,
 195–96, 203; in modern era, 190;
 "thinking" during, 168
Epistemology, ontology and, 199–200
Eriugena, John Scotus, 59, 303
Eros, 26, 74, 95
Eros and Civilization (Marcuse), 86,
 94–95
Eschatology: desire and, 26, 27; Judeo-
 Christian, 115; of justice, 133–34;
 Kearney on, 292–93; Levinas,
 Emmanuel, on, 74, 81; messianic, 81,
 150; ontology and, 26, 27, 254; phenomenology and, 258–59; Ricoeur
 on, 103, 116–17; universalism and,
 222
An Essay on Liberation (Marcuse), 94
Essay on Personal Peace (Kant), 222
Étant Donne [Being Given] (Marion),
 16–17
Ethics: Arendt on, 263; Aristotle's Nicomachean Ethics on, 34–35, 184; of
 attestation, 45; Bible and, 72; dis-
 course/discussion, 46–47, 52, 222;
 ethical "I" in, 77–78, 81–82; ethos as,
 35; God and, 72, 76, 82–83, 301;
 Greek, 184; Heidegger on, 43–44,
 77, 84; Kearney on, 262–64; language and, 79–80; Levinas on, 44,
 72–84; Lyotard on, 194, 200–201;
 metaphysics and, 79; morals and,
 80–81; nature v., 76; ontology and,
 43–44, 72–74, 76–78, 84, 184, 258;
 other and, 72, 75–76, 79, 81–82;
 peace and, 81–82; philosophy and,
 81; poetics and, 262–64; politics and,
 184–85, 194, 196, 200–202, 237–38,
 272–73, 304; religion and, 76,
 238–39; terrorism and, 278–79
Ethiopia, 272
Ethos, 35

Habermas, 174, 177; on Heidegger, 167, 168, 175, 179, 180, 181, 185–86, 187, 190; on hermeneutics and dialogue, 174–82, 328; on hermeneutics and Greeks, 167–71, 172–75; on hermeneutics and politics, 182–87; on hermeneutics and science, 168, 170–71, 175, 187–89, 190; on hermeneutics and theology, 170–71, 189–90; on hermeneutics as choice, 167–69; on hermeneutics, future of, 190–91; on Husserl, 168, 175, 177, 178, 180–81, 186; on influences, 167–69; Kearney on, 246, 251, 255, 298, 328; on language, 169, 172–73, 181–82; on mathematics, 168–69; on metaphysics, 171, 176, 178–79; on phenomenology, 168–69; on philosophical texts, 173–74; on phonocentrism, 175, 176; on Plato, 167, 168, 174; on "praxis," 183–85; on rhetoric, 168, 181–82; on Ricoeur, 174–75; on truth, 187–88; *Truth and Method* by, 175, 182; on understanding/explanation, 188–89
Gandhi, Mohandas Karamchand, 243
Genesis 11, 226
Genette, Gerard, 101
German idealism, 246, 264
The German Ideology (Marx), 105
German language, 169
Germany: culture of, 118; historians from, 49; nineteenth-century theology in, 189; plurality of subsystems in, 40; romanticism of, 169; Social Democrats in, 101
Gift, Christian, 284–87, 293, 312
Gilson, Etienne, 138
Ginsberg, Allen, 91
Glas (Derrida), 153–54
Gnosticism, 324
God, 260; Being and, 45, 83, 189–90, 238, 312; of Bible, 82; Breton on, 127–29, 132, 133–34, 259; burning bush as, 30; death of, 194, 202; Derrida on, 8–9, 11–13; desire and, 82–83, 294, 297; ethics and, 72, 76, 82–83, 301; Gadamer on, 187,

189–90; Hegel on, 27, 202; hermeneutics of, 12, 17–19, 234; as historical process, 23–24; Kearney on, 233–35, 237–41, 243–45, 253–60, 284–304, 306–307, 313–14, 316, 321–22, 324–25; Kristeva on, 164, 166; language and, 226, 227; man's coexistence with, 74; of messianism, 5; metaphysical characteristics of, 302; Middle Ages on, 225; phenomenology of, 15, 254; possibilizing of, 291–92, 301–302; question of, 17, 19, 69–70; stranger as, 164; time and, 74–75; transfiguring of, 289–90; in United States, 243; Yahweh as, 60, 235
The God Who May Be (Kearney), 11, 13, 15, 36–37, 42, 232, 233, 237, 253, 254, 255–56, 286, 291, 295–96, 307, 321
God Without Being (Marion), 17, 21
Goethe, Johann Wolfgang von, 168, 178
Gramsci, Antonio, 196
Grandeur, 38
Gratton, Peter, 283
Greece, ancient: "big lie" in, 41; concept of Being in, 71, 190; criticizing of democracy in, 167–68; *oikos* (home) in, 38; polis, 167–68; tripartite ideology in, 56
Greek language, 127, 169, 172
Greek mythology, 56, 58–59, 107–109, 121, 123
Greek philosophy, 70–71, 72; ethics/ontology and, 74, 76, 184, 258; hermeneutics and, 167–71, 172–75; Judeo-Christian tradition and, 70–71, 72, 116, 121, 128–29, 139–40, 148, 233–34, 236, 260, 302–303
Greek tragedy, 41
Gregory of Nazianzus, 21
Gregory of Nyssa, 21, 26
Greisch, Jean, 16, 247, 253
Griffith, Arthur, 309
Griffith, D. W., 280
Grisward, Jöel, 59
Grondin, Jean, 16

Gutenberg, Johannes, 174

237, 253, 254, 255–56, 286, 291,
295–96, 307, 321; on Habermas, 238;
Hallifax colloquy with, 253–60; on
Hegel, 246–47, 251, 286, 291, 301,
307, 309, 324; on Heidegger, 231–32,
242, 251, 253, 257, 258, 259–60, 261,
264, 282–83, 285, 286, 298, 313, 328;
on hermeneutics of religion, 232–45,
253–60, 254, 256, 257; on himself,
305–18; on Husserl, 231, 239, 263,
265, 284–85; on imagination,
261–83, 263, 266, 267, 298, 308,
316–17, 320, 325; on influences,
261–62, 305–308; on Ireland,
310–11, 314–15, 319, 320–21,
322–23; on Jesus, 235–36; on
Judaism, 232–37, 244, 254–56,
258–60, 284–85, 298, 302, 304; on
justice, 240, 243, 252, 254–55, 300;
on Kant, 231, 233, 238, 239, 262–66,
281, 285, 307; on Levinas, 232,
236–37, 238, 247, 252, 253, 258, 260,
262, 265, 274, 282–83, 288, 300, 307,
308, 328, 331; on media culture,
268–83; on Merleau-Ponty, 266–68,
276, 282, 283, 285, 322; on messianism, 234–35, 239, 284, 291, 292, 297,
304; *Myth and Terror* by, 120; on
"negation of negation," 264–66; on
ontology, 251; on philosophy,
308–309, 310; on philosophy and literature, 260–61, 307; on philosophy
and politics, 307, 308, 314–15; on
philosophy and religion, 231–33,
245, 307, 315–16; on philosophy as
dialogue, 327–32; on philosophy as
therapy, 306; on poetics/ethics,
262–64; *Poetics of Imagining* by, 264,
316, 318; *Poetics of Modernity* by, 262;
Poetics of the Possible by, 240, 253,
254, 258, 262, 293; on Ricoeur, 232,
239, 247–48, 251, 253, 259–60,
261–62, 271, 278, 307, 308, 314, 328,
330–31; on Rorty, 238, 239–40;
Sam's Fall by, 319, 320, 324; on
Sartre, 241, 247, 261, 264–68, 306,
318; self and, 246–52, 268; Stony
Brook colloquy with, 261–83; *On*

Stories by, 7, 33–37, 250; *Strangers,
Gods and Monsters* by, 13, 247, 250,
253, 255, 256, 258, 298, 318, 321; on
Vattimo, 237–38; Villanova colloquy
with, 231–45; *Wake of Imagination* by,
275, 316, 318; *Walking at Sea Level*
by, 302, 320, 323, 324
Keller, Catherine, 286
Kemp, Peter, 247
Khōra, 296, 299; Derrida on, 12–14;
desire and, 26–27
Kierkegaard, Søren Aabye, 83, 180,
199, 247, 262, 300, 313, 323–24
Knowledge: absolute, 108; desire v.,
24–25; phenomenology of, 68
Kojeve, Alexandre, 247
Kosselek, Reinhart, 48; *History of the
Concept of History* by, 112
Kristeva, Julia, 29, 103, 159–66, 311;
on Catholic Church, 162; on Christianity, 162, 163, 164; on cosmopolitanism, 159, 161, 162, 163; on death
wish, 165–66; on Enlightenment,
159, 163–64, 165; on European identity, 159–62, 163; on God, 164, 166;
on Marxism, 162, 165–66; on nationalism, 160, 161–62, 165–66; *The Old
Man and the Wolves* by, 161; on pain,
307, 308; on psychoanalysis, 164–65,
308; on religion, 163–64, 166; on singularity, 162–65; on violence,
165–66
Kubrick, Stanley, 279

Lacan, Jacques, 26, 311, 314, 318
Language: Americanization of, 214;
Derrida on, 142–43, 147, 154–56; as
difference, 142–43, 155–56; Eco on,
225–28; English, in United States,
227; ethical, 79–80; French, 213–14;
Gadamer on, 169, 172–73, 181–82;
German, 169; God and, 226, 227;
Greek, 127, 169, 172; hermeneutics
of, 106–107, 110, 113–14, 124,
181–82; Latin, 127, 169, 172,
213–14; lingua franc and, 213–14;
national, 210, 213–14; philosophy as
question of, 70–71, 72; politics and,

philosophy, 198–99; on politics, 192–93, 194, 197–99, 201–3; on postmodernism, 192–97, 202, 203–4; on role of intellectual, 196–97

MacCabe, Colin, *The Revolution of the Word* by, 151
McCana, Proinsias, 59
Machiavelli, Niccolò, 39
McLuhan, Marshall, 208
Maimonides, Moses, 168, 176
Mallarmé, Stéphane, 136, 141
Malraux, André, 107
Manolopoulos, Mark, Boston colloquy with, 284–304
Manson, Charlie, 299–300
Marcel, Gabriel, 69, 138, 239
Marcuse, Herbert: on art/politics, 85–98; on beauty, 93–95, 97; *Counterrevolution and Revolt* by, 87, 90, 91, 94; *Eros and Civilization* by, 86, 94–95; *An Essay on Liberation* by, 94; influence of Heidegger on, 95–96; on Marxism, 85–94, 95, 331
Marion, Jean-Luc, 257, 258, 297; v. Derrida, 284–88, 295–96; *De surcroît [In Excess: Studies of Saturated Phenomena]* by, 17; *Étant Donne [Being Given]* by, 16–17; *God Without Being* by, 17, 21; on hermeneutics of revelation, 15–32
Maritain, Jacques, 138
Marxism, 83–84, 126, 241; art and, 85–94, 95; Breton on, 132–33, 137; capitalism and, 112; Christianity and, 132–33, 306; Frankfurt School and, 88, 114, 331; Hegel and, 113–14; Kristeva on, 162, 165–66; Levinas on, 83–84; Lyotard on, 192–93, 195; Marcuse and, 85–94, 95, 331; Ricoeur, Paul, on, 100–101, 111–13, 115–16
Marx, Karl, 85–86, 90, 95, 137; Freud and, 95, 273; *The German Ideology* by, 105
Mathematics: Gadamer on, 168–69; history of, 17; logic, 136; relations, 128; zero question in, 131

Matter and Memory (Bergson), 50
Matthew 10:9, 132
Meaning, in world, 66–67
Media culture, 268–83; philosophers in, 282–83
Mediation, hermeneutics of, 11
Melancholy, mourning and, 35–36, 41–42, 318–19
Melanchton, Philipp, 171
La mémoire, l'histoire, l'oubli [Memory, History, the Lapse of Memory] (Ricoeur), 35
Memory, 240; authority's reliance on, 37; future and, 109; history and, 47–51; imagination and, 49–51, 266; loneliness of, 318; mourning and, 35–37; of nation, 49; Pascal on, 50; recovered, 271; repressed, 313–14; Ricoeur on, 47–52, 220, 221
"Memory and Forgetting" (Ricoeur), 49
Merleau-Ponty, Maurice, 27; on Being, 127; Kearney on, 266–68, 276, 282, 283, 285, 322; Levinas on, 68; Lyotard on, 192; Ricoeur on, 104
Messianism: eschatology and, 81, 150; Frankfurt School and, 95; God of, 5; indeterminacy of, 5; Judaism and, 95; Kearney on, 234–35, 239, 284, 291, 292, 297, 304
La Métaphore vive [The Rule of the Metaphor] (Ricoeur), 99, 105
Metaphysics: Aristotelian, 23, 82; "Being as Being" in, 126, 128, 129, 134; Christian, 260; deconstruction and, 31, 84; Derrida on, 142–43, 148–49, 153–54; desire as "backstage" of, 25; end of, 257; ethics and, 79; Gadamer on, 171, 176, 178–79; God and, 302; Heidegger on, 65–66, 70, 71; of Lévi-Strauss, 107; postmetaphysical movements and, 23; of presence, 258; Ricoeur on, 42–43; Scholastic, 23; technology and, 66; theology and, 19–21, 31; will in, 26
Metaphysics (Aristotle), 42, 43, 45, 128
Michael Collins (film), 280
Michelet, Jules, 280
Middle Ages, 224–25

Middle East. *See* Arab states
Mill, John Stuart, 162
Mimesis, 34, 35
Modernity, Derrida on, 144
Moliére, 213
Montaigne, Michel de, 50, 204
Montesquieu, Charles de, 114, 163, 220
Moon landing, 282
Morality, 80–81, 162, 185, 301–302
Mounier, Emmanuel, 110, 138
Mourning: melancholy tied to, 35–36, 41–42, 318–19; memory and, 35–37
"Mourning and Melancholia" (Freud), 34–35, 41, 318–19
Mummia, Abu Jamal, 241
Music: African-American, 90; of Dylan, Bob, 91; rock, 87, 90; by Verdi, 93
Muslim narratives, 298
Mysticism: Christian, 132; forms of, 303; mystical humanism and, 87; theology and, 23, 297; Wittgenstein on, 306
Myth and Terror (Kearney), 120
Mythe et epopée (Dumézi), 58
Mythology: Celtic, 119, 124; comparative, 54; demythologization and, 122; Dumézi on, 54, 56–59; of Fall, 123; Greek, 56, 58–59, 107–109, 121, 123; Hebraic, 121; Ricoeur on, 117–25
Mythos, 34
Myths, Dreams, Mysteries (Eliade), 119–20

The Name of the Rose (Eco), 225
Narrative: biblical, 108; Christian, 298; *grand*, 194; hermeneutics and, 100, 103, 110, 328; history and, 46–51, 100–117; imagination, 298; in Ireland, 46, 48–49; Jewish, 298; Judeo-Christian, 103; literature as, 102, 103–104, 105–106, 107–109; little, 195; Lyotard on, 194–95; Muslim, 298; religious, 238–45; Ricoeur on, 33–37, 46–52, 90, 99–110, 247, 328
Nasser, Gamal Abdel, 69
Nationalism: Irish v. British, 310; Kristeva on, 160, 161–62, 165–66; Ricoeur on, 217–18

Nations, memory of, 49
Nation-states, 39–41, 217–18
NATO (North Atlantic Treaty Organization), 10
Natural Born Killers, 279–80, 281
Nature, ethics v., 76
Nazis: death camps of, 34, 50, 239, 270–71; democracy's victory over, 40; Gnostic doctrine of, 324. *See also* Hitler, Adolf
Needs: biological, 57, 61; Jewish proverb on, 75–76
"Negation of negation," 264–66
Neoconservatism, 195–96
Neoplatonism, 24, 126, 131–32, 138, 268
New Age religion, 257, 260, 299, 323, 324
New York Times, 274
Nicomachean Ethics (Aristotle), 34–35, 184
Nietzsche, Friedrich, 141, 152, 178, 262, 271, 273, 306, 308
Nihilism, 154–55, 194, 237
Nixon, Richard, 41
Northern Ireland, 3, 120, 217, 272, 311
Nouvel Observateur, 69
Nugent, Andrew, 306

Odyssey (Homer), 109
Oikos (home), 38
The Old Man and the Wolves (Kristeva), 161
Old Testament, exclusivism in, 259
O'Leary, Joseph, 253
O'Murchadha, Felix, Hallifax colloquy with, 253–60
Oneself as Another (Ricoeur), 42, 43–44, 247
On Justification (Boltanski), 38
On Stories (Kearney), 7, 33–37, 250
Ontology: of action, 44–45; epistemology and, 199–200; eschatology and, 26, 27, 254; ethics and, 43–44, 72–74, 76–78, 84, 184, 258; Greek philosophy and, 74, 76, 184, 258; Heidegger on, 43–44, 77, 84; Hellenic concept of, 129; Kearney on,

251; *other in,* 75; of substance (Aristotle's), 178, 183

O'Reagan, Miceal, 311–12, 321

Orwell, George, 89, 197

Other/otherness: Derrida on, 7–8, 11–12, 139–40, 148, 154; ethics and, 72, 75–76, 79, 81–82; hermeneutics of revelation and, 18, 28–29, 32; Islam as, 7; Levinas on, 28, 69, 72, 75–76, 77, 79, 81–82; in love, 29; in ontology, 75; self and, 75–76, 246–52; United States use of, 7–8, 11–12

Paganism, 257–58; Celtic, 59, 60; in early Christianity, 59–60; Greek-German, 259

Paine, Thomas, 309

Pakistan, 3

Palestine, 3, 6

Pardons, 41

Paris, as epitome of France, 206

Partridge, Simon, 309–10

Pascal, Blaise, 50

Past: future of, 48, 103; grammar of, 49; political re-reading of, 100–101; two meanings of, 51

Peace, 81–82

Pearse, Padraig, 309

Phallogocentrism, 152–53

Phenomenology: of being able, 44, 45; of body, 322; of Breton, 126–27, 130–31; comparative, 18–22, 54–55; Derrida on, 141; eschatology and, 258–59; of existence, 100; Gadamer on, 168–69; of God, 15, 254; of Heidegger, 15, 27, 65–66, 67–68, 95–96, 125, 129, 168–69, 231–32; hermeneutics and, 15–18, 21, 23, 27–29, 30, 31–32, 100, 247–48; of Husserl, 15, 27, 66, 67–68, 77, 104, 109, 125, 129–30, 131, 168–69, 231, 284–85; of imagination, 261, 263, 266, 267; on knowledge, 68; Levinas on, 65, 66–69, 70, 77; Lyotard on, 192; of religion, 18–22, 258

The Phenomenology of Internal Time Consciousness (Husserl), 77

Phenomenon, saturated: Augustine and, 23, 25; Dante and, 25; four types of, 16, 17; judging, 16–17; Marion on, 15–32; temporality in, 32; theology and, 17–22

Philosophers, media on, 282–83

Philosophical Investigations (Wittgenstein), 110

Philosophy, 84, 308–309, 310; analytic, 124–25; as *a priori* doctrine, 20; Breton on, 126, 135–38; Christian, 138, 189, 190, 284; Derrida on, 145–46, 149–50, 153; as dialogue, 327–32; of difference, 136; ethical, 81; faith in, 258–59, 260, 316; German, 66; Greek, 70–71, 72, 74, 76, 116, 121, 128–29, 139–40, 148, 167–71, 172–75, 184, 233–34, 236, 258, 260, 302–303; language question of, 70–71, 72; literature and, 260–61, 307; Lyotard on, 198–99; phenomenology and modern, 66–67; poetry v., 135–36, 153; politics and, 307, 308, 314–15; postmetaphysical movements in, 23; religion and, 69–71, 231–33, 245, 307, 315–16; "seeing" in, 29; teaching of, 188–89; technology and, 65–66; tentativeness of, 27–28; as therapy, 306; "Value," 188

Phonocentrism, 176

Physics (Aristotle), 178

Picasso, Pablo, 89, 93, 209

Plato, 65, 144, 213; on desire, 26, 307; *eros* of, 26, 74; Gadamer on, 167, 168, 174; Levinas on, 23, 24; Neoplatonism and, 24, 126, 131–32, 138, 268; as ontotheology, 23; *The Republic* by, 59, 148, 167; *Sophist* by, 148; *Symposium* by, 26

Platonic idealism, 203

Poetics: ethics and, 262–64; of imagination, 127; theology and, 135

Poetics (Aristotle), 34, 102

Poetics of Imagining (Kearney), 264, 316, 318

Poetics of Modernity (Kearney), 262

Poetics of the Possible (Kearney), 240, 253, 254, 258, 262, 293

of, 16, 51–52, 100, 103, 104–6, 108, 110, 113, 117, 119, 122, 124, 125, 328, 330–31; on himself, 46; *History and Truth* by, 110, 116; on hope, 58; on imagination, 106–7, 109–10, 111; Kearney on, 232, 239, 247–48, 251, 253, 259–60, 261–62, 271, 278, 307, 308, 314, 328, 330–31; on language, 99–117, 124–25; *Lectures on Ideology and Utopia* by, 48; on Lévi-Strauss, 101, 102, 107, 118; on life stories/narrative, 33–37, 46–52, 99–110; on Marxism, 100–101, 111–13, 115–16; *La mémoire, l'histoire, l'oubli [Memory, History, the Lapse of Memory]* by, 35; on memory, 47–52, 220, 221; "Memory and Forgetting" by, 49; on Merleau-Ponty, 104; *La Métaphore vive [The Rule of the Metaphor]* by, 99, 105; on metaphysics, 42–43; on myth, 117–25; on nationalism, 217–18; *Oneself as Another* by, 42, 43–44, 247; on possibility, 42–45; on societies, 107, 117–19; *The Symbolism of Evil* by, 117, 119, 122, 123, 124; *Temps et récit [Time and Narrative]* by, 36, 90, 247; on testimony, 50–51; *Thinking Biblically* by, 43; on time, 99–100, 102–103; on universality, 217, 221–22

Riefenstahl, Leni, 280

Rights, Kant's theory of, 41

Rilke, Rainer Maria, 215

Robinson, Mary, 309

Roman Empire, 48, 205, 228

Romanticism: age of, 171; German, 169, 246; postmodernism and, 250

Romero, Bishop, 243

Rome, tripartate ideology in, 56–57

Rorty, Richard, 238, 239–40

Rosenzweig, Franz, 234

Rousseau, Jean Jacques, 39, 309

Rushdie, Salman, 318; *The Satanic Verses* by, 277

Russell, Bertrand, 128, 196

Russian Formalists, 101

Said, Edward, 233

Said, the, 79–80

Sam's Fall (Kearney), 319, 320, 324

Sanderson, James, 283

Sartre, Jean-Paul, 192, 247; on Being, 127; *Being and Nothingness* by, 68, 241; Foucault breaking from, 250; on Hell, 308; Kearney on, 241, 247, 261, 264–68, 306, 318; Levinas on, 68–69; *L'Imaginaire [Imagination]*, 68; *The Psychology of Imagination* by, 49

The Satanic Verses (Rushdie), 277

Saturated phenomenon. *See* Phenomenon, saturated

Schama, Simon, 280

Schelling, Friedrich, 43, 136

Schindler's List, 34

Schlegel, Friedrich, 178

Schleiermacher, Friedrich, 169, 298, 328

Schöenberg, Arnold, 199

Scholasticism, 43, 130, 136, 172, 260

Science: Derrida on, 146–47; as element of language, 147; Gadamer, on hermeneutics and, 168, 170–71, 175, 187–89, 190; history of, 17; Islam and, 8–9; language ignored by, 73; logocentrism of, 147–49; technology and, 65

Scorcese, Martin, 277

Scotus, John, 21

Scripture, 256, 260

Searle, John, 30

Seeing, 29, 30–32

Sein und Zeit [Being and Time] (Heidegger), 30–31, 195

Self: identity, 35; Kearney on, 246–52; *other* and, 75–76, 246–52; postmodernism and, 247; world and, 268

September 11: African-American assimilation after, 10–11; terrible logic of, 317–18; United States response to, 4–5, 6–7, 10–11; West v. Islam after, 3–4. *See also* bin Laden, Osama; Terrorism

Shakespeare, William, 107–108, 195, 213, 320, 327

Sharon, Ariel, 6

Shoah (film), 34

Singularity, 162–65

Perspectives in Continental Philosophy
John D. Caputo, series editor